Crisis Communications

Crisis Communications: A Casebook Approach presents case studies of organizational, corporate, and individual crises, and analyzes the communication responses to these situations. Demonstrating how professionals prepare for and respond to crises, as well as how they develop communications plans, this essential text explores crucial issues concerning communication with the news media, employees, and consumers in times of crisis.

Author Kathleen Fearn-Banks examines the steps of choosing the appropriate words to convey a message, selecting the method and channels for delivering the message, and identifying and targeting the most appropriate publics or audiences. She also addresses such important topics as avoiding potential mismanagement of communication in crisis situations.

Key features of this fourth edition are:

- Six new cases, including several international crises;
- Current discussion of communications technology as it relates to crises; and
- A companion website with additional cases as well as supplemental materials for students and classroom resources for instructors. Please visit www.routledge.com/textbooks/fearn-banks.

A Student Workbook is also available for use with this volume, providing additional pedagogy for each chapter, including discussion questions, activities, key terms, case exercises, and worksheets.

Utilizing both classic and contemporary cases of real-world situations, *Crisis Communications* provides students in public relations and business with real-world perspectives and valuable insights for professional responses to crises. It is intended for use in crisis communications, crisis management, and PR case studies courses.

Kathleen Fearn-Banks is Professor of Communication in the Department of Communication at the University of Washington.

Communication Series
Jennings Bryant/Dolf Zillmann, General Editors

Selected Titles in Public Relations (James E. Grunig, advisory editor) include:

Austin/Pinkleton
Strategic Public Relations Management: Planning and Managing Effective Communication Programs, Second Edition

Berger/Reber
Gaining Influence in Public Relations: The Role of Resistance in Practice

Botan/Hazleton
Public Relations Theory II

Hearit
Crisis Management by Apology: Corporate Response to Allegations of Wrongdoing

McKee/Lamb
Applied Public Relations: Cases in Stakeholder Management, Second Edition

Crisis Communications

A Casebook Approach
Fourth Edition

Kathleen Fearn-Banks
University of Washington

Routledge
Taylor & Francis Group

NEW YORK AND LONDON

First edition published 1996
by Lawrence Erlbaum Associates Inc.

Second edition 2001
Third edition 2007

This edition published 2011
by Routledge
711 Third Avenue, New York, NY 10017

Simultaneously published in the UK
by Routledge
2 Park Square, Milton Park, Abingdon, Oxon OX14 4RN

Routledge is an imprint of the Taylor & Francis Group, an informa business

© 2011 Taylor & Francis

The right of Kathleen Fearn-Banks to be identified as author of this
work has been asserted by her in accordance with sections 77 and 78
of the Copyright, Designs and Patents Act 1988.

Typeset in Sabon by
Florence Production Ltd, Stoodleigh, Devon, UK
Printed and bound in the United States of America
by Edwards Brothers Malloy

Library of Congress Cataloging in Publication Data
Fearn-Banks, Kathleen.
 Crisis communications: a casebook approach/Kathleen Fearn-Banks—
 4th ed.
 p. cm.
 Includes index.
 1. Public relations—Management—Case studies. 2. Crisis
management—Case studies. 3. Advertising—Case studies. I. Title.
HD59.F37 2010
659.2—dc22 2010014680

ISBN 13: 978–0–415–88058–9 (hbk)
ISBN 13: 978–0–415–88059–6 (pbk)
ISBN 13: 978–0–203–84952–1 (ebk)

Brief Contents

 Company 320

Appendix B Crisis Communications Plan for Seattle's Union
 Gospel Mission 340

Appendix C Crisis Communications Plan for a Fictitious
 Small Business 347

 Sources 366
 Index 377

Full Contents

Preface

This, the fourth edition of *Crisis Communications: A Casebook Approach*, like the previous editions, is concerned with how organizations, companies, and individuals cope with the communications aspect of crisis management. How do they, or should they, communicate with the news media, employees, and consumers? They must choose the best possible words to convey their message, the best possible method of delivering the message, and the precise and most appropriate public(s) or audience(s). There are obviously many more methods of communications as time passes; this makes the choices of methods challenging. However, the ideals and principles remain—doing what is fair and honest.

Six new case studies are included in this volume. "Häagen-Dazs and Honey Bees" is about the worldwide disappearance of honey bees, the foods and food products we will be without unless something is done, and the work that the ice cream manufacturer Häagen-Dazs is doing to help propel the study that will, hopefully, find a solution. "Holland America Line and Cruise Crises" shows us how limitless the kinds and numbers of crises one organization may endure are. "Saginaw Valley State University and the Theater Controversy" centers on a Michigan university's fight to serve its students and teach others about tolerance. "US Airways and the Emergency Landing in the Hudson" is the familiar crisis from the unfamiliar point of view of the communication team at US Airways. "Yuhan-Kimberly and Baby Wet Wipes" is one of two additional crises outside of the U.S., and it is about how the Korean-based company used communications when consumers perceived one of their products as harmful to infants.

The other crisis originating outside the U.S. is from Canada; "Maple Leaf Foods and the Battle against Listeria" centers on how that company took the high road when consumers became ill and died from their products laden with the bacteria. There is a chapter, "Social Media and Crisis Communications," on the newest technology rage and a chapter, "Individuals in Crisis," on what public individuals do and should do when involved in scandal. A chapter on how to develop a crisis communications

plan remains, updated to include social media. There are three crisis communications plans in the appendices and all have been revised to include the new technology. Two are generic—the large company and the small business—and the third is an actual crisis campaign plan for a nonprofit, Seattle's Union Gospel Mission.

Four case studies have been removed from the print edition and can now be accessed on the website, www.routledge.com/textbooks/fearn-banks. Most remaining chapters and case studies have been updated.

Acknowledgments

I thank the crisis communicators and their staff members who helped provide me with the information for the case studies. At Yuhan-Kimberly in Seoul, Korea, the assistance was provided by S. W. Son, E. W. Lee, Y. I. Kim, K. H. Kang, J. W. Shin, K. S. Cho, J. W. Lee, J. W. Leekim. Dr. Yang-ho Choi of Chosun University introduced me to the crisis at Yuhan-Kimberly. My former student, Boram Park, also assisted in translating from Korean. For Maple Leaf Foods in Toronto, I was assisted by Linda Kuhn, Jeannette Jones, and Linda Smith. Häagen-Dazs simply asked to be recognized as "The Häagen-Dazs Brand team." For Saginaw Valley State University, I was assisted by Eric Peterson, J. J. Boehm, and Gene Hamilton as well as Justin Engel and Janet Martineau of the *Saginaw News*.

Erik Elvejord and Michael Versteeg at Holland America Line found time to help despite their work schedules.

Sister Mary Lou Specha, PBVM, of Reconcile New Orleans kept me apprised of the progress of the youths she serves. Kathy Gill of the University of Washington's Master's Degree in Digital Media program and Ron Schott of Spring Creek Group were my social media experts. Henry Marsh, Ruth Marsh, and Osie Thornton, Jr. in Michigan, Gerald Brown in Los Angeles, Agnes Marsh in Louisville, and Elva Miller in Blacksburg, Virginia, sent me information and material. Gina Arnold was my artist.

I thank Sharon Thomas-Hearns and Jeff Lilley at Seattle's Union Gospel Mission for permitting us to publish their crisis communications plan.

Very helpful University of Washington student researchers were Zach Buck, James Tosch, Katie McElroy, Rachel Huntsberger, Kristin Marie Scheidegger, Amina Saleh, M. S. Erickson, and students in COM 452 Crisis Communications. The Department of Communication's reference librarian Jessica Albano is indispensable to students and to me. Staff members Patricia Humphrey and Robin Brooks helped organize the cases. Kristina Bowman, Nika Pelc, and her staff of computer support specialists are always helpful.

Professor Albert Sampson of Argosy University has been an excellent, dutiful proofreader for all four editions. I thank him and also Routledge editor Linda Bathgate who has been supportive from the beginning.

Chapter One

Crisis Communications Today

People who pick up a book on crisis communications are aware of social media. Perhaps they do not use them or use them only socially. Perhaps, they don't know how to use them or don't know if they should use them. However, they are aware that social media exist and are major communications tools in the second decade of the 21st century.

Between the date this book goes to press and the date it is in book stores there will undoubtedly be new networks and usages of social media. Many experienced crisis communicators are exploring, developing, and learning how best to use social media. Chapter 5, "Social Media and Crisis Communications" of this textbook addresses how organizations and companies have used Twitter, Facebook, MySpace, YouTube, blogs, and other social media to cope with crises. The chapter includes advice on using social media and cites some crises caused by the use of social media.

Crisis communications demands that one uses the best crafted message delivered by the most effective method to the precise public (audience). This has not changed. What has changed is the fact that social media make it possible for faster communication than traditional methods and to a very precise, often chosen, public. Whereas we used to have a "golden hour" to disseminate crucial information about a crisis, now we have a "golden few minutes" before publics expect information. The message still needs to be carefully written—mistakes on social media can live forever—but social media encourage rapid and frequent two-way communication between an organization and its segmented publics, without a gatekeeper. Social media can build positive relationships with these publics.

So what the new technology has done is present new methods of communicating faster, possibly better and possibly not. It has not eliminated the need for traditional methods. And it has not changed the facts of human behavior—ethical and professional standards, the basic tenets of crisis communications.

What is a Crisis and What is Crisis Communications?

A *crisis* is a major occurrence with a potentially negative outcome affecting the organization, company, or industry, as well as its publics, products, services, or good name. A crisis interrupts normal business transactions and can sometimes threaten the existence of the organization. A crisis can be a strike, terrorism, a fire, a boycott, product tampering, product failure, or numerous other events (see the list in Chapter 15, p. 308). The size of the organization is irrelevant. It can be a multinational corporation, a one-person business, or even an individual.

Public relations (PR) professionals often say, "I have a crisis every day." This is an exaggeration, of course. The term *crisis* denotes something more serious than a "problem." Public relations people deal with problems— solving them or avoiding them. By definition, however, a crisis interrupts the normal flow of business, so a crisis cannot be a normal part of this flow.

On the other hand, a crisis is not necessarily so catastrophic that the life of the organization is destroyed. Exxon suffered the crisis of crises after its oil spill in 1989. It still suffers from a bad image, but it continues to thrive in business. (See the Exxon case in Chapter 7.)

This book advises you to plan for the worst that can happen, whether it be a crisis or a problem, and it brings us to another expression: "Be prepared." This book shows you how to prepare yourself and your organization to cope with crises that may occur. It deals with preparations made far in advance, as well as with strategies and tactics to be used during a crisis. It examines the experiences of public relations professionals in crises, describing what they did, what they wished they had done, and what hampered their progress. You can learn from their successes and failures.

In a crisis, in contrast to a problem, emotions are on edge, brains are not fully functioning, and events are occurring so rapidly that drafting a plan during a crisis is unthinkable. Simply following one is difficult.

Crisis management is a process of strategic planning for a crisis or negative turning point, a process that removes some of the risk and uncertainty from the negative occurrence and thereby allows the organization to be in greater control of its own destiny.

Crisis communications is the dialog between the organization and its public(s) prior to, during, and after the negative occurrence. The dialog details strategies and tactics designed to minimize damage to the image of the organization.

Effective crisis management includes crisis communications that not only can alleviate or eliminate the crisis but also can sometimes bring the organization a more positive reputation than it had before the crisis.

Public relations deals with publics. *Publics* are the specific audiences targeted by programs. People frequently use the term "general public," but public relations professionals are usually more specific in their targeting. Examples of corporate publics include the following: employees; customers; stockholders; community members; board members; unions; and retirees.

Proactive public relations programs can be used to build relationships with certain publics. They can prevent crises; they can also make these publics supportive when there is a crisis. Trust is at the heart of each type of public relations.

These programs might be the following:

- *Media relations*: Building a positive relationship with the news media so they know you are reliable, professional, accurate, and ethical. Tactics for the news media would include not only news releases but also pitch letters, backgrounders, media advisories, media tours, news conferences, and others.
- *Community relations*: Building a positive relationship with community leaders, organizations, families, individuals. Tactics may include advisory boards, open houses, speakers' bureaus, public service announcements, CSR (corporate social responsibility) activities, exhibits, scholarships.
- *Employee/internal relations*: Building a bond with employees even if there are only one or two, making employees feel a part of the organization. These would be volunteers in nonprofit organizations. Tactics would be the use of an intranet, newsletters, and other house organs, closed circuit television, e-mail and other social media, contests, awards, gifts.
- *Consumer relations*: Building a mutual bond between the company and its customers. A returns policy, tours, sales advantages, brochures, posters/flyers, open houses, educational material, and a complaint system are possibilities.

There can also be programs for government relations, labor relations, international relations, investor relations, and others. An organization depends on these publics for survival because they have some stake in the organization.

Public relations is concerned with reputation. It exists to avoid a negative image and to create or enhance a positive reputation. It is largely the fear of a negative image that causes organizations to develop public relations departments, hire public relations agencies, or both. Too often, an organization does not consider utilizing public relations until it is in a crisis. Then it wants a speedy recovery.

Research shows that companies with ongoing two-way communications often avoid crises or endure crises of shorter duration or of lesser magnitude (see Chapter 2, "Crisis Communications Theory"). Research also shows that companies with a crisis management and/or crisis communications plan come out of a crisis with a more positive image than companies without such a plan.

Whether an organization is a large multinational company or a small business, a *crisis communications plan* is needed. A crisis communications plan is preferably a part of a company-wide *crisis management plan* that includes sections on evacuation, work sites, equipment, and so on. If a company does not have a crisis management plan, a crisis communications plan is still advisable—even urgent.

The media to which you have tried unsuccessfully to pitch ideas for news stories, the media that toss "perfect" news releases in the trash, the media that never return phone calls—those media will call on you in a crisis. They will probably not telephone in advance. They will show up on your premises "in your face." The media, seeing themselves as advocates for the people, can be the principal adversaries in a crisis.

This is a time when public relations takes front and center—in a very crucial way. This is not to say that public relations will operate independently—that might be a greater disaster. It is a time, however, when the CEO (chief executive) may listen to the PR pro whose name he can never remember.

Sometimes, even in a crisis, the head of the company or organization does not listen because business schools often teach CEOs to make their own decisions. There are many documented cases of disasters during which CEOs acted independently. The Exxon crisis is an example. Exxon's CEO, Lawrence Rawl, did not respond as the media and environmentalists would have preferred. He did not accept responsibility as rapidly as critics felt he should have. He did not fly to Valdez to express concern. All the moves the public relations experts would advise, Rawl ignored. Rawl is not alone among corporate heads in his response, but the number of bad responses is declining as organizations learn the effects of public opinion.

In a crisis, when everyone else is in a state of panic, public relations practitioners must offer a calming presence: "This is not as bad as it seems," or "This could be worse. We cannot turn crises into catastrophes. This is what we do . . ."

The Five Stages of a Crisis

A crisis has five stages:

1. Detection
2. Prevention/preparation

3. Containment
4. Recovery
5. Learning.

Detection

The detection phase may begin with noting warning signs, or what Barton (1993) referred to as *prodromes* or the *prodromal stage*. Some crises have no noticeable prodromes, but many do.

When an organization in the same business as yours suffers a crisis, it is a warning to your organization. The 1982 Tylenol tampering case was a prodrome to other manufacturers of over-the-counter drugs. Most companies heeded that warning and now use tamper-proof containers. Imagine how many crises were avoided by noticing that what happened to Tylenol could happen to other companies.

On the other hand, Johnson & Johnson itself had little warning before it was hit with this crisis. No one had ever before poisoned an over-the-counter painkiller; it was not a crisis Johnson & Johnson had anticipated. The only warning the company had was a phone call from a journalist from the *Chicago Tribune*, taken by a Johnson & Johnson public relations staff member. The journalist asked questions about the company's holdings, the spelling of names, and so forth. The employee reported the call to supervisors, who called the newspaper and found out that there were deaths attributed to Tylenol (see Chapter 7, "Johnson & Johnson and the Tylenol Murders").

The *Exxon Valdez* oil spill was a prodrome to other companies as well as Exxon itself. Oil companies now know better how to prevent spills, how to clean up spills, and how to react to the public after spills.

There are other less obvious prodromes. Employee discontent over any issue is a sign of a brewing crisis. Perhaps there is an increase in complaints about work hours, work conditions, or unreasonable supervisors. Any one of these and many more issues can be an early sign of a work stoppage. The same prodromes can be early signs of workplace violence.

An organization should watch for prodromes and make attempts to stop a crisis at this stage, before it develops into a full-blown crisis. To detect these early signs, organizations form employee committees that function like lighthouse keepers watching for vessels at sea, watchdogs, or whistle-blowers. These whistle-blowers report warning signs to organization officials who can implement plans to avoid the impending crisis or at least have time to prepare to address the media or other publics.

Crisis detection also refers to a system within the organization in which key personnel are immediately notified of a crisis. An organization has a considerable advantage if it knows about a crisis before its publics

do, especially before the news media get the tip. This gives the organization time to draft a statement, make preparations for a news conference, notify the crisis team, and call in spokespersons. As mentioned earlier, the phone call from a *Chicago Tribune* journalist gave Johnson & Johnson some lead time before the public knew about the Tylenol murders.

Crisis Prevention

Ongoing public relations programs and regular two-way communications build relationships with key publics and thereby prevent crises, lessen the blows of crises, or limit the duration of crises.

The establishment of a corporate culture conducive to the positive and open interaction of members also minimizes crises, as does including crisis management in the strategic planning process (see Chapter 2, "Crisis Communications Theory").

There are other specific tactics and actions that an organization may adopt to prevent crises. These tactics must be communicated to appropriate publics. A company must not only do what is right. *It also must tell its publics that it is taking appropriate action.* This may appear to be bragging, but if the company does not reveal ethical and professional business practices, publics will never know. Crisis prevention tactics include the following:

1. Fostering the continued development of organizational policies that allow for updates and changes based on variances of publics and mission.
2. Reducing the use of hazardous material and processes.
3. Initiating safety training and providing rewards for employees with stellar safety records.
4. Allowing the free flow of information from employees to management with no punishment of employees who deliver bad news.
5. Following up on past crises or problems.
6. Attending community meetings.
7. Developing a community board with key outside members who are public opinion leaders.
8. Circulating a newsletter to frequent consumers.
9. Offering scholarships to employees and their children as well as to other children in the community.
10. Hosting community or employee picnics.
11. Sponsoring community activities, such as Little League teams and charities.

In communications, diligence can sometimes prevent crises. A public relations executive in the Midwest tells of a telephone call from a West

Coast journalist at 5 p.m., just as she was leaving for the weekend. She could easily have refused the call, but she decided to take it. The reporter was preparing to write a story for a big-city newspaper about the failure of a product manufactured by the PR executive's company. The story was one that could have sparked a full-scale crisis. The PR person took the time to locate information that proved the information to be baseless. The reporter was satisfied and the crisis that could have been was averted.

If all members of the management staff are trained to be media savvy, numerous crises can be prevented. Using the story above, the PR executive could have consulted a respected expert on the issue to refute the charges and nip them in the bud. Public relations personnel and key organizational leaders should always be aware of who these experts are and of how to reach them in emergencies. Prompt responses to media inquiries are also a plus.

Crisis Preparation

Crisis preparation is necessary for dealing with crises that cannot be prevented. Pepsi had no way of anticipating the scare in which hypodermic syringes were found in cans of Diet Pepsi. The presence of these syringes in the cans cried "AIDS," and fear of the illness and death far surpassed brand loyalty.

The crisis communications plan is the primary tool of preparedness (see Chapter 15, "The Crisis Communications Plan"). This plan tells each key person on the crisis team what his or her role is, whom to notify, how to reach people, what to say, and so on. The crisis communications plan provides a functioning collective brain for all persons involved in a crisis, persons who may not operate at normal capacity due to the shock or emotions of the crisis event.

Containment

Containment refers to the effort to limit the duration of the crisis or to keep it from spreading to other areas affecting the organization.

Pepsi used an advertisement to end its crisis. After several hoaxes had been exposed without the discovery of one documented case of a syringe in a can after the original incident, the company decided the crisis was over and told the world so. And it was.

Foodmaker, parent company of the Jack-in-the-Box fast-food chain, was charged by PR critics with delaying the resolution of the E. coli crisis that killed several children and one adult in 1993 because the company did not take responsibility for the tainted meat soon enough. However, as long as people, especially children, were sick and dying, there was no way Foodmaker could curtail the crisis. It was contained to the Pacific

Northwest and did not affect all outlets of the chain, and Jack-in-the-Box communicated to consumers that other food products in the restaurants were not contaminated.

Recovery

Recovery involves efforts to return the company to business as usual. Organizations want to leave the crisis behind and restore normalcy as soon as possible. Recovery may also mean restoring the confidence of key publics, which means communicating a return to normal business.

Snapps, a fast-food restaurant in Fort Pierce, Florida, suffered from a rumor that one of its managers had AIDS and had infected hamburgers. To implement recovery, health department officials participated in a news conference telling the public that all managers had been tested, that none had the AIDS virus, and that the virus could not be transmitted through hamburgers (see Chapter 6, "Rumors and Cybercrises").

Exxon attempted to recover from the *Valdez* oil spill by making efforts to persuade tourists that Alaska was still a beautiful place to visit. It is particularly interesting that Exxon looked beyond its own recovery to the way its crisis had affected the tourism industry.

Learning

The learning phase is a process of examining the crisis and determining what was lost, what was gained, and how the organization performed in the crisis. It is an evaluative procedure designed to make the crisis a prodrome for the future.

One might think that this is like closing the barn door after the cows have escaped. Any farmer will tell you that once the cows are back in the barn, they will escape again unless you close the door this time. The fact that a company has suffered one crisis is no indication that it will not happen again. Johnson & Johnson, after its second tampering crisis, learned its lesson by selling over-the-counter medications in tamper-proof containers. Other companies followed suit. Public relations personnel set about the task of telling the public about the new safety containers.

Another example of the learning phase is illustrated by the case of the U.S. airlines that were plagued with hijackings during the 1960s and 1970s. The airlines set up metal detectors at airports for persons boarding planes. The procedure was extended to cover employees after an irate employee boarded a plane with a gun, shot a supervisor, and caused a fatal crash. The airlines' public relations personnel informed passengers of the new safety procedures.

The learning phase brings about change that helps prevent future crises.

Public Opinion

In a crisis, the public perceives truth to be whatever public opinion says. An organization in crisis must prove to its publics, and often to the general public, that the prevailing negative opinion is not factual. In contrast to a U.S. court of law where a person is innocent until proven guilty, in the court of public opinion, a person or organization is guilty until proven innocent.

Public opinion is difficult to define, but it is based on individuals' attitudes toward specific issues. These attitudes are based on age, educational level, religion, country, state, city, neighborhood, family background and traditions, social class, and racial background. All of these help to form each individual's attitudes, and a predominance of similar attitudes makes up public opinion.

On any given issue, people are in favor, against, neutral, or so disinterested that they could not care less. Most people, unfortunately, fall into the last category. Public relations aims to reinforce positive attitudes, change negative attitudes, and provide information in a way that causes the unopinionated and neutral to form the opinion most conducive to the organization's function.

An organization has no choice in accepting a crisis. A crisis is forced on it, and the organization must cope with it. Organizations can ignore a crisis and hope it will go away. Occasionally, it does. More often, it does not. A crisis ignored is an organization failing.

The essential role of crisis communications is to affect the public opinion process and to be instrumental in establishing and communicating proof that the prevailing "truth" is not factual or not wholly factual. Then explanations of how much is true must follow. If the organization is actually at fault, owning up to it is usually the best policy. The public is forgiving if measures are taken to prevent recurrence.

The news media are prime tools for changing public opinion. The media can reach the masses in a short period of time because most Americans utilize some form of the news media, primarily television. Radio is popular during prime traffic hours. Public relations experts are trained in knowing how to reach the media, when and how to call a news conference, when and how to conduct one-on-one interviews, and when and how to disseminate written material.

Crisis communications, like public relations, is not merely the distribution of news releases. Nor is it only media relations. Frequently, community relations, consumer relations, employee relations, investor relations, government relations, and many other kinds of public relations are involved.

Mini-Case: White Star Line's *Titanic* Sinks

To illustrate terms, let's examine a well-known crisis: the sinking of the *Titanic* in 1912.

Titanic was one of several ships of the White Star Line, which had a primary rival, the Cunard Line. The Cunard Line had two famously fast ships—the *Lusitania* and the *Mauritania*. White Star decided not to compete with Cunard on speed but to surpass it, as far as public opinion was concerned, in size, elegance, sumptuousness, and safety.

The White Star Line planned to launch three ships—the *Olympic*, the *Titanic*, and the *Gigantic*, in that order. In the area of media relations, advance publicity praised the immensely luxurious ships. Postcards went out claiming the *Titanic* was "the largest moving object in the world." A promotional brochure claimed the *Olympic* and the *Titanic* were "designed to be unsinkable" (Ziakas, 1999, p. 109). The trade journal *The Shipbuilder* bragged about the *Titanic*'s opulence—its grand staircase, its elevators, its Turkish baths, and, of course, its "unsinkable" construction.

Titanic personnel were chosen to appeal to a celebrated and wealthy clientele, the targeted public. Captain E. J. Smith, called the "millionaire's captain," was the highest-paid captain on the seas and a celebrity in his own right. The musicians were the tops in their field and could play a wide range of music. White Star felt it had thought of everything and had attained the highest form of customer relations.

Crisis management plans and crisis communications plans were believed to be unnecessary. After all, if the ship couldn't sink, what could happen? There were medical facilities on board should any passengers suffer a heart attack or some other unforeseen illness. The ship had state-of-the-art communications equipment; if help was needed, personnel could radio other ships.

We've learned that it was always possible, though unlikely, that the ship would sink. A long gash in the hull was the worst case scenario, and that is exactly what happened. So, the non-planners were short-sighted. What about fires? Certainly the ship could burn. An adequate number of lifeboats would still be needed. In fact, a fire out of control on a ship could have been a worse disaster.

A crisis management plan would have detailed what would be done in the event of fire and other tragedies—how evacuation would take place, how practice drills would be conducted for the crew and possibly for passengers, who would lower the lifeboats, who would ensure that passengers were guided safely to the closest lifeboats and ships, who would contact persons ashore by radio, when crew members would save themselves, and so on. A crisis management plan would also have included making sure effective insurance policies were in place. In today's

crises, one must be sure that payrolls can be met; special insurances may be necessary to cover computers.

The crisis management plan would have included the crisis communications plan. The crisis communications plan would have included notification of the home office, where personnel acting as public relations professionals would, in turn, notify the press, White Star Line executives and employees, and passengers' relatives. These were also key publics. (The term *public relations* was not used at the time, although that management function has always been important to the success of any company or organization.)

The crisis communications plan would have also included details about who would be the spokesperson once the passengers were brought to safety. If Captain Smith had survived, he would have been the best spokesperson. As it was, Smith went down with the ship. However, the managing director of White Star, J. Bruce Ismay, was aboard, survived, and was rescued from a lifeboat sent from the *Carpathia*. Many felt he should have given his place on the lifeboat to a passenger. However, because he survived, he should have been the spokesperson. Instead, he hid in the luxurious quarters of the *Carpathia*'s physician until the ship docked in New York, hoping to avoid the other survivors who huddled on floors and under tables.

There were two persons connected to White Star who participated in the media communications. Harold Bride, a radio operator on the *Titanic* who worked for Marconi Wireless Telegraph Company, was among the passengers picked up by the *Carpathia*. He wrote a first-person account of the tragedy that he sent to the *New York Times* by wire from the rescue ship. Phillip A. S. Franklin, who had been hired to head White Star's New York office, called together a kind of crisis communications team. This came after David Sarnoff, also a Marconi employee, heard the signal from the *Olympic* that the *Titanic* had run into an iceberg and was sinking fast; Sarnoff gave his story to the Associated Press. Franklin attempted to stop the Associated Press from running the story, saying that even though the ship had run into an iceberg, he had "absolute confidence in the *Titanic*. . . . We are not worried about the ship but we are sorry for the inconvenience of the passengers" (Ziakis, 1999, p. 116).

The morning before the sinking, the *New York Times* ran a story announcing that the "The New Giantess *Titanic*" would soon arrive in New York. The story was a PR person's dream, a proactive story aimed primarily at a public of potential passengers and at educating and informing the general public, thereby assuring that when asked, "What is the biggest, most elegant ship afloat?" anyone would say, "The *Titanic*." The *Times* story described the ship's impressive size, luxury, and illustrious passengers aboard its maiden voyage.

On April 15, White Star was in a reactive mode, as is almost always the case in a crisis. Presented with information from the Bride and Sarnoff stories, the *New York Times* ran a story with this headline:

NEW-LINER *TITANIC* HITS AN ICEBERG;
SINKING BY THE BOW AT MIDNIGHT;
WOMEN PUT OFF IN LIFEBOATS;
LAST WIRELESS AT 12:27 A.M. BLURRED

A later *New York Times* headline read as follows:

TITANIC SINKS FOUR HOURS AFTER HITTING ICEBERG
866 RESCUED BY *CARPATHIA*, PROBABLY 1250 PERISH
ISMAY SAFE, MRS. ASTOR MAYBE, NOTED NAMES MISSING

Other newspapers' April 15 headlines indicated that the editors were much less aware of accurate details of the story. The *New York Sun*'s headline was "All Saved From *Titanic* After Collision." The *Washington Post* apparently chose to believe the spokesperson for White Star, Franklin. The *Post*'s headline was the following:

TITANIC'S 1470 PASSENGERS ARE NOW BEING
TRANSFERRED IN LIFEBOATS TO CUNARD LINE
Twenty Boat Loads Have Already
Been Transferred to the Catania,
of the Cunard Line. . . . No Loss of
Life is Feared. . . . Officials Confident
Throughout Long Period of Suspense . . . Halifax
Hears That *Titanic* is on Her Way to That Port.

(Note that newspapers made estimates of the numbers of passengers rescued and deceased in early coverage. Also, the *Washington Post* thought the rescue ship was *Catania*, not *Carpathia*.)

The *Manchester Guardian*, on April 16, wrote about the miscommunications of White Star. Newspapers love to write about corporate mistakes; it's the stuff of which interesting articles are made. Under the headline "The Day's Strange Reports in America," the story was a timeline of every arrogant message from White Star's Franklin and from other reports. One message from the Government Marine Agency in Halifax said that the *Titanic* was sinking, whereas a message from Franklin said that "all passengers are saved, and the *Virginian* is towing the *Titanic* towards Halifax" (Ziakas, 1999, p. 117).

Franklin finally received a telegram confirming that the ship had sunk, and he later described his reactions:

> ... it was such a terrible shock that it took us a few minutes to get ourselves together. Then at once I telephoned, myself; two of our directors, Mr. Steele and Mr. Morgan, Jr. and at the same time went downstairs to the reporters. I got off the first line and a half where it said: "The *Titanic* sank at two o'clock a.m." and there was not a reporter left in the room—they were so anxious to get out and telephone the news.
>
> <div align="right">(Ziakas, 1999, p. 117)</div>

At Pier 54 in New York harbor, the surviving passengers came ashore and were regarded as celebrities from that point on. An embarrassed and tearful Franklin went aboard *Carpathia* to meet with Ismay, who was in a state of mental and physical collapse. Ismay and Franklin drafted White Star's official reaction to the disaster and came ashore long after the passengers had left. Ismay and Franklin also were present at a stressful media availability event and later issued a formal statement (shown in Figure 1.1).

In the presence and under the shadow of a catastrophe so overwhelming my feelings are too deep for expression in words. I can only say that the White Star Line, its offices and employees will do everything humanly possible to alleviate the suffering and sorrow of the survivors and of the relatives and friends of those who perished.

The Titanic was the last word in shipbuilding. Every regulation prescribed by the British Board of Trade had been strictly complied with, the master, officers, and the crew were the most experienced and skillful in the British service.

I am informed that a committee of the United States had been appointed to investigate the circumstances of the accident. I heartily welcome the most complete and exhaustive inquiry, and any aid that I or my associates or our builders or navigators can render is at the service of the public and the governments of both the United States and Great Britain. Under the circumstances I must respectfully defer making any further statement at this time.

Figure 1.1 Formal statement made by J. Bruce Ismay, managing director of White Star, following the sinking of the *Titanic*. Ismay was aboard the doomed ship and issued this statement after consultation with Phillip A. S. Franklin, who headed White Star's New York office (Ziakas, 1999, p. 120).

The surviving passengers issued their own statement, which read in part:

> We, the undersigned surviving passengers from the steamship *Titanic*, in order to forestall any sensational or exaggerated statements, deem it our duty to give the press a statement of facts that have come to our knowledge and that we believe to be true. We feel it is our duty to call the attention of the public to what we consider the inadequate supply of live-saving appliances provided for on modern passenger steamships, and recommend that immediate steps be taken to compel passenger steamers to carry sufficient boats to accommodate the maximum number of people carried on board.
> (Ziakas, 1999, pp. 120–121)

The survivors were viewed as heroes, as was Captain Smith, who went down with the ship. Ismay was cleared of any wrongdoing by both British and U.S. inquiries, but his reputation never recovered. In motion pictures about the *Titanic*, Ismay was portrayed as a villain. The denotation of *Titanic* was "huge, colossal," whereas its connotation was "doom." White Star Line became synonymous with bad management. It suffered financial problems during the European Depression and, in the 1930s, merged with Cunard, with Cunard holding 62% of the shares. Both flags were flown on the ships until 1957, when the White Star flag was withdrawn. White Star liquidated its ships, and Cunard bought the remaining shares. By 1958, White Star no longer existed. Cunard went on to produce the *Queen Mary*, the *Queen Elizabeth*, and the *Queen Elizabeth II*. The *Queen Elizabeth II* still makes transatlantic crossings.

Prodromes for the *Titanic* tragedy were ships that had sunk previously. White Star thought it had made, in the construction of the ship, all the necessary adjustments in response to warning signs. The company concentrated on the positives rather than the negatives. It did not examine the worst case scenario: "What if this doesn't work?" That question was apparently never asked or heeded.

Prevention and preparation would have included making sure there were enough lifeboats and developing crisis management and crisis communications plans. Containment would have meant recognizing the danger as soon as the iceberg was sighted and putting into effect the crisis management and crisis communications plans. However, much arrogance ("This ship is unsinkable") existed. Although there were a limited number of lifeboats, many went unfilled because of poor crisis management. There was apparently time—if there had been a plan to be carried out—to save many more passengers.

Total recovery was not likely in this crisis. The reputation of White Star remained damaged after nearly a century had passed. If the company

had done anything right in the pre-launching, the sinking, or the post-sinking, there might have been a possibility of the recovery of their reputation.

In some cases, a company in crisis can seem to be a victim of crises, but this was not true in the sinking of the *Titanic*. The company was guilty of its own negligence and arrogance.

Chapter Two

Crisis Communications Theory

Academic researchers study the methods and procedures of professional communicators and develop theories of what is and what is not effective. Professionals rarely study theory but many have "tried and true" methods of practice that are, in effect, theory. Often, these practices of professionals are the same theories that academicians have studied and named.

A *theory* is used to explain what will work, what decisions should be made and how, what actions are likely to result and how, and how things relate. It is a prediction based on what has happened before. Theory-based practice is preferable because, in most aspects of life, we learn from our previous experiences and the experiences of others. Theorists have examined the actions of numerous practitioners and culled their findings into succinct theories.

Theories exist in various fields. Crisis communicators can benefit from many theories in the social sciences. The relatively new fields of crisis communications and public relations are developing their own theories, but theories applied to crisis communications are often theories in communications (including persuasion and rhetoric), sociology, and psychology.

Theories also tend to change, so it is necessary to regularly test them. Variables and relationships and conditions change, and results are sometimes vastly different in subsequent tests. Also, theories build on previous theories. Often, in using a theory, the researcher recognizes a missing element that does not necessarily find fault with the original theory but is deemed worthy of a new or more multifaceted theory.

Some theories are described in this chapter. They are followed by the predominant public relations/crisis communication theory called the *excellence theory*, proposed by James E. Grunig and Todd Hunt in 1984.

Apologia Theory

When an organization has been accused of a misdeed, its reaction to its publics is often called *apologia*. It is, as one would assume, an effort to

defend reputation and protect image. But it is not necessarily an apology. The organization's effort may deny, explain, or apologize for the action through communication discourse.

If a soft drink manufacturer, for example, is accused of using inferior ingredients in its products, the apologia might contradict the charges by explaining what ingredients were actually used. The aim is to counteract a negative or damaging charge. Publics—the news media, consumers, employees, and key opinion leaders—may express disappointment with the company and expect some explanation, if not a full apology.

The organization may insist that the charges are false and totally deny them. Or the organization may communicate to its public(s) that it did not "intend" to commit the misdeed. This is called *redefinition*. Publics tend to forgive if the organization's policies are above reproach and somehow, someway, something unforeseen happened. One individual, whose employment may subsequently be terminated, might be blamed. However, the public's forgiveness is not guaranteed. If the organization can show how it has taken steps to prevent the occurrence or the recurrence of the misdeed, all *may* be forgiven.

Apologia strategy may also include informing publics that the organization might *seem to have* committed a misdeed but actually has not. This is called *dissociation*. Facts explaining should follow. In the example above, if the soft drink's color has changed slightly, the manufacturer might explain that the ingredients have not changed but the food coloring is different; all ingredients are still pure and perfect. The organization, if faced with a large number of complaints, might also explain that it is returning to the former food coloring. That would be using dissociation and explanation.

A third strategy might be the actual apology: "We are guilty. We are sorry. Please forgive us." This is called *conciliation*.

Muslims in Turkey, Iraq, and Palestine territories wanted Pope Benedict to make a conciliation in 2006 when he cited a medieval text that characterized some of the teachings of the Prophet Muhammad as "evil and inhuman," particularly "his command to spread by the word the faith." The pope said he was "deeply sorry," but the complainers from the Muslim countries felt the apology was insincere and made merely to protect his public image. The pontiff said the comments were those he cited from an old source, not his opinion (Associated Press, 2009).

A man in Washington State was frustrated because his wife was missing. He called 911, and an employee of the county sheriff told him his missing wife didn't "meet the criteria for a search" and that he should "check the jails and hospitals." The man threatened to get the news media involved and did. As the public's concern grew, after two days a tracking was done using cell phone technology. The woman's car had gone over

an embankment where no one from the street could see it in foliage; she was trapped in the car but alive. The sheriff, representing her department, apologized "for not doing a better job of explaining the process" to the man. This was redefinition. The sheriff did not admit that her department and employee had any culpability in the man's crisis or that "the criteria" would change. She said the process should have been explained better (Castro, 2007).

Image Restoration Theory

This theory builds on the apologia theory. In this theory, the organization determines what is threatening reputation or image and also determines which publics must be addressed and persuaded in order to maintain and restore positive image.

Organizations sometimes take the attitude "Don't bring me bad news!" They may refuse to read or watch negative news coverage in specific publications or they may close their eyes to consumers or other publics. In refusing to know what some people think of them, they cannot possibly know how to respond. Organizations should seek to read bad news just as much as they keep positive news clippings and read them carefully.

When it comes to publics, the organization must know which publics have negative impressions and what the extent of their knowledge is. Does the public know all the facts, some of the facts, half-truths, lies? One must know where these publics stand before they can be targeted for communication. In most public relations campaigns, the first step is research. The same holds true for crisis communications.

On the other hand, one must determine if the publics know anything at all that might damage reputation. Sometimes it is better to remain silent on the issue. At other times it is best to tell your own bad news. This is a judgment call but a crucial judgment call determined by carefully researching one's publics continually.

An example of image restoration took place when Wal-Mart realized in 2009 that it was getting bad press. Apparently many people felt that the huge company had a serious case of corporate greed, that it would do anything to earn money.

To build its customers' trust, executives decided the company should have an open information policy, one in which customers would know the origins of the products sold in the stores. The policy was part of a sustainability agenda that also included requiring suppliers in China, the U.S., and the United Kingdom to comply with environmental laws. It also included having stronger audits, offering awards to energy-efficient suppliers, and urging the suppliers to come up with quality merchandise with no returns due to defects.

Decision Theory

Decision theory is concerned with counseling management and other leaders to make the most effective decision. Decision theory may be applied to all areas of management, but it is useful in public relations management and crisis communication. The theory is especially applicable to issues management and the effort to prevent a crisis.

Decisions are made under various conditions. The outcome may be certain, vague, ambiguous, or risky. The theory suggests that the decision maker should consider the possible benefit of each alternative; this is called *maximizing*. How useful is one alternative compared to others?

The best decision possible garners the greatest benefit, the greatest utility for the organization. Often, decision theorists note that decision makers do not opt for the greatest benefit but settle for the decision that will satisfy minimum requirements, usually because they do not have adequate data with which to formulate decisions. This practice is called *satisficing*.

Obviously, when trying to build long-standing relationships it is better to maximize than to satisfice. When satisficing, a public or publics may not be happy with the decision, or the decision may be temporary, a Band-Aid solution to a cancer in the organization.

Diffusion Theory

Also called *diffusion of innovations theory*, this theory examines how new procedures, practices, and objects are adopted and accepted by companies and individuals.

Diffusion theory has a five-step process: awareness (the body is exposed to the idea), interest (the body develops interest in the idea), evaluation (pros and cons are determined and considered), trial (the idea is implemented, perhaps temporarily to determine its effectiveness), and adoption or failure to adopt (acceptance or rejection of the idea, change, or innovation).

Whether something is adopted or not depends on three variables:

1. *The Past.* What has happened previously? What are past problems and needs? Basically, you must know where you are before you make decisions to make changes, to go forward.
2. *The Decision Makers.* What are the characteristics of the decision-making body that make it open to or closed to change? Are there close-minded persons with great influence over others? How do experience, age, education, and other socioeconomic variables impact the decision-making process? Is the body made up of all leaders and no followers?

3. *The Innovation/Change*. Does the innovation show more obvious advantages and few disadvantages over present practice or procedure? Does the innovation call for drastic change or can it be easily assimilated into current practice?

The *change agents*, often communicators or public relations professionals, try to move the body forward toward adoption. They often use the mass media during the awareness and interest stages. During evaluation and trial, personal contacts are valuable.

An example of *diffusion theory* in crisis communications might be a theater with an aging clientele suffering from poor single ticket sales and declining subscriptions. The plays have, for years, been the classics. Theater management wants to offer more contemporary plays to attract a younger audience, but they also want to keep the faithful clientele. Communicators might make announcements through the news media of this effort showing reasons in the *awareness stage*. In the *interest stage*, they might have focus groups of persons from Generation X and seniors.

In the *evaluation stage*, the focus groups are studied, and comments are offered by members of the executive and community boards. In the *trial stage*, one contemporary cutting-edge play is produced with careful publicity, interaction, and communications with leaders of both groups attending to help them understand. Follow-up interviews are conducted. The same effort is made to get the younger group to understand and appreciate a chosen classic.

The *adoption stage* results if most efforts succeed; during the following season, perhaps two contemporary plays may be offered.

Excellence Theory

Most recent public relations research builds on the *excellence theory* developed by J. Grunig and Hunt (1984) and later expanded by J. Grunig and L. Grunig (1992). The excellence theory is based on types of public relations practices called "models." The four models defined by J. Grunig and Hunt provide a way of classifying the types of public relations that individuals and organizations may practice.

In a spectrum of excellence of public relations programs, Model 1 would be the least desirable. Model 4 would be the most desirable, or could be said to be the "most excellent." Models 2 and 3 fall between these two extremes.

Model 1—Press Agentry/Publicity Model

In this model, public relations practitioners are interested in making their organizations or products known. They may or may not use truthful

statements. Falsehoods, half-truths, and incomplete facts are all permissible. The practitioners' abiding slogan, "All publicity is good publicity," indicates a one-way transfer of information from the organization to the publics. Little or no research is required. There is no feedback.

J. Grunig and Hunt (1984) revealed that this model was used by 15% of public relations practitioners. Later, J. Grunig and L. Grunig (1992) found the earlier data to be inaccurate and reported that most public relations practitioners, unfortunately, still fall into this category.

As practitioners become more knowledgeable and as the profession of public relations grows in respect, the number of practitioners using this model is expected to decrease.

Model 2—Public Information Model

This model is characterized by the desire to report information journalistically. It is different from Model 1 in that truth is essential. Most public relations practice in government agencies today falls into this category. Companies that simply distribute news releases are examples of this model. The practitioner is often called a flack.

This model also involves a one-way transfer of information from the organization to the publics. Little or no research is required. There may be some type of evaluation, such as readership surveys or the counting of news clips. Model 2 is most common in corporations.

Model 3—Two-Way Asymmetric Model

In this model, also called the *scientific persuasion model*, the public relations practitioner uses social science theory and research, such as surveys and polls, to help persuade publics to accept the organization's point of view. There is some feedback, but the organization does not change as a result of communications management. In asymmetric public relations programs of this type, the organization rules. It always knows best. Its attitude is that publics should adhere to the organization's viewpoints. An example of asymmetric action is a letter informing a public of a new policy or a recorded telephone message with no technology available for returning messages.

Model 4—Two-Way Symmetric Model

The public relations practitioner in this model, also called the *mutual understanding model*, is an intermediary between the organization and its publics. The practitioner tries to achieve a dialogue, not a monologue as in the other models. Either management or the publics may make changes in behavior as a result of the communications program.

Research and social science theory are used not to persuade but to communicate. Effective public relations programs based on this model are said to be "excellent" programs.

Symmetrical public relations programs negotiate, compromise, bargain, listen, and engage in dialogue. The organization knows what the publics want and need; the publics, in turn, understand the organization's needs and desires. An example is talking to consumers by telephone or at a public meeting in which the consumers can talk back and changes result.

In crises, organizations are frequently forced, by circumstances, to practice symmetrical communications with adversarial publics. Although most organizations practice Models 1 and 2, research by J. Grunig and L. Grunig (1992) revealed that PR practitioners would prefer to practice Model 4 if they had the expertise to do so and if their organizations were receptive to that practice.

The preceding classifications are not precise. For example, an organization may practice Model 2 and Model 4. If the organization practices Model 2 more than Model 4, it is considered a Model 2 public relations operation.

The new social media networks are a boon to the possibilities of two-way symmetrical practice. An organization can, if it desires, listen to its publics and make changes in its programs on the basis of those communications. It can also use them to explain its policies to these publics. After listeria-tainted meat had killed several people, the Canadian company concerned—Maple Leaf Foods—responded to a consumer on the corporate blog, explaining the precaution the company had instituted to ensure that this would not occur again. When it responded to that one irate blogger, other consumers read it.

If a company uses social media to count kudos from its publics and not to carefully consider change for mutual benefit, the social media interchange is Model 3.

Grunig and Repper on the Excellence Theory

J. Grunig and Repper (1992) identified theories on strategic management, publics, and issues as having two primary propositions. Both are conducive to a study of crisis communications programs:

1. Public relations is most likely to be excellent (contribute to organizational effectiveness) when it is an integral part of an organization's strategic management process and when public relations is managed strategically.
2. Public relations is managed strategically when it identifies stakeholders (separates active publics from stakeholder categories) and resolves issues created by the interaction of organization and publics

through symmetrical communications programs early in the development of issues.

These propositions mean that excellent public relations programs, as well as excellent crisis communications programs, have the following characteristics:

1. The public relations head is an important part of the top management of the organization.
2. Programs are designed to build relationships with all key stakeholders of an organization or company.
3. Public relations, through research, identifies who the organization's key stakeholders are and ranks them in order of importance. They may be customers, the media, employees, competitors, unions, special interest groups, vendors, suppliers, environmental groups, consumer advocates, and critics, to name a few.
4. An ongoing public relations plan is developed for each key stakeholder. This necessarily goes beyond media relations into a Model 4 program (two-way symmetrical program). These programs can sometimes prevent crises. At other times, they can help lessen the severity of crises.
5. In segmentation, public relations breaks down large publics into smaller subpublics with which it can communicate more effectively about issues or problems. These publics are usually, but not always, active rather than passive. Active publics seek out information and are more likely than passive publics to act on an issue. For example, if an organization wants to gear a program to all public schoolchildren, it might direct its program to the National Education Association or the American Federation of Teachers, organizations consisting of members who are educators and who can reach all public schoolchildren. Organizations that do not segment their stakeholders might send a news release to metropolitan newspapers, hoping that teachers will read the resulting article and communicate its contents to the children in their classes.
6. Issues management is part of a two-way symmetrical program that is best handled by the public relations department. (Although issues management is, in many cases, handled by public affairs or corporate communications departments, which are separate and apart from public relations departments that handle only media relations, Grunig and Repper's theory does not advise this separation.) A public makes an issue when it perceives that a problem is brewing or already exists. In issues management, the public relations department anticipates the issues that are potential crises and ranks them in order of possible damage to the organization. Then strategies and tactics are developed

and implemented to lessen the likelihood of crises. The crucial element here is early identification of potential crises, like treating a sniffle before it becomes the flu. The treatment might involve making allies with potential adversaries or meeting with community activists to explain a procedure that might be construed as damaging to consumers. Consequently, the odds are enhanced that an issue can benefit the organization rather than hamper it.

Marra and the Excellence Theory

Marra (1992), in an attempt to build on and validate a model of excellent crisis public relations, suggested that organizations develop a theoretically based crisis public relations model that would allow practitioners to identify which variables could be adjusted to make a crisis communication plan (CCP) work and which variables, if not adjusted, would cause it to fail. Marra argued that this knowledge could allow public relations practitioners to know before a crisis what will or will not work. He identified strategies and techniques common to excellent responses to crises with the following hypotheses:

1. An organization having strong and well-developed relationships with its key publics prior to a crisis will suffer less financial, emotional, or perceptual damage than an organization with weak and poorly developed relationships with its key publics prior to a crisis. Key publics would not only be the media but also employees, customers, community members, and so forth.
2. Organizations with weak precrisis relationships are those with asymmetrical practices; that is, they are Model 1, 2, or 3 organizations. Therefore, an organization that uses two-way symmetrical crisis communications procedures will suffer less financial, emotional, or perceptual damage than the Model 1, 2, or 3 organization or the organization that uses silence as a crisis response.
3. An organization that establishes and puts into effect continuing risk communications activities and prepares crisis communications plans prior to crises will have stronger relationships with key publics, use two-way symmetrical crisis public relations practices, and as a result suffer less financial, emotional, and perceptual damage than the organization that does not.
4. An organization with communication ideologies that encourage, support, and champion crisis management preparations, crisis communications plans and actions, and two-way symmetrical communications practices will suffer less financial, emotional, and perceptual damage than the organization that does not.

CRISIS COMMUNICATIONS VOCABULARY

Strategy—An approach on how one handles a problem.

Stakeholders—People who are linked to an organization or who have an interest in an organization and are affected by the decisions made by that organization. Examples of company stakeholders are employees, stockholders, communities, and government officials.

Strategic publics—Stakeholders who are crucial to an organization. The organization cannot function without them. Examples are boards of directors, investors, and unions.

Strategically managed public relations—Communications programs designed to build relationships with strategic publics, the crucial stakeholders of an organization.

Segmentation—The division of a market, population, or a large public into groups whose members are bound by mutual interests, concerns, and characteristics.

Risk communications—An ongoing program of informing and educating various publics (usually external publics) about issues that can affect, negatively or positively, an organization's success. The program builds solid relationships between an organization and its key publics, the publics on which an organization's survival depends. These relationships must be established prior to a crisis. It is too late after a crisis erupts.

Organizational ideology—An organization's philosophy, its working climate, its corporate culture. Each person's experience with the organization—no matter how small or large—puts him or her in contact with that organization's ideology, or corporate culture. The elements of that culture (such as norms of dress, formal rules, informal codes of conduct, taboos, jokes, language, etc.) make up an invisible, internalized whip that cracks and tells people what they can do, what they cannot do, what they can say, and what they cannot say in their dealings with the organization. It is inescapable that the culture determines to some degree how people within the organization behave. Popular examples of organizational ideology include "Look busy whether you are or not" and "The boss is always right." Johnson & Johnson relied on its organizational ideology in 1982 when, without a crisis management or communications plan, it followed its credo after several people died from poisoned Tylenol capsules.

Communications ideology—The organization's philosophy and attitudes of behavior in communicating with publics. Again, Johnson & Johnson's public relations program during the tampering case is an example. The company's basic rule in coping with the media, and thereby with the consuming public, was "open and honest information." It is difficult for a public relations department of a major corporation to have a communications ideology different from the organizational ideology. A productive public relations operation necessarily suffers from an unproductive organizational ideology and vice versa. (This is further examined in Chapter 7, "Exxon and the *Valdez* Oil Spill.")

Figure 2.1 To comprehend crisis communication theory, certain terms must first be understood.

Fearn-Banks and the Excellence Theory

Two additional characteristics are suggested (Fearn-Banks, 1996):

1. An organization that anticipates, through crisis inventory (see Chapter 15), the precise type of crisis will suffer less financial, emotional, and perceptual damage than the organization that does not.
2. An organization that maintains the reputation of having an overall "open and honest" policy with stakeholders and the news media will suffer less financial, emotional, and perceptual damage than the organization that does not. (This is a specific area covered broadly in Marra's fourth characteristic.)

Summary

Various theories suggest attributes and characteristics of programs that are likely either to prevent crises or enable organizations to recover from crises more swiftly than organizations without those characteristics. Strong among all the theories is the necessity for planning ahead. Also prominent is maintaining strong relationships with publics (including the news media).

Persons with public relations savvy are likely to say, "This is obvious. People who are prepared should withstand a crisis better." Nevertheless, the likelihood of a crisis is not seen as obvious by many organizational heads. Most companies still do not plan for crises and take the attitude that "it hasn't happened, so it probably won't happen." However, it does happen, more often than not. After an organization without a plan or a program has suffered a crisis, it then sees the need for crisis planning and proactive public relations programs.

Communications to Prevent Crises

Warning signs, called *prodromes*, are crucial because prevention is the best cure for a crisis. Strong community relations programs that get positive coverage in the media and endear your company to its publics will help this effort. Actually, ongoing proactive public relations programs of any kind are insurance policies against crises.

A strong people-centered corporate culture, rather than a profit-centered one, is also an effective crisis prevention tool. Corporate culture is the way an organization does business, its unwritten but firmly established values. The corporate culture must be established in such a way that honest, open communication is a basic value. Problems such as the CEO not speaking to the head of public relations and ignoring complaints from consumers are signals of an impending crisis that can be devastating. Employees who are stressed from overburdened workloads can ignite a crisis as well.

When on a fact-finding mission among internal publics to determine likely prodromes, listen attentively to others. You need to listen to what is said and to note how it is said, under what circumstances, and who said it. Watch facial expressions; they may be indicative of a story beyond the information you actually gather. Employees may fear reprisals from superiors or want to avoid "ratting" or whistle-blowing. There are numerous reasons for omissions, half-truths, and lies. A diligent researcher will see clues and hints of a need for further investigation.

An example of this was exhibited when a specific brand of automobile was found to be dangerously defective. It was discovered, after numerous cars had rolled off the assembly line and been sold, that the workers on the line knew about the defect. They were afraid to pull their supervisors' coattails, afraid of the workplace culture of "Kill the messenger of any news that causes a slowdown."

The News Media

Before a crisis, or at the onset of a crisis, you must anticipate what the news media need and want. Looking at the big picture, the media want

to sell newspapers and win ratings wars. The media give the public what it wants to know rather than what it needs to know. There is a fine line between news and entertainment, and crises make for entertaining news. The public is perceived to enjoy watching, reading about, uncovering, and lambasting organizations, companies, and individuals who might have done harm to people or, even worse, to animals.

Never say, "No comment!" to the public; refusing to comment appears to be an admission of hiding information or even guilt. If you do not respond, the public does not hear your side of the story and will conclude, "Company X refused to comment and, therefore, it must have done something terrible." If there is some legal reason for not revealing certain information, explain this as much as possible and promise to reveal the information at a specific time. Do all you can to make that information available at the time you specified.

Do not assume that the crisis story will go away. The media can do their stories without you. They can build a case against your organization, portrayed as "the bad guy," by talking with disgruntled employees, volunteers, and customers, and, even more often, by seeking out disgruntled former employees, former volunteers, and former customers. The media can also use computer files and call up long-forgotten problems and mistakes and, in a few seconds, regurgitate them and place them before the eyes and ears of the public. The people thus hear the negative story.

In a TV interview, Carl Bernstein (1994), who with Bob Woodward investigated the Watergate crisis for the *Washington Post*, said, "There are always people, if you work hard enough, who will want to tell the truth." In other words, do not wage a war with an enemy who buys ink by the barrel, paper by the ton, and controls the airwaves.

Internal Publics

Companies and organizations are wise to develop programs designed to achieve the following objectives with internal publics, particularly with employees:

1. Employees must learn what positive performance is and how it will benefit the organization and the employee. Employees need job descriptions and perhaps instructions on how their jobs should be done. In some public relations departments, employees admit that they write news releases on a "monkey see, monkey do" system—they use previous news releases and make new ones fit the same format, a kind of formula writing. This may work occasionally, but each news release should have its own unique elements and style. If an employee needs a formula to write a news release, it may be time

for writing classes. Demonstrations, practice, and special training or a reference manual may also be helpful.

2. Employees also need to know the consequences of a job well done and of a job poorly done, including consequences to the company and to the individual employee. It is important for all employees to feel as if they are part of the company. It's a feeling of "we," not "they."

3. Employees must learn what the job priorities are. Employees and management could have various opinions of which jobs or tasks are priorities. It is important for both employees and management to be on the same page. Either side may adjust to the other, but it is important that management and employees agree on priorities. This, again, requires effective communication.

4. Positive performance must be rewarded. Employees perform well when their work is recognized and rewarded. Conversely, they perform poorly when their work is not rewarded. Although managers say the paycheck is enough, they are the very managers likely to suffer crises arising from internal conflict. Research shows that positive reinforcement results in continued effective performance. Rewards may include money, trophies, certificates, an afternoon off, a free lunch, compliments, announcements on a bulletin board, a temporary parking place of honor, and other forms of employee recognition. Even a minor recognition in the form of a letter, memo, or e-mail message can be effective and encouraging when it is provided on a regular, perhaps daily, basis. Such a message might say, for example, "You worked very hard to get that report completed on time and I appreciate your hard work."

5. Conversely, poor employee performance should be punished. If an employee not doing his or her job well is never reprimanded, the good workers become discouraged. Proper communications with poor performers include formal or informal documents and face-to-face conversations, but they should never include public humiliation.

6. Punishment for good work must be avoided. Many times in companies, an employee who does work well is given more work to do. An employee who makes useful suggestions winds up having to carry out the suggestions. An employee who comes in early or stays late is despised by other workers. These are examples of punishing employees for exceptional work. First, communication is necessary to reward the good performance; second, an effort should be made to provide the training, mentoring, and advising necessary to bring the other employees up to the standard set by the exceptional worker.

7. Help employees cope with personal problems. Whether management likes it or not, employees will have personal problems that may interfere with their work. Management should learn to recognize the

symptoms of a personal crisis. A personal crisis may exist when an employee does the following: spends an unusual amount of time on the telephone, makes an unusual number of errors, is unproductive, abuses equipment, arrives late or leaves early, stares blankly into space, yells and is otherwise irritable, or spends excessive time in the restroom.

Because personal crises can turn into company crises, it is imperative to help employees cope with the issues affecting their performance. Allowing employees time off for personal business (with or without make-ups) is one way to handle these situations; providing on-site psychologists and advisers is another. Some companies even have on-site physicians and dentists available to employees to save time away from the job.

Large companies have employee relations departments to cope with issues surrounding employee problems and employee benefits. Many companies provide outstanding benefits that are a real plus in earning employee loyalty. They may also provide stock options and extensive vacation time. J. P. Morgan grants a free lunch. Fel-Pro pays $3,000 a year to send employees' children to college. Johnson & Johnson has a benefit whereby employees who have worked there for at least 5 years get an extra week's paid vacation when they get married. Johnson & Johnson also has a child-care center and on-site fitness center.

Customers/Consumers

Generally, a business has five primary objectives designed to build sales and gain loyal customers. These objectives are the following:

1. *Keep the old customers.* Longtime contented customers bring other customers. Programs such as the frequent-flyer programs and exclusive discounts are examples of programs designed to reward consumers for loyalty to a company, brand, or product. Other communications, such as newsletters and individual letters, are also frequently used. Assuring loyal customers of the constant effort to have quality products and services as well as competitive prices is important.
2. *Attract new customers.* Good prices, excellent quality, and word-of-mouth referrals from loyal consumers help to attract new customers. Interpersonal contact with sales staff and other employees is also effective in this area. Open houses and other special events bring the company to the attention of potential customers. Publicity about the company's outreach programs also attracts new customers.
3. *Market new services and products.* Customers and consumers want to see that a company or organization is constantly making efforts

to better itself in every area. They want to know what the new products and services are, why they are better than the older ones, and that prices are reasonable.

4. *Handle complaints swiftly.* A customer who complains and is subsequently satisfied will return and bring other customers. One who does not complain or is not satisfied after a complaint will switch loyalty to a competitor. If four people complain, one can usually assume that there are 24 others who were dissatisfied and did not speak out. Complaints in some organizations are handled by a middle person who mediates between the complainant and the company. He or she may simply say, "We're sorry and will make amends." Or a letter might be written explaining the company's actions. The overall message to the customer is: "We want you to be happy. We want your business."

5. *Educate customers.* Companies develop programs to educate customers about products and services. A store with a new line of cotton garments might inform customers—through ads, publicity, newsletters, and web pages—of the advantages of cotton, how to recognize well-made garments, and so on.

6. *Organize outreach programs.* In the area of community relations, companies and organizations adopt outreach programs in an effort to build loyalty among persons in the community surrounding its place of business. This may include making donations to nonprofits, schools, and the like. Or it may mean actually getting involved: A drug store may offer colon cancer screening. The police department might mentor fatherless teens. McDonald's runs the Ronald McDonald Houses providing temporary houses for families while their sick children are treated at nearby hospitals. The Internal Revenue Service includes photos of missing children on its income tax forms. In outreach programs, it is important to publicize your efforts—if your purpose is to build positive relationships with the community. Some organizations feel that publicizing their good deeds is bragging. If you do not publicize, only those people who have benefitted will know about your actions.

The Nordstrom Consumer Policy

The Nordstrom chain is known for its "customer is first" policy, a prototype and model for other retail stores. A Nordstrom store manager said, "Employees are instructed to make a decision that favors the customer before the company. They are never criticized for doing too much for a customer, [but] they are criticized for doing too little" (Spector & McCarthy, 2000, p. 88).

The company works on the principle that if it takes care of customers' needs and concern first, the dollars will come. The corporate organizational chart shows customers at the top of an inverted pyramid and the co-chairs at the bottom. Perhaps the most well-known aspect of Nordstrom customer relations is its returns policy: If a customer is dissatisfied with a Nordstrom purchase for any reason, the store takes it back with no questions asked. Bruce Nordstrom advised his salespeople:

> If a customer were to come into the store with a pair of 5-year-old shoes and complain that the shoes were worn out and she wants her money back, you have the right to use your best judgment to give my money away. As a matter of fact, I order you to give my money away.
>
> (Spector & McCarthy, 2000, p. 98)

Although the returns policy invites consumer abuse, Nordstrom believes that 98% of its customers are honest and should not be punished for the dishonesty of a few. This policy has forced other retail stores to adopt a more liberal returns policy to compete with Nordstrom.

Employees, customers, and even other publics (boards of directors, advisory boards) may be included in regular communications through social media, such as Facebook groups.

Chapter Four

Communications When the Crisis Strikes

When there is a crisis, there must be communication with the news media, social media publics, internal publics, external publics, and lawyers. All these communications should begin as soon as possible in the "golden hour," the first hour following notification that a crisis has occurred.

The International Telecommunications Union and other sources provided data for the World Internet Usage Statistics as of December 31, 2009. Their Internet Big Picture revealed 76.2% of North Americans had Internet usage. Australia had a 60.8 percentage; Europe, 53.0; the Middle East, 28.8; Latin America, 31.9; Asia, 20.1; and Africa, 8.7. All continents showed considerable growth (World Internet usage statistics, n.d.).

Nevertheless, that does not mean social media and websites are more important tools of communication than the traditional news media. As much as Internet use has increased, we still cannot ignore that television is in 98% of homes in the U.S. Some were lost when television went digital in 2009, but television is basically in all U.S. homes. The percentage is high in other countries, too (Media trend track, 2009). Another consideration is that television viewers get crisis information without seeking it. A family can be watching their favorite sitcom when breaking news interrupts. If people read newspapers—and there are still millions who do—they see news stories they were not necessarily seeking. Conversely, with online media, you don't get any information unless you actively seek it yourself.

News can sometimes be circulated faster by social media than by traditional news media (see Chapter 5, "Social Media and Crisis Communications"). Reporters must spend time getting to a crisis site and then transmit a story while bloggers already at the site, with little or no expertise in reporting, can get information transmitted immediately. It may be accurate; it may be misinformation. The trained reporter, hopefully, will find more complete information than the blogger or the Facebook friend. He or she will know what questions to ask and what answers to seek.

Still, without doubt, both social media and traditional media must be targets of communications as swiftly as possible. Ideally, the two should

be contacted simultaneously and immediately because if accurate data is not disseminated, inaccurate data is. If the crisis is online, then online communications is probably best (see Domino's Pizza, Chapter 12, page 258). If your communications staff is too small to permit simultaneous communication, then a decision must be made as to which is more urgent for your business.

Communicating with the News Media

There are three possible results of a crisis: (a) The organization is put out of business, ruined, possibly sued, and key executives are possibly charged with crimes; (b) the organization continues to exist, but it has lost some image and respect in its publics' eyes, and perhaps a great deal of financial position; (c) the organization, in a hard-fought battle, has won a war of public opinion and is seen as favorably as before or perhaps more favorably.

Some types of organization suffer crises, loss of reputations, and great financial loss but never seem to go out of business no matter what they do. Governments are usually in that category, and they often lose lead officials after a crisis—the captain must go down but not the ship. Hospitals are also in this category—no matter what misdeeds they do, they usually stay in business.

Information about a crisis reaches publics through the media more than through any other means. An organization may have to work very hard to get the media's attention during normal times; its public relations personnel may struggle even to get a news release used. However, during times of crisis, it will be the media who will be seeking out PR personnel or other company representatives.

It is true, unfortunately, that bad news sells. This has always been true. Even Shakespeare wrote about it in Julius Caesar: "The evil men do lives after them. The good is oft interred with their bones." A negative story is deemed more newsworthy than a positive one; the media consider your positive news "puffery."

It is the PR practitioner's dream that every news publication and every electronic news outlet will run prominent stories saying, "Company A is the greatest. Its products and services are the greatest, and it has the best PR people imaginable."

Plan a system in advance whereby you are notified of erupting crises. You want to be among the first, if not the first, to know. This can be done by instructing company telephone operators to reach you 24 hours a day, leaving a voice-mail greeting on your personal line during non-business hours, and cultivating friendly relations with key personnel in the media, the fire department, and the police department—people who can notify you in the event of a crisis affecting your organization.

Stages of a Crisis in the News Media

News media coverage of a crisis usually falls into four stages. The crisis communicators should realize these stages and be prepared to provide correct information and make explanations at each stage.

Stage 1 is breaking news. It is the immediate shocking or dramatic impact. Detailed information is usually not available; misinformation is often broadcast and printed. For example, in the Fort Hood shooting incident in November, 2009, the first news stories said the gunman had been killed; he had not. Reporters are covering the shock of it all.

Stage 1 ends when causes and explanation are presented. News stories then center on those explanations. This can mean one day on TV news and newspaper pages, not to mention social media conversations, or it can mean several days. The Exxon oil spill (see Chapter 7) stayed in Stage 1 for a long period of time because reporters were stuck in Alaska with nothing else to cover except the dead sea life.

Natural disasters also have prolonged Stage 1 news coverage. The January 2010 earthquake in Haiti suffered Stage 1 for a couple of weeks. As long as survivors were being pulled out of the rubble and as long as relief was delayed, the stories continued. Fortunately for Haitians, as people all over the world watched and read about the disasters, they felt inclined to make donations.

Stage 2 begins when concrete details are becoming available. In the Haitian tragedy, an accounting of the fatalities and the funds being raised was a sign of Stage 2. In the Columbine school shooting in Littleton, Colorado (see Chapter 13), Stage 2 began when descriptions of the personalities of the shooters and stories of survival became available.

Stage 3 often involves analysis of the crisis and its aftermath. How are victims coping? What is being done to remedy the situation? More is said about how and why. In the Columbine crisis, Stage 3 stories were about how the gunmen planned the attacks and memorials for the victims.

Stage 4 is an evaluation and critique of the crisis. Were warning signs heeded? In most natural disasters and frequently in other crises, stories are done about how the company, city, or country was warned that the crisis would occur. Katrina, the Asian tsunami, and the Haitian earthquake had warning signs. At Columbine, the youthful gunmen displayed signs of maladjustment. This stage also signals a return to normalcy and a consideration of what lessons have been learned.

Stage 4 usually includes anniversary stories—at first yearly, and then perhaps every 10 years, 20, 30, etc. The 9/11/2001 tragedy is revisited every year in September. The attack on Pearl Harbor is still revisited each year but to a greater degree in 10-year increments. The 2000 Alaska Airlines crash over the Pacific Ocean was revisited in January, 2010 in Seattle newspapers, the headquarters of the airline. The news media keep tickler files to remind them to revisit crises.

Sometimes a crisis grows out of another crisis, and that goes through stages also. After the 9/11 tragedy, concern erupted about what was happening to the enormous donations made to survivors, and this became another crisis.

What the News Media Want to Know

- What happened?
- Were there any deaths or injuries?
- What is the extent of the damage?
- Is there a danger of future injuries or damage?
- Why did it happen?
- Who or what is responsible?
- What is being done about it?
- When will it be over?
- Has it happened before?
- Were there any warning signs of the problem?

If your organization has erred, it is usually best to reveal the mistake at once, apologize, and make amends. The story may end right away as long as the crisis itself is not continuing. Cover-ups make a crisis persist. Whether your company has erred or not, do all you can to get control of the situation as much as possible and as soon as possible. When you release your own bad news, you decrease the likelihood of rumor, supposition, half-truths, and misinformation.

If the disaster or crisis has already resulted in injury or death, or if it poses a threat to the safety or well-being of groups or individuals, contact the media immediately and indicate that you are looking into the situation, that you "just found out 5 minutes ago." This way, the media representative will realize both the crucial aspect of the problem and that your company cares about people and understands the media's needs. This action may buy you an ally as well.

If the situation is not urgent (be certain of this), it is advisable to look into the situation, to make attempts to fully understand what took place, and to have answers prepared for the media's questions.

If reporters contact you first and you are unaware of the crisis, do not rattle on without knowing details. Ask if you can call back in a few minutes, saying frankly, "I need to find out what's going on." Get the facts and then call the reporter back at the appointed time to communicate them.

Remember that the media and the public are entitled to have the facts about a crisis. The idea is to help the media cover the story accurately and with minimum criticism of the organization or company. The overall goal is to keep or get the public's trust through the media. The media need you for information for interesting stories. Your organization needs

the media to communicate with the public en masse. By keeping this symbiotic relationship in mind, the public relations professional will be in a more proactive position during a crisis and feel more in control of the organization's bad news.

The spirit of cooperation must be established. In a crisis, there are three types of response to a media request:

1. We know and here's all the information.
2. We don't know everything at this time. Here's what we know. We'll find out more and let you know.
3. We have no idea, but we'll find out and tell you.

Give the media access to the material they need: background information, statistics, photographs, and spokespersons.

Apology

Know the difference between an apology and an excuse. An excuse passes blame to others; an apology does not. Do not say, "We didn't realize . . ." when you should have realized. An apology is a sincere admission that you are sorry for whatever happened. When people, especially children, were sick and dying from the E. coli that had tainted Jack-in-the-Box hamburgers, an excuse was not what the consumer public wanted to hear. Saying the meat-packer was responsible for the E. coli infections was not an apology. If your company had sold such a product, you would owe the public an apology: "We are sorry. We will do everything we can to make amends. We take responsibility for medical treatments" (see "Apologia Theory" in Chapter 2, "Crisis Communications Theory" and also Chapter 14, "Individuals in Crises.")

Spokespersons

Identify one primary spokesperson for your company. Designating one primary spokesperson reduces the possibility of conflicting statements, organization values, or explanations being released to the media. Speaking with one voice is more crucial in a crisis than during normal operations.

The CEO is considered by most public relations professionals to be the spokesperson of choice during a crisis, especially if people have been injured, if there is danger of physical harm, or if there are millions of dollars in damages. The CEO usually has the most credibility with publics and the media. He or she is seen as a true representative of the company, as a person who can make decisions, and speak for the company. If the company has a heart, it is the CEO's; at least, that's the public's perception.

Alternative spokespersons should be selected in the event the primary spokesperson is not available during a crisis. Supportive spokespersons, people who can speak authoritatively on technical subjects, are frequently of value, too. For example, if patrons of a restaurant get food poisoning, a physician might serve as a supportive spokesperson responsible for telling the public about symptoms and treatments.

External Experts as Spokespersons

When there is an opportunity to let impartial experts speak about your company's diligence, sense of responsibility, or innocence in a crisis, permit them to be spokespersons. In the Snapps restaurant case (see Chapter 6), medical officials spoke at news conferences telling the public that AIDS could not be spread to food by an HIV-positive food handler

News Conferences

If a news conference is warranted and can be arranged swiftly, arrange one. Be certain to have a prepared statement read and distributed to the media. This assists you in setting the tone for the rest of the session.

Spokespersons, whether the CEO, other top executives, experts, or public relations professionals, should have major talking points. Also called *key messages* and *speaking points*, these talking points are one-or two-sentence summaries used to remind you of messages you want to be sure to get across to the public. They might provide details about the crisis or positive information about the company, such as the company's safety record, safety procedures, evacuation procedures, and other information that says, "We are very concerned; we care."

Be mindful during a crisis, however, that it is not the time to bring up unrelated community service projects, no matter how many you have. When lives are in jeopardy, no one wants to hear about how much money you give annually to scholarships.

Spokespersons should rehearse their statements and talking points enough to be comfortable with the information, to be comfortable in front of TV cameras, and so prepared that he or she need only glance occasionally at notes. Preferably, before a crisis, practice sessions should be held in which employees ask the most difficult, rude, pointed questions of the spokespersons to simulate an actual crisis news conference.

Do not prolong the crisis by calling an unnecessary news conference or by engaging in other activities that can keep the crisis in the news. During a crisis, you want to get off the news pages and broadcasts.

10 Do's for Media Interviews

When dealing with the media or when being interviewed by the media, whether in a one-on-one situation or at a news conference, note the following 10 do's for media interviews:

1. Do listen to the whole question before answering.
2. Do use everyday language, not the jargon of your business or profession. Even if the reporters use the jargon, use the common vernacular unless the interview is with a professional publication.
3. Do maintain an attitude showing you are calm, courteous, responsive, direct, positive, truthful, concerned, and, if necessary, repentant and apologetic.
4. Do understand the reporter's job. Respect deadlines and return phone calls promptly.
5. Do be accessible and pleasant.
6. Do try to treat the reporter as a partner, an ally in maintaining or restoring the company's good image.
7. Do tell the truth, the whole truth. Misleading or omitted facts are also forms of lying. (Some seasoned public relations practitioners disagree with this position and even insist that no organization in a crisis is ever totally open and honest with the media or anyone else from the outside. This is an arguable point in a moot debate. Even these skeptics would agree that it is important to appear open and honest.)
8. Do look the reporter in the eye. In your response, address each reporter by name if possible.
9. Do use your crisis communications plan.
10. Do keep employees informed of the crisis. They may be volunteer spokespersons.

10 Do Not's for Media Interviews

At the same time, there are do not's when dealing with the media:

1. Do not be a wimp! Being concerned and empathetic does not mean that you must shake in your boots.
2. Do not guess or speculate. Either you know or you don't.
3. Do not get overly upset about being quoted out of context. Unless a complete transcript of your interview is printed, you are almost always quoted out of context to a degree. If the quote is completely wrong or libelous, that is another matter. Asking an editor for a retraction or correction is permissible if a reporter has been undoubtedly biased. A friendly letter delivered immediately and followed by

a phone call is generally most effective. "Demanding" a retraction should usually be a lawyer's job, as is a charge of libel. Proving libel is difficult and costly.

4. Do not play favorites with the media. Always favoring one newspaper or one television station is bad business. It can haunt you later.

5. Do not pull advertising from a newspaper because reporters are not cooperative. The purpose of advertising is not to help the newspaper anyway.

6. Do not consider your news release "golden." It will be changed except in small-staffed newspapers. If it is written well with real news, you have done the best you can do.

7. Do not stick to a story if it has changed, just to be consistent. The media realize that things change. Johnson & Johnson experienced this during the Tylenol crisis (see Chapter 7). It had initially announced there was no cyanide in its plant but later discovered that there was. Johnson & Johnson's public relations staff told the media the truth. No publication made a big deal over it.

8. Do not be trapped into predicting the future.

9. Do not wear sunglasses or chew gum.

10. Do not smoke—unless you are in a place such as Winston-Salem, North Carolina, where the economy is based on cigarette sales and smoking is a way of life.

Truth is Essential: The Dissemination of Error

When there is no time for research, when the news media tell you the news, or when the spokesperson must speak to the news media before there are any real answers, what should you do? In these cases, make it clear you have no definitive information. Do not reveal assumptions. Tell the truths that are certain, saying repeatedly, "I just learned about this, so I don't have all the answers." If you know, for example, that your company practices safety precautions, say so: "This company is very concerned about employee safety. There are hard and fast rules. There are rewards for safety records. If anything happened, it was not because of a lack of concern for safety. But we are very sorry that it happened." An early, earnest response can sometimes set the tone for how the public will perceive the company in a crisis. In these days when news is disseminated instantly, it is more important than ever to make sure the information is accurate. This is a concern of communicators and news media.

An illustration of what happens when miscommunications are spread is the Sago Mine tragedy in January 2006. Twelve men died in the mine blast; another was rescued barely alive.

The tragedy was compounded because the families and friends of the miners, after waiting and hoping that the toxic fumes detected were not

where the men were believed to be, were told that 12 men had survived and only 1 had died. Then, 3 hours later they found that the good news was wrong and the bad news was right, that 12 had died. Understandably, they were devastated.

The miscommunications occurred like the children's game of "Telephone." A worker in the mine communicated by two-way radio that 12 were deceased but as the message traveled like a chain to various points through the mine to the ground above, the details were reversed. An official called 911 in anticipation of the rescue and asked for medical crews. This was the phone conversation:

> *911 operator*: What am I telling them (the medical crews)?
> *Mine official*: 12 and bringing them out.
> *911 operator*: And they're alive?
> *Mine official*: As far as I know.

"As far as I know" is not confirmation. However, people—and there were apparently many people—on the scene were so eager to get good news that they clung to what they wanted to hear and delivered the good news to the people waiting at the church. It also went to the gathered news media who assumed it came from someone in authority. Newspapers and television news broadcasts went with the story as heard.

It was never revealed where the mistake occurred, and it was obviously a mistake—not a lie and not a cruel trick as some people thought immediately. Management of the mine should have had a way of being certain before giving information. They possibly did, but the head of the mine, interviewed on television news (CNN), seemed to have been misled himself.

The news media know with whom to check for official word, so their participation in informing the world is less forgivable. It is likely that each news outlet was afraid his or her operation would be the only one not carrying the great story of survival. Heads would roll! Without doubt, some reporters worried about whether it was fact, but the story had wings and was traveling all over the world.

Hopefully, news outlets saw their error and will have set up systems whereby this will not happen again. Considering social media, cell phones, Blackberries, and various other technologies, the dissemination of errors can be swift and disastrous.

Trick Questions

Although news reporters must make sure their information is accurate, communications professionals representing companies in crisis must be careful of their response to reporters. A media critic once said, "Being

interviewed is like playing Russian roulette. You never know which question will kill you." Sometimes reporters stray from the typical "who, what, where, when, and why" questions. Metzler (1994) identified several types of questions that reporters have been known to ask. Metzler's questions as well as a few others follow.

Speculative questions begin with "if." These can be embarrassing and dangerous. For example, a reporter may ask, "If the earthquake had happened during business hours, how many people would have been killed or injured?"

Leading questions imply that the reporter already has the answer; you are merely to verify it. For example, "You do agree that the company could have avoided this tragedy, right?"

Loaded questions are designed to elicit an emotional response. Some television reporters thrive on these because responses to them make for more exciting videos. A sample might be, "Isn't it true that you knew there was asbestos in the ceiling and failed to do anything about it?" In the case of a loaded question, rephrase it and answer your own question. You could say, "Do you mean, 'Were we aware there was asbestos?' No, we were not."

Naïve questions indicate that the reporter has not done any homework and does not know what to ask. "Tell me, what does your company do?" is an example. Reporters who ask such questions are dangerous because they desperately need a story. Make sure they get the story you want them to have. Give them media materials such as press kits, "backgrounders," biographies, and news releases.

False questions intentionally contain inaccurate details. If the question is "You fired half of your over-50 staff, right?" the public relations professional, knowing the statistic is wrong, could counter with, "No, only 40%," not realizing the reporter was aiming for that information all along.

Know-it-all questions begin with "We have the story. I just need a few wrap-up facts." The reporter may want you merely to confirm an already formed viewpoint. He or she may not have a story at all but wants you to release only "the dirt."

Silence, or an absence of questioning, is used by reporters who want you to spill your guts, to talk on and on. Many people tend to babble because there is silence. Remember, silence is the reporter's problem, not yours. Use this opportunity to reinforce positive statements or continue to be silent.

Accusatory questions are designed to force you to blame others. Never fall for this. Maintain your innocence if that is true, but do not cast blame on others. The court of public opinion does not react kindly to this.

Multiple-part questions can be confusing to you as well as to the public. Ask which part you should answer first. Then answer each part as a

separate question. Also, you can say, "I'll take the first part first." Then restate it yourself the way you want to answer it. Do the same for each subsequent part.

Jargonistic questions are those in which technical words or professional jargon are used. In response, use everyday language. Jargon builds a barrier between you and your publics and erodes their trust.

Chummy questions are those in which the reporter, pretending to be your buddy, may ask, "Say, pal, off the record, what do you think . . .?" The PR practitioner should remember that nothing is off the record and should be careful about supposed friendships.

Labeling questions aim to make issues negative or simplistic by seeming to ask for clarity, as in "Would you call the company's work schedule 'stressful'?" You should not accept the reporter's labels unless they are fair and accurate.

Good-bye questions are posed at the end of an interview and may even come after the camera or tape recorder is turned off. The reporter shakes hands and says, "By the way . . ." Watch out for what follows. The interview is not necessarily over. Remember—in all media questioning—to be positive, concerned, empathetic, and apologetic, if necessary.

Reporters

The preceding discussion of trick questions may seem to be a warning that reporters are sinister creatures whose life goal is to harass public relations practitioners. This is usually not the case.

There are jerks in every profession, including the news media. If you stay in public relations long enough, you will come in contact with them. Know who the jerks and enemies are. Sometimes you can work around them by dealing with other reporters. Other times, you can follow the advice of former President John F. Kennedy: "Forgive your enemies, but never forget their names."

There are also those journalists who apparently make themselves feel better by labeling public relations people "flacks." There is no reason to take this to heart. Reporters do not hate you or your profession. In fact, many of them will seek public relations jobs.

Newspaper and broadcast journalists, in record numbers, are becoming public relations practitioners. Newspapers are failing. Most on-the-air personnel in television cannot expect to have jobs in their middle age. Everyone is downsizing. Public relations is the fastest growing communications profession, largely because of crises and the forecast of crises to come.

Reporters are frequently not knowledgeable about, or interested in, the issues they cover. A story may have been assigned to them. Their task is to bring back an interesting story, a story that will get them a

promotion, a raise, an extended contract, an Emmy, or a Peabody. They want their stories prominently displayed in the newspaper or at the top of the broadcast. They want to get this award-winning story back before the deadline. All would rather that you assist them than be an obstacle to them. Obstacles make awards and raises difficult to obtain.

After reporters have filed stories, they are frequently finished with them. They do not write the newspaper headlines that you hate—that's the job of editors you rarely, if ever, see. Sometimes, if the story continues, other reporters will be assigned.

If you are breaking the news of a crisis or a development in a crisis and you know of reporters who are known to be fair and accurate, you can sometimes give them your story. This does not mean that if you dislike the reporter assigned, you can call another. This works only when no other reporters are involved, and you cannot be charged with playing favorites.

Choosing the news outlet for bad news is not an unheard-of or new tactic. When death was imminent, physicians attending to King George V injected lethal doses of drugs into his veins to hasten his death. They wanted him to die in time to make the deadlines of *The Times,* a morning newspaper in London, considered more responsible than what were, in 1936, considered the "inferior news organs of the afternoon."

In dealing with reporters, one must consider the pressures they are going through, especially when covering an emotional story.

Communicating with Lawyers

Lawyers frequently advise clients in crisis to: (a) be silent, say nothing, circle the wagons; (b) say as little as possible but reveal what information you have as quickly as possible; (c) deny blame and guilt; (d) shift blame to others or share it with others; and (e) remember that anything you say can be used against you in a court of law.

A public relations counsel suggests that a client be open and honest. "No comment" is perceived by the public as an admission of guilt. Anything you do not say can be used against you in the court of public opinion.

Both professions must be heard and considered. There are times when lawyers are right; spokespersons can speak too much. There are times when speaking up pays dividends in both courts of law and the court of public opinion.

Courts of law proclaim that a person is innocent until proven guilty, whereas the court of public opinion often declares a person guilty until proven innocent. When your company loses in the court of public opinion, it also loses its reputation, good name, and positive image—the very qualities that make for its success.

The public believes that an innocent person can answer a police officer's questions without having a lawyer present. After all, what does the person have to hide? The public also believes that this innocent person can go on the stand and plead his or her innocence, showing emotion in the process. However, lawyers frequently advise clients to refrain from all these actions and reactions. Some lawyers think public relations is publicity, getting somebody's name in the newspaper. Others know what public relations really is, but they choose to ignore it.

Sometimes lawyers may be cautious at a time when public relations professionals feel that open communication with publics is crucial to the positive conclusion of a crisis. The lawyer's job, after all, is to protect the company, organization, or individual. Sometimes public relations counsels may not anticipate threats to their own clients.

Lawyers know that any persons with knowledge of the organization in trouble can be called into court for depositions against the client. Sometimes communication with publics can put the organization in a perilous situation.

A case of law versus public relations occurred in 1985, when a Delta Airlines plane crashed. After the crash, high-ranking Delta employees showed great concern for survivors and families of victims. They sent flowers. They visited. They attended funerals. The company's public relations effort was so impressive that many lawsuits were avoided as a result. Nevertheless, some lawsuits were filed. In court, the lawyers for Delta were said to be vicious. They accused one plaintiff of being a cocaine addict and of having a child who was not her husband's. They implied that another victim, a homosexual, might have died soon of AIDS. Irate news stories resulted in the company being called a "monster." At least one newspaper wrote prominently of the airline's "Jekyll–Hyde" behavior.

Delta was upset over the negative publicity, but its lawyers insisted that they had to introduce relevant information, acquired legitimately, to fight money-hungry personal injury lawyers (Thompson & Hess, 1986). A solution to such a dilemma is a bond of mutual understanding, a marriage of the two fields, a careful balance.

The legal profession is much older than the recognized field of public relations (although, in effect, public relations has been practiced for centuries). As a profession, public relations is moving toward a day when professionals will have to pass a kind of "bar exam." The Accreditation in Public Relations (APR) credentialing offered by the Public Relations Society of America is a step toward this certification.

Lawyers are becoming more adept at public relations. The American Bar Association provides media training for its primary officers. It realizes that a defendant can win a battle in a court of law and lose it in the court of public opinion. In recent crises, lawyers have apparently learned

the value of communicating. Rarely does a corporate spokesperson in a crisis refuse to address the news media. Usually, the company in crisis goes further and even puts information about the crisis on its website and in blogs and other social media.

In 1991, for instance, a crisis team consisting of public relations and legal representation for Snapps restaurant in Florida made a decision not to prosecute or sue a teenager who had helped spread a rumor that caused a drastic loss of business (see Chapter 6). The members of the team decided that although they might win a victory in court, it would be a case of winning the battle and losing the war. The teenager had apologized publicly and admitted she was truly sorry that her actions had caused the crisis; she had simply been trying to warn her friends whom she believed might be in danger. The public might have boycotted the restaurant had further action been taken against her. It would have been a matter of the powerful restaurant ruining the life of a well-meaning child who made a mistake in judgment.

Conversely, a defendant can lose in court and win in the battle of public opinion. Sometimes the latter offers a brighter future. This was the case when Mayor Marion Barry of Washington, DC, was convicted of a drug charge, served time in prison, and then returned to the nation's capital to resume his political career. Although few voters doubted that Barry was a drug user, there was resounding public resentment of the way he was supposedly "setup" for the arrest. Anger at those believed to be responsible for the "setup" translated into support in the court of public opinion for Barry, who was reelected as mayor in 1994.

More and more, lawyers are influencing public opinion outside the courtroom. We have seen the results of this when a lawyer representing a prisoner convicted of a serious crime persuades *60 Minutes* or *20/20* to tell a story of the innocence of the client. The lawyer may have exhausted all legal channels or the client may have been unable to afford the legal battle. An effective letter to the television news magazine may change everything.

The public is often not aware of how the news magazine series got the story; true public relations professionals (or lawyers performing public relations acts) are more concerned with their client's needs than with promoting their own visibility. Thus, a televised account of a "poor, innocent" man imprisoned for years for a crime he did not commit is a public relations tool that appeals to the court of public opinion. In many cases, on the basis of the convincing television profile, viewers appeal to courts for new trials, or judges grant new trials in anticipation of public reaction. Sometimes the prisoner is subsequently freed.

The necessity of merging law and public relations leads to an even greater need for precrisis planning by representatives in both fields. Effective precrisis planning sets up scenarios for each type of crisis likely

to affect the organization. Different strategies and tactics are outlined for each kind of crisis. Examples are reflected in such statements as these: "If there is a loss of life, we will . . ."; "If there is no loss of life, we will . . ."; "If the media is unaware of the story, we will . . ."; "If the media is pressing, we will . . ."

A balance between public relations and law should, as much as possible, be determined before the crisis. A balance often cannot be accomplished effectively after the manufacturing plant has exploded. The PR professional should communicate with the organization's lawyer before communicating with external publics, even if it's not a matter of getting permission.

Lawyers who have not adapted to public relations procedures should be advised that some key stakeholders can be dealt with personally, whereas some key stakeholders will get negative impressions from the news media and social media.

Refusing to talk to reporters will not make the story go away. Reporters will get a story—and it may not be the story the company wants told. The board of directors of the United Way of America was not aware of this when, in 1991, its CEO, William Aramony, was accused of excessive spending. No one on the board would talk to the media. The story started as a brief section in a long, basically flattering article about Aramony in one newspaper. Editors of other newspapers read the article, focused only on the negative aspects, and soon public perceptions of misuse were nationwide.

The news media is a conduit to the public. The public rarely has any real evidence, at least not as much as juries in courtrooms do. Even though the public is well aware that reporters err, people still tend to believe what they see and read in the media. They make decisions based on sound bites and articles selected and written by reporters.

The court of law and the court of public opinion will remain crucial in deciding the fate of individuals, groups, organizations, and corporations. Both the public relations professional and the lawyer must learn to put clients in the best light in both courts to gain the best possible outcome to a crisis.

Communicating with Internal Publics

Internal publics include all classifications of employees—labor, management, hourly workers, interns—as well as retirees and stockholders. In a non-profit organization, volunteers are also an internal public. Internal publics are crucial in a crisis because they are the most believable spokespersons. Because internal publics may not be hired or paid to speak for the company, the news media seek them out for comment.

In many businesses, such as retail stores, employees are a link between the company and the consumer public. They are the principal representatives of the company and have the power to make a potential customer a loyal customer or to make a loyal customer a former customer.

Communication with internal publics before, during, and after a crisis is vital. For each internal public, you must choose the correct message and the correct medium.

Once a crisis has occurred, employees and other internal publics must be advised of what has happened early in the notification process. Whenever possible, internal publics should not learn of the crisis from the news media and they should know about it before external publics do. If the crisis occurs after office hours, all managers notified are aware of others they should inform. Those notified by those managers have others to contact, and so on. The telephone tree must be in place before a crisis. As a crisis develops, the employee public, called a *functional public*, should be kept apprised of what is occurring at every step. Common methods for keeping employees informed include meetings, closed-circuit television programs, e-mail, the public address system, and bulletin boards.

Many companies can utilize their intranet, internal networks designed to improve productivity and the circulation of proprietary information. The intranet is better than the Internet in the case of crises because it allows the company or organization to communicate only with its own people, whereas anyone can access the Internet.

Crisis communications researcher W. Timothy Coombs (1999) advises that "the beauty of the intranet is the speed of accessing information" (p. 85). The crisis team can access information directly with keystrokes on a computer instead of going through telephone calls or through other means. Information may be stored on the intranet, updated regularly, and any employee can access it. Coombs also warns that all information cannot be collected by using the intranet. Some interpersonal communications may be necessary, but the relevant data can be stored there after it is gathered.

During a crisis, internal publics generally want to know what they can or should do. During the Snapps restaurant rumor crisis (see Chapter 6), managers volunteered to take AIDS tests to prove that no manager could have spread the AIDS virus through food products. If it is important for employees to make some effort to continue the business, convey that to employees and tell them why. If there are crisis tasks employees need to take on, they should be preadvised and pretrained. If the nature of the crisis eliminates jobs—either temporarily or permanently—employees need to be carefully told what options are available and what the future is likely to hold.

As in normal operating mode, it is crucial that employees feel a sense of "we-ness" during a crisis, that they are part of the battle. Many companies order employees to remain silent about company issues relating to the crisis; they are especially told not to talk to the news media. They are told to let the appointed spokesperson do all the speaking. Often this is an advisable move; too many people can make for a confusing story. However, some companies and organizations do not fear the situation will get out of hand and encourage their employees to talk to the media, confident that employees like their jobs and their company.

Communicating with External Publics

External publics include consumers/customers, community members, government officials, labor unions, dealers, suppliers, trade associations, competitors, and other outside people related in some way to an organization. As in all types of communications, it is important to strategically plan the correct message and the appropriate medium for communicating with each external public, both before and during a crisis.

Organizations tend to form alliances with key external groups that will make members of these groups feel like they are part of the company. The airlines have been very successful with the frequent-flyer programs, so much so that other businesses are trying "frequent" programs too. Boards of directors and community advisory boards are also popular efforts at bridging the gaps between companies and organizations and the business world and the community, respectively.

Organizations should communicate with loyal consumers more directly than through the news media to inform them of the crisis and progress toward normalcy. Various methods must be evaluated—social media networks are popular methods, also letters, newsletters, notices on websites, telephone calls, and so on. You want customers to remain loyal throughout the crisis and continue to patronize the organization. So tell them all the five Ws of the crisis—who, what, when, where, and why.

Like consumers, community members will want to know what happened, what the cause was, what is being done, when the crisis will be over, and so forth. Community members can be reached through key community leaders on advisory boards. Flyers can be circulated in communities and posters can be put up in public places and on bulletin boards.

Labor representatives and government officials should be among the first notified. Key messages should be conveyed to them because these people, depending on the nature of the crisis, may be called on by the news media to comment.

Communicating Directly with the Masses

With new communications technology, it is possible to get information out to the masses. The Internet makes it possible to communicate with vast numbers of people through Twitter, Facebook, e-mail, blogs, websites, and any new methods that have been developed since this edition was written. This is mind-boggling when people living today recall when the manual typewriter was the most modern writing tool. There was a job title called typist. Newspaper printing meant setting each letter in type on brass dies individually on a Linotype machine. Newspaper boys delivered and persuaded people to buy the newspapers. Radio was the best broadcasting tool, not television, not satellites. When computers were born, they were giant machines that occupied a huge room. Now, in a flash, one person can send a message read by thousands, even millions of people.

This is progress, but few people have considered how this swift dissemination of information should mean new policies of accuracy. Historically, research tells us that people believe the written word more than the spoken word. This is because the articles in newspapers go through layers of editors before they are published. Most books (except self-published books) go through fact checkers before they are published. So people are inclined to think of data on the Internet as factual when it's not necessarily so. Some information has gone through editors but other information has come straight from the writer, who may be biased or wrong. Readers and researchers must discern what is true and credible.

Because information on the Internet remains primarily textual, some people may be inclined to think of it as factual. However, research findings from the University of Southern California's Annenberg School's Center for the Digital Future suggest that experienced information-seekers rank media and government sites as more reliable than those published by individuals.

The growing demand for news has made the Internet a valuable source of supplemental information. The traditional news media are still the primary sources of news for the unwired American, but as many as two-thirds of Internet users have accessed some of their news online and about one-third do so three or more times a week. In addition, the tragedies of September 11, 2001 made it clear that news-seekers want more immediacy than newspapers, commercial television, cable television, and radio can offer.

On the morning of September 11, 2001, the 24-hour news services reported to more than 100 million people. According to Nielsen Media Research, nearly 50% of all television households watched CNN's coverage. The commercial stations also had high ratings that day. However, according to researchers Paul N. Rappoport and James Alleman

(2003), the demand for more coverage and instantaneous updates led large numbers of people to the Internet. They say there is anecdotal evidence that the Internet, that day, became overwhelmed and left users without access or reasonable connections, but when it did catch up, it was an effective means of supplementary news.

Between 9 a.m. and 10 a.m. Eastern time, MSNBC.com experienced a 50% increase in traffic; CNN.com, a 450% increase. The sites were ill prepared for such surges as more than 30 million people sought online news. Many sites urged people to go to television and some had a written statement saying, "Many online services are not available, because of high demand." Internet sources have and probably will become more capable of handling the task.

Nevertheless, researchers conclude that the public has accepted online news sites as sources of credible news, although most Americans obtain their news from television—local, network, and cable.

Among the values of Internet news sources, according to Rappoport and Alleman, are the following: (a) information sources may be tailored to meet the specific objectives of the user; (b) the user may get the news at any time, no more "News at 11"; (c) news may be linked to other sources; (d) in-depth analyses may be available, even more in-depth than newspapers because the medium is not restricted by column inches or minutes of airtime.

Organizational and corporate websites provide background information and, in a crisis, what the organization believes is the truth. This gives the information-seeker the organization's side of the story. A website is normally a one-way means of communications, but the Internet can easily link one to other points of view.

Blogs

Blogs, or weblogs, are a type of website that consists of commentary from the author (or authors) with comments from various readers. The writing style is usually more casual and often more personal than traditional organizational or corporate communication. Blogs are one form of personal publishing and have several distinctive characteristics:

- Reverse chronological journaling (format).
- Regular, date-stamped entries (timeliness).
- Links to related news articles, documents, blog entries with each entry (attribution).
- Archived entries (old content remains accessible).
- Links to related blogs (blogrolling).
- RSS or XML feed (ease of syndication).
- Passion (voice).

A website is rather standard as an organizational communications tool, and blogging is growing in usefulness and importance. Because blogs can easily facilitate dialog between information-giver and information-seeker, they may be more believable than a traditional website. Blogs are good for public relations purposes, to provide accurate information for persons seeking information about your organization.

Blogs are akin to buzz. Whatever subjects or issues are occupying the minds of the public can be brought to the attention of many on a blog. Political blogs are popular, but all kinds of blogs are developing—from commercial business to education to basic gossip. In addition, the person wishing to post his or her opinion about an issue will find the blog more accessible than other forms of electronic expression.

Companies and organizations are being urged to develop blogs to garner web-based commentary about their products or services from consumers. The numbers of blogs are growing constantly and they can be accessed by search engines such as Google, Yahoo!, Technorati.com, or GlobeofBlogs.com. Technorati is one of the oldest blog search engines whereas GlobeofBlogs classifies blogs by subject. Information published in blogspace is disseminated faster than more traditional forms of communications through a technology called RSS (Real Simple Syndication). Textual blogs have given birth to video blogs and audio blogs, often known as podcasts.

In some cases, companies may need to have a blog format to show their publics that they are savvy about current technology. Companies and organizations may also find a blog to be the preferred publishing medium when an issue is constantly changing and it is urgent to get the latest information out as soon as possible.

Blog expert Kathy Gill asks, "What does the audience expect when they visit the website?" If the public is technically savvy, it will expect information in a blog format. Gill also notes that the voice of a blog is "personal" and cautions that "personal" is difficult for some organizations that require various levels of approval and sign-off. They tend to distrust having an unmoderated voice speak for them. In blogspace and in a crisis, there is often no time for multilayered decisions.

Blogging software makes the process of creating and updating a professional-looking web page relatively easy and less expensive when compared to a webmaster setting up a site. Some companies offer free hosting for blogging services. These blogs can be linked to other data on the Internet, other blogs, a corporate website, news articles, photo images, and audio files. The blogosphere is the word for the blog network with blogs interconnected to other blogs on the Internet.

There are five basic types of blogs:

1. *The corporate/organizational blog* provides commentary about a specific company or organization. Key executives usually are the bloggers, and their goal is to tell their own story, to correct misinformation of others. It is considered unethical for a corporate executive or employee to respond to a blog without revealing who he or she is and the connection to the organization. Will PR professionals ghost-write blogs? Probably. However, if the information seems like puffery, the readers will soon distrust it.
2. *Subject blogs* are comments relating to various subjects or issues written by experts on these subjects. Smudde (2005) says these blogs are like white papers or keynote addresses "as if to impart sage wisdom."
3. *Industry blogs* are centered on the status quo of a particular industry or field and otherwise are similar to subject blogs.
4. *Publication blogs* come from media sources such as newspapers, magazines, and other publications. Editors and reporters are the bloggers and sometimes readers. They are usually a way of keeping up to date on a continuing news story.
5. *Personal blogs* express opinions of individuals on any matter they choose to discuss, often politics, issues in the news, or products, especially high-technology ones. Smudde says personal blogs are the most potent type because subjects covered can be beneficial and helpful or hurtful to an organization's reputation.

The Harvard Business School's online tool "Working Knowledge" suggests the following reasons (in italics) for a company having its own blogs:

1. *You can influence the public conversation about your company.* Journalists can locate accurate information, the information you want them to have. You can correct misinformation and provide new information.
2. *You can enhance brand visibility and credibility.* This can give the company a human voice. Debbie Weil of BlogWrite for CEOs advises that companies not let their PR departments write blogs. This is true if the blogs are puffery, but not true if the PR writers can present the facts. Some PR firms are already offering expertise in "blog relations."
3. *You can achieve customer intimacy* because customers can speak directly to you, whether positive or negative comments. This is a kind of electronic, immediate, suggestion box.

Newspapers have begun to have blogs to supplement their publications. Different from an online edition of the paper, the blogs are updates on specific issues, continuing stories that may change several times before the next issue of the newspaper. Years ago, metropolitan daily newspapers used to do many editions throughout the day to always have the latest news; however, shrinking budgets and shrinking readership have ended that level of production.

Crisis communications researcher Amiso George (2005) at Texas Christian University writes of a newspaper's blog:

> The *Nevada Appeal*, Carson City, Nevada, newspaper developed its first web log before breaking news on its website www.Nevada Appeal.com to keep the public updated on the Waterfall Fires of 2004. From the onset of the fires on July 14 until containment on July 20, the newspaper provided frequently updated information on the fires. The paper's editor, Barry Smith, said that the initial coverage of the story followed traditional news coverage format, until he realized quickly that merely updating the news was no longer enough ... The paper updated the web log 50–60 times a day for the duration of the fire. Smith noted that the web log generated "terrific response" from people outside the Carson City and Reno, Nevada areas as people were interested in getting details of the fire and checking up on loved ones.

The *Times-Picayune* in New Orleans set up a blog for its readers. During the Katrina disaster in September, 2005, the presses did not run for a few days. Instead, reporters and editors published only online and used blogging software to "report" the news. As in New York after September 11, 2001, local bloggers provided their own news of what was happening to New Orleans. Survivors told very poignant, graphic stories without having a reporter as an intermediary. It was a kind of participatory journalism; everyone can be a reporter in the blogosphere. (See also "Hurricane Katrina and New Orleans," in Chapter 10.)

Chapter Five

Social Media and Crisis Communications

An increasing number of companies, organizations, and individuals are using social media outlets to gauge the sentiments of their publics, prevent crises, or cope with crises. In early 2010, Facebook, Twitter, and YouTube were the most utilized by crisis communicators and public relations professionals. The following are cases in which these and other social media were used.

Southwest Airlines

A Southwest Airlines flight made an emergency landing in Charleston, West Virginia, in July, 2009. The passengers were safe, but airline officials were not certain how passengers viewed the experience. Southwest had what it called an "emergency media team" that scanned Twitter, Facebook, blogs, and websites to ascertain passengers' reactions. The team found mostly positive commentary. So Southwest used that information to post tweets praising the work of the crew and the attitude of the passengers onboard.

Linda Rutherford, Vice President, Communications and Strategic Outreach, said the company would have reacted differently had the comments been negative. They would have still complimented the crew for the safe landing but in a different manner.

Coca-Cola Company

While monitoring Twitter, the Coca-Cola Company found a post from a frustrated customer; it revealed that the customer was having difficulty redeeming a prize from a My Coke reward program. The customer's profile showed more than 10,000 followers on Twitter. Adam Brown, head of the social media for the company, posted an apology on the customer's Twitter profile and offered to assist in getting the prize. The customer received the prize and, in appreciation, changed his Twitter avatar to a photo of himself holding a Coke.

JetBlue

Tony Wagner, a social media director for an academic group, used his skills to get a better seat on a JetBlue flight. He and his family were heading to San Francisco on JetBlue, and he discovered he would not be seated with his wife and child. The customer service agent was of no assistance, so Wagner posted a plea on his Twitter account. JetBlue tweeted back in 19 minutes and flagged his tickets as a priority. He got better seating. Morgan Johnston, a spokesman for JetBlue, said that disgruntled customers "tend to be the biggest opportunities" to show how consumer-friendly the company is. The then 770,000 followers on the JetBlue Twitter account saw the company trying to please one customer.

Wildfires in California and Australia

During California wildfires in fall, 2009, people were keeping their friends, relatives, and neighbors apprised of their whereabouts and the proximity of the fires through Facebook and Twitter and other social media. They also posted links to Google Maps so others could track the movement of the fires toward businesses, residences, and schools.

The American Red Cross used Twitter during the California wildfires to distribute information about preparedness and resources. Twitter was also used to connect to employees and volunteers to inform them of shelter availability and food and water distribution sites.

After fires in Victoria, Australia, Prime Minister Kevin Rudd posted messages to his 7,000 Twitter followers urging them to donate money and blood to victims. For the same fires, MySpace contacted more than two million users registered with a local group to inform them about emergency contacts and how to make donations. Several groups were created on Facebook to support families of those killed in the fires.

Government Agencies and the Peanut Butter Crisis

In December, 2008, tainted peanut butter made by the Peanut Butter Corporation of America was causing salmonella poisoning; eight people had already died and 500 were sickened. Three government agencies—The Centers for Disease Control and Prevention (CDC), the Food and Drug Administration (FDA), and the Department of Health and Human Services (DHHS)—needed to get warnings to the vast public quickly in order to curtail deaths and additional illnesses. The FDA had created a database of recalled products and looked to the CDC to spread the word because the CDC had the IT infrastructure to inform the public quickly.

They were using traditional media, but after a brainstorming conference call, they decided social media should also be used to tell consumers to

refrain from eating the infected peanut butter. They used the following: Twitter, podcasts, blogs, widgets, mobile alerts, and online videos.

The widget was created and then posted on websites run by other government agencies and by private organizations. The widget allowed users to search the FDA's database, and it was used 1.4 million times in 9 days. A subject-specific blog was launched on the FDA website. The posts were from health professionals and CDC officials, and featured video on how to avoid the banned products. A video was placed on YouTube to show people how to protect themselves against the tainted peanut butter.

Fargo Flooding

In March, 2009, the Red River in Fargo, North Dakota, was rising from floodwaters and was threatening the homes and businesses of the city's 92,000 citizens. The highest the river had ever crested was 40.1 feet in 1897, but this time it was expected to crest at 43 feet. The city was preparing to evacuate; four nursing homes began moving residents. Rescues were already taking place in rural areas south of the town as residents were stranded by the flood. A savvy citizen, Kevin Tobosa, urged city officials to set up a Facebook group and post a plea for sandbaggers. In a brief time, 4,550 Facebook friends had volunteered. They scrambled through freezing cold weather to load the sandbags before the sand froze and make the city's dike a foot higher. They saved the city.

Virginia Tech University and the Shooting Incident

The Virginia Tech campus was attacked by a lone gunman, a troubled student, in 2007. When the shooting ended, 32 students and faculty members were dead and also the gunman. The incident shows how social media is challenging the roles of traditional new media and authorities including the police, administrators, and public information officers because before any of these authorities could get information out, social media users were disseminating data, in effect serving as citizen journalists.

The college web server was down. Cell phones were jammed. Emergency service agencies were still in the dark when Wikipedia posted accurate facts of the event on its web page. Contributors to the campus newspaper, the *Collegiate Times*, posted blog entries on their parent company's website.

Students communicated with each other and parents by Facebook. They posted news and photos of the day's tragedy. There was a group site called "I'm Okay at VT." Facebook reportedly had 500 groups that included the Virginia Tech shooting subject. This was a turning point for Facebook, which had been previously viewed as a fun network.

Students uploaded photos to the Flickr photo-sharing line.

There were also blog posts on campus during the incident. One was a guy keeping people updated on his girlfriend, who was trapped in a classroom while the gunman was raging in an adjacent classroom.

A freshman, Bryce Carter, hiding in a dorm room, posted video he shot of police cars outside his window and blogged his friend on his personal blog, which was usually dedicated to partying, the environment, and sports.

Dr. Jeannette Sutton of Colorado University, Boulder, said the social media sites were able to identify all the names of the deceased accurately, before the official announcement was made. They provided information to the news media.

Social Media as Bad News

Citizen journalists are a godsend when they are geographically close to the site of a breaking news story and can pass accurate information on to news-anxious people or to the actual news media. People in Asian countries told the world about the tsunami in December, 2004 before the news media could arrive. An amateur videographer named Zapruder even caught the John F. Kennedy assassination on film. It happens even more frequently now that there is a cell phone with photographic ability in nearly every hand.

Social media can spread information quickly, but it can also spread misinformation just as quickly. The middle man is eliminated in the news gathering process. Trained journalists have editors who determine whether their stories are published or broadcast. Citizen journalists have nothing and no one preventing them from disseminating misinformation to a global audience in seconds.

Twitter Trouble

A Twitter hoax circulated after the Haitian earthquake in January, 2010. The false rumor (see Chapter 6, "Rumors and Cybercrises," page 63) was that airlines were flying doctors and nurses to Haiti free of charge to assist with relief efforts. A spokesperson denied the rumor by e-mail.

Another rumor on Twitter was that UPS would ship for free any packages under 50 pounds to Haiti. UPS debunked the rumor on a blog post on its website saying it could not deliver packages even if it was paid because roads were blocked.

Facebook Foils

A Canadian woman was on sick leave from her job due to depression. She had photos of herself on her Facebook page enjoying her own

birthday party, having fun at a Chippendales club, and on a sunny vacation. Her insurance company saw the photos and cut her benefits. She said the photos did not mean she was not depressed. She vowed to fight.

MySpace Mischief

In 2006, a 13-year-old Missouri girl took her own life after a neighborhood mother with a fraudulent MySpace account pretended to be a boy who befriended the girl for a while and then rejected her saying she was "fat" and "a slut." The girl, unable to accept the rejection, hanged herself.

E-Mail Error

The Admissions Department at the University of California, San Diego admitted responsibility for sending out erroneous e-mails to 28,000 students congratulating them on their admission when they had not been admitted. The error occurred after 47,000 applicants had been denied admission previously. Only 18,000 of those rejected were to be accepted after reconsideration.

Writing Social Media Messages

Social media is not only an effective method for monitoring and participating in proactive pubic discourse but also a tool for participatory crisis or emergency communications. The basic difference between crafting messages for more traditional methods of communicating and crafting messages for social media is the speed with which one can communicate information and misinformation.

Blogs, Twitter, Facebook, and podcasts are used to convey messages. They can build trust or they can destroy trust depending upon how they are used. More than ever, rules of writing are important and they will remain important no matter what social media are created.

The following are guidelines for social media writing. Most—marked by *—are guidelines for traditional media also:

- *Know your subject well. If you don't, research it well. Talk to experts.
- *Know your public(s). What knowledge do they have about the subject? You don't want to talk down to them, but you want to use all information needed to get them on your side.
- *What is the best method of communication? What is the best way to reach your targeted publics? Which social media network should

be used? Or is your public reached best by other methods? Believe it or not, there are still people who do not live by social media. One agency learned that baby boomers, its primary public, do not spend much time on the Internet even though they have computers and an Internet service.

- *Don't forget ancient tools such as telephones and direct mail. If your public is not large, a personal phone call could make a consumer feel important to the company; long-distance calling is relatively inexpensive or free these days. The same might be true of a real letter delivered by the U.S. Postal Service or other couriers. Letters can have more permanence than any computer generated product.

- Monitor social media to see what is being said about your subjects and who is communicating. Participate in the discussion. In Twitter, you may have only a few followers, but all your followers may have dozens or hundreds. By communicating you are building relation- ships, building a community. Some PR agencies make lists of tweets and blogs about their clients and give the list to the clients weekly so that they will know what the issues are.

- *When you begin to write, have the reader in mind. If you have monitored and participated in discussion, you have a good idea of who the reader is.

- *Think before you write. You need to think of your objective. What do you want to happen as a result of this effort?

- *Adopt a style. The most frequently used style book is the *Associated Press Style Guide*. Make sure you have the most recent edition. There are differences and changes in accepted style.

- *Make sure everything is accurate. Good writing is moot if the facts are wrong. If you make a mistake in social media, it is possible that thousands of readers are misinformed forever. There are no editors as in traditional media.

- *Make sure everything is clearly understood. A reader should not have to read something more than once to understand it. Social media are rapid methods of communication—rapid writing, rapid reading. People comprehend immediately or they don't read.

- *Be brief. Twitter limits you to 140 characters, but brevity is important in all social media. Each word should be essential.

- *Watch noun/pronoun agreement. This is the mistake made most by novice writers. A singular noun takes a singular pronoun; a plural noun takes a plural pronoun. For example, the following sentences are wrong. "The company tries to satisfy their consumers. They send them coupons every month." "Company" is singular. It takes a singular verb "tries" and can be substituted by the pronoun "its" and in the subsequent sentence another "It." So the sentences should be, "The company tries to satisfy its consumers. It sends them . . ."

Avatar—A computer user's representation of himself/herself; can be words, a name, or an image.

Blog—A contraction of the words Web and log, usually maintained by an individual or group with regular text, image, or video entries.

Blogroll—A list of other blogs or websites that a blogger recommends, usually found in a sidebar list.

Citizen journalists—Persons contributing information to sites. They may or may not have journalistic skills.

Comments—A section that follows a blog post, which allows readers to provide reactions to the content of the post or to other comments.

DM—direct message; a private message between Twitter users.

Emoticon—An image expressing the writer's mood (smile or frown) through the use of punctuation marks and letters/numbers.

Facebook—http://facebook.com; a free and popular online meeting place where "friends" can send each other messages. Users can join networks by city, workplace, college, etc.

Facebook friends—users on Facebook linked to others.

Facebook wall—a means of public messaging. There are personal walls accessible by profiles and group walls that enable people with similar interests to come together. Groups are the central use for crisis communications in this form of social media.

Flickr—An image and video hosting website; it claims to host more than 4 billion messages.

Follow—To add a Twitter account to the tweets that you see on your home page; unlike Facebook, the relationship is not necessarily reciprocal.

Hashtag—Keyword or term assigned to a piece of data or subject.

Koobface—A social media virus that infects computers when a video link is clicked. It can steal personal data and also trick the user into buying fake antivirus software.

Lexicon—Searches Facebook for keywords.

Monitter—Provides real-time monitoring of TwitterSpace.

MySpace—www.myspace.com; a free online social networking site with roots in music and entertainment.

Podcast—A series of digital media files (audio or video) maintained centrally on the distributor's server as a web feed. The listener can access the feed and download it.

ReTweet—When one Twitter member retransmits another member's message.

RSS—Real Simple Syndication, a family of XML formats designed to make it easy for consumers to know when frequently updated websites have new content.

Tweet—A message on Twitter.

Twitter—http://twitter.com; a free online service that allows members to share instant messages in 140 or fewer characters.

Twitterspeak—The language of Twitter.

Widget—An application that can be embedded into a third party website by any user who has rights of authorship, sharing information from one site to another by copying and pasting the code into one's own profile.

Wikipedia—Open source encyclopedia, allows anyone to contribute to entries.

YouTube—Video sharing and content syndication site founded in 2005 and owned by Google; it boasts more than 1 million video views per day.

Figure 5.1 Social media glossary.

- *Do not use redundancies. "The company hired a new technology manager." "New" is not needed; the company did not hire an old one. It could be "hired a second technology manager" or "hired its first technology manager" or simply "hired a technology manager."
- *Don't use emoticons—such as smiley faces—and abbreviations such as "icur" for "I see you are" in business communications.
- *Do use legitimate abbreviations such as "PR" in place of public relations.
- *Don't rely on your spell-checker. It doesn't find all typos. When public relations becomes pubic relations, you're in trouble.
- *Edit and proofread. It's often effective to have a second party proofread. The writer has been looking at the document too long (even if writing is swift) to notice errors. Be careful of multiple editors and writing by committee. Remember a camel is a horse designed by a committee.

Chapter Six

Rumors and Cybercrises

As we make progress in technology, we also advance the possibilities of rumor. The Internet is a great source of information and news, but it is an even greater source of misinformation and rumor. Opinion, guesses, assumptions as well as rumor present tragic consequences to people who are victimized because Internet users often believe everything they read is true. This was not the case with print media and it is even further from the truth on the Internet. Internet data just looks like factual information.

What Internet blogs, sites, and social media have done is provide faster, easier ways to circulate rumors and thereby cause crises for organizations and individuals.

A premature fact rumor (see "Types of Rumor," page 72) circulated on theater blogs in late 2009 written by anonymous "insiders" who posted claims that producers of the Broadway musical "Ragtime" had told the cast to prepare for closing the show. The show was not doing well at the box office, but producers had not given the actors notice. In fact, producer Kevin McCollum said, "The advertising was continuing, the investors had not pulled out or indicated they would."

McCollum did not suspect a conspiracy, a "malicious rumor." He expected it was a real estate move. When a show is not hot, speculation erupts about which theater will be available for the next show. However, when the speculation goes online, it also encourages possible patrons to forget about trying to see the show. Who wants tickets they cannot use even if they can get refunds?

Considering the increasing number of theatergoers who look to the blogs for reviews and information, this was a blow. "Compounding this is the fact that the methods of sharing and delivering hearsay have never been so frictionless," said McCollum. "There are far more outlets for rumors today and it's much easier to write a story about bad news than good news."

The show closed in early 2010. How much damage was done by the rumors is not known.

Of course, the new technology can also be used to fight rumor. This happened in 2007, when rumors circulated by word of mouth that tourist spots in California were closing due to wildfires. The California Travel and Tourism Commission (CTTC), helped by Edelman Public Relations, in addition to news conferences, monitored and participated in social media conversations to dispel the rumors. They also posted video footage of the recovery of burned tourist sites on its website.

Word-of-Mouth Rumors, E-mail Rumors, Rogue Websites, and Blogs

An unfounded rumor can be the most damaging attack an organization or company can experience. A rumor can put a company out of business; it can greatly affect the bottom line. In a mild form, it can be a nuisance that requires time and thought to determine whether to fight it and how to fight it. And because time is money, this too affects the bottom line.

There are three unique problems when coping with rumor:

1. You usually have no idea how the rumor started—was it an irate customer, a competitor, a person with nothing better to do or someone's conversation that was merely misunderstood?
2. You usually have no idea how widespread the rumor is or how long it has been circulating.
3. You have to determine carefully whether it is best to ignore the rumor or fight it—will fighting the rumor spread it more than leaving it alone?

Communications research often seeks to determine where people get their information, what sources are most trusted. Generally, more people get their news from television than from newspapers. Newspaper articles are more believable than advertising, but most people do not read newspapers. In recent years, we have discovered that the source of information most trusted by the American public is "other people." *The New York Times* can print a fact. *PBS Newshour* may broadcast the same fact. However, "Bubba, my cousin's next-door neighbor," can say something contrary and Bubba will be more believed. Internet sources are a combination of Bubbas and *The New York Times*, and to many people, they look the same. This attitude fuels rumor and makes rumor all the more dangerous.

The Nature of Rumors

Crises can, and often do, begin with rumors. In fact, a crisis can actually be a negative rumor. "Deep-sixing" rumors is an important task in crisis control and crisis communications.

A rumor is information passed by word of mouth and electronic communications with no verification of fact and no credible source. Rumors can be positive or negative. They can be absolutely false or partly false, or they can be undeniably true or premature facts. "There's a ring of truth in every rumor"—because people know and believe that expression, they tend to believe there is truth in rumors that are patently false and even ridiculous.

A rumor can begin as in the children's game "Gossip" (or "Telephone"), in which Child 1 whispers something to Child 2, who repeats it to Child 3, and so on. By the time the message reaches Child 10, it is usually unrelated to the original message. This is rumor spread innocently, but rumor can also be spread maliciously and intentionally.

The victim of malicious rumor rarely knows how the rumor started or who has heard it. This makes it difficult to curtail its spreading, which happens quickly and often with disastrous consequences.

How Rumors Start

One of the difficulties in establishing the source of a rumor is the realization that each person who passes it on may change it and thus be a contributing part of its source. The sources usually cited for rumors are rarely the actual sources. The rumors themselves may cite a specific person or institution that sounds credible, but the source is not readily available for verification. For example, the teller of a rumor might say, "I read it in last week's paper!" "What paper?" we ask. Not many people will go back and look for an article in last week's newspaper, especially considering that "last week" is also a vague term. Or the rumor teller may insist, "My aunt in Chicago was there when it happened!" This sounds convincing. But who will call the aunt and get specific details? Is there really an aunt at all?

Rumors are often started innocently. This was the case when talk show host Johnny Carson on his late-night show told a joke about a shortage of bathroom tissue. People heard about the shortage but not that it was a joke. There was a run on bathroom tissue in grocery stores. Soon the shelves were empty; the stock was depleted. This rumor was merely annoying to grocery stores and customers who remained tissueless.

However, some rumors started innocently can cause real damage. For instance, consider the Cable News Network (CNN) story about the Individual Retirement Account (IRA) that cited McDonald's as an example of corporations contributing to employee IRAs. In Great Britain, that story circulated as a rumor that said that McDonald's supported the Irish Republican Army—also called the IRA. Members of Parliament received numerous letters attacking McDonald's for financing attacks on British soldiers and civilians.

The following sections discuss two case studies of how companies coped with word-of-mouth rumors.

Mini-Case: Procter & Gamble and the Satanism Rumor

Procter & Gamble's original logo dates back to 1850; it depicted the man in the moon and 13 stars (representing the 13 original colonies) around the moon. The logo identified Crest toothpaste, Tide detergent, Pampers diapers—all the P&G products. Then in 1979, there was a rumor that the company had been purchased by the Unification Church headed by the Rev. Sun Moon (followers of the church are called "Moonies"). At first, calls came in to the Consumer Services Department's toll-free number. The company denied the rumor to consumers on the phone and also called news organizations in certain areas. Soon, the rumor changed to claim that P&G was involved in devil-worshipping, that the design of the man in the moon and 13 stars representing the original American colonies was a symbol of Satanism.

The Moonie rumor faded away and the Satanism rumor grew. A P&G executive, according to the rumor, went on a TV show and admitted a pact with the devil to gain success for the company. (The same rumor circulated about McDonald's and other companies.) Also, fliers were circulated, usually misspelling the company's name, claiming that 10% of the company's earnings went to the Church of Satan and advocating a boycott of P&G. Some church heads believed the rumors and advised their congregations to stop buying products from P&G.

The rumor went further and suggested that there was a 666 sign, the sign of the beast from the Book of Revelation in the Bible. Some saw 6's in the curls of the man in the moon when held up to a mirror. P&G was afraid to fight the rumor publicly because it would tell more people about it than already had heard about it. P&G sought the cooperation of religious leaders Jerry Falwell and Billy Graham who spoke up for the company and sent out letters to 48,000 churches.

Rumors subsided but sometimes recur. Some people were prosecuted, and that helped the public realize the rumors were false. Usually, charges were dropped after apologies.

The company started to phase out the logo in the mid-1980s, except on company letterheads and publications. It wasn't worth the trouble, and it had already cost $100,000 to fight the rumors associated with it.

Case: Snapps Restaurant and the AIDS Rumor

Rarely does a company call a news conference to fight a rumor. There are several reasons for this. Companies would ideally prefer to reach only

the people who have heard the rumor—and not one person more. This is a difficult-to-impossible task. Nevertheless, many times, the rumor is limited to a specific location. With a news conference, however, the media wind up spreading the rumor to people who have never heard it. Also, some companies reason that if the rumor is not spread by the media, it is not likely to reach the crucial public by the media either. The people who spread and believe the rumor may not read newspapers or watch television news.

The Snapps fast-food chain departed from both of these tenets in 1991, when it held a history-making news conference to fight a rumor about one of its restaurants. In Fort Pierce, Florida, Snapps confronted a rumor that one of its managers had AIDS and had contaminated hamburger meat. The Ohio-based chain had opened its first Florida restaurant in Fort Pierce in 1990. About an hour's drive north of Palm Beach, Fort Pierce is a middle-class city of 40,000 residents.

The location of Fort Pierce was important: Nearby Jensen Beach, Florida, was where Kimberly Bergalis allegedly contracted the AIDS virus from her dentist. Because Bergalis was the first person known to have contracted AIDS from a health-care professional, the incident was widely publicized. Furthermore, because of their proximity to the case, the people of Fort Pierce were probably more concerned with this case than many other people. The incident also aroused other questions about how the virus might be spread.

The rumor spread by way of a crudely handwritten flyer (see Figure 6.1). The flyer was circulated primarily among students in two public high schools, thereby targeting a large chunk of Snapps's clientele. The Fort Pierce Snapps restaurant saw its business drop by 50%. The Snapps corporate office in Columbus, Ohio, sent Regional Vice President Donald G. Gilbert to remedy the crisis.

Gilbert formed a damage-control task force that included a lawyer, a private investigator, and Richard M. Gruenwald, a public relations consultant for Dick Gruenwald Associates of nearby Palm Beach Gardens. The team worked closely with Rod Cardiff, a physician and director of the St. Lucie County Health Unit. Gilbert, the Snapps home office, and Fort Pierce Snapps owners Jack and Jeff Roschman monitored and approved actions of the task force.

The team's first task was to find the source of the rumor. The private investigator felt certain that a student in one of the schools had written the flyer. Police procedure called for a complaint to be filed before the police could enter the case. The investigator and the lawyer were able to collect enough information to file the complaint.

The next step was to have the restaurant's managers tested for AIDS. This decision had legal implications. By law, the managers would have to volunteer to be tested; the company could not force them to do so.

> Don't Eat Snapps, the manager has aids and he cuts he's finger and let the blood drip in the hamburger meat. don't die Early.

Figure 6.1 The handwritten flyer circulated at Fort Pierce high schools that helped spread the rumor that a manager at a popular restaurant was infected with the AIDS virus and that persons who dined at the restaurant might become contaminated. All managers were voluntarily tested and none tested positive for the virus. The health department cooperated with the restaurant's public relations efforts and, during a news conference, explained that the disease could not be spread in that manner. Reprinted by permission of Snapps Restaurant.

All seven managers volunteered, including one who had recently been transferred from the Fort Pierce restaurant to one in another city. The law also required that the test results be sent to the people who took the tests, not to the employer. The procedure took a week. The results indicated that all seven managers, as expected, tested negative for the AIDS virus.

Meanwhile, the Fort Pierce restaurant continued to lose business. Layoffs were threatened if business did not improve. "This was a double-edged sword," said Gilbert. "We had to be sure of our facts, have everything in place for the complaint filing and act quickly, as business was continuing to go downhill." Gruenwald, the public relations counsel, and his associate, John Futch, suggested a press conference. "We all agreed that a press conference would bring everything out in the open," said Gruenwald. "The problem was there. Why hide it?"

Snapps made public relations history when it became the first fast-food chain to address an AIDS rumor by going on the offensive and holding a news conference (see Figure 6.2). "We were most impressed with the way that management accepted our recommendations," said Gruenwald. To add credibility to the occasion, the press conference was held in the St. Lucie Health Unit's office, and the unit's director spoke on behalf of the franchise. At the conference, an announcement was made that the chain was offering a $5,000 reward for information leading to the arrest of the person or persons who started the rumor. The news conference was attended by company executives as well as the county health director, who announced that all Snapps managers had tested negative for the virus. He further stated that AIDS could not be transmitted through food and that it was safe to eat at Snapps.

Two West Palm Beach television stations led their 6 p.m. newscasts with the Snapps news conference story, including interviews with customers. Employees talked about how their jobs were affected. Associated Press and Knight-Ridder News Service picked up the story and it was used in newspapers all over Florida as well as in many newspapers out of state.

"The press was most cooperative and news coverage was excellent," Gilbert said. Gruenwald, looking back, said his philosophy was that "if you cooperate with the media, they—for the most part—will cooperate with you."

Other newspapers picked up the *Miami Herald* story; its lead emphasized the unusual public relations tactic: "In a highly unusual move, an Ohio-based fast-food restaurant went public yesterday to confront a rumor that one of its managers had AIDS and had contaminated hamburger meat." The article went on to comment on the restaurant's denial, the offered reward, and the fact that AIDS could not be transmitted through food. It also pointed out that other fast-food restaurants had been plagued by AIDS rumors, but Snapps was the first to fight the rumor through a news conference (see Figure 6.2).

The private investigator discovered that a 16-year-old female high school student had written and distributed the flyer, apparently after a class discussion on AIDS. "The girl admitted to writing the flyer," said Gilbert, "but we determined that the student's action came after the

STORE'S BUSINESS CUT 50 PERCENT BY AIDS RUMOR

By PHIL LONG
HERALD STAFF WRITER

PORT PIERCE—In a highly unusual move, an Ohio-based fast food restaurant went public Wednesday to confront a rumor that one of its managers had AIDS and had contaminated hamburger meat.

"The rumor is totally false," said Don Gilbert, regional vice president at Snapps, a company with 44 stores, mostly in Ohio.

"All of our managers have been tested and none has AIDS," he said.

But in a little over a month since the rumor started, business in Florida's only Snapps store has dropped almost 50 percent, Gilbert said. Five of the store's 40 positions remain unfilled, and employee hours have been cut. Layoffs are possible, he said.

The firm is promising a $5,000 reward for information leading to the arrest of the person who photocopied or circulated a crude, hand-drawn flier that accuses the manager of having AIDS and contaminating hamburger meat with his blood.

In what may have been the first press conference of its kind involving a national food chain, Gilbert met reporters in the lobby of the health department. He was flanked by the county's health director, Snapps employees, a company attorney and a police detective.

Snapps managers have been tested and they don't have any trace of the virus, said Dr. Rod Cardiff, director of the St. Lucie Public Health Unit.

'There is nothing unsafe about Snapps," he said. "AIDS is not transmitted through food. There is no danger with going to Snapps and eating there."

Fort Pierce police Lt Irving Hamrick, who suspects that a teenager is responsible because the fliers have been circulated at the county's two public high schools, said his department is investigating.

Prosecutor Linda Craft said the person responsible for the flier could face up to a year in jail on the misdemeanor charge of criminal defamation, it is illegal to publish anything that causes "hatred, contempt, ridicule or obloquy," to an individual, Craft said.

"They are not only affecting my job, but the jobs of many other people employed by Snapps," said Anita Farley, a Snapps worker who has been with the restaurant since it opened in July.

AIDS rumors are not new. McDonald's and Burger King have faced them before. Neither have gone quite so public . . .

■

Figure 6.2 An excerpt of a news story about the Snapps crisis appearing in the *Miami Herald*, May 9, 1991. Note the reporter recognized that the news conference was not a common method of fighting such rumors. Reprinted by permission of the *Miami Herald*.

AIDS rumor had been circulating in the community and she didn't start the rumor."

"The student, through her parents and attorney, agreed to issue an apology," said Gilbert. "We used the apology in a press release and a full-page ad in the local newspaper."

The minor, who said she wrote the flyer because she was concerned about her friends and wanted to do them a favor, wrote the following apology:

> I apologize to the community in helping to spread a rumor about Snapps, a local fast food restaurant. As a young person who has taken a course concerning AIDS and having great concern for the people in the community, I took it upon myself to prepare a flyer concerning Snapps without knowing whether the information I received as a rumor was true. I now realize that I was wrong and I apologize to Snapps, its managers and employees. It was not my intent to harm their business and I am sorry that Snapps' business has suffered as a result of the rumor. I have since returned to eat at Snapps and I encourage others to do so as well.
> Sincerely,
> C. J., a minor

Because the student was a minor, her identity was never made public. State Attorney Bruce Colton said a rumor could violate state laws that made libel a misdemeanor punishable by up to a year in jail. Prosecutor Linda Craft said the person responsible for the flyer could face up to a year in jail on the misdemeanor charge of criminal defamation (Knight-Ridder, 1991).

Gruenwald advised the company not to press charges against the girl. "It was never felt that the girl acted maliciously," he said. "Also, she did not start the rumor. It had been circulating before she wrote the flyer. If we had filed charges, we could win the battle, but not the war of public opinion. The public apology would bring her sympathy and perhaps a boycott to the restaurant. Then, the case might drag out, thus hurting the chances for a return to normalcy."

The media carried the story of the apology with headlines as follows:

Palm Beach Post—"Student Apologizes for Restaurant Rumor" (Reeder, 1991).

Stuart News (Stuart, Florida)—"Student Apologizes for AIDS Rumor About Eatery" (Cheek, 1991).

Miami Herald—"Student Apologizes for Spreading Rumor About Restaurant" (Long, 1991b).

As in most crises cases, recovery stories are not featured as prominently, nor are they as long, as the original stories.

Snapps management continued an aggressive effort to win back customers. Its advertising agency, Haunty & Welter of Columbus, Ohio, launched a strong radio and newspaper, and later, television campaign with a free hamburger weekend on June 1 and 2, 1991. "This was a tremendous success," said Gruenwald. "The girl who wrote the flyer, who we called 'C.J.,' attended the event." More than 15,000 free hamburgers were served. The event was promoted in a news release and resulting stories using C.J.'s apology (see Figures 6.3 and 6.4).

"If we had to do it all over, we would have followed the same crisis management and damage control program. In retrospect, this was an excellent example of crisis teamwork, everyone working together for the common good," concluded Gruenwald.

Gruenwald said the source of the rumor was never found. The restaurant changed names and managed to stay in business, although it never fully recovered its popularity.

Types of Rumor

There are six various types of rumor. The *intentional rumor* is started to achieve a purpose. The financial community thrives on intentional rumor. There are rumors to make stocks rise and rumors to make them decline. People might start rumors to help their own businesses. For example, a young, aggressive manager of a new restaurant getting off to a slow start in a campus community started a rumor at the college that a famous rock star was related to the owner and that the rock star might drop in that night. Needless to say, business boomed that evening, with patrons hoping to see the celebrity who never showed up. When patrons asked if the rock star would show up, the manager responded, "You never know." He offered each patron who asked a free drink. No one left angry. The manager said the ploy was a marketing technique to get people into the restaurant for the first time. He felt the food, the ambiance, and the service would get them back in the future.

The *premature-fact rumor* is an early version of what will eventually become the truth. In the workplace, for example, employees might hear and pass on rumors about layoffs that eventually turn out to be fact. Denying this type of rumor can be more damaging than being silent.

The *malicious rumor* is often started to damage competitors' businesses. For example, someone says, "The stew in the restaurant across the street is made up of last week's leftovers." This rumor may or may not be true. It may be true of half of the restaurants in town. Yet when told to the right people at the right time, the rumor spreads and causes a decline in patronage.

NEWS

DICK
GRUENWALD
ASSOCIATES
PUBLIC RELATIONS
4362 Northlake Boulevard, Suite 109
Palm Beach Gardens, Florida 33410
(407) 622-3200
FAX: (407) 627-6403

June 3, 1991

SNAPPS SERVES
15,000 FREE HAMBURGERS
OVER WEEKEND

FORT PIERCE --Snapps Restaurant celebrated its first anni-
versary in Fort Pierce giving away 15,000 free hamburgers Satur-
day and Sunday.

It was quite a turn-around for the drive-in eatery that saw
its business drop dramatically with a rumor that one of its
managers had AIDS.

Last week Snapps management announced that a Fort Pierce
teen-ager, identified only as "C J", had apologized for writing
and distributing a flier stating that a Snapps manager had AIDS.
"C J was one of our customers over the weekend," regional vice
president Donald Gilbert said.

Since the apology announcment, business has picked up but
still has a long way to go to return to normal, Gilbert said.

The weekend event was most encouraging, Gilbert said. There
were several large groups including one church with more than 100
kids and a compact car with 13 kids.

‡

For media information: Dick Gruenwald

Figure 6.3 One of several news releases distributed by the public relations firm hired
by an Ohio-based restaurant to manage the crisis in Fort Pierce. Reprinted
by permission of Snapps Restaurant.

The *outrageous rumor* is so unbelievable that people react by saying,
"It has to be true! Who would create such a story?" The Snapple Beverage
Company was the target in 1993 of an outrageous rumor that claimed
the "k" on its product labels, which stood for "kosher," actually stood
for Ku Klux Klan.

EATERY PLAGUED BY RUMOR FIGHTS BACK

STUART NEWS

FORT PIERCE—A Fort Pierce eatery gave away 15,000 hamburgers last weekend, battling recent rumors that an employee at Snapps restaurant tainted food with the AIDS virus.

Among the many people eating at the restaurant at 25th Street and Orange Avenue was a teenager known only as "C.J." The Fort Pierce Westwood High School student apologized recently for distributing a flier warning fellow students not to eat at Snapps.

Snapps Regional Vice President Donald Gilbert said the weekend promotion was a dramatic turnaround for the eatery, which saw business plummet because of the untrue rumor.

County health officials said food cannot be tainted by the AIDS virus. All the Snapps managers tested negative for the fatal virus.

Figure 6.4 A news story in the nearby *Stuart News*, June 5 1991, about the restaurant's crisis recovery process. Copyright ©1991 *Stuart News*. Reprinted by permission.

The *nearly true rumor* is so named because it is partly true. People hear it, attach credibility to a part of the story, and then draw a conclusion that the entire rumor must be true. This could have been the case when in the early 1990s a rumor circulated nationally that Reebok, during apartheid, was manufacturing and selling its products in South Africa. This was a crisis for Reebok because the company featured African American athletes in its commercials and marketed to African American consumers. It was true that Reebok once had manufacturing plants in South Africa, but the plants had been closed in 1986.

The *birthday rumor* is one that continues to emerge over and over again. It is as regular as birthdays.

The six primary categories of rumors can overlap. The outrageous rumor may also be malicious. The premature-fact rumor may be intentional, and so forth. One rumor that fits both the nearly true and the birthday categories is the ancient rumor that Chinese restaurants cook dogs. It is true that in China dogs are a delicacy, but that does not mean that owners of Chinese restaurants in the United States are out hunting your pets. This rumor can be traced to the 1850s in the United States and even earlier in Great Britain. The same rumor has now been told of Vietnamese cuisine in Texas, Mexican cuisine in Southern California, and Native American cuisine in Wisconsin.

How Rumors Spread

Rumors can spread throughout the United States, turn stomachs, perpetuate negative images, and cost millions of dollars in lost revenue. Corporations have to fight in the press, in the courts, and, in the case of Procter & Gamble, in the churches to stop the rumors.

A rumor spreads because people believe it is news and because the "news" has some emotional relationship to their lives. The rumor somehow seems plausible. Often the rumor refers to something causing distress or fear, and the rumor tellers who spread it are hoping to relieve their fear or distress by giving a reasonable explanation or denial.

Dr. Allan J. Kimmel (2004), of Fitchburg State College, in Massachusetts, studied 229 college students. The students passed on rumors about AIDS because they were personally relevant and upsetting. "The more frightened people were by a rumor, the more likely they were to repeat it," Kimmel said. "In repeating something that makes you nervous, you may learn some contrary fact that will calm you. On the other hand, it can escalate your fears if the person you tell believes it" (p. 51).

Rumors are also spread because people distrust the "establishment"—organizations, governments, and big corporations—or because the rumor tellers want to be thought of as people "in the know." Information is power. Telling rumors may give people who feel they lack power a sense that they are powerful. Therefore, people who have trouble making a success of their lives and careers are most likely to believe and spread rumors.

Detecting a Rumor and Preventing its Spread

Step-by-step instructions on what to do in the case of rumors are difficult, if not impossible, to provide. Variables such as potential damage, geographic location, type of organization affected, the nature of the rumor, and what crucial publics are affected require each organization's response to be tailored to the situation.

However, some general suggestions can be given for avoiding a crisis brought on by rumors as well as for fighting rumors that are already circulating. Be mindful, nevertheless, that this is not an exact science. Some of the suggestions are conflicting because there are various schools of thought on how to handle the problem.

The following suggestions are general steps organizations may take to minimize the chances of a crisis caused by rumor:

1. Because the victim of a rumor is often the last to hear it, establish a rumor center or rumor hotline to report any rumors circulating. Employees and customers/consumers would report a negative rumor

as soon as it is heard. Periodic focus groups of 10 to 12 people—employees, consumers, retailers, distributors, other related publics —might be held. Historically, hotlines have been special telephones. Telephones, though still often useful and immediate, are joined in their usefulness by social media, blogging, e-mail, text messaging, and the use of Blackberries. If necessary, a system of anonymous reporting might make a person more inclined to make a report.

2. Periodically train representatives of the organization or company in rumor control. These should be the people who would process and initiate the investigation of rumors; in a large company they might be hired for this purpose, or rumor control might be part of the job description for carefully chosen employees or organizational volunteers. These persons should be rumor-sensitive and well aware of the company's position with all publics. They should keep records of details of rumors and inform and advise management of tactics and responses to make. Communications here might be secret until communications action plans are made.

3. Conduct rumor workshops prior to the circulation of rumors to advise personnel on what actions should be taken in the event of a damaging rumor. Develop a rumor communications plan not unlike a crisis communications plan. Consider what rumors might be most damaging to your organization or company. Study rumors that have caused problems for companies similar to your own. Important to the plan is anticipating the role of the news media and online media. Is this the type of story that will be appealing? Will TV news use it in a sensational way? Anticipate trick questions such as "Isn't it true where there's smoke there's fire?" Many people might believe that a rumor is so unbelievable that it must be true. What would be the response? Can you prove the rumor is not true? If so, how?

4. Make sure the company or organization has such strong positive relationships with its key publics that the publics will at least doubt a negative rumor, if not totally disbelieve it.

5. Keep employees informed; remember that all employees and internal members are spokespersons. Employees left in the dark are fertile ground for the growth of rumors commonly spread by "the grapevine." Even if events that are bad news, such as layoffs, are a possibility in the near future, give employees real information and promise to keep them up to date. This is more advantageous than letting rumors circulate, because the rumors take on imagined and more negative characteristics than the truth. Informed employees can be a company's strongest supporters and loudest defenders. McDonald's followed this advice when a rumor circulated that there were worms in its hamburgers. It was a well-known rumor that had plagued Wendy's earlier. McDonald's personnel, on a one-to-one basis with

patrons who asked, denied the presence of worms. In addition, the employees recorded the names and phone numbers of those patrons. The strategy was intended to make customers knowledgeable about the company and, therefore, less likely to spread the rumor.

6. Evaluate the extent of a rumor. How damaging can it possibly become? Think negatively, imagining the worst case scenario. Determine the best action, if any.

Fighting the Rumor

The following suggestions are general steps organizations may take to fight a negative rumor that is already circulating:

1. When a rumor seems to be developing or circulating, disseminate to publics complete, accurate information that is contradictory to the message of the rumor. Do not mention the rumor itself. You do not want to advance its circulation. Your information should imply strongly that the rumor is untrue. This may reduce exposure to the rumor. Be advised, however, that fewer people are likely to see the positive news than the negative news.

2. After a rumor has circulated, analyze it. What is its probable origin? Why was it started? What is its possible impact? What are people saying? Are the rumor-mongers fired employees, irate customers, competitors or what? How many varieties of the same rumor are circulating? How does it circulate—word-of-mouth, e-mail, or Internet? Have the news media carried the rumor? Are people blogging about it? Does the rumor pose a threat to the success or existence of the organization? Those that do not pose a threat may be handled in a low-key manner without publicity. What are the geographical limitations of the rumor? Will it go away, either temporarily or permanently? Will it mushroom?

3. Do nothing. Sometimes denial draws more attention than silence. Some rumors do go away. When choosing this strategy, be careful that, if the rumor persists, it will not be damaging.

 Gerber Products chose to hang tough and be silent in 1986 when a grocery store charged that a customer had found a fragment of glass in a baby food jar. Gerber's test lab found no traces of glass in the jar, and the store had lost the fragment supposedly found in it. The FDA tested 40,000 unopened jars of Gerber baby food and concluded that no glass existed. Gerber relied on its state-of-the-art equipment designed to filter out any foreign objects larger than four-thousandths of an inch. It also X-rayed for possible breakage in the production line. There was no proof that there was glass in the jar.

Gerber felt it had proved the rumor false. Although the rumor continued to spread all over the United States, Gerber stood tough on refusing a recall. The rumor eventually died, and Gerber recovered sales, something the company felt it could not have done had there been a recall.

4. Deny the rumor publicly and vehemently, and prove it has no basis in truth. Once the rumor is shown to be unsubstantiated, a person who passes it on might be challenged with "That is absolutely untrue. I know because . . ." However, if the rumor is already widespread and potentially serious, a news conference is in order. The purpose is to show how erroneous the rumor is. In this news conference, do not repeat the rumor itself unnecessarily.

 Effective public relations is less expensive and the resulting articles usually more believable than advertisements. However, Allan J. Kimmel (2004), in his guide to understanding and combating rumor, *Rumors and Rumor Control*, warned against easy use of urging the news media to fight the battle, when saying that once the news media have the story, the organization loses control of the message and it may not be delivered to the publics in the intended way. Crucial data may be omitted or not stressed.

 Remember that a simple denial is not as interesting or as juicy as the original rumor. Just "saying" it's not so is boring. Rumor-mongers expect you to deny it. Why would you admit something so negative? Your denial must be persuasive and convincing.

5. To be convincing, get an outside expert on the subject to discredit the rumor. The expert should be a person with strong credentials who speaks with authority—a university professor, a leading physician, or some other professional.

6. Place ads in high-circulation publications. This is a powerful tool for reaching great numbers of people—if your message is convincing. If the message is not convincing, the ad may promote the rumor. Before placing an ad, be sure the rumor is totally untrue, not premature. In the latter case, ads can cause more harm than good.

Social Media Rumors

Where word-of-mouth rumors have put companies in crises for years, electronic rumors have given rumors wings. Social media and e-mail rumors can spread to thousands of people in seconds and, just like spoken rumor, they can change elements of the story with each transmission. The culture of cyberspace includes many individuals who apparently believe what they read on the Internet even when just the opposite seems to be the case. Although rules and laws will eventually be put into effect, at the beginning of the 21st century anybody can write

about almost anything on the Internet and to an even greater degree via e-mail. Some people, such as competitors, use social media and e-mail rumor with vicious intent; others use it merely to warn their friends. The transmission of e-mail rumors can be extremely damaging to businesses, organizations, and people in public life.

An e-mail rumor circulated in the late 1990s claiming that a customer ate chocolate-chip cookies from a café in a Neiman Marcus store, asked the waitress for the cookie recipe, and was told it would cost "two-fifty." Thinking that meant $2.50, the customer agreed, but found later that $250 had been charged to her credit card. According to the rumor, she said the store would not correct the discrepancy because she could have copied the recipe, so she was stuck with the charge. In revenge, she decided to tell everyone she could about the recipe and thereby circulated it by e-mail to people she knew and asked them to circulate it to everyone they knew. In a short time, the recipe and story were everywhere. However, the story is false. The Neiman Marcus store mentioned does not even have a café. Yet the e-mail rumor was widely transmitted and believed.

Another widely circulated e-mail rumor asserts that Kentucky Fried Chicken changed its name to KFC because it could not use the word "chicken" since what it sells is not chicken but "genetically manipulated organisms." The rumor further asserts that "the so-called chickens are kept alive by tubes inserted in their bodies to pump blood and nutrients throughout their structure. They have no beaks, no feathers, no feet."

As in most e-mail rumors, the writer of the KFC e-mail cited a believable source but got the facts wrong: "Listen to their commercials, I guarantee you will not see or hear the word 'chicken.' I find this disturbing." Actually the word "chicken" is used repeatedly in the commercials. The company changed its name to KFC to eliminate the word "fried" because some of their products are not fried and the company wants to appeal to a more health-conscious consumer public.

KFC officials released the following statement to the news media: "The hoax is intended to destroy the trust that you have placed in KFC to provide high-quality chicken meals at all of our restaurants. Although we hope that readers of the hoax will recognize it as obviously false, we take this or any other attack on the quality of KFC's product seriously" (Noack, 2000).

Battling Online Rumors

In 1999, the Public Affairs Office at the University of Texas Medical Branch (UTMB) at Galveston set up a web page to fight rumors. Faced with a fiscal problem and a projected deficit, several hundred jobs had already been eliminated and other jobs would be eliminated in the future.

The campus rumor mill was abuzz with gossip about which programs would be cut. The Public Affairs Office realized the rumors were sapping morale and threatening productivity. "Our biweekly employee newsletter, with its slower response time, didn't seem like the proper vehicle," said Chris Comer, UTMB's director of communications (Lucey, 1999, p. 6).

The university webmaster and art director worked together to create a website called "Rumors and Trumors." Accessed through a flying saucer button on the university's homepage, the site permitted employees to ask about the rumors they heard. The Public Affairs Office then tracked down and posted the answers. The site became a trusted and effective source for employees. Hundreds of rumors were explained or zapped, and morale was improved.

Fighting back with a proactive website is one tactic. If the company has a website and does not address a circulated rumor on it, it may make the company appear guilty. This happened in July 1996 when TWA Flight 800 went down off the coast of Long Island. The TWA website did not address the rumor circulating widely that the plane was shot down by a missile during a nearby U.S. military exercise. Alaska Airlines, on the other hand, put details of its 2000 crash online within an hour of the accident.

Janal (1998) advised three tactics for fighting all cybercrises, including e-mail rumors: pay attention, read the rumor and think about it, and put up a fight. Companies and organizations should be ever vigilant, watching for e-mail rumors. Encourage employees to notify the public relations department, or another designated department, when they notice e-mail or word-of-mouth rumors. If the complaint is legitimate, an appropriate solution to the complaint, and perhaps publicity about the correction, should be posted on the company's website, through the news media, or through some more appropriate outlet. If the rumor is unfounded and the source of the rumor is known, respond to the rumor. If the source is not known, respond to the listserv or Internet service provider (ISP) associated with the e-mail message that distributed the rumor. Fight in the news media and on websites. But do not wait for the rumor to go away. "To many people," said Janal, "silence equals assent."

At times, a decision must be made between fighting a rumor with public relations and fighting a rumor with lawyers. Public relations is the first step. If that does not work or is not feasible, call the lawyers.

Many companies establish a policy forbidding employees from making statements about the company while they are employed or after they depart. Employee comments on an attack site violate that agreement and expose the employees to punitive measures. This may work well in some environments, but it seems difficult to enforce, particularly with fired or other former employees who are frequently the culprits behind e-mail rumors.

Another tactic is to ignore the problem. Most Internet experts do not embrace this as a tactic and say it would be like a duck sitting in the water hoping the hunter's shot will miss. However, companies have been successful with it—watching and waiting and riding the problem out. If this tactic is taken, ongoing monitoring of the situation is crucial.

Kotcher (1999) advised the following:

1. Your company must respond to the e-mail rumor. If you remain silent, the only side of the story revealed is your enemy's.
2. Think strategically. Devise the best plan for the problem.
3. Speak with one voice. A clear, consistent message is mandatory.
4. Communicate your concern. Even if you are not guilty of the charges, be concerned.
5. Adopt an appropriate tone. Choose formal or informal language depending on the nature of the crisis.
6. Seize the opportunity. This is a chance not only to diffuse the crisis but also to build new alliances and reach goals.

Mini-Case: Microsoft Fights Fake E-Mailed News Release

The fake e-mailed news release began like this:

MICROSOFT BIDS TO ACQUIRE CATHOLIC CHURCH

VATICAN CITY (AP)—In a joint press conference in St. Peter's Square this morning, Microsoft Corporation and the Vatican announced that the Redmond software giant will acquire the Roman Catholic Church in exchange for an unspecified number of shares of Microsoft common stock. If the deal goes through, it will be the first time a computer software company has acquired a major world religion.

(Janal, 1998, pp. 270–273)

The fake news release went on to say that Bill Gates and Steve Ballmer would be invested in the College of Cardinals, and Gates was quoted as saying, "The combined resources of Microsoft and the Catholic Church will allow us to make religion easier and more fun for a broader range of people." The release also claimed that there would be a new software application called "Microsoft Church," that the deal would give Microsoft online rights to the Bible, and that comedian Don Novello, playing his *Saturday Night Live* character, Father Guido Sarducci, hosted the announcement that was broadcast by satellite to 700 sites worldwide.

If anything remotely like this were true, which is ludicrous, it would have been a front-page, top of the newscast story. So how could anyone believe it on an e-mail transmission? So many people believed it, or, at least, thought it might be true, that they contacted Microsoft for confirmation. The fake news release also made the news. The company had to issue a news release denying the rumor.

Mini-Case: The Killer Banana Rumor

A rumor circulated both on the Internet and via e-mail claimed that bananas from Costa Rica were infected with "necrotizing fasciitis," or flesh-eating bacteria, and that the entire Costa Rica monkey population had been wiped out because of the bananas. It warned the public to stop eating bananas and to seek medical attention if they had eaten a banana and had come down with a fever. The bacteria, it said, could "eat" 2 to 3 centimeters of flesh per hour, making amputation likely and death possible.

The message, like most e-mail rumors involving food, said the message could be confirmed by the Centers for Disease Control and Prevention (CDC). Rumors tend to carry an expert's name to make the outrageous rumor seem believable. When contacted, a spokesperson for the CDC said, "This is a false report."

APBNews.com reported on the incident, saying a trade group was trying to squelch the rumor. Tim Debus of the International Banana Association (IBA), an organization directly affected by the rumor, called it "Just another case of Internet terrorism like the recent hacker attacks on popular websites." The National Necrotizing Foundation, which researches such diseases and offers support and education services, said it was not possible for the disease to spread in the way the hoax claimed (Noack, 2000).

Debus indicated that the IBA, concerned that the prank could disrupt the economy, made efforts to get the word out that the allegations were false.

Rogue Websites

Rogue websites are normally created by disgruntled individuals with the intention of bringing attention to an issue or several issues concerning a corporation or organization. The company attacked in the rogue site must consider whether to respond and if it responds, how. Sometimes no response seems appropriate because the site appears to be simply vicious, but the company must determine, as best it can, whether readers will actually believe the claims made. Are Internet users sophisticated enough to realize that information on any website, especially a rogue website, is not necessarily factual?

Dr. Louis K. Falk, in his research on rogue websites, classifies such sites into five categories. The five categories are the following:

1. Sites in which consumers are unhappy with the performance of the company. Examples include a rogue website that targeted Wal-Mart; it featured complaints and comments from customers and employees and claimed that "a considerable amount of content on this site is from other sites around the world."
2. Sites in which consumers are unhappy with the policies of the company. Examples include a rogue site aimed at Pepsi that featured complaints that the company supported animal cruelty because it placed ads at bullfights.
3 Sites in which consumers or former employees have negative feelings toward the company. Examples include a disgruntled former employee of Burger King who set up a website to complain about creatures in the salad, low wages, and office politics. The information was so rambling that the discerning reader got the impression "Somebody got fired and has a vendetta against Burger King." Burger King would probably be advised to ignore the site. Another rogue site complained that McDonald's was not environmentally concerned because it killed animals, damaged the planet, harmed the health of consumers, and paid employees low salaries. Few customers of McDonald's likely cared, as anyone concerned about killing animals for food doesn't order Big Macs.
4. Sites in which consumers create humor pages, also called "spoof sites." Examples include a site aimed at making fun of Taco Bell that clearly states its intentions. The webmaster says, at the top of the homepage, "I am not Taco Bell. I'm just a freak that likes to eat their food. If you want to write to Taco Bell, please go to tacobell.com. This page is meant to be a fun page." The site's criticism is so minimal, the reader may wonder if Taco Bell might have masterminded the site itself. In one central spot, the hot sauce is criticized for not being hot and the quality of the meat in Taco Bell Lunchables is questioned. But the webmaster admits that the humor comes from his or her marijuana use as well as his or her relationship with Taco Bell.
5. Sites in which an index is created for complaints of multiple businesses. An example is www.sprawl-busters.com, which battles large-scale retail stores and megastores such as Wal-Mart, K-Mart, and Target.

Another type of Internet crisis can develop when a company's own website is invaded. This occurred when a medical products company in Michigan discovered that hackers had posted on its own website a false

news release saying the company was merging with a pharmaceutical firm. Stocks for both companies rose on the NASDAQ index after the fake posting. The medical products company indicated it would pursue the hackers and reassess its security.

The rogue sites that seem designed to destroy a company are often called attack sites or antisites. Many times, the web address is made up of the company name followed by the word sucks—as in yourcompany sucks.com.

How Do Companies Prevent Rogue Websites?

Cyberexperts advise companies to purchase several domain names, including buying up the "sucks sites." This is only a temporary remedy because the clever webmaster can merely set up a rogue site using "stinks" instead of "sucks," making Xcompanystinks.com. Then there are numerous other synonyms that can be used. The irate webmaster can also purchase Xcompanyreallysucks.com and Xcompanystillsucks.com.

Site suffixes have been a problem, too. For example, "whitehouse.gov" is the website address of the real White House in Washington, DC, but a spoof site, "whitehouse.org," was set up, and also a pornography site at "whitehouse.com." It would seem that government Internet and web experts could have prevented these occurrences by anticipating the need to control both sites.

Another Internet address problem occurred when Sno-Isle Regional Library in Snohomish County, Washington, set up a website for bibliophiles to reserve books. There is a hyphen in the address. If the hyphen was not typed in the address, the computer user would get a pornography site. The address of the pornography site is not sexy and seems to have no relevance to its site. The library suspected that the pornography site webmaster wanted the library to purchase the address or merely wanted to play a trick on the library. So the library's legal representative entered the picture.

In November 1999, the Federal Anticybersquatting Consumer Protection Act was signed into law. It allows the holder of a copyright or trademark to sue cybersquatters who have registered copyrighted domain names, and it forces them to relinquish those Internet addresses.

The most important prevention method is acquiring a federal trademark registration for the company name. The first company or the first person to register the name holds the rights. It is also advisable to register the company trademark and product name under all possible domain name variations (.com, .org, .net, etc.). Companies are advised to register their names with and without hyphens. For example, 1-800-dentists.com and 1800dentists.com are two websites owned by two different companies. Confusion is apparent.

If your company has a federal registration for its name, and if another company or webmaster has taken the name as its domain name, write to the domain name holder and tell him or her that he or she is infringing on your trademark. If he or she fails to transfer the domain name, go to Network Solutions, Inc. (NSI), the organization responsible for the administration of domain names in the United States and Canada. Present NSI with a certified copy of the federal registration and ask to place the domain on hold. Neither party will be able to conduct business at that website until the dispute is settled. If the problem continues, a suit in federal court is the next step.

Use a monitoring service. These services help companies track online problems and manage their reputations through online resources and interactions. A Phoenix-based division of WavePhore, called "eWatch," prowls websites and assists companies with damage control when criticism hits the Internet.

What to Do After an Attack Site Is Up

If a company is the victim of an attack site, Falk suggests the following tactics:

1. Do not overreact; the problem may not be as bad as it seems.
2. Assess the problem. Consider whether the information is true or false, whether many key stakeholders have seen the site, and whether the persons making the claim are credible.
3. Analyze the attack site.
 (a) Do not pretend you are a consumer; webmasters of rogue sites recognize misleading communications.
 (b) Get a picture of how damaging the site is. How are you affected? Learn all you can about the attitudes of your publics and the issues most important to them.
 (c) Contact the webmaster of the attack site by telephone, face to face, or through e-mail. This gives you someone to hold accountable and helps develop a relationship with him or her if that is helpful. It also tends to force people to observe a higher standard.
 (d) If the issue is big enough, contact your key stakeholders. This allows you to build a personal relationship with them and educate them about the attack site.
4. Drive the discussion by allowing your employees to be interviewed on your website. Make your company the expert on information about your company. Even if there is a negative aspect, admit to it and tell what your company is doing about it.

If there is no doubt that the site is an attempt to damage the company's reputation, Kim Bayne (as cited in Janal, 1998, p. 240) suggests the following steps:

1. Make a complete mirror of the attacking websites for reference purposes.
2. Find out the webmaster's point of view. Is the webmaster a disgruntled customer, an ex-employee, a competitor, or a prankster?
3. Create rebuttal pages at the company's website to address all accusations and implications. However, don't post the rebuttal pages at the company's site until you have gauged the public's reaction, or you may unwittingly stimulate interest in the attack site.
4. Prepare written statements for your crisis communications team, and make sure all team members agree on how to route inquiries about this particular website, should it become an issue.
5. Telephone the webmaster and explain your concerns about the misinformation. Do not be accusatory, angry, or threatening. Ask him or her to remove the site. Explain that you would like the opportunity to present your company's view in an unbiased manner at the attack site. Use your communications skills first to try to resolve the problem.
6. If for any reason you are unable to communicate with the webmaster, it's time for your company to draft a nice letter spelling out the situation and asking for resolution by a specific date.
7. Still not getting results? I'd apply the "three strikes" rule here. If after the third attempt to "play nice," you still don't get results, then it's time to get your company lawyer involved (Janal, 1998, p. 240).

The mini-cases discussed in the following sections involve rogue websites.

Mini-Case: Alaska Airlines and the Good and Bad News Websites

After the 2000 crash of Alaska Airlines Flight 261, Alaska Airlines was one of the first major companies to put its bad news on its own website within an hour of it happening. The story was placed on the employee site because several persons on the flight were nonrevenue passengers, primarily employees. However, Alaska had to battle fraudulent sites also.

Two fraudulent websites were created to solicit donations for the families of the passengers and crew. The webmaster of the first rogue site used the Alaska Airlines logo to masquerade his or her site as an official Alaska Airlines page. Visitors who downloaded the fake contribution form

unleashed a computer virus that allowed outsiders access to information on their computers.

Company executives were tipped off about the rogue site by an e-mail message. Needless to say, the company, still in shock over the tragedy, was doubly shocked. Company spokesperson Brian Petro said, "We just couldn't understand. It was unimaginable someone would do something like that" (Stiffler, 2000, p. A10). Alaska Airlines contacted the rogue site's Internet provider and asked that the site be removed. The ISP, Costa Rica-based Freehomepages.com, complied.

A second rogue site asked for Social Security numbers of Alaska Airlines employees under the guise of donating to coworkers. The site was also purged. It is not known how many Internet users fell prey to the fraud. Alaska Airlines also issued two news releases about the fraudulent sites. The releases warned the public that the sites were fraudulent and vicious and revealed information about the official site, www.alaskaair.com, and fund-raising efforts.

Mini-Case: Dunkin' Donuts Adopts a Rogue Website

The webmaster of a rogue site aimed at Dunkin' Donuts said he or she had "way too much time on [his] hands" and posted some thoughts about Dunkin' Donuts on a personal website. Within a few weeks, the site had "an unusual [but welcome] influx of visitors." The webmaster learned through the referrer log at Yahoo! that all of these visitors went through Yahoo! to access the site. The webmaster also learned that Dunkin' Donuts did not have its own website, so Yahoo! indexed the rogue site as a "consumer opinion" website about Dunkin' Donuts.

The site started getting "500 hits and a dozen e-mails a week," it said. Then the webmaster requested and was granted the use of the domain name "dunkindonuts.org" and moved the content previously posted on his personal website to the new official website. The site made news (Segal & Mayer, 1999, p. A01).

It must be said here that 500 hits are not necessarily 500 complaints. People stumble onto sites. Curiosity leads them to sites. Also, one person may "hit" a site more than once, so it doesn't even mean that 500 people visited the site. And the webmaster himself admits on the page that some of the hits come from people who "are from Dunkin' Donuts headquarters doing 'damage control,' 'lurking,' or eavesdropping."

Dunkin' Donuts started to respond to the comments on the rogue site. Jennifer Rosenberg, a Dunkin' Donuts spokesperson, was quoted on the top line of the rogue site as saying, "If this was where customers were going to post their comments, we thought it was important for us to go ahead and address them." Soon after, Dunkin' Donuts made arrangements to acquire the site for its own use.

Mini-Case: America Online and a "Sucks" Site

This "sucks" site charged America Online (AOL) with being "the MTV of the Internet . . . competitive on prices, but disastrously poor in service." The site contained several pages of detailed and focused text. James M. Egelhof was identified as the rogue site's webmaster.

An AOL webmaster wrote a letter to Cloud 9, the ISP of Egelhof's site, saying the site violated the ISP's rules: "Both as an Internet user and as an AOL employee, I find his web page to be offensive and disturbing. Because Mr. Egelhof has chosen to use a noninteractive medium to express his opinions, he is not providing an avenue for an AOL response to these allegations, and thus his communication can be considered harassment [a violation of the ISP's rules]."

Another violation was of the ISP's rule that users may not use the system to distribute and/or store illegal copies of commercial software. The AOL webmaster's letter to Cloud 9 continued: "The use of AOL online art in this site is extensive. Please remove the graphics on these pages to avoid possible legal action. I am currently contacting our legal department to determine if they (sic) would consider Mr. Egelhof's opinions to be libelous and to discover precedents for legal action in this medium."

Egelhof maintained that AOL's threats were groundless and that he had broken no law. He said he checked with his attorney about the harassment and libel threats and was told they were "garbage." He said he was also advised "that when a large corporation uses lawsuits (or the threat of them) to try to silence critics, that there are grounds for a harassment suit against the corporation."

At this point, there was much talk about the incident in several newsgroups, and the number of visits to the rogue site increased, Egelhof said, from 20 to 360 daily. As the talk continued, AOL Vice President Lyn Chitow posted an apology and mailed it to those who complained about the company. The main points of the apology were the following:

1. "We are not in the business of censorship and believe strongly in individual freedom of speech."
2. "We know we are not perfect and welcome feedback about how to make it better."
3. "The author of the [rogue] web pages was expressing his view of America Online, and I personally found it insightful and helpful as we strive to make it the best service it can be."

Interestingly, the AOL webmaster who took Egelhof to task offered him a job, saying "We are looking for folks who know (the) web."

Blogs

Blogs can be positive or negative. Blogs used to be personal online diaries but they have grown to become expressions of opinion on any subject. Beginning with the September 11 attacks of 2001, and continuing with all great disasters, including the Asian tsunami in late 2004 and Hurricane Katrina in 2005, bloggers (persons who write blogs) brought to the Internet numerous revealing personal stories that helped us get the big, broader picture of the tragedies. However, the basic nature of blogging can be dangerous.

Why is it dangerous?

1. A 2005 study by the Carnegie Corporation revealed that 44% of 18- to 34-year-olds get their news from online sources, including an increasing number of sites in the blogosphere. By early 2005, 32 million Internet users had accessed blogs.
2. Even though most bloggers and most Internet users who read blogs are well educated, it is difficult to differentiate a blog site set up by a news medium and one set up by an irate person or organization.
3. A blogger is not necessarily employed by a news medium or trained or experienced in the basic tenets of journalism—balanced and objective coverage. A blog is closer to a letter to the editor than a news story. Yet there is no editor to assure checks and balances as in traditional newspapers, television, and radio news. Bloggers can and do write whatever they wish, and their writing may be full of errors, flaws, and innuendo.

This means that organizations and companies must monitor blog sites in order to know what publics are saying about them, just as they monitor phone calls, letters, rumors, and complaints.

One blog crisis occurred when a Google employee posted a complaint about his salary on his Google blog. He was subsequently fired for divulging proprietary information to a vast external public. This caused companies to develop rules governing what can and cannot be said on a blog site.

Conclusion

As the Internet's many possibilities emerge, there will be more and more opportunities for attacks. Hopefully, laws will be established to protect while still providing freedom of speech and expression. The basic lesson to be learned in all forms of communication—from word-of-mouth to word-of-electronics—is "Watch, Listen, Learn."

Chapter Seven

"Textbook" Crises

The Johnson & Johnson Tylenol case and the *Exxon Valdez* oil spills case, both in the 1980s, set the stage for the development of the field of crisis communications. Up to and including these landmark cases, organizations and companies, for the most part, handled their crises as best they could, without crisis management or crisis communications plans.

These crises made the organizations realize that there should be plans, and were the key examples of what to do and what not to do. Johnson & Johnson was reputed to be the stellar company and Exxon to be the prime example of what was bad in communications and public relations. Actually, the case studies reveal that Johnson & Johnson made a mistake in its handling of the crisis, though it was honest about the mistake. And Exxon, though still blamed for the tragic, widespread oil spill, was not solely responsible and made some positive moves to help the state of Alaska recover.

Case: Johnson & Johnson and the Tylenol Murders

Before September 30, 1982, manufacturers felt that if they made a good product and dealt fairly with consumers, retailers, employees, and other publics, they could maintain a positive image and be considered consumer-friendly, a good company with which to do business.

Johnson & Johnson was one of those companies. It was an old and trusted company. With 165 companies in 53 countries throughout the world, it made baby products, baby powder, lotions, shampoos, cotton swabs, adhesive bandages, surgical instruments, Reach toothbrushes, Ortho-Novum birth control pills, and pharmaceuticals in the World Health Organization list of essential drugs. Johnson & Johnson was a household name.

The corporation also had a positive image among its employees. It was listed as one of the 100 best places to work. The company credo was

written by the son of the company's founder in the 1940s (see Figure 7.1). The credo said that the company had four responsibilities in the following order of priority: to the consumer, to the employees, to the communities, and to the stockholders.

The company also had continually good relationships with the media. Little did it realize just how crucial those relationships would become.

September 30 began like any other workday at the headquarters in New Brunswick, NJ. Then a fateful telephone call came in.

A reporter from the *Chicago Sun-Times* telephoned a public relations staff member asking such questions as "How long has Tylenol been on the market?" and "What is Tylenol's share of the market?"

The reporter did not know why he had been asked to prepare background information on Tylenol. Someone else was writing the story. An editor had merely assigned him to do background research to use in the main story. The Johnson & Johnson staffer, who then alerted most of the department, thought the call was a bit strange and reported it to Public Relations Director Robert Kniffin. Kniffin called Arthur Quilty, an executive committee member who had responsibility for McNeil Consumer Products Corporation, a subsidiary. Quilty alerted James Burke, CEO. The reporter later called back and explained there had been reported deaths from the intake of Extra Strength Tylenol.

Corporate Vice President Lawrence Foster, who was on vacation, called in, as was his daily practice, and when he learned what had happened, he immediately returned to the office and took charge of the public relations activities.

The corporation had no specific crisis communications plan—few companies did at the time. It did have an emergency plan and call list for such incidents as plant fires. The first step was to notify the chain of command.

There was an immediate meeting in Burke's office with top executives, including Lawrence Foster, head of public relations; David Clare, president and chairman of Johnson & Johnson's executive committee; Joseph Chiesea, president of McNeil Consumer Products Company; and David Collins, chairman of McNeil.

At that meeting, Foster dispatched Kniffin to McNeil's headquarters nearby. Collins, who had been president of McNeil Pharmaceuticals and knew the subsidiary well, was sent to McNeil by Burke. This would actually have been the next step in a crisis communications plan—had there been such a plan.

The executives all said that it was a period of great fear. There were no warnings, no prodromes. Nothing like this had ever happened to them or any other company that provides products for human consumption. What was going on? Was there a psychopathic murderer in the plant?

Our Credo

We believe our first responsibility is to the doctors, nurses and patients,
to mothers and fathers and all others who use our products and services.
In meeting their needs everything we do must be of high quality.
We must constantly strive to reduce our costs
in order to maintain reasonable prices.
Customers' orders must be serviced promptly and accurately.
Our suppliers and distributors must have an opportunity
to make a fair profit.

We are responsible to our employees,
the men and women who work with us throughout the world.
Everyone must be considered as an individual.
We must respect their dignity and recognize their merit.
They must have a sense of security in their jobs.
Compensation must be fair and adequate,
and working conditions clean, orderly and safe.
We must be mindful of ways to help our employees fulfill
their family responsibilities.
Employees must feel free to make suggestions and complaints.
There must be equal opportunity for employment, development
and advancement for those qualified.
We must provide competent management,
and their actions must be just and ethical.

We are responsible to the communities in which we live and work
and to the world community as well.
We must be good citizens — support good works and charities
and bear our fair share of taxes.
We must encourage civic improvements and better health and education.
We must maintain in good order
the property we are privileged to use,
protecting the environment and natural resources.

Our final responsibility is to our stockholders.
Business must make a sound profit.
We must experiment with new ideas.
Research must be carried on, innovative programs developed
and mistakes paid for.
New equipment must be purchased, new facilities provided
and new products launched.
Reserves must be created to provide for adverse times.
When we operate according to these principles,
the stockholders should realize a fair return.

Johnson & Johnson

Figure 7.1 The Johnson & Johnson credo that guided the company's crisis team
through the ordeal of saving the company's image, even as news accounts
reported that the company's Tylenol product was killing consumers.
Reprinted by permission of Johnson & Johnson.

When the story ran in the media, the public also was afraid. The very idea that a person could take a capsule for a headache and die was terrorizing. People were saying, "I have a terrible headache, but I'm alive." Even consumers outside the Chicago area were afraid of Tylenol capsules, if not also afraid of all over-the-counter pain medications.

Collins immediately set up a seven-member crisis team. The team's first task was to find out what sickness it was actually facing. Then it would determine how to go about the healing process. The crisis team handled decisions in the area of communications and was in charge of all strategies and tactics. With Burke's approval, the team decided to recall all Tylenol capsules from stores in the Chicago area.

Cyanide turned out to be the cause of the deaths. The recalled batch was tested and two additional cyanide-laced capsules were discovered. Still, the team and company were uncertain of how the cyanide got into the capsules. It indeed hoped that the criminality was not in the company, but there was no certainty.

Johnson & Johnson had one overriding priority: Warn the public. The company did just that by being completely open and cooperative with the media in getting the news out.

Foster said he believed that three points marked the reason Johnson & Johnson was successful in coping with the crisis:

1. The company was open to the media.
2. It was willing to recall the product no matter what that meant to the company.
3. It appealed to the American sense of fair play and asked for the public's trust.

Foster was responsible for the communications aspect of the crisis team's work. The team was concerned with aiding police and the FBI in finding the responsible party and in dealing with the Food and Drug Administration (FDA).

First, the crisis team identified its key publics:

1. Consumers (through the media).
2. The medical profession.
3. Employees and other internal groups.
4. The FDA.

All publics were notified initially, and the team kept in touch with them throughout the crisis.

The first story appeared in the morning edition of the *Chicago Sun-Times* on October 1. The *Chicago Tribune* ran a story that same afternoon under a banner headline:

OTHER REMEDY MAY BE SAFE, BUT CUSTOMERS DON'T BUY IT

CHICAGO TRIBUNE

DUST IS COLLECTING on some drugstore shelves in the Chicago area, and people apparently are learning to live with headaches in the wake of last week's tragedy involving Extra Strength Tylenol laced with cyanide.

An informal survey of drugstores throughout the Chicago area showed that sales of most acetaminophen products have dropped while sales of aspirin have increased slightly. Acetaminophen is the nonaspirin substance used in Tylenol and other pain relievers.

"In general acetominophen products are not selling. Point blank. Done in. Dead. Aspirin products are picking up a bit, but the scare seems to have spread through the shelves," said pharmacist Paul Bablak of the Hinsdale Medical Center Pharmacy. "We're collecting a lot of dust on our shelves. People are scared, and you really can't blame them."

If the fear of cyanide poisoning can be measured by the stillpacked medication shelves at drugstores, then the fever is spreading through the metropolitan area, several other pharmacists said.

"I think everybody's walking around with headaches," said Jerry Denny, a pharmacist at Family Pharmacy in west suburban La Grange. "All the acetaminophen products are just sitting on the shelves. Even generic acetaminophen is moving slowly."

The slow sales were found not only in smaller, private drugstores but also in chain stores. Jane Armstrong, director of consumer affairs for the Jewel Foods Co., which operates almost 200 Jewel grocery stores and Osco drugstores in the Chicago area, said, "It's too early to tell what's happening to other acetaminophen products. We have noticed an increase in aspirin sales, although it's not a groundswell at this point."

The results have been the same for major drug wholesalers in the area. Drug buyers from several large wholesalers said they expect orders to increase for aspirin and the substitute acetaminophen products once fear subsides, but they added that it is too soon to accurately measure the effect of the tragedy on drug sales.

Figure 7.2 One of four news stories appearing in the *Chicago Tribune* on October 1, 1982, the first day of news coverage of the Tylenol crisis. Note that the story did not mention Johnson & Johnson. Chicago Tribune Company. Reproduced by permission.

5 Deaths Tied to Pills
Fear Killer Put Cyanide in Tylenol

A study of the *Tribune*'s coverage revealed that the newspaper was as supportive of Johnson & Johnson as it could have been in the telling of the bad news. Its support is especially noteworthy compared to later newspapers and television broadcasts, which basically attacked companies in crisis. The opening pages of two *Tribune* stories are shown in Figures 7.2 and 7.3. The company's executives, the police, the FBI, and the newspapers knew from the start that the tampering could possibly have happened at the plant. Nevertheless, there was no insinuation of this in the *Tribune*'s coverage.

STORES AROUND NATION PULL TYLENOL CAPSULES

By BARBARA MAHANEY

CHICAGO TRIBUNE

STORES NATIONWIDE quickly ordered personnel Thursday to strip their shelves of Extra-Strength Tylenol capsules and hospital spokesmen reported rashes of phone calls after cyanide-tainted capsules were linked in three deaths and possibly two others in suburban Chicago.

The nation's largest grocery chain, Safeway, in Oakland, Calif., ordered all stores to remove bottles of the over-the-counter pain killer in the 96,000-bottle lot-MC 3000-which was recalled by McNeil Consumer Products Co., of Fort Washington, PA.

All 1,000 Revco Discount Drug Centers and 400 CVS pharmacies in New England pulled every bottle of Extra-Strength Tylenol. "We have pulled it off our shelves completely," said Bernie Thomas of Perry Drug Stores, Inc., which operated 124 stores in five states, including 98 in Michigan.

Meanwhile, poison centers and hospitals were reported swamped with thousands of calls from worried consumers, many of whom said they took Tylenol capsules from the recalled lot, but apparently suffered no ill effects.

"We've had questions ranging from 'Do you know anything about Tylenol being contaminated' to 'Oh my God, I just took Extra-Strength Tylenol, am I going to die?'" said Cathy Piccillo of the Indiana Poison Center, which received 50 phone calls.

Figure 7.3 Another of the four stories appearing in the *Chicago Tribune* on the first day of coverage of the Tylenol crisis. Again, there was no mention of Johnson & Johnson. Chicago Tribune Company. Reprinted by permission.

The name Johnson & Johnson was not mentioned on page 1. In the continuation of the story on page 2, nearly buried in the middle of 12 column-inches of copy, was the following statement:

> A spokesperson for Johnson & Johnson, parent firm of the company that makes Tylenol, said Thursday evening his firm "launched an investigation this morning to track down the capsules."
>
> The spokesman, Robert Andrews, and two other Johnson & Johnson officials met for an hour and a half with Elk Grove Village detectives and evidence technicians.
>
> He said his firm is "collectively shocked."
> (Houston & Griffin, 1982, p. 2)

There were four *Tribune* stories about the Tylenol crisis in that one issue. Other than in the preceding quoted passage, all other mentions of the company were of McNeil Consumer Products Company, not as familiar a name to consumers as Johnson & Johnson.

The captions for the related photographs on pages 1 and 2 of the *Tribune* also did not mention the company. The caption on page 2 indicated that medical examiners believed "the capsules were tampered with after leaving the manufacturer's plant in Pennsylvania" (Shanker & Grady, 1982, p. 2).

On Saturday, October 2, the headline in the *Chicago Tribune* was "Stewardess is 7th Capsule Poison Victim." The page-1 headline was not the dominant headline on the page. A bomb explosion that had killed hundreds of people in Tehran, Iran, took that honor. There were two other stories about the Tylenol crisis—one about the efforts to track the source of the poison, and another about funeral services for the victims.

On Sunday, October 3, the Tribune's front-page banner headline, "Shoplifter Is Sought in Poisoning Probe," referred to a story about a man who had been arrested a couple of months before for stealing Tylenol. The story continued on page 4 with excerpts referring to the Johnson & Johnson plants. The first excerpt read as follows:

> Consumers nationwide were urged to stop using Extra Strength Tylenol capsules. Johnson & Johnson, parent company of the pain-killer's manufacturer, announced it is recalling all Extra Strength Tylenol in the Chicago area.
> (Shanker & Grady, 1982, p. 4)

The second excerpt took the following form:

> Investigators have been unable to determine how and where the cyanide capsules were placed in any of the suspect containers—

whether the killer infiltrated the drug company's sophisticated manufacturing and distribution system at some point between plants in Pennsylvania and Texas and warehouses elsewhere or whether the killer removed and replaced containers once they had been placed on the shelves of local stores.

Stein said he could not rule out "factory error" because of the reported disclosure by Lawrence Foster, a spokesman for Johnson & Johnson.

Foster said potassium cyanide is used in chemical tests at some of McNeil's laboratories, but not in the manufacturing process. The labs are remote from the manufacturing areas and cyanide would be detected even if someone tried to introduce it during manufacturing, he said.

(Shanker & Grady, 1982, p. 4)

There was another front-page story in the October 3 *Tribune*, this one about a 12-year-old who had died from the poison 4 days before.

Johnson & Johnson installed 33 telephones to communicate with publics during the crisis. Pretaped statements were placed on special toll-free telephone lines to expedite news gathering. The messages were regularly updated. A full-page advertisement was placed in major Chicago newspapers offering consumers an exchange of Tylenol capsules for Tylenol tablets.

During the first week of the crisis, Kniffin handled the media from McNeil, whereas Foster was in charge at headquarters. Approximately 180,000 news stories ran in newspapers nationally. The story was at the top of television and radio newscasts.

Two thousand telephone calls were taken from the media. Thirty thousand calls from consumers came in during the first months following the deaths.

Still there were glitches.

During the first 3 days, as the *Chicago Tribune* articles showed, Foster issued a statement to reporters that there was no cyanide in the manufacturing plants. A few days later, the Associated Press heard that there was cyanide in the manufacturing plants and called Foster to confirm the report. After checking again, Foster discovered that indeed a small amount of cyanide was used in the manufacturing plant for quality-assurance testing of some kind. However, the cyanide was kept in a completely separate facility from the production line. Also, none of it was missing. There was no way that it could have gotten into the capsules accidentally. Even if it had, it would have been so dispersed as to be harmless.

Foster called the Associated Press and told it the truth. He had a reputation for being honest, fair, and ethical. He could not afford a cover-

up. When he told the wire service that there was no way the cyanide could have gotten into the capsules, the reporters believed him and agreed not to run the story—unless some other news outlet got the information, too.

Sure enough, the *Newark Star-Ledger* got word of the information, called Johnson & Johnson for confirmation, and again Foster said, "Trust me." The reporter agreed.

Keeping his promise to the Associated Press, Foster called and told the wire service that the *Newark Star-Ledger* had the information but had also agreed not to run it. The Associated Press agreed once more not to run the story unless still another newspaper or TV station got the information. After all, the *Star-Ledger* was basically a neighbor to the company.

However, when the *New York Times* got the information, Foster decided to give up. He called both the Associated Press and the *Star-Ledger* and asked them to use discretion in running the story. The resulting stories had very little impact. They were run in insignificant places in the Sunday newspapers, and the facts were not blown out of proportion (as had happened with other crises). The newspapers merely reported the information as Foster had revealed it.

With this, Foster realized that his positive dealings with the media over the years had paid off. The story could have made front-page headlines everywhere, but it did not because the media trusted the public relations professional from their past dealings with him.

The FBI and the FDA never found any evidence of tampering at the two Johnson & Johnson plants. They found that the contaminated capsules had come from both plants—one in Texas, the other in Pennsylvania. This was proof that no person at Johnson & Johnson had ever been in contact with all the capsules. It was not an inside job. The finger now pointed to some external, malicious psychopath who bought the Tylenol, laced it with cyanide, and placed it back in the containers and on the shelves of stores.

After the crisis team discovered what had transpired, its members were relieved to be assured that the contamination could not have occurred in the plants. The task of the team now turned to saving Tylenol and restoring sales. Because of the company's diversified product line, the team was not worried that Johnson & Johnson would go under. Sales were not down for other Johnson & Johnson products. There was no boycott against the company. However, there was a fear of Tylenol capsules. The future of Tylenol was at stake.

To reach the employees who were concerned about their company's future, CEO Burke spoke to an assembly at McNeil and promised that Extra Strength Tylenol was coming back. Employees wore "We're Coming Back" buttons. Those employees who had been manufacturing

Tylenol were given other temporary jobs. Videotaped reports of activities were shown to employees explaining what was going on with the crisis.

Information packages were sent electronically—by fax, telegram, and other methods—to major distributors, who, in a short time, notified half a million retailers and medical professionals.

Up to this point, there was a debate over whether to recall the product. The FBI and the FDA advised against a recall because it would mean giving in to the criminals.

The decision not to recall would have worked if it had not been for a copycat crime that took place in northern California on October 5. The company decided then that removing the product from all stores was the only way to show the public that it was concerned about the welfare of its customers. On October 5, all Tylenol products were removed from stores nationwide.

Later, there were approximately 250 copycat reports, all of which were found to be groundless.

During the recovery period, a decision was made to repackage the product. A 60-second television commercial featuring the medical director at McNeil notifying consumers of the upcoming return of Tylenol aired in October and November to an estimated 85% of U.S. television households.

The triple-seal safety package devised for the product was announced at a November 11 news conference transmitted by satellite to 29 different sites where reporters were gathered. Burke also announced the availability of coupons that could be used toward the purchase of any Tylenol product and a special toll-free telephone number through which consumers could learn about the special promotion. More than 200,000 calls came in to the toll-free information number. Coverage of the press conference in the *Kansas City Times* applauded Burke and the company for their efforts and described the new Tylenol safety package as having "glued flaps . . . that must be forcibly opened. Inside, a tight plastic seal surrounds the cap and an inner foil seal wraps over the mouth of the bottle" (Goodman, 1982, p. A3). Johnson & Johnson could not have paid for better news coverage.

Johnson & Johnson executives did interviews with network television shows, such as *Donahue*, *60 Minutes*, and *Nightline*, as well as with major newspapers and magazines, such as the *Wall Street Journal* and *Fortune*.

As a result of the crisis, all Tylenol capsules were discontinued, as were capsules of other brand names. Tamper-proof, triple-sealed safety containers were swiftly placed on the shelves of retailers 10 weeks after the withdrawal. Other manufacturers followed suit.

The crisis cost the company more than $100 million. Tylenol regained 100% of the market share it had before the crisis. Seven people died. Other lives were saved by the company's decision to recall all the capsules

in the Chicago area. The Tylenol murderer was never found. A $100,000 reward offered by Johnson & Johnson still remains unclaimed.

An October 11, 1982 *Washington Post* front-page article praised Johnson & Johnson's crisis response:

> Johnson & Johnson has effectively demonstrated how a major business ought to handle a disaster . . . what executives have done is communicate the message that the company is candid, contrite and compassionate, committed to solving the murders and protecting the public.
>
> (Knight, 1982, p. 1)

Johnson & Johnson has expanded and also acquired numerous other companies in the United States and abroad since the tampering incident. Fifty-eight mergers and acquisitions were made in the decade spanning 1994 to 2004. This added more than 50 companies and product lines to the Johnson & Johnson name. International affiliates of the company were founded in China (Xian, 1985; Shanghai, 1990), Hungary (1990), Poland (1990), Russia (1990), and the Czech Republic (1991).

In 2004, the company had more than 110,000 employees worldwide. When *Fortune* ranked its 10 Most Admired Companies in 2002, Johnson & Johnson was number 7. Harris Interactive ranks companies according to its National Corporate Reputation Survey, and Johnson & Johnson ranked first for 6 consecutive years (1998–2004).

Johnson & Johnson was named "The Most Respected Company" in 2009 in a *Barron's* magazine online survey. It was "One of the Best Places To Work" according to the Human Rights Commission, was ranked #1 by *DiversityInc* magazine, and has been one of the "Top 100 Companies for Working Mothers" since *Working Mother* magazine began the annual list in 1975.

In November, 2009, Johnson & Johnson issued a voluntary recall of five product lots of Tylenol Arthritis Pain formula caplets because consumers complained of a moldy smell, nausea, stomach pain, and diarrhea. In December, the company recalled all lots of the painkiller with the red EZ-OPEN CAP. The moldy smell apparently resulted from the presence of trace amounts of a chemical called 2,4,6-tribromoanisole used to treat the wooden pallets that transport and store packaging materials. The same chemical can give wine a corky, musty smell. The side effects were said to be "temporary and non-serious."

In January, 2010, Johnson & Johnson issued a third and even more extensive recall of batches of Tylenol, and also of Motrin and St. Joseph's aspirin—all because of the moldy sickening smell.

Johnson & Johnson's McNeil consumer health care division, which sells a range of medicinal products including Sudafed and Mylanta,

posted $16 billion in sales in 2008 according to the company's annual report. The company was ranked 29th in the Fortune 500 list for 2009.

As late as January, 2010, the FBI was still investigating the 1982 Tylenol crime. The prime suspect, James Lewis, provided DNA samples on the orders of a Massachusetts judge. Lewis resides in Boston. Shortly after the murders, he was convicted of extortion for demanding $1 million to "stop the killing." He served 12 years in prison and was released in 1995. Lewis told a Massachusetts TV show he is innocent of murder.

Case: Exxon and the *Valdez* Oil Spill

In the late 1980s, Exxon was one of the five largest companies in the United States, with sales of $80 billion. Exxon CEO Lawrence G. Rawl had been employed at Exxon for 37 years before getting the top job in 1986. He was considered a strong leader who disliked publicity and the media.

The *Valdez* oil spill crisis started shortly after midnight on Friday, March 24, 1989. The *Exxon Valdez*, a 987-foot oil tanker, was headed for Long Beach, California, from Prince William Sound off the coast of Alaska. A reporter later described the ship as "longer than three football fields, [and] loaded to the top with enough oil to fill the Rose Bowl almost halfway to the top" (Turning Point, 1994).

The weather was calm. The water was beautiful. During daylight hours, an abundance of sea life could be seen. It was the time of the migration that brings to the area the largest concentration of migratory fowl in the entire world. Sea otters, seals, whales, salmon, herring, and halibut inhabited the Sound.

Just before midnight, the local pilot, who had guided the tanker out of the harbor, went off duty. Captain Joseph Hazelwood, in command, put the supertanker on autopilot and headed straight for Bligh Reef, one of several well-known hazardous areas in Prince William Sound. Hazelwood had sailed the route more than 100 times. Some said he could do it nearly blindfolded. He had been with Exxon for 21 years, 10 of them as captain.

On this night, Hazelwood left his post at the bridge and put Third Mate Gregory Cousins in charge, telling him to keep the tanker on course for 3 minutes, then turn right, thus avoiding the reef. Although Cousins was qualified to take command during normal times, government investigators later said that he was not qualified to take command at that critical period when the ship had to be steered in a very precise maneuver.

Cousins waited too long before ordering the turn, and the *Exxon Valdez* headed for the submerged rocks. He told Captain Hazelwood, "I think we're in serious trouble." Hazelwood radioed the Coast Guard with

the message, "We've fetched up hard aground. . . . Evidently, we're leaking some oil" (Smith, 1992, p. 84). Cousins and Hazelwood had just made the two understatements of 1989.

The tanker had run aground on the rocks of Bligh Reef, ripping open a hole in the hull nearly as long as the ship itself. Over the next hours and days, 11 million gallons of crude oil poured out into Prince William Sound. The oil spread relentlessly. Some said the oil slick was 10 feet wide and 4 miles long—the worst oil spill ever in American waters.

Obviously, the beautiful waters were no longer beautiful, but more importantly, sea life perished. It was estimated that 1 million migratory fowl and one-third of the sea otter population—about 2,500—died. Seals and sea lions also fell victim to the slick. Some sources revealed that 2 million animals died as a result of the oil, although this did not include halibut, pink salmon, herring, clams, and worms that remained uncounted. Some scientists claimed that wildlife may still remain poisoned by the oil years later. Others later said Prince William Sound totally recovered from the spill.

The weekend news reports came from local media and through the three major television networks. By Monday, media people from all over the world began to pour into the town of Valdez. The media frenzy had begun. (Examples of the news coverage are shown in Figure 7.4.) In addition, hundreds of environmentalists arrived in Valdez to help save the animals, the beaches, and the water. Concern was rampant.

Don Cornet, who later became Exxon's public relations manager, was Alaska coordinator for Exxon at that time; he reported to the head of public affairs and rushed to the scene as soon as he got word of the accident. The company's immediate strategy was to focus on the clean-up effort. Exxon's theory was that the initial spill was regrettable, but that at this point the most crucial task was to clean it up as swiftly as possible and restore normalcy to the area.

Frank Iarossi, then-president of Exxon Shipping (the grounded tanker came from its shipyards), was Exxon's main representative at the Valdez site. CEO Rawl was nowhere to be found. Iarossi dealt with the logistics of the spill response. Early on, he pointed a finger at Captain Hazelwood. Years later, there was still some confusion over whether Hazelwood had been drinking that night, but it was a fact that his driver's license had been revoked for drunken driving and that he had once been hospitalized for alcohol treatment. He denies he was drunk and no court has ever proven he was. At any rate, Hazelwood was fired. Third Mate Cousins blamed the crisis on "poor seamanship" ("The Big Spill," 1990).

Some Exxon employees placed the blame on Exxon's corporate culture. They said that to save money the company had cut crews, and that the short-staffed crews worked long hours and got little sleep. They felt that human fatigue was responsible for the accident. Moving the oil was a

CRUDE OIL FOULS SOUND
Oil officials react slowly to disaster

BY LARRY CAMPBELL
DAILY NEWS REPORTER

VALDEZ—As the largest oil spill in the history of the United States entered its second day, only a feeble containment effort has been mounted and a crowd of state, federal and oil company officials remained undecided about how to clean up the mess.

A 32-square-mile, multi-hued sheen continued to float and spread atop the waters of Prince William Sound. The Sound is surrounded by land on three sides. Two large islands, Hinchinbrook and Montague, lie across its open, southern end. That means that unless the spilled oil can be dealt with, it is a near-certainty that it will wash ashore somewhere in the Sound.

Valdez residents grew increasingly critical Friday of what seemed to be sluggish movement by Alyeska Pipeline Service Co., which operates the oil terminal here, and Exxon Shipping Co. in dealing with the spill. Nearly 24 hours after the Exxon Valdez ran aground on Bligh Reef about 25 miles southwest of here, officials had done little to contain the spill or clean up what was beyond containment.

Oil keeps spreading in Sound State says
Alyeska's cleanup effort inadequate, slow

BY LARRY CAMPBELL
DAILY NEWS REPORTER

VALDEZ—State, federal and oil company officials ended Saturday as they had begun it, no closer to a solution to the problems posed by more than 11 million gallons of North Slope crude oil washing around the fish-and-wildlife-rich, enclosed waters of Prince William Sound.

But while the oil of the nation's largest spill was left mostly unmolested, the chief of the state Department of Environmental Conservation assailed the Alyeska Pipeline Service Co. for its failure to respond quickly to the disaster.

Figure 7.4 Excerpts from front-page news stories appearing in the *Anchorage Daily News* on March 25, 1989, the day after the oil spill from the *Exxon Valdez*.

cardinal rule, they said, and employees who did not work fast and long enough feared losing their jobs.

Smith (1992) said that in 1986, the *Exxon Valdez* was designed for a crew of 33. Yet on the fateful night of the spill, the crew numbered only 19.

According to requirements of the State of Alaska, the Alyeska Pipeline Service Company, a consortium of several companies working on Alaska's North Slope, was responsible for the initial response to the spill. Exxon, Atlantic Richfield (ARCO), British Petroleum (BP), and five other companies initially participated in the response. Exxon soon after took over the clean-up efforts from the other companies.

At the start of the crisis, Cornet set up a media center in Valdez, a remote town with limited facilities, equipment, and accommodations. Critics charged that the media center should have been in New York or Chicago, a city that could better accommodate such a large gathering of reporters and photographers. Others insisted that it had to be at the site, regardless of the difficulties. The media said that photographs and videos of the spill, citizens of Alaska, and government officials were all necessary to the stories communicated to the public.

Contradictory statements about the seriousness of the crisis were issued from various news sources. One statement said the damage was minimal. Another said the damage was substantial.

Four days after the spill, local fishermen in the village of Cordova were angry because clean-up efforts had not worked. They and the media were not happy about the response. Iarossi held a press conference without first being briefed by public relations personnel; he was verbally slaughtered. Brian Dunphy, another spokesperson for Exxon Shipping, said that he would not verify the extent of the damage or what was being done about it, a statement that was not well received.

CEO Rawl still declined to go to the site. He said that he felt "technologically obsolete." The media, the fishermen, the environmentalists, and the public were irate. Customers began to cancel their Exxon credit cards. The media continued to attack more vociferously. Exxon had not anticipated the intensity of the public's concern about the environmental crisis, nor had it anticipated such a large spill or the difficulties with clean-up and communications.

Exxon's Concern for Alaska

In 1989, George Mason, APR, was vice president of Bradley/McAfee Public Relations, Alaska's largest public relations firm. The firm was part of Bradley Advertising, the state's largest advertising agency. (The company's name was later changed to Bradley/Reid Communications.)

"Alyeska Pipeline Service Company was our largest account, and we'd held it for 14 years," said Mason, who was not personally responsible for the account but had, on occasion, handled crisis communications for the client.

When the *Exxon Valdez* ran aground on the night of March 24, 1989, Mason contacted Alyeska's public relations director, John Rattermann, to offer assistance. "What is often forgotten in the news stories," he said, "is that Alyeska was responsible for [the] initial response in the event of a spill."

The day after the angry public meeting, Mason flew to Valdez to meet with Don Cornet, Alaska coordinator for Exxon. "In my opinion," said Mason, "Mr. Cornet had already grasped the futility of the situation as far as the degree of damage Exxon's image had suffered. He seemed to accept this and had begun to look ahead to the long-term future."

Cornet asked Mason to develop and implement strategies for three areas that he expected would be of future concern: (a) the tourism industry, Alaska's third-largest industry (oil was the state's largest industry); (b) the animal rescue centers Exxon had already begun to set up on Valdez; (c) the seafood industry, Alaska's second-largest industry.

Mason agreed to handle the first two and referred the third to a public relations agency in Anchorage that handled the state's seafood account.

Exxon's Animal Rescue Centers

Mason went to one of the animal rescue centers, where there was additional mayhem. Teams of wildlife professionals and their equipment had been flown into Valdez. They were trying to set up the center to help rescue some of the animals.

"Reporters and interested community people were given free access to the facility, again in an effort to cooperate," recalled Mason. "However, the result was impossible. On more than one occasion, eager reporters, mostly freelancers trying to make a buck, were in the way, and in some instances had stepped on injured birds being treated."

Again, Mason, in agreement with the head of the animal rescue center, put security guards to work. This time, it was the media and others not connected with the rescue effort who were kept out. The facility was roped off. Then media tours were arranged and guidelines were constructed to guarantee the protection of the animals.

Mason subcontracted a staff member to do the same work with a second animal rescue center in Seward, Alaska. He subcontracted others to act as community liaisons in other communities. "The purpose here," said Mason, "was to ensure credible connection between Exxon and the community."

Exxon's Success at Restoring Tourism

Mason headed the tourism campaign himself. He already knew, from previous research, that the greatest concern was that the spill had occurred in spring, the peak time of year when tourists make plans for vacations.

"We suspected," he said, "that the televised reports of thick oil and dead animals would seriously impact decisions of tourists contemplating travel in Alaska. An early survey of vendors statewide confirmed our fears."

Mason said that the tourism industry telephoned from all over Alaska. The fear was that American tourists would think that the spill had marred all of Alaska. Cancellations were also rampant. Some callers asked, "How deep is the oil in Fairbanks?" Fairbanks is a city nowhere near the oil spill.

Mason designed a crisis plan that was further developed and fine-tuned by a team of experts, including public relations heads of Westours and Princess cruise lines. The plan was quickly funded by Exxon and approved by the Alaska Tourism Marketing Council, a combined state and industry group.

The crisis plan involved bringing travel writers to Alaska to witness the conditions and encouraging them to travel within the state to report what destinations were and were not affected by the spill. A telephone hotline was also instituted for travel editors to get information swiftly.

News conferences were held in New York, Los Angeles, San Francisco, and Seattle with feeds to major television network programs. The news conferences in San Francisco and Los Angeles were organized by Ketchum Public Relations offices in those cities. Erik V. Peterson, APR, who was formerly Mason's boss in Alaska, did the groundwork for the Seattle news conference. The agency Padilla, Speer, Beardsley set up the New York press conference. Alaska Governor Cooper participated in the news conferences in Seattle and San Francisco and was a very credible participant because he had been so publicly critical of the spill. When he said, "Alaska is beautiful," people believed him.

At the same time, Exxon funded an advertising campaign developed jointly by Mason's agency and McCann-Erickson of Seattle. The public relations campaign reached an estimated 50 million Americans. The advertising campaign reached even more. Both were successful in diffusing negative travel publicity.

That season, Alaska's tourism set a new record. It was 5% higher than it had been the year before the spill. The public relations campaign won a Silver Anvil Commendation from the Public Relations Society of America, as well as numerous other national and regional awards.

"None of it [the tourism and the animal rescue efforts] would have been possible were it not for the cooperation and support of Exxon," said Mason: "The lesson I learned from that crisis and have since applied

to other crises is that once the crisis begins and the public hysteria begins, it is too late to worry about your PR. All you can really do is hang on, get on with the work, and continue to do what you think is best and most honest."

After the Crisis

Rawl eventually issued a statement via television telling the public what chemicals would be used to clean up the spill. He made no apologies to the fishermen whose livelihoods had been affected. He showed no emotion over the impact of the disaster.

Ten days after the spill, Exxon released full-page ads expressing concern and vowing to clean up the spill. Still, the company did not accept responsibility for the damage. Three weeks after the spill, the CEO went to Alaska, apparently no longer feeling "technologically obsolete."

All oil companies operating in Alaskan waters now have crisis plans approved by the state. In 1989, Alyeska Pipeline Service Company's plan anticipated a much smaller oil spill and allotted only 5 hours for containment. A primary response in these plans was the use of dispersants as well as in situ burning for clean-up. The Coast Guard and the Alaska state government could not decide on the use of dispersants for the *Exxon Valdez* spill, and this debate prolonged the clean-up. A dispersant test was attempted on the Monday following the Friday night spill, but harsh weather prevented its completion. In addition, the spill was so massive that there were not enough dispersants in Alaska to deal with the problem.

A month after the spill, Exxon finally had the equipment for a full-scale clean-up, which was not completed until 1992. Some Alaskans said there was still evidence of the oil in the Sound. In 1994, Exxon issued information to the media showing that predictions of long-term damage resulting from the spill were exaggerated, and that there was oil from other sources in Prince William Sound. Independent scientific studies seemed to confirm this, but oil from these sources was minuscule compared to that from the *Exxon Valdez*.

Although various controversies about the Exxon spill remained, one thing was certain: The *Exxon Valdez* was a warning sign, a prodrome for other oil companies. Later, BP suffered an oil spill in the Pacific Ocean off the coast of Huntington Beach, south of Los Angeles. BP reacted with haste, even getting underwater photographers to capture images of the hole in the ship for the media.

In a few days, the BP accident was no longer news. This spill, however, was in no way as massive or as difficult as the Exxon spill. It should also be noted that Exxon sent personnel and equipment to help work on the clean-up of this BP spill.

Rawl resigned in 1993 and Lee Raymond became Exxon's chairman. In 1989, the position of public relations manager did not exist at the company. In organizational restructuring under Raymond, Cornet took this position. In this new organizational hierarchy, there were fewer layers between the CEO and the public relations department. Cornet reported to the head of public affairs, who reported directly to Raymond.

Although Hazelwood was acquitted of operating the tanker while intoxicated, he was convicted of negligent discharge of oil (a misdemeanor), fined $50,000, and ordered to perform community service. After 8 years of appeals, in 1998 the Alaska Court of Appeals upheld Hazelwood's sentence of 1,000 hours of community work ("Sentence Upheld Over Oil Spill," 1998). After being fired from Exxon and sued, he was unable to find work as a ship's captain, though his credentials and skills were highly praised. He worked for a time in New York as a claims adjuster for his lawyers. In 1999, at 52, he began to do his community service and was scheduled to complete 200 hours a year for 5 years (*Exxon Valdez* Captain Finally Will Do Community Service," 1999). Although he resents being fired by Exxon and sees himself as a victim, Hazelwood said, "I felt terrible about my involvement . . . as any normal human being would" ("Serving Time," 1999).

Cousins, the third mate who was left by Hazelwood with the responsibility of steering the ship away from Bligh Reef, continued on his ladder of success to become a second mate on a U.S.-flagged bulk ship (Nalder, 1999).

Ten years after the *Exxon Valdez* oil spill, the largest marine disaster in U.S. history, scientists announced that Alaska's Prince William Sound was recovering, although full ecological recovery had not been achieved. According to scientists, humans could not do much more to hurry the recovery. Only two of the 28 kinds of herring were declared recovered. Although sea otters were recovering, it could take decades to make a full comeback in some of the area's most heavily oiled bays (Watson, 1999).

Exxon was ordered by a federal court to pay $5 billion to fishermen and others damaged by the oil spill. Although saying it "deeply regrets" the spill, Exxon argued that there were limits to its deep pockets. It cited the $2.1 billion in clean-up expenses and another $1 billion in fines, criminal restitutions, and civil settlements to state and federal governments as sufficient punishment for the damage, saying that a greater amount would send a "perverse message" after all the company had done to mitigate the accident's effects (Connelly, 1999).

Environmental organizations, particularly Greenpeace, MoveOn.org, the Alaska Coalition, and the Sierra Club still demonstrate against Exxon because of the spill and also with regard to issues such as global warming. John Passacantando, director of Greenpeace, said while demonstrating in 90-degree weather at a Washington, DC, gas station, "It's going to

get hotter thanks to Exxon-Mobil, thanks to them more than any other company on the planet." The manager of the gas station said he had noticed no impact in business at the pumps. Exxon says it is investing in new technologies to reduce greenhouse-gas emissions and produce cleaner fuels (Ruskin, 2005).

Since 2005

In 2009, Exxon Mobil was ranked first in the list of *Fortune* 500 companies (it had ranked second in 2008). WalMart ranked second in 2009 while oil giants Chevron and ConocoPhillips were ranked third and fourth. Exxon's revenues were up 18.8% over the previous year despite a drop in the price of oil. Its profit was up 11.4% at more than $45 million.

In June, 2009, the 9th U.S. Court of Appeals in San Francisco ordered Exxon to pay more than $500 million in interest on punitive damages for the oil spill. The sum was nearly double the payout to 33,000 Alaska natives, fishermen, and business owners harmed by the 1989 crisis. Each would get an average of $15,000.

Still this sum was the result of several cuts. Exxon was, in 1994, ordered by a jury to pay $5 billion. In 2006, a federal appeals court cut that in half to $2.5 billion. Then the Supreme Court slashed that amount to $507.5 million. Exxon maintained that the interest rate should be calculated from the date the punitive damages were set, but the court decided the interest would be based on the original settlement.

Exxon could appeal again, but a lawyer for the company said, "What we want more than anything now is just to bring this case to a close."

(This book was in press when BP oil caused what President Obama called "the worst environmental disaster America has ever faced" in April, 2010.)

Culture Crises

Foreign and Domestic

Communicators must understand and heed cultural beliefs and practices before developing plans, programs, and messages. There are corporate and organizational cultures, cultures within one's own country, and foreign culture. All demand attention. In this chapter, we first examine an issue of tolerance at a Michigan university. Next we look at the HIV/AIDS crisis in several African countries where the human death toll has been astronomical and until a cure or an immunization is discovered, communications is the key to prevention. Then we take a look at strong traditions in a Texas university. The crisis "Yuhan-Kimberly and Baby Wet Wipes," beginning on page 236, could also be in this category of culture crises.

Case: Saginaw Valley State University and the Theater Controversy

Saginaw Valley State University (SVSU) is located in the heart of the Tri-Cities of Saginaw, Midland, and Bay City in mid-Michigan about 90 miles north of Detroit.

Not as famous as the Big Ten football powerhouse, the University of Michigan, 90 miles to the east, SVSU is proud of its football team, a member of NCAA Division II, which had six playoff appearances in a 10-year period and had five players go to the NFL in 2008.

SVSU, the youngest of the state's 15 public universities, is also proud of its phenomenal growth since its birth in 1963. It is proud to be the most affordable public university in Michigan, with annual tuition and fees at $6,900 in 2009–2010. It prides itself on personal attention to students with an average class size of 25 students.

And it is proud of its numerous programs, among them its Theater Department.

In January, 2010, the Theater Department, for the second straight year, hosted the regional Kennedy Center American College Theater Festival. More than 1,500 participants from colleges and universities in five

states (Illinois, Indiana, Michigan, Ohio, and Wisconsin) attended the competition.

Each year the Theater Department—faculty and students—plans a schedule of plays to be presented. The goal is to present a wide variety to showcase the talents of theater majors and also to attract an admiring audience.

In the 2006–2007 school year, the plays selected were the following: *Fat Pig, A Christmas Carol, The Princess and the Pea,* and *Angels in America Part One: Millennium Approaches.* The selection was made to have some fare for everybody. Some patrons would choose one or more of the plays; serious theatergoers would see them all. *Angels in America* won a Pulitzer for playwright Tony Kushner. Its themes are homosexuality and the early days of the HIV/AIDS crisis.

The crisis for SVSU began after the play's director, Professor Richard B. Roberts, enthusiastically spoke with *Saginaw News* reporter Janet I. Martineau about the upcoming play. He told Martineau and she wrote, in the April 14, 2007 edition of the newspaper, that the play was one "clearly no community theater north of Detroit would touch. And not only is it untouchable but it's also x-rated and suitable only for ages 16 and up." Roberts was referring to conservative individuals and groups in small towns and rural areas outside of Detroit, the state's only large and clearly diverse city.

The play features full-frontal male nudity and the actors frequently use the "F" word—"without either being gratuitous," Roberts told the reporter. "And we are doing it all. It is our responsibility to provide our students with cutting-edge material to perform, with shows that stretch them."

Numerous colleges and universities across the U.S. have produced *Angels in America,* and some have had problems resulting from conservative publics. Kushner recalls problems at The Catholic University in Washington, DC, Wabash College in Indiana, and Kilgore College in Texas among others. Professor Anthony Hill, of the Department of Theater at The Ohio State University, said both Part I and Part II have been produced successfully and without furor on the stage of Thurber Theater. He said, "Students and faculty are usually accepting of cutting-edge drama and the city of Columbus is known to be 'gay-friendly.'"

Of the two lead actors in the SVSU production, one is gay and the other straight. Caleb M. Knutson, then 19, is straight, but said, "I figured if I can play a role I don't 100% believe in, then I will stretch 100% as an actor." The other actor, Chad W. Baker, then 21 and admittedly gay, said "When I was cast, . . . I was afraid the actor cast opposite me, if he were straight, would be uncomfortable with me being gay. And we, as actors, need to look comfortable because, in the play, we've been lovers for four years" (see Figure 8.1).

Figure 8.1 Chad W. Baker (left in tee shirt) and Caleb Knutson played the leads in the gay-themed play *Angels in America Part One: Millennium Approaches* at the Saginaw Valley State University Theater for Performing Arts in 2007. They both faced challenges as actors in that Baker is gay and Knutson is not, but were determined to do it. The Saginaw News, 2007. All rights reserved. Reprinted with permission.

In addition to playing homosexuals, a female was cast as a rabbi and a white person as black.

The play was scheduled to run two consecutive weekends, April 20–22 and April 27–29. Roberts also mentioned in the article that ran in the April 14 edition that "we are the only theater in mid-Michigan that can get away with it because while we want people to come see the show, we're not tied to ticket sales to survive."

This was true because the production was part of the university's academic program. However, there was also no intention to alienate local patrons. Still, he did not want to hide the controversy from the public. He knew the value of producing plays that cause people to think, to discuss, to grow and perhaps change attitudes that help develop harmonious relationships within the community. Controversy was the reason for the play.

Nevertheless, the reference to not being tied to ticket revenue was what Eugene Hamilton, special assistant to the university president and head of government relations, calls "the spark that lit the firestorm that would follow."

Phone calls and e-mails began to come in to the president's office. On April 19, a letter signed by several Michigan state legislators, spurred by their constituents, arrived expressing "disappointment that the university would sponsor a play with this content [full frontal nudity and vulgar language]." It further said they were "appalled that our tax dollars would have any part in funding such a display." One lawmaker sought to withhold all of the university's state funding ($28 million) if the play opened.

Realizing his response to the e-mails, phone calls and letters would be identical, President Eric Gilbertson and J. J. Boehm, Director of Media Relations, crafted an open letter responding to the issue on the SVSU website (see Figure 8.2).

Basically, the open letter spoke about the wide variety of plays done by the Theater Department. The key point was the following:

> All in all, our students have had a wonderful range of opportunities to experience the varieties of theater. But part of any comprehensive range of performance art must also include pieces that may be more controversial, unnerving, occasionally even raw. Their experiences would be sheltered and incomplete without exposure to contemporary plays that raise troublesome questions—even in controversial ways.

Hamilton said, "Whenever an individual or a media outlet asked questions about the play, they were referred to the website. There were no press conferences and the president did no interviews."

Boehm, on the other hand, said he did dozens of interviews, including one on WJR Radio in Detroit. "I simply answered the phone in my office and I was immediately on the air live in a conversation with the state representative seeking to withhold our funding." Boehm said the news coverage of the play before and after it opened was as far away as New York and San Francisco, a wider circle of coverage than SVSU normally receives:

> My comments quickly spread across the Internet, showing how rapidly word can travel in today's information age, especially the following remark, "This is a Pulitzer Prize-winning play, not some piece of second-rate sleaze we picked up somewhere."

The play went on as scheduled to capacity audiences, great applause, and several curtain calls. Martineau of the *Saginaw News* wrote in her

AN OPEN LETTER

I appreciate your thoughtful expression of concern. It is a freedom of expression issue, but some additional context may also be helpful in your assessment of our theater program at SVSU.

Our Theater Department has attempted to give our students a balanced and varied array of performance opportunities. In the past few years, they have performed children's productions ("Princess and the Pea," "Young Black Beauty,") musicals ("Oliver," "Man of La Mancha," "Fiddler on the Roof") comedies ("I Ought to be in Pictures," "I Love You, You're Perfect, Now Change"), seasonal works ("A Christmas Carol") and even informal performances for kids at the Saginaw Children's Zoo.

All in all, our students have had a wonderful range of opportunities to experience the varieties of theater. But part of any comprehensive range of performance art must also include pieces that may be more controversial, unnerving, occasionally even raw. Their experiences would be sheltered and incomplete without exposure to contemporary plays that raise troublesome questions—even in controversial ways.

"Angels in America," is such a play, but it was carefully chosen. It also won a Pulitzer Prize and several other awards, and has served as the basis for a television mini-series.

In the local news report about this production, the Director tried to give the readers fair warning as to what was in the play so that all of us could make an informal judgment about whether we wanted to attend. I appreciate his doing that. Certainly no one should be lured into a performance only to be offended.

And so, I suspect we may simply have to remain in disagreement about this matter. But even as I am not willing to censor this kind of artistic expression, you too are free to express your disapproval. And I do respect your point of view in this regard.

Again, thank you for your message and your thoughtfulness in expressing it.

Sincerely,
Eric Gilbertson

President
Saginaw Valley State University

Figure 8.2 When some members of the community questioned whether a controversial play should be produced at Saginaw Valley State University in Michigan, the university president posted this open letter on the campus website and all doubters were referred to it. *Saginaw News.* Reprinted with permission.

review, "There is nothing more fun or pleasurable, after 40 years in this reviewing business than discovering a great play for the first time and getting lost in its magic." She went further to tell her readers, "There is nothing to fear about this work other than dealing with your own fears." She also pointed to the "sarcastic witty dialogue" and praised the actors saying, "There are no misses in the cast of 14."

Playwright Kushner wrote two e-mails. The first, just before the second weekend, was to the cast, urging the actors to stay focused despite the "mean-spirited attacks that can be upsetting, infuriating, even frightening, and which can make it difficult to stay focused on the reasons you decided to do the play in the first place."

The second e-mail was to President Gilbertson on the final day of the production saying he admired his integrity, his decision to "accept as part of his job description protecting the atmosphere of open discussion, free from intimidation, essential to the life of the mind." He criticized state representatives for having "nothing better to do with their time than trying to censor a college theater production."

On May 8, after the play had closed, the *Bay City Times* said, in a short editorial titled "Freedom of Expression at SVSU Stands Against Gusts of Intolerance":

> One man's filth is another's fertilizer. Most Americans can appreciate that; well, anyway, those not handicapped by whatever blinders they choose to wear. The play's opponents were free, of course, to vent their raging intolerance. Pres. Gilbertson and the university didn't bend an inch. The show went on as scheduled. Bravo!

President Gilbertson received additional e-mails, mostly positive, thanking him for supporting the production despite opposition, applauding his leadership and support of the arts and freedom of speech. Standing on principle is admirable, but it is also important to know one's publics. Who are the patrons? How do taxpayers and community leaders feel? What will be the reaction of the news media? There are places, colleges included, where such a play would not be as successful. Gilbertson knew the people SVSU serves. That is the best advice: To be well acquainted with the people you serve.

Boehm received the Ruby Award from the First State Bank—awarded to "the brightest professionals under the age of 40 who have made their mark in their professions and are having an impact throughout the tri-cities"—for his public relations work, including crisis communications for this theater project. He said, "While $28 million is no insignificant sum, to SVSU its reputation and image are infinitely more valuable and these emerged from the ordeal intact." On top of that, the university did not lose the funding.

Case: AIDS in Africa

A United Nations report, in 2008, estimated that sub-Saharan Africa remained the most heavily affected by HIV/AIDS. As many as 22.4 million people are living with HIV. New infections in 2008 were 25% lower than the disease's peak in 1995 partly because medical treatments allow increased longevity. An estimated 1.4 million people died in sub-Saharan Africa in 2008.

Approximately 2 million children have the infection. About 12 million have lost one or both parents. By the year 2010, experts say there will be 40 million orphans who will have grown up with little, if any, social structure.

HIV prevalence rates (the percentage of the adult population living with HIV) vary by country; West Africa is relatively less affected but is not out of danger. The prevalence rate in Nigeria was low at one time but has increased in recent years. In Eastern Africa, Uganda lowered its prevalence rate through well-planned campaigns including communications.

The United Nations estimates that the next two decades could see 89 million new cases of the disease on the African continent—or up to 10% of the population.

The UN recommends a campaign costing $200 billion. However, funding and donations are not the only requirements; there must be very effective communications programs to persuade people to change their lifestyles.

This case study looks at crisis communications aimed broadly at Africans in various countries, people who have the HIV virus and need to accept treatment and those who are not yet infected and need to accept prevention techniques.

Considering that abstinence and safe sex are determined to be the methods of preventing AIDS and that medical treatments can help infected persons to live with HIV, communications to persuade people to take these actions is necessary. As in all crises, to be effective, the communicators, whether organizational leaders or communications experts, must choose the best message targeting the precise segmented publics by the best possible method of communications.

Compounding this is the urgency of considering the culture of the publics to be reached and served. Cultural backgrounds and traditions, including sexual practices, have remained constant for generations. Even educated Africans say, "We cannot ignore our elders." So, although medical science searches for cures and treatments for HIV and AIDS, social scientists must research this previously rarely studied subject of African cultures. Sexual myths, taboos, and traditions cannot be easily combated.

A *disconnect* is sure to occur if well-meaning persons from other countries are sent to African countries to basically change a way of life.

This communications process is called *parachuting*. To avoid parachuting, it is necessary for foreign professionals to partner with local organizations, agencies, or officials who understand the culture and the people and are trusted by the people. Too often, "do-gooders" sympathize with the African plight when they should empathize. Sympathy is feeling compassion and concern for others, whereas empathy is more intellectual; it involves the understanding of thoughts and feelings and sensitivity. Even in one's own country, it is important to empathize when communicating with people of other races, religions, social status, and walks of life. Often people say to others suffering some loss, "I know how you feel." Actually, they don't know; they can't know. They can imagine how one feels. They can have concern, compassion, or sympathy. But empathy is not that easily achieved. It requires carefully studying a culture, a plight. It's more than a simple feeling.

Some of the practices and taboos of African countries will seem strange to outsiders. Some practices in your culture are strange to people in other countries. A person who feels superior with an attitude of "I shall help these unfortunate souls because I am so above this problem" is likely to fail in the communicating process.

One must accept the fact that for generations—more generations than there has been a United States of America—people have followed tribal traditions that are precious to them because of their longevity. Their lives are built on love for ancestors, elders, traditions, and history. True, some practices must change for them to survive, but getting them to make these changes requires a careful plan sensitively executed.

Some of the taboos, cultural practices, and traditions follow. They are not specific to one country and are not manifested exactly the same way in each country. These practices, identified by various organizations and individuals researching the HIV/AIDS crisis (see Sources, p. 366) are not characteristic of all persons in any country or region, but have been determined to be problematic in the fight against HIV/AIDS when they do occur. The challenge of the communicator is to help eliminate a specific practice while respecting and sustaining the culture:

1. A man who is HIV-positive can be cured if he has sex with a virgin; most virgins are, obviously, little girls.
2. There is great sexual inequality. Women feel powerless to reject or disagree with their husbands about sexual acts. "Women's lib" is a concept they do not know.
3. A person known to have AIDS is often stigmatized or physically abused by others. Wives are often terrified to tell their husbands they are HIV-positive even when their husbands infected them. A woman in South Africa admitted on television that she had AIDS. When she returned home, she was beaten to death by people in her village.

4. Men say, "Having sex with a condom is like eating a banana with the peel."
5. A man buys a bride from her family, making her his property. If a wife dies, the man can demand to marry (and sleep with) her sister because he has paid to have a wife.
6. In some countries, when a man dies, his wife is automatically the property of his brothers, just like his house, land, and cattle. Many wives are infected in these inherited marriages when their brothers-in-law are HIV-positive.
7. Sugar daddies are appealing to young girls who want material possessions; the girls who are very poor often see no possibility of ever having a simple change of clothing unless they perform sexual favors. These sugar daddies often carry the HIV virus.
8. If a person is well dressed and clean looking, he or she could not possibly have the HIV virus.
9. If someone dies of AIDS, relatives blame the death on witchcraft from an enemy.
10. Nursing mothers who are HIV-positive continue to breast-feed their babies, exposing them to the virus, because the stigma of being known to have the virus is unbearable.
11. In six countries, approximately 15 million people are at risk of starvation. These countries are Zimbabwe, Zambia, Swaziland, Lesotho, Malawi, and Mozambique. The convergence of hunger and HIV increases the vulnerability to infection and disease. Malnutrition and HIV weaken the immune system. Also, hunger is immediately felt and women will do anything, including prostitution, to feed themselves and their families.

The rest of the chapter addresses these countries: Uganda, Botswana, Zambia, South Africa, Zimbabwe, and Swaziland. The culture, including facts about geography, government, and languages, are mentioned, as well as the tactics used to fight HIV/AIDS. Crisis communicators supposedly considered these facts before planning the tactics. For example, if 75% of HIV-infected people have no access to television, it would be senseless to make television the primary method of communications. If people do not trust outsiders, it would be senseless for strangers to try to change their practices.

Uganda

Uganda has done more than most countries in the world to slow the spread of HIV.

AIDS, commonly called "slim disease," emerged in Uganda in 1982. Great human suffering resulted as elsewhere in sub-Saharan Africa.

Approximately 2 million people died; the government estimated that 1.5 million children were orphaned.

Yoweri Museveni seized power from dictator Milton Obote in 1986 and became president of Uganda. He learned of the dreadful HIV/ AIDS statistics and was appalled. He established the country's first AIDS Control Program. He also asked for help from researchers and public health organizations worldwide, announcing that Uganda would participate in African vaccine trials. He involved religious and traditional leaders, community groups, and nongovernmental agencies, in a unified effort to slow the spread of the disease and provide care and support for the victims.

The program had some success. In 1994, the president's efforts resulted in survey results showing that there were fewer cases of casual sex, more frequent condom use, and youth who waited until an older age to be sexually active. More important, the HIV infection rate dropped.

Since 1993, HIV infection rates have been halved for pregnant women, a prime indicator of the spread of the disease, and decreased by a third among men seeking treatment for sexually transmitted infections (STIs). In Kampala, the capital, the HIV rate of pregnant women seeking prenatal treatment went from 31% in 1993 to 14% by 1998. The rate for men studied went from 46% in 1992 to 30% in 1998.

Nevertheless, there is and has been a high risk of infection due to cultural practices and factors. Consider these cultural practices:

1. It is acceptable that the groom's father have sex with the bride. Sometimes other members of the groom's clan may also have sex with the bride and nothing is said. It is possible that these men may have the HIV virus.
2. A widow can be inherited by any of a man's surviving brothers. However, wife inheritance, along with polygamy, has begun to fade due to HIV/AIDS and exposure to Western culture.
3. A 16-year-old girl said she was "heir" to her aunt. This meant that when her aunt died, she had to marry her uncle (her aunt's husband) and care for his children. Both the aunt and the uncle were HIV-positive and the girl also became infected by her husband-uncle (who also died) and she subsequently infected one of the two sons she bore. She was not promiscuous; it was her duty; it was tradition.
4. Truck drivers stop regularly for sex from women who need the money to feed their families. This, too, is tradition. The women infect their husbands and boyfriends who then infect other women.
5. In rural areas (88% of the population), people value appearing wealthy. This includes owning livestock, bicycles, and, still to a degree, multiple wives.

Additional cultural practices may affect communications—particularly religion and sports. Most Ugandans are Christian—Catholics and Protestants primarily, but some are Pentecostals. Sudanic people in the West Nile region (one of four main linguistic lines) are primarily Muslim.

Soccer is the most popular sport but basketball and netball (basketball for girls) are also played. Omweso is a popular strategy board game played with seeds and stones.

So strategies and tactics have had to be developed to change traditions and alter tribal culture.

Strategy

Some say Uganda used the "ABC" strategy to prevent the sexual transmission of the HIV virus. "A" stands for Abstain; "B" stands for Be Faithful; and "C" stands for Condomize, but the use of ABC as a slogan seems to originate in Botswana. However, Uganda did use the elements of the ABC approach in its successful program.

There are various definitions of the ABC approach. UNAIDS, the United Nations AIDS agency, defines "A" as abstinence or delaying first sex, "B" as being safer by being faithful to one partner or by reducing the number of partners, and "C" as correct and consistent use of condoms for sexually active young people, couples in which one partner is HIV-positive, prostitutes and their clients, and anyone engaged in sexual activity with partners who may have been exposed to HIV. The President's Emergency Plan for AIDS Relief (PEPFAR) defines "A" as abstinence for youth until marriage, "B" as being tested and being faithful in marriage and monogamous relationships, and "C" as correct and consistent use of condoms for those with high-risk behaviors. The latter includes prostitutes, substance abusers, couples in which one partner has HIV, and does not include youth in general.

The government of Uganda launched a media campaign aimed primarily, but not exclusively, at youth. They were encouraged to abstain from sex if they were virgins and to return to abstinence if they were sexually active. Persons who were sexually active, whether married or not, were encouraged to adopt a policy of "zero grazing," which means staying with one partner and not having casual sex. Those who would not or felt they could not abstain were encouraged to use condoms. All the population—not just youth—were encouraged to use condoms (see Figure 8.3).

Tactics

An aggressive media campaign was launched. Radio broadcast the message and the urgency. Rallies were held; posters were put up in key

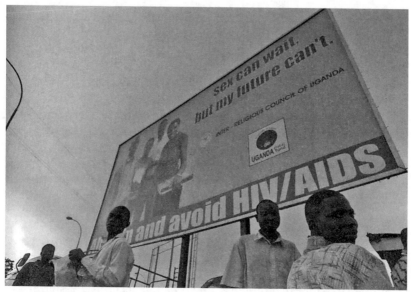

Figure 8.3 In Kampala, Ugandans stand next to a street advertisement promoting AIDS awareness, in December 2005. In an effort to curtail the numbers of victims, the Church of Uganda has been very active in promoting abstinence, especially among teenagers, and faithfulness among married people. Photo by Marco Di Lauro. Reprinted by permission of Getty Images.

spots. Teachers were trained to educate students on HIV and AIDS. Community leaders and faith-based organizations, especially churches, were encouraged to work with the government in getting citizens to reduce the increase of HIV cases and eliminate the tradition of death.

Messages were drafted differently to impress different groups depending on their cultures and needs and their ability to comply. Discussion groups were organized to answer questions and to hear challenges. Questions regarding fear and stigma of having the disease were anticipated and addressed so that people would not hesitate to be checked and treated.

A television medical drama, Centre 4, was produced and aired in 13 episodes. Aimed at men and women aged 18 to 36, the production aired in 2002. An audience of 110 million in Uganda and 20 other African countries could see the drama. HIV/AIDS and other crucial health issues such as malaria immunization and safe childbirth were explored in the storylines. The initial design began with a workshop for representatives of the Uganda Ministry of Health (MOH) and other health organizations. Mediae (a television production company) and Johns Hopkins University Center for Communications Programs collaborated on the production.

In 2001, flyers publicizing the TV drama were distributed in Uganda seeking persons to apply for training positions as scriptwriters, directors,

sound technicians, camera operators, editors, and other production staff members. Also in the same year, profiles of the main characters and storylines were developed for each of the episodes. Three Ugandan scriptwriters participated, as well as health specialists from MOH.

Communication through personal and social networks of friends and family was dominant as far back as 1989. Aunts and other figures were instrumental in talking to young girls and in creating a dialog about sexual behaviors and HIV.

Religious leaders and faith-based organizations served as educators and developed prevention activities early in the fight.

Population Services International (PSI), based in Washington, DC, launched clubs for Uganda university women called Go Getters, in 2004. The clubs worked with 669 women in their first year at three universities and used 60 peers to encourage the women to gain confidence in themselves and to set long-term goals. There were presentations by women who were role models. Employment opportunities were revealed as well as information on how to get the skills for those jobs. Internships were offered. More than 40 girls found employment as a result of the Go Getters clubs.

Numerous workshops and websites were organized for key publics. One was an AIDS website competition between 60 Ugandan schools. Teachers participated in workshops in Cape Town, South Africa, and Washington, DC. AIDS orphans were offered a workshop to help them learn to generate income and entrepreneurship skills. There were many other workshops.

Uganda used between 8 and 100 million condoms annually. Safe sex and the use of free condoms was widely considered the reason for the success of the prevention program that helped reduce rates from as high as 30% of the population in the early 1990s to about 6% in 2005. However, a 1995 study showed that 48% of men and women in Uganda reported that they stuck to one partner; 11% of women and 14% of men said they stopped all sex; and 2.9% of men and 12.5% of women said they had started using condoms. If this study is accurate and if it covers the entire country, it means that the success of the campaign was not based on condoms but on abstinence or being faithful.

Under President George W. Bush's Presidential Emergency Plan for AIDS Relief, Uganda was funded about $31.8 million. The cornerstone of the Bush prevention strategy was the promotion of sexual abstinence, not safe sex. The Ugandan First Lady, Janet Museveni—said to be "an extremely conservative evangelical Christian"—attacked the use of condoms and those who distribute them. After years of success, there was a fear that condom use would become "restigmatized," according to the Center for Health and Gender Equity.

In October 2005, a condom shortage in Uganda was reported. Apparently both the U.S. government and the Uganda government had allowed the condom supplies to decrease. A reported 32 million quality-approved condoms remained impounded in government warehouses. AIDS activists in Uganda wrote a letter to the MOH claiming that for more than a year, access to condoms had decreased dramatically and that programs should embrace a full range of HIV prevention (condoms) instead of focusing only on abstinence.

Virgin Scholarships

In 2005, a Ugandan lawmaker, Sulaiman Madada, proposed a plan to promote a new morality among young girls in the Kayunga district of Uganda. This district has one of the highest HIV/AIDS infection rates in the country. Girls who could prove they were virgins would have their university fees paid by him.

Madada said his purpose was to counteract the attraction of young girls who see sex as a way out of poverty. One 13-year-old girl said that an older man had offered to take care of her in return for sex. Because she owned only "one dress and one knickers," she said she was "thinking about it. I want to take a sugar daddy and just go. I need someone to take care of me." Her mother, who had been forced into marriage at 15, wanted her daughter to stay in school and said, "Don't go to the old men."

Said Madada, "Our area has high incidences of early marriage and defilement and sugar daddies." He said he hoped the program would grow and help steer young women away from sexual arrangements that could ruin their lives and often cause their deaths.

Government billboards went up reading, "Saving yourself for marriage is the right thing to do." Posters in schools read, "Beware of sugar daddies." The United States gave Uganda grants to promote abstinence.

The scholarships were offered to teenaged girls who could prove their virginity through gynecological exams. This stipulation caused some concern among Ugandans who say the virginity tests are not always accurate and that if girls fail them, they may be ostracized. Other critics say the testing is traumatizing and could stigmatize girls who have been raped.

Since 2005

UNAIDS estimated that in Uganda there was a decline in the infection rate from about 15% in the early 1990s to 5% in 2001. Consequently, Uganda was studied to determine why rates had dropped. Most believed it was the ABC program, which was focused on unmarried youth.

However, from 2006 to 2008, it was discovered that the prevalence rate was creeping up again to around 6.4%.

A UNAIDS survey determined that 43% of new HIV infections were centered among married victims. This meant a shift in the campaigns toward promoting fidelity in marriage. Experts also speculated that people had grown complacent about HIV because antiretroviral (ARV) drugs mean that HIV is no longer an automatic death sentence. Research also showed that the rate is higher among people in urban areas than rural and higher among women than men.

New Tactics

Billboards, television and radio spots, wristbands, and viral text messages encourage people to be "Reliable, Exceptional and Dependable." The campaign pushes for what they call "passionate fidelity ambassadors." Supporters wear something red to signal their backing of the program, titled "Go Red."

Another program encourages those infected to secure the future of their children by teaching them to write wills and record information, advice, and other messages for their children. Older children are trained to care for younger siblings and to manage households. This program is challenging because in many places it is taboo to discuss death.

The Stay Negative Campaign is aimed at encouraging people to protect themselves and their partners. It advocates conversation and being tested, and it distributes free condoms. All of this is communicated through popular music and through leaders' speeches with the theme "Get Tested. Stay Healthy. Stay Negative."

Botswana

Botswana is one of the countries hardest hit by the AIDS pandemic, largely because the disease was ignored for so many years. UNAIDS estimated in 2003 that there were 350,000 HIV-infected Batswana (people of Botswana) out of a population of 1.6 million, or 36.5%. In the entire world only Swaziland has a higher rate.

HIV/AIDS lowered the life expectancy in Botswana from 72 to 39 years of age. Out of the total population, 40% is under 15.

Cultural Challenges

1. Women feel they do not have the power over their husbands to control decisions about sexuality. They also feel pressured to conform to tradition by their parents, their in-laws, and the elders in their tribes.

2. Traditional healers use herbal medicines and charms and provide widely respected alternatives to modern medicine.
3. Many skilled health professionals in Botswana have taken jobs elsewhere—many in the United States where there was a shortage of nurses and considerably higher salaries and benefits. Consequently 90% of the physicians are from other countries and do not speak Setswana, the primary local language. English is the official language of government and education, but more people speak Setswana. The foreign physicians also do not understand the culture of the country.

Positive Conditions

1. Independent newspapers have freedom of the press and wide circulation, an opportunity for communications. Also, schools receive copies of the *Daily News* from the government.
2. In 1987 school fees were eliminated for primary and secondary schools, so education is offered to most children, making the schools a good source of AIDS education.

AIDS Strikes Silently

The first case in Botswana was reported in 1985, and at that time AIDS was considered essentially a male homosexual disease affecting people elsewhere. In the late 1980s, screening of blood through blood transfusion was instituted. From 1989 through 1997, information about how the disease is spread was circulated, but the target public was still not focused. President Festus Mogae and his government developed the Botswana National Policy on AIDS.

The government adopted the ABC approach (see "Uganda" in this chapter) and had billboards reading "Avoiding AIDS disease is as easy as Abstain, Be Faithful, Condomize." Posters and billboards were plentiful all over Botswana. One health official said, "The country has been bombarded with HIV messages, but there hasn't been a change in behavior." The problem was the publics who needed to be targeted by the slogan did not understand what it meant and it was not clear what publics were targeted. The disease became known as the "radio disease" because people heard about it on the radio but paid no attention. HIV and AIDS were spreading while Botswana was not looking.

Then between 1997 and 2002, there was an effort to identify key publics after realizing the disease affected all levels of society. Botswana was the first African country to provide ARV therapy to its citizens. The government of Botswana is credited with lessening the stigma because it supports free ARV therapy and the Prevention of Mother to Child Transmission (PMTCT) program. In the latter, mothers go into ARV

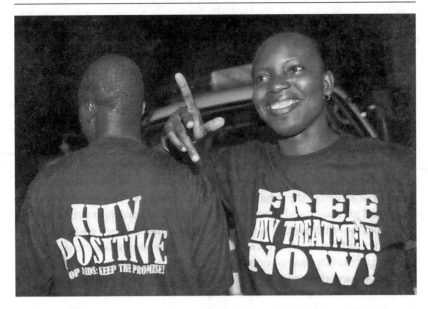

Figure 8.4 Rose Olutu (right), a single parent with the HIV virus, said "I don't mind telling people about my status. It goes a long way when you put a human face on your problem." Olutu contracted the virus while working as a laboratory attendant. In this photo, she and an infected colleague participate along with hundreds of delegates from all over Africa in the 14th International Conference on HIV/AIDS and Sexually Transmitted Infections held in Abuja, Nigeria, in December 2005. Photo by Pius Utomi Ekpei/AFP/Getty Images. Reprinted by permission of Getty Images.

therapy, and their infants are provided with formula so that the women will not breast-feed and thereby pass the virus to the babies.

By the end of 2004, more than 35,000 Batswana were receiving ARV drugs thanks to organizations such as the Bill and Melinda Gates Foundation and the Merck Company; each committed to $50 million through the African Comprehensive HIV/AIDS Partnership (ACHAP). ACHAP is a collaboration between the Gates Foundation, Merck, and the Government of Botswana.

Tactics

Botswana has had at least two television shows with AIDS prevention themes. One is the show *Talk Back*, a product of the Botswana Ministry of Education and its Teacher Capacity Building (TCB). It is a 1-hour weekly program broadcast live; it features interactivity between teachers and viewers through phone-ins, e-mail, and letters. The show includes a documentary or video clip on HIV/AIDS shot in different areas of

Botswana in Setswana and in English. This makes the show a country-wide participation show. Then, there is further interaction and feedback through workshops and seminars at various education sites around the country.

Another weekly television show is *Re Mmogo* (meaning "We are together in this"), which is an educational HIV/AIDS awareness program. It reveals and examines new approaches to win the war against the disease and tackles issues that might contribute toward positive behavior change. The show hopes to further destigmatize the disease.

There is also a radio drama, *Makgabaneng*. It is similar to a soap opera in the United States, and the characters were developed to draw the listener into wanting to know what happened to them next. The characters lived in a small town where a third of the inhabitants are HIV-positive. The HIV storyline was introduced gradually, so listeners would be so engaged in the dramatic entanglements of the characters that they would not realize there was a hidden lesson. It was a sneaky but effective method of getting listeners to pay attention, and the 100 episodes of the drama were therefore a combination of entertainment and education.

Stellar among the programs in Botswana is a beauty pageant called "Miss HIV Stigma Free." All the contestants are women who are HIV-positive and of a variety of sizes, shapes, and ages. The winners are seen as spokespersons and a symbol of the fact that a full life is possible even with AIDS. The pageant is featured on CNN and the BBC each year, and is a model for other African countries.

The Youth Health Organisation (YOHO) is a nongovernmental organization (NGO) that provides sex education through school plays and other Botswana-specific AIDS-related materials.

Discussions about prevention, living with AIDS, and caring for AIDS patients were encouraged by improving the knowledge of teachers, who could thereby help to take the mystery and stigma out of the fight against AIDS. This meant challenging cultural beliefs and traditions.

Peer education was a strategy in getting males and females to buy condoms. These sessions were set up at shopping malls, night spots, fairs, and festivals, as well as schools.

"Know Your Status" was a campaign to get Batswana between 18 and 49 to be counseled and/or tested voluntarily. Many centers in convenient places were provided for this service; results were immediate and confidential. The target public learned about the centers from bus stop signs, print ads, billboards, banners, and radio programs. Between 2000 and 2003, 65,000 citizens used the centers. Botswana was therefore the first country in Africa to have national voluntary routine HIV tests.

Educational videos were released to educate citizens about the impact of ARV drug therapy. They were shown to patients in waiting rooms and in presentations at hospitals and clinics, thereby reaching

HIV-positive patients and families of HIV patients. Approximately 90% of patients in the drug regimen adhered to it. So the videos did their job.

The "Get-Involved" campaign uses mass media to facilitate behavior change. It calls for ads at bus shelters; the ads show photographs of persons engaged in high-risk behavior, with Botswana proverbs and a hotline number giving the target audience an opportunity to call and get help or to volunteer to help. Volunteers receive training in how to be grassroots counselors. They distribute condoms and informational materials.

Since 2005

By 2008, 11,000 Batswana had died of AIDS. As many as 20% of all children in the country were expected to be orphans by the year 2010 due to AIDS deaths. More than 15,000 children and 280,000 adults had the HIV virus.

New Tactics

The Botswana government developed a campaign to circumcise 500,000 men by 2012 and an additional 460,000 by 2014, which, according to the *Journal of the International AIDS Society*, will prevent nearly 70,000 new HIV cases by 2025. The campaign is publicized through television and radio advertisements to encourage circumcision at local clinics.

The National MCP (Multiple and Concurrent Partnership) Campaign was proposed in 2009 with the goal of an AIDS-free generation with zero infections (new) in 2016. The campaign targets young women, 18–24, engaged in MCP for personal or material gain; men, 25–35, engaged in MCP for sexual variety; and cross-generational sexual partnerships between older men and young vulnerable women.

After gathering data from numerous qualitative studies, it was determined that both deep-seated cultural traditions and modern phenomena are drivers of MCP.

The following are some of the messages designed for the target groups:

- Overlapping sexual relationships are risky.
- Masculinity is not defined by the numbers of sexual partners.
- Men must learn to communicate about sex and relationships with their sexual partners rather than seek additional partners.
- Young girls must be empowered to refuse sexual advances from older men offering gifts and money.
- Help girls seek social support from authorities.

Methods of communicating were to be:

- Churches and faith-based organizations.
- Community theater and debates.
- Mass media spots and jingles.
- Peer education.
- Small group discussion.
- One-on-one discussion.
- Sports, music, other leisure activities.

Zambia

Zambia, in the heart of subequatorial Africa, has some of the world's most devastating statistics about HIV/AIDS. Out of its population of 11 million, one in every six adults has the infection.

The country's first reported AIDS case was in 1984. By the end of 2003, 89,000 had died and 820,000 were living with the disease or the infection. Most of the victims were female. Life expectancy at birth is less than 40 years. The deceased left 630,000 orphaned children. Half the population is under 15 and 85,000 children are infected.

Unlike many countries in Africa, Europe, and the West, most Zambians with the disease are not the underprivileged and uneducated. Numerous teachers and other educated professionals have the virus. Nevertheless, there are great numbers of poor, uneducated Zambians who are in need of information and training on how to manage their lives with HIV.

As in other African countries, most HIV infections in Zambia result from unprotected sex. There are numerous cultural practices that compound the prevention problem; these are some of them:

1. Gender inequity prevails. Women and girls are expected to be submissive. Older women teach young girls, sometimes through song and dance, how to please their husbands. The bride learns to obey and cannot refuse her husband sex, even if she knows he is HIV-positive. If women are infected, they can and do infect their unborn children and are stigmatized by the community for promiscuity even if their husbands had the disease first.
2. Extended families exist in which a father's brothers are also considered fathers and a mother's sisters are also considered mothers. All of the children of these extended fathers and mothers are considered as sisters and brothers, not cousins as U.S. culture dictates. The father is the traditional head of the family but if the father must work out of town, it is not unusual for women to head the household. Often while striving to survive under dire circumstances, guidance in how to prevent disease is lacking. Sometimes, if AIDS has taken adults in the family, the older children head the household.

3. Many Zambians mix indigenous beliefs with a practice of Christianity or Islam. Approximately 80% of Zambians are Christians; about 10% are Muslim. A smaller number practice only indigenous beliefs; among them witchcraft remains strong especially in villages.

4. Sex for sale is prominent in Zambia. Nearly a third of the male population has had sex with prostitutes. Nearly a fifth of the female population has sold sexual favors as a regular way of living or for occasional needs of money. Truck driving, a popular occupation in Zambia, causes drivers to be away from home for long periods. Some are HIV-positive and engage in temporary relationships and spread the disease (see Figure 8.5).

5. Soccer is the most important sport. Zambians play mankala, a strategy game with marbles and stones. Church activities are important in rural areas (60% of the population).

6. Zambians value education but often cannot afford to send children to school. The government pays teachers' salaries but parents must buy uniforms and books.

7. Television is available in cities and large towns. Rural areas get radio, and much news is passed by word of mouth. Newspapers are not distributed in rural areas, but if someone gets one, it is passed around.

Figure 8.5 Sex workers in Africa are a key to lowering the rates of AIDS/HIV infections. Most of them depend on the trade for the necessities of life, not to mention occasional frills such as make-up and dresses. Here, several sex workers are educated on the dangers of HIV and how to avoid infection. Photo reprinted by permission of the Bill and Melinda Gates Foundation.

In the late 1980s, Zambia began an aggressive educational campaign. The slogan, "Sex thrills, but AIDS kills," was circulated on posters and pamphlets. The warnings were out there, but many misconceptions remained:

1. HIV/AIDS cannot be avoided.
2. Mosquitoes carry the virus.
3. The virus and disease come from witchcraft or sorcery and it is imperative to find out who is responsible.
4. Sharing a meal with an HIV-positive person will put one at risk.
5. People who get HIV have "weak blood."

The challenge is to change attitudes and behaviors to curtail the spread of the infection and to teach Zambians how to have responsible sexual relationships. Because much of the population is under 15, children are a primary public. The Ministry of Education was slow to get started with the campaign, but in recent years, there has been an effort for more support. There are problems involved. One is that 72 languages are spoken in Zambia and AIDS-related materials must be translated into these languages and into Braille. Another problem is that if parents cannot afford school uniforms and books, only the oldest boy goes to school, so often girls, the main victims of HIV/AIDS, are not in school to see and hear the warnings and advice.

The third problem is that many teachers and school officials have the virus or the disease. Teachers once threatened a strike because they did not get their paychecks. Of the two government officials responsible for payroll, one was ill from an AIDS-related illness, and the other was attending the funeral of a colleague who had died from the disease. These problems create a crisis within the crisis because schools are often the best way to reach uninfected youth and to persuade them to reject old ways of life and accept new attitudes.

A study of how Zambians acquired information about sexual warnings, HIV, and AIDS reveals that most found out from friends, family, overheard conversations, gossip, and word of mouth—not from schools anyway. So AIDS activists in Zambia determined that they must reach the youth through means beyond the school chalkboard.

There was a stigma attached to those who are known to have the virus, so many people were afraid to take the tests. Some had the virus and were unknowingly exposing others to it. Then, two well-known politicians—Former President Kenneth Kaunda and Vice President Nevers Mumba—consented to take the HIV tests publicly. Both tested negative. This inspired others to take the test, learn their status, and, if necessary, seek confidential counseling and treatment.

Television, radio, and the press were used for people in cities and large towns, but only radio is available in rural areas. In those areas, interactive sessions using music and drama or role-playing or group discussions were organized.

Anti-AIDS clubs organized by both schools and outside organizations were used with 25,000 students. In these clubs, games, dramas, and role-playing were used to get the points across. Organizations also used trained peer educators to work with street children, commercial sex workers, and the military.

The Washington, DC-based organization Population Services International (PSI) implemented a prevention program called Corridors of Hope in 35 African nations, including Zambia. The intention was AIDS prevention by the social marketing of condoms. Activities centered on prostitutes, truckers, informal traders, uniformed officials, and adolescent girls. Zambia's Society for Family Health promoted the program and made efforts to remove the stigma attached to the use of condoms. The condoms were promoted as part of a very successful safe-sex awareness campaign through radio, television, print, and outdoor advertising. Large musical events such as "Chirundu Live" delivered the message about prevention and the use of condoms. The show was so successful that it expanded to other cities in Zambia.

Since 2005

At the end of 2007, 46% of the 330,000 people who needed antiretroviral drugs were receiving them. But nearly two-thirds of youth, ages 15 to 24, could not identify ways of preventing HIV, nor could they reject misconceptions about HIV transmission. Only 28% of Zambians aged 15 to 49 knew their status. Education of youth is considered the "window of hope" for Zambia.

There are conflicts over whether young people should be told about condoms at all. Many say abstinence should be the goal until they marry. Consequently, there are many campaigns to persuade youth that condoms do not work.

In 2005, the Zambian government admitted it does not encourage mandatory testing as suggested by Zambia's National AIDS Council (NAC), but it did agree to encourage voluntary testing and routine testing for at-risk patients.

New Tactics

In April, 2009, the NAC launched an organizational website aimed at disseminating information on HIV/AIDS to stakeholders. Health Deputy Minister Mwendoi Akakandelwa hopes to better address concurrent

sexual partners, discordant couples, male circumcision, and men having sex with men. It is believed that Zambians will feel this site is more credible to their culture than external sites.

In 2007, evidence was revealed that social marketing condom ads and radio and television programs on family planning and HIV were successful in reaching large numbers of Zambians. The results also show that condom campaigns were more effective for males than females.

Also in 2007, a radio serial drama *Gama Cuulu* was launched in the Southern Province. The drama is managed by the Centers for Disease Control and Prevention (CDC) and is funded by the President's (U.S.) Emergency Plan for AIDS Relief (PEPFAR). The show encourages listeners to adopt safer behaviors and to encourage and to talk more openly about HIV/AIDS issues. With a script in the chiTonga (stet) language, it has six main characters who face hurdles as they strive to practice health behavior.

South Africa

The first two official deaths from AIDS in South Africa were recorded in 1982. In 2009, 5–7 million were living with HIV and AIDS, more than in any other country. In 2008, more than 250,000 South Africans died of AIDS. An estimated 280,000 under 15 were living with the disease in 2007.

The country is the worst affected because of several factors. Among them are the following: poverty and unemployment; low status of women; high mobility (mostly migrant labor); what persons in the West would call sexual promiscuity; the legacy of apartheid; stigma and discrimination; misconceptions about HIV/AIDS; cultural beliefs and practices; and lack of leadership.

President Thabo Mbeki, unlike presidents of most countries in sub-Saharan Africa, has not led the fight against the disease. He is reported to have said that widely used anti-AIDS drugs are "poison," that prevention and treatment programs are plots by the West to eliminate black Africans, and that AIDS might not be caused by the HIV virus.

Making the fight against HIV more difficult to understand, Roman Catholic bishops from South Africa, Botswana, and Swaziland, all hit hard by AIDS, held a semiannual meeting in South Africa in 2001. Realizing that the Pope disapproved of condoms, the bishops' purpose for meeting was to determine whether they would approve the use of condoms for AIDS prevention. After 5 days of closed-door meetings, they emerged and announced that promotion of condoms was immoral, that condoms undermined abstinence and marital fidelity and that condoms might even spread the disease. Most South Africans are Christians so this was shattering. This was doubly shattering and shocking to AIDS

prevention activists because the Catholic Church provides more direct care for AIDS patients and their loved ones than any other institution. Paul Delay of USAID (United States Agency for International Development) said, "What we've asked of the churches, particularly the Catholic Church, is that if you can't say anything nice about condoms, don't say anything at all. Concentrate on abstinence and fidelity but don't say that condoms don't work . . ."

In 2002, former U.S. president Jimmy Carter and Bill Gates, Sr. (the father of Microsoft's Gates) went to South Africa, and offered Mbeki what Carter called "a chance to be a hero instead of a villain" through introducing antiretrovirals for treatment and adopting a prevention plan. Carter and Gates expressed disappointment with their meeting. Mbeki said the ARV drugs were too expensive, difficult to take, and dangerous, that South Africa was and should be more concerned about poverty that still remained after white rule ended.

In August 2003, activists at the opening of a national AIDS conference in Durban, South Africa, jeered the country's health minister, Tshabalala-Msimang, yelling, "Shame on you!" They displayed signs and placards reading "Save Our Youth, Save Our Future, Treat AIDS Now." Tshabalala-Msimang said that she advocated a diet of beetroot, olive oil, African potato, and garlic for HIV victims. She became known as

Figure 8.6 In Johannesburg, South Africa, schoolgirls play "The Magical AIDS journey," a board game created by a South African social worker to help children with HIV or AIDS-infected parents learn to process their feelings about the disease. Photo by Naashon Zalik/Getty Images News/Getty Images. Reprinted with permission of Getty Images.

Dr. Beetroot. Mbeki told the *Washington Post* that he didn't know anybody who had died of AIDS. In late 2003, the Mbeki government made a decision to initiate a HIV/AIDS program that included the distribution of free ARV drugs, yet critics say it was late—too late.

Even with the plan to use the ARV drugs, the challenges—most cultural—remained. Among them were the following:

1. Men are socialized to believe that women are inferior, and women are socialized to be submissive, meaning they have no power to insist on condoms or to refuse sex at all.
2. Abstinence and monogamy are often considered unmanly. Violence against women is manly.
3. A South African woman has a one in three chance of being raped; so the country has the highest sexual violence statistics in the world. Genital injuries resulting from forced sex increase the likelihood of HIV infection.
4. Women who have no male partners are the lowest in the class system. This encourages women with abusive husbands to keep them at any cost. Also, women who have "too much knowledge" about sex are considered immoral. So, if a woman insists on the use of condom, she is either considered too informed or suspected of having an extramarital affair.
5. The early fight against HIV/AIDS was lost while South Africans fought against apartheid, which was a longtime issue, a passion for most black South Africans. Blacks comprise 77% of the population. When Mandela was freed and the country erupted in celebration as he became president, the HIV virus was growing rapidly.
6. Millions of men work as miners in a migrant workers program left over from apartheid, during which the government relied on cheap black labor. Away from home for long periods of time, the men live in hostels and are given easy access to commercial sex workers and little access to condoms. They are infected by the virus and then go home and pass it to their wives.
7. Homosexuals are subject to violent attacks, so few admit their sexual preference or identity and are fearful of seeking protection or treatment.
8. About 80% of South Africans consult traditional healers and use traditional health remedies. These healers treat symptoms successfully, though temporarily, and claim to have cured their patient.

Tactics

Various organizations, both external and internal, are engaged in crisis communications tactics. Some of the communications are through the

mass media, but in many cases the publics targeted do not have access to the broadcast media or newspapers, especially in countries with high rates of poverty. So, organizations must strive to find the best method to deliver their messages to the segments of the broad public that will benefit.

The following are some of the tactics used:

1. The government made efforts to integrate traditional healers into the national health care system. This was necessarily one-on-one communication as well as getting community organizations to work with the healers in counseling, testing, and promoting good nutrition. Later some of the healers even recommended patients to clinic workers and vice versa. This effort shows signs of sustained success, though the battle is not won.

2. The Medical Research Council set up free HIV testing and free condoms for miners. Couple counseling was offered as well as education awareness and ARV treatment. Mining companies are being urged to make family-friendly housing so that families may remain close.

3. Former South African President Nelson Mandela went public in 2005 and announced that his 54-year-old son had died of AIDS. This was considered a brave move because use of the term AIDS was taboo. Associates of Mandela, 86 at the time, said he knew of his estranged son's illness but refrained from discussing it openly, though he visited his son in hospital. He said, "We must not hide." Later in 2005, Mandela began a "46664" (his number during his 27 years in prison) anti-AIDS campaign. He was MC of a pop concert in Norway attended by more than 15,000 people and held to benefit the AIDS fight. Musical celebrities from around the world entertained.

4. To reach persons worried about stigma, in 2004 the International Cricket Council and its players in South Africa embarked on a series of activities designed to help reduce the stigma attached to the epidemic. They wore red ribbons as a sign of solidarity and were joined by cricket players from Australia, West Indies, England, Sri Lanka, India, and Pakistan. On their HIV/AIDS Awareness Day, the players visited an AIDS center and garnered attention from the news media.

5. Another program utilized the mass media. An estimated 99% of South Africans have access to radio, 75% have access to television, and 7% read newspapers. As many as 69% of young people (40% of the population is under 20) watch television 5 or more days per week. Consequently, a national campaign using television, billboards, newspapers, and magazines was launched. Knowing South African

youth are attracted to American culture, sexy ads and branding techniques were used to advocate LoveLife, a lifestyle that is cool and hip and safe. The images were like those on a rap album and were designed to compete for attention with products such as Coca-Cola or Levi's. Slogans that encouraged teens to discuss sex with their families were also included. Nelson Mandela endorsed the campaign; critics say the ads are too sophisticated or too subtle. Research determined that young South Africans recognize the effort and of those, two-thirds said they have delayed or abstained from sex as a result.

Since 2005

In 2009, there were more than 5.7 million HIV/AIDS cases in South Africa, with as many as 1,800 reported daily, and 900 deaths daily. New infections among mature age groups in South Africa are still high, but infections among teenagers seemed on the decline in 2009.

A study by the Harvard School of Public Health in 2008 revealed that the South African government could have prevented 365,000 AIDS deaths in the early years of this century if it had provided antiretroviral drugs. This failure resulted from President Thabo Mbeki's and Minister of Health Tshabalala-Msimang's denials that the HIV virus causes AIDS.

In 2008, President Mbeki resigned and was replaced by Kgalema Motlanthe, who was to complete Mbeki's term, due to end in May, 2009. He hired Tshabalala-Msimang ("Dr. Beetroot") as Minister in the Presidency. Jacob Zuma was elected president in May, 2009. He promised a new era in the fight against the disease and to expand testing and treatment for HIV/AIDS. On World AIDS Day (December 1, 2009) at a ceremony in Pretoria, he said, "Let there be no more shame, no more blame, no more discrimination and no more stigma."

New Tactics

At least 90% of people carry a mobile phone and that number is increasing. So Project Masiluleke was set up in 2008 to send text messages by the millions and in all 13 languages to increase HIV/AIDS awareness, testing, and treatment. Pilot projects saw immediate results with a decided increase in the numbers of calls to the National AIDS Helpline.

Local celebrities Sipho "Hotstix" Mabuse, Seiphemo Rapulana, soccer star Shoes Moshoeu, and comedian Kenneth Nkosi participated in a round table discussion at the fourth Southern African AIDS conference in 2009, and agreed to urge their peers to help spread the messages of HIV prevention and safe sex.

Soul City, a pilot program targeting 8 to 12 year-olds, used television and radio dramas to discuss issues such as social norms, health, and HIV/AIDS.

In 2009, the Khuza Award, determined by a vote of 3,000 youth aged 8 to 22, went to the animated "Scrutinize," and HIV prevention programs. The Khuza is South Africa's biggest research-based youth marketing and communications award. Young people indicated they love the humorous ads, and the campaign also had high a "talkability" factor.

A survey asking men to tap answers into a Palm Pilot device revealed that one in four men in South Africa admitted to rape and confessed to attacking more than one victim. The Medical Research Council of South Africa says the responses were very frank and provide hope that this may be a first step in changing the culture where sexual entitlement of men is rooted in the ideal of manhood.

Zimbabwe

In 2008, one in seven adults in Zimbabwe was living with HIV. Between 2002 and 2006, the population decreased by 4 million people. In 2006, women, who were the most affected, had a life expectancy of 34, the lowest in the world. By 2011, that life expectancy could drop to 30. There were more orphans in Zimbabwe than anywhere in the world, according to UNICEF in 2010.

Children orphaned by AIDS number more than 980,000 and 120,000 children are living with the HIV infection. Of the total of all hospital admissions 70% are HIV related. Infection rates are highest for people aged 25 or under, especially teenagers and women who are most vulnerable.

HIV/AIDS activists, attempting to be as optimistic as possible, say that although 25% of the population is infected, 75% of the population is HIV negative, and it is these people they need to reach with safe sex and abstinence programs.

There are sociological findings that contribute to the challenges. Among them are the following:

1. The population is largely Christian and more Roman Catholic than any other denomination. The Vatican is opposed to condoms and therefore many of the people are confused as to whom to believe.
2. English is the official language of the educated population but people in rural areas speak in their native languages—usually Shona and Ndebele. Many health care workers cannot speak those languages.
3. The country is crippled by drought, a shortage of food, unemployment, and poverty. Concern about a confusing and mysterious disease is not as urgent as having food to eat.

4. The meaning of the term "be faithful" is difficult to comprehend. Being faithful to one person is only effective if one's partner is also faithful and uninfected. The culture in Zimbabwe has long permitted men, but not women, to have multiple sexual partners. Also, young people consider faithfulness to mean dating one person at a time— no matter how frequently one relationship may follow another. Actually, this is also a source of confusion in the United States. When the advice is that people with multiple sex partners are more likely to be infected, many do not realize that if the one partner they have sex with in their entire lives is HIV-positive, they might be infected too.

5. The school system is a major center of fighting the virus in Zimbabwe and a major center of the crisis. Teachers are the career group with the highest infection rate so they are not effective role models. They have not been adequately trained in coping with HIV/AIDS themselves. Also, sick teachers lose their jobs after excessive absences. Some, therefore, force themselves to meet their classes even when they are chronically ill. So the quality of education also suffers.

6. Long distances between home and school result in some students, especially girls, seeking temporary housing closer to schools. This is called "bush boarding," and it often results in prostitution, which increases the risk of HIV infection. When girls have sex with older men in return for shelter or money, it is called "food for work" or "survival sex."

7. School enrollment levels are also affected because girls, who are more susceptible to the disease, often drop out to care for the sick in their families or they are often unable to pay school fees because of sicknesses in their family, or unemployment or abject poverty.

8. Research shows that persons not in school are five times more likely to have sex than those in school, so children are urged to stay in school not only to get an education that will make them more upwardly mobile but also to learn the lessons of HIV/AIDS.

9. The schools in 80% of Zimbabwe, in rural areas, do not have televisions or access to any electricity, so training programs that require electronic equipment are not useful. Urban schools and homes may have television. Most people even in rural areas have radio at home and can comprehend if programs are broadcast in their native languages.

Tactics

The Zimbabwe National Family Planning Council (ZNFPC), with technical assistance from Johns Hopkins University's Population Communication Services, launched a program aimed at getting young people

to adopt new behaviors: abstinence or the use of condoms. The campaign was based on the Steps to Behavior Change framework that has five stages: knowledge, approval, intention, practice, and advocacy. Effective communications campaigns determined at which stage the segmented publics would become targets of "approval" campaigns. Once publics approved, they would be targeted by "intention" and so on. Each step led to the next. For example, the youth campaign (for those aged 10 to 24) was at the knowledge stage and the slogans mentioned in all its activities and printed matter were "Have self-control," "Value your body," and "Respect yourself."

More than 10,000 posters were distributed with slogans such as "You may think you are ready for sex, but are you ready for the consequences?" Leaflets were produced on abstinence, saying "no" to sex, and postponing sex; 19,000 were distributed. Most youth in Zimbabwe had access to radio so a 1-hour radio variety series, *Youth for Real*, was produced and broadcast nationwide weekly. The episodes mixed entertainment such as music and drama with advice. There was also a segment in which listeners could call in and ask questions of counselors or physicians. Two community theater troupes performed interactive dramas daily at schools, churches, and shopping centers. Peer educators were trained to advise people in their own age group, mostly in schools.

Other organizations also joined in with the knowledge and approval stages. The Grassroot Soccer Foundation (GRSF) trained 14 well-known soccer players to educate at-risk youth about HIV/AIDS in nine schools in Bulawayo, Zimbabwe. GRSF targeted seventh-graders to improve their knowledge, attitudes, and perceptions of HIV/AIDS. Students reported that they intended to use their knowledge. The program was completed by 3,000 children.

In an exchange program funded by the American Federation of Teachers, "Teachers Helping Teachers, Combat HIV-AIDS in Africa," teachers from Zimbabwe and Kenya came to the United States for intensive 2-week sessions of learning about HIV/AIDS and how it spreads. The teachers from Zimbabwe and Kenya also shared their various experiences with the disease, though Kenya's statistics (a 13.5 prevalence rate) was less troubling. They were all encouraged to return home and teach other teachers and students. The same program produced a Zimbabwe publication, *Teacher's Voice*, which also aims to educate teachers about the disease. Each edition explores a basic fact.

To reach the HIV-positive in Zimbabwe, PSI received funding from USAID to do an anti-stigma media program titled, "Don't Be Negative About Being Positive." It was featured on television, radio, newspapers, and posters, beginning in 2005. Persons who are HIV-positive are provided with a platform to frankly discuss their situation and to challenge discrimination.

Since 2005

In 2007, Zimbabwe, though still in crisis, had a drop in HIV rates, one of the most significant declines. Despite a high level of awareness, HIV/AIDS remains highly stigmatized in Zimbabwe, but people feel that the stigma is diminishing. The "Don't Be Negative About Being Positive" campaign won the 2005 Global Media Award for its organizers.

The statistics are worse for women than men because of social inequality. According to UNAIDS, in 2006, 60% of adults in Zimbabwe with HIV were women. Women are poorer, less educated, and more dependent. Programs that ignore these facts are doomed to fail.

Life expectancy for women is 34, the lowest in the world. The overall population decreased by 4 million between 2002 and 2006. Starvation plays a role, but a Zimbabwean physician explained, "Put simply, people are still dying of AIDS before they can starve to death." Also, women in rural areas have limited access to antiretroviral drugs and they depend on herbal remedies. Sometimes, they don't understand the disease, and at other times their husbands discourage them from taking the drugs.

New Tactics

Women's football (soccer) teams made up of openly HIV-positive players are increasing in number. Two top teams are the ARV Swallows (ARV stands for antiretroviral) and the Sporting ART (ART stands for antiretroviral treatment). They are positive role models because they are open about being infected, and their success in the sport shows how healthy one can be while taking HIV drugs. They distribute literature and male and female condoms at the games; the supply is depleted after every game.

A public health television commercial featuring Davies Mazodze, a college lecturer speaking openly about his HIV status, is a popular mass media campaign and has generated dialogue and discussion about everyone's vulnerability to HIV.

More than 70 barbers and 2,000 hairdressers in Zimbabwe have been trained to provide information about male and female condoms and to sell them. They earn a small commission on all they sell.

In 2009, the Children's Performing Arts workshop in Harare presented a participatory theatre production to address issues related to HIV/AIDS and young women. "Act Out: Tackling HIV and AIDS Through Theatre Communications" fused theater with discussion to engage the audience. At a high school in St. Augustine, students participated in a workshop run by a Zimbabwe theater group.

One hope for beating the disease is that more and more information may be disseminated online. Internet penetration in Zimbabwe went

from 6.7% to 10.9% between 2005 and 2008. Most people access the Internet through colleges, schools, cybercafés, workplaces, and some access it at home.

Swaziland

In 2005 the Kingdom of Swaziland had the highest rate of HIV infection in the world. The first case of AIDS there was reported in 1987. Since then the disease has spread rapidly.

About one-third of the 480,000 adult Swazis are HIV-positive out of a total population of 1 million. The age group from 20 to 30 is the most affected. Out of young people aged 15 to 19, 29% are HIV-positive. Of adults aged between 30 and 39, 40% tested positive. As many as 42.6% of pregnant women tested were HIV-positive.

Situations and Challenges

1. Unlike some other African countries (such as Uganda), it is still taboo to admit HIV-positive status in Swaziland. Polygamy is still practiced and supported by the royal family, and people still think they can avoid the infection and practice polygamy. In the old tradition, boys are expected to seek sex and girls are expected to comply, but the new environment is beginning to shun that tradition.

2. Research reveals that poverty and culture are the biggest issues in the fight against HIV/AIDS. Swazis are warm people, but they have some lack of trust for foreigners and persons in the political arena.

3. Extended families, headed by the eldest male (usually a grandfather if there is one), make decisions involving the entire family. Adult unmarried children and some married sons remain in the extended family. Women have little voice, but they are beginning to take jobs out of necessity. HIV/AIDS has affected the family structure.

4. Churches and other faith-based organizations are coming forward to help the fight against HIV. Swazis are primarily Christians who mix religious principles and indigenous practices. A minister in rural Mliba said, "A heavy mantle of shame cloaks AIDS in Swaziland. It is the duty of churches to bring about moral guidance to the issue. AIDS isn't about sin, it's about a virus."

5. ARV drugs have been introduced, but many health workers fear that HIV prevention is being ignored while treatment is emphasized.

6. Swaziland's National Emergency Response Council on HIV/AIDS (NERCHA) determined through research that when targeting people between the ages of 20 and 30 who had already had sexual experiences, the anti-AIDS effort should concentrate on encouraging self-protection and not on abstinence.

7. The epidemic affects Swazi children in two ways. First, they are orphaned, and then they often contract the disease through child abuse. There was a 50% rise in reported cases of incest between 2003 and 2005. This does not mean a drastic increase in cases, but rather that reporting became more acceptable.

8. Protectors were put in place in some urban areas. These were people whom children could trust and could tell them about abusive incidents. The protectors would tell them how to recognize dangers, what to do, and that they did not have to accept abuse. But in villages in rural areas it was not possible for outsiders to be accepted.

9. The people of this country are very mobile traveling across the country and outside for work. This would include migrant miners who may be away from home as long as a year. Many travel to South Africa to work in mines. Most of these men encounter commercial sex workers.

10. In 2005, Swazi King Mswati III abandoned a campaign to urge girls to remain virgins. The campaign began in 2001 and urged young girls to avoid marriage and remain virginal for 5 years. It was a modern version of the tradition of "uMcwasho, the badge of the virgin." No reason was given for the king's action but it is believed the program was not popular among youth. In a jubilant ceremony, thousands of young girls removed the "virgin tassels" they wore to signify chastity.

Tactics

Billboards and posters were installed by NERCHA in schools, clinics, and libraries, at bus stops, and as full-page ads in newspapers. They showed a confident, smartly dressed professional woman. The message was, "I am not going to share my partner with anybody." The organization's communications director explained, "The woman cannot control what her partner does, but she is warning him that if he does take another girlfriend, he will lose her." It's a message of independence—that a girl can stand up to cultural pressures and say "No" to men despite the cultural pressures. Gcebile, a 22-year-old office worker commented, "I am like the woman in the billboard. I took charge of my life in order to save it when I found my boyfriend was cheating on me; it became a case of self-preservation triumphing over the love I held for that boy." NERCHA's program is built on the hope that many women will respond as Gcebile.

A UNICEF representative, Alan Brody, used folklore traditions to communicate with Swazi children aged 12 and older. A story titled, "How the Children of Chakijane Put an End to Brother Snake's Abuse" was first performed by professional actors in churches. Later, children played

the roles themselves. The characters in the play are animals; a deceitful snake convinces a rabbit that bedding his 12-year-old daughter is acceptable. There is humor in the play, but the overall effect is devastation. The daughter rabbit dies, the father is banished, and the villagers behead the snake. However, it leads to much more open discussion than real-life abuse can bring about. When done in a village, the discussion often leads to the audience electing a village protector who tells the story to other children from a book published by UNICEF. This way, bonds of trust and resulting communication develop.

The play has been done for various adult groups also—the unemployed, community elders, Christians, male groups, female groups. Each time, the audience can translate the allegory to their own lives.

Posters read, "Be faithful to your polygamous family." If all the partners are faithful to each other then HIV is not a threat. However, if one partner strays and is infected, all the partners are at risk.

On a visit to Matsapha, Swaziland, in July, 2005, U.S. Global AIDS coordinator Randall Tobias and principal secretary of Swaziland's Ministry of Health and Social Welfare Dr. John Kunene underwent public AIDS testing from a PSI center to show the Swazis how easy the test is.

Since 2005

There was a slight decline when the prevalence rate dropped from 42.6% in 2004 to 39.2% in 2006. There seems to be conflict among Swazis over whether prevention is possible. Some say condoms are advised, men have them, but they do not use them. The government pushes condoms; community leaders push abstinence. They call condoms "unSwazi."

New Tactics

In 2009, the AIDS Healthcare Foundation (AHF) launched a free "Love Condom" campaign utilizing television and newspapers. There was early indication that those who saw the coverage requested condoms.

In June, 2009, the Partnership Framework on HIV and AIDS was formed. The purpose of this five-year (2009–2013) collaborative effort of the government of the Kingdom of Swaziland and the government of the United States is to provide a strategic agenda to contribute to the PEPFAR goals for prevention, care, and treatment. A key intervention area in the plan calls for focusing on better linking mass media approaches with sustained community-based prevention activities.

PEPFAR also launched a love test to encourage couples to be tested for HIV as a way of showing love for each other.

Conclusion

Worldwide, the HIV/AIDS crisis has not ended; it just happens to be worse in African countries. The essential evaluation of the fight is a measurement of whether there are fewer cases of infections and fewer deaths. This will require years to determine. Earlier positive indications will be celebrated—an increase in the use of condoms; a decrease in the pregnancy rate of young girls, which is a signal of abstinence; and people verbalizing their concern about the crisis and their determination to do something about it.

Case: Texas A&M University and the Bonfire Tragedy

Eleven Texas A&M University students and one alumnus were killed and 27 others were injured when the traditional Aggie bonfire they were building collapsed at 2:42 a.m. on November 18, 1999. The burning of the bonfire and the celebration surrounding it were part of a detailed 2-day timeline of events leading to the November 26 football game with the University of Texas. The bonfire would represent the Aggies' burning determination to defeat its archrival, commonly called (in lowercase letters) "t.u."

The tragedy made big news in Texas but also made newspapers and broadcast news nationally and internationally. *USA Today* quoted the university's president, Ray C. Bowen, as expressing "unspeakable grief." *The Philadelphia Inquirer*'s headline read, "Collapse Kills 11 at Texas A&M" (Jones, 1999). The twelfth victim died the next day. And in France, *Le Matin* had the headline "Une pyramide meurtrière" ("A pyramid of death").

The 32-page *Bonfire Briefing Book* detailed the history of the event as well as the precautions, maps, charts, and diagrams for erecting the 55-foot tall, 45-foot wide log monument. The erection of the bonfire pyramid had begun on October 3, 1999, with the cutting of trees from land that farmers needed cleared; an estimated 6,000 to 8,000 logs were to be used. On October 30, the center pole, made of two utility poles, arrived, and on November 6, the center pole was raised and anchored 10 feet in the ground, 55 feet above. "Stacking" logs would take 2 to 3 weeks. There would be six stacks with the fifth and sixth stacks wired together on the day before the bonfire (see Figure 8.7). The book included a detailed timeline of the festivities planned for November 25, down to the arrangement of the media vehicles, the football team's arrival, when the torches would be thrown and the bonfire lit, and which yells the cheerleaders would do. But in 1999 the day of festivities never came. The accident occurred during the stacking phase.

Figure 8.7 An artist's sketch of the bonfire built by students shows the telephone poles spliced together to make the center pole that supports the structure. The spliced poles are also embedded underground. The logs on each stack are held together in groups of three with baling wire. Drawing by Gina Arnold.

Tradition and Culture

The bonfire tradition at Texas A&M began in 1909, with the first bonfire made from a simple trash heap. Tradition is the operative word; it is capitalized in some Texas A&M publications. Many, especially non-Texans, wondered, "All these years of building the bonfire and there's no expertise?" "What's the big deal?" "What a wasteful reason to die!"

"Students are a university's most precious resource. How can we risk them?" "Why waste people and trees?" "Start a new tradition—build a house for Habitat for Humanity." "It's simple—People were killed; stop the tradition." But it was not so simple because the bonfire was part of the Texas A&M culture.

Five thousand students put in 125,000 work hours each year to build the bonfire. Aggies participated every year, and from 1935 on, the bonfire was a monument of logs, growing bigger every year until 1970, when a limit was placed on its size. University alumni and community members returned each year to see the bonfire blaze. In 1963, the bonfire was canceled because of the assassination of President John Kennedy, so in 1994 the class of 1964 was invited to participate in the lighting of the bonfire; the students came in large numbers, eager to have their moment.

Some students risk their grades to take time to build the bonfire. A&M student John Comstock, the last accident victim to be released (in April 2000) from the hospital, had been pinned under the rubble for 7 hours. His injuries left him partially paralyzed, and his left leg had to be amputated above the knee. Still, he said he wanted the bonfire tradition to continue. Some parents of students who were killed also wanted the tradition to continue. Former U.S. President George H. W. Bush, whose library is located on the Texas A&M campus, was asked if the tradition should continue. He replied, "Absolutely" (Kirsch, 1999b).

Aggies say "you have to be there" to understand the spirit and the tradition of the bonfire, that the experience is beyond words or description. They call it the "Spirit of Aggieland." They say it keeps Aggies of today and yesterday in a tight bond.

There had been prodromes to the 1999 bonfire tragedy. In 1955, an Aggie on all-night duty at the bonfire construction site was hit and killed by a truck. He is called the "first Bonfire hero," not its first victim. In 1957, a few days before the scheduled burning, the bonfire stack fell while the Aggies were lunching. No one was hurt. In 1981, an Aggie was killed after he rode a tractor to the cutting site; he hit a bump, was thrown off the tractor, and was crushed beneath its wheels. In 1994, following heavy rains, the stack of logs shifted and had to be rebuilt.

Proponents of the bonfire discount that the 1999 tragedy is a warning of what could happen again. They argue that the bonfire can be built more safely and that the tradition must continue. After all, in Texas in 1999, 11 students died in traffic accidents. University students die playing football, but there is no move to abolish the game. Accidents happen (Tang, 2000).

External and Internal Communications

In 1999, it was not Cynthia Lawson's decision to continue or not to continue the bonfire tradition. As executive director of university relations

at Texas A&M University, it was her job and her staff's job to head external and internal communications. Lawson (see Figure 8.8) reported directly to President Bowen, who reported to the chancellor of the Texas A&M system. The chancellor reported to the Board of Regents.

Lawson's staff consisted of 21 persons whose duties included national, international, state, and local news and information, institutional communications, strategic planning, photography, graphic design, video services, and other public relations and communications duties.

Texas A&M University, located in the small college town of Bryan/ College Station, is among the top 20 U.S. universities and a major research university. The Office of University Relations disseminates to

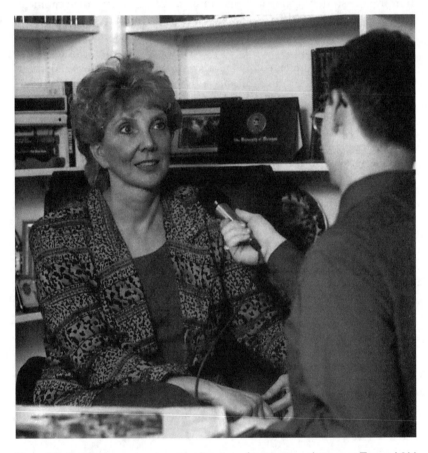

Figure 8.8 Cynthia Lawson, executive director of university relations at Texas A&M University, had been in her position only 5 months when the bonfire accident occurred. Reprinted with permission of Texas A&M Office of University Relations.

national outlets research findings related to the work of the various departments in the university in relevant publications. News releases vary from local and state media to wire services and national media. Lawson said that before her arrival at Texas A&M, "there had been a few other national stories about hazing incidents or the relocation of a pig farm to make room for President Bush's library and Presidential Conference Center."

Having been in her position for only 5 months, Lawson had not been a part of the longtime bonfire tradition and had not seen the actual structure, although everyone on campus and in the College Station vicinity could watch the daily building of the bonfire on the web. A digital camera was focused on the construction most of the time. Most residents of the state are aware of the bonfire after it is lit.

On November 18, 1999, around 2:50 a.m., Lawson got a call from the university's Critical Incidence Response Team, telling her there had been an accident, the bonfire had fallen, and students were injured. She did not know, at that time, that there were deaths. "I had no idea of the magnitude of the project nor could I place any meaningful significance [symbolic or otherwise] as to what the collapse actually meant," she said.

Lawson's first task was to telephone selected members of her staff; then she headed for the site of the tragedy. She did not have to call key administrators because the Critical Incidence Response Team had that responsibility. The university president told Lawson to make all the communications decisions, saying that she was "the expert" and that it was "her call." Lawson saw this as an act of faith on Bowen's part, because even though she had been highly recommended for the position, they did not know each other. She was appreciative.

A&M had only a skeletal crisis communications plan in place, a one-page document advising personnel of the critical nature of effective communications during a crisis and mentioning what it called "one-minute manager" admonitions, such as "Be honest. Be accurate. Do not speculate." As Lawson explained, what helped her to a greater degree was her prior experience with crisis planning:

> I worked in Public Affairs at the Detroit Edison Company back in the 1970s and 1980s. During that time, Detroit Edison was constructing a nuclear power plant. Part of my responsibilities was being involved with and ultimately managing the Joint Public Information Team.
>
> This team was created to handle a media crisis in the event of an accident at the nuclear power plant. As I recall, a "mock crisis" was created once or twice a year. County and state officials, as well as FEMA and Edison employees, were involved in the effort. Even the news media participated in the effort by asking tough questions.

The purpose was to coordinate the information released during a nuclear crisis. I recall that we used to be called in the middle of the night. We knew the week, but not the day or time.

The drill was gruesome—all day long. The circumstances of the accident were never the same. Sometimes [in the drill] no one was hurt; other times, people were killed. We never knew the direction of the nuclear plume and what the consequences of that particular scenario were. Mock press conferences were held; faxes were released. An entire Joint Public Information Center was set up with equipment, and so on. It was as real as one can get and yet not be real. I even remember vice presidents getting angry at me for pushing them to release "pretend information" that the press would want and need.

The skills I learned in these practices long ago were ingrained in me. I knew what I had to do. It was automatic.

However, as we see later, Lawson said she would make some changes if she had to do it again.

Another factor that helped Lawson with the crisis communications was that she had spent the first months of her position connecting with key community leaders. There was no organized advisory board, but there were these community leaders who, she said, "were invaluable during the crisis." One of them was Royce Hickman, president of the Bryan/College Station Chamber of Commerce. He came to the fallen bonfire and asked what he could do to help. Hickman helped arrange for food for student workers and the news media. He also arranged for a masseur/masseuse to treat workers who were becoming weary.

Home Depot contacted Hickman to offer its services. Houston Cellular offered cell phones and backup batteries to the Office of University Relations, and before the day was over, these phones were being used by the fire department, police department, and rescue workers whose cell phone batteries had died.

Relationships with the news media also paid off. "There were many 'media types' on campus who had connections with media throughout the state. Lane Stephenson, Deputy Director for University Relations, and Sherylon Carroll, Associate Director for University Relations, had extensive contacts and relationships. I had developed relationships with the local media, but national and regional contacts were virtually nonexistent,"Lawson said.

As at most universities, a number of people at Texas A&M had public relations expertise. Lawson estimated that there were about 20 such people, and they deferred to her and her office for media response. "This cooperation was a first at the university," she said. "This is important in a university setting. Unlike a corporation that may send forth an edict ordering that no one talk to the news media except the public relations

officers, in a university academic freedom seeks to prevail to its fullest extent. Everyone has something to say and a need to talk. With a few exceptions, this did not happen. And I am glad. Otherwise, we could not have controlled the message as well as we did."
Lawson continued:

> Most of the first day of the crisis was spent answering media questions and arranging interviews for reporters. There was a never-ending parade of news personnel. Since they did not arrive at the same time, it required repetition of information to bring them up to speed throughout the early morning hours of the crisis. Key members of my staff and I tried to do this one-on-one. So, to keep some control of the scene and to keep from having a "circus" atmosphere, I advised the media that I would come back every hour on the half hour to advise them of new developments. Also, I told them that if new information developed before the appointed time, I would immediately come and advise them. Then, I was careful to keep my promise.

Volunteer Help

Lawson held four or five news conferences throughout the first day and brought with her, at various times, President Bowen, Vice President of Student Affairs J. Malon Southerland, Bonfire Adviser Rusty Thompson, Student Body President Will Hurd, and Bart Humphreys, a public relations official representing the joint city–county rescue operations. Because there were students by the thousands around the site, the media had easy access to students. Hurd made himself available throughout the day of the crisis and during the aftermath. He was also helpful in identifying for reporters those students who were especially effective at being interviewed and could be counted on for helping to convey the types of messages the university wanted.

The key messages were the following: (a) concern for the parents of the injured and dead students; (b) facts about the bonfire tradition; (c) facts about the bonfire accident; and (d) an understanding of and appreciation for the "Aggie Spirit" and the "specialness" of the Texas A&M family.

In addition to getting warm clothing for the workers, newspeople were helpful in numerous other ways. When university officials needed to urge students to telephone their parents to tell them they were not injured, the electronic media got the word out. They also urged the community to refrain from needless telephone calls to avoid jamming phone lines. When a hotline was installed for parents, the news media announced it. When night fell and the temperature dropped, the media put out a call

for coats and sweatshirts for workers, and more than enough soon arrived. Then the call went out to stop. Lawson said, "The media was a tremendous asset in so many ways to the success of the rescue operation. We were truly indebted."

Another asset was the cooperation of university legal representatives. "General counsel were on the site, and I spoke to them briefly," Lawson explained. "They did not try to counsel me with respect to what I or others should or should not say. Texas A&M, fortunately, takes the position that we must do the right thing. We must be truthful regardless of the consequences. There was no attempt to cover up or be deceitful. If inaccurate information went out, we corrected it as soon as it was brought to our attention."

Information Communicated

An instance of incorrect information being disseminated occurred when Rusty Thompson, the bonfire adviser, estimated the height of the stack at the time of the collapse. The truth was, according to Lawson, that no one had gone out and measured the stack, so the actual height was not known. As it turned out, Thompson's guess was inaccurate. It was corrected.

The university has an ongoing communications vehicle called the "Aggie Hotline." It began as a means of communicating with faculty and staff via the web. On the first day of the crisis, the Office of University Relations immediately developed a web page for the bonfire accident. The Association of Former Students also had a web page that it used to communicate with its constituents. The hotline and the two web pages were used to update information on a regular basis throughout the bonfire crisis and for months afterward. All internal publics with Internet access—students, faculty, staff, parents, community leaders, the Board of Regents, government officials—could and did access these electronic sources on a regular basis.

In addition, the Texas A&M University PBS television station, KAMU-TV, was at the site to provide coverage of the crisis. Students tuned into the university TV station as well as to other local stations. Informal systems of communications, such as residence hall councils, the student government, and student activity leaders, were used to inform students of a candlelight vigil, a Thursday night memorial service, and other events. The aftermath of the crisis was covered by the student newspaper, the *Battalion*, a morning daily. In its first edition following the start of the crisis, the *Battalion* reported the names of the deceased and injured students, but because the "why" and "how" of the crisis were not known, no other hard news was included. Other coverage included eyewitness testimony and feature material or "soft news."

The chronic stage of the crisis, when the accident made front-page national news, lasted about 2 weeks. However, the story remained in the news until the Christmas break. There were inquiries almost daily for several months. Although the national and regional coverage soon subsided, coverage in Texas continued daily for many months more.

Texas A&M University made all documents, memos, and other pertinent information available to the press through the university library. "Initially," said Lawson, "general counsel was not comfortable with the decision to release the information to the public in the library. The reality was that the president made the decision that this was the right thing to do. General counsel was given the task of logging and disseminating all of the information. Everything was released except pictures from the morgue of the deceased students. The media can get those, too, on request."

The most important public, during the first days of the crisis, was the parents of the deceased and injured students. Once a deceased or injured student was identified, his or her parents were telephoned and informed. If the parents lived close enough to the university, a personal visit was made. It was only after parents were notified that student information was given to the news media and posted on the website. Parents of injured students were visited frequently in the hospital. Periodic visits were made months later to student John Comstock, who remained in rehabilitation, and to other students and parents as needed.

As days passed, information was provided to parents via phone calls, visits, or letters depending on the nature of the information and the urgency. The types of information the university needed to send included instructions for receiving special funds available for funeral arrangements, hospital bills, and lodging, and the announcement of the creation of the Bonfire Commission, meetings of the Bonfire Commission, and so on. The parents were also informed of negative or hurtful stories in the press (e.g., there were stories that some students were under the influence of alcohol). All of these communications to parents were disseminated by the vice president of the Office of Student Affairs.

Texas A&M at College Station is a member of a consortium of 12 universities that make up the Texas A&M University system. The system has its own public relations director who, according to Lawson, "came to the site, stayed by my side, and kept the regents informed, primarily by cell phone." Some of the regents came to the crisis site. They also were kept apprised by accessing the web page and watching and listening to news reports. After the first day of the crisis, the president and chancellor kept the Board of Regents informed through phone calls and board meetings.

Both Texas A&M University and the university system have vice presidents of governmental affairs. Both officers came to the crisis site

and stayed throughout most of the day. They communicated regularly to state legislative leaders by phone. After the crisis ended, the legislature was updated via memos from the two governmental affairs officers, personal visits, phone calls, and the website.

Within a few days of the start of the crisis, University President Bowen made a decision to appoint a person outside the university to head an independent commission to investigate the cause of the bonfire accident. There were discussions about who that person should be and what qualities the person should have. University officials felt this was the right thing to do no matter what the commission's report might reveal. The independent commission, later called the Special Commission on the 1999 Aggie Bonfire, would be more credible to the public, alumni, parents, community, and taxpayers than if the university conducted its own internal investigation.

Leo E. Linbeck, Jr., a trusted Houston businessman with a stellar reputation who was active in civic affairs, was asked to head the commission. Four other members were chosen by Linbeck; they were from El Paso, Dallas, Austin, and Fort Worth. Lawson's office sent out media advisories under commission letterhead announcing the meetings. The advisories told the press the agenda of each meeting and gave details as to how the press might cover it.

The media began to line up interviews for the commission report months before the report was due. Lawson's office prepared for the national media attention she knew the report would bring. She also geared up for the national media attention after the announcement was made about the future of the bonfire. Either way, it was expected to be good news–bad news–welcome news to some, disappointing news to others. Lawson's staff also realized it would again be sought after on the 1-year anniversary of the bonfire accident, November 18, 2000.

Psychological Counseling for Staff Members

Bowen strongly urged psychological counseling for all university employees who were at the bonfire site at the time of the accident. Others within the university community were also urged to seek such help. "I had encouraged all of them to make personal appointments with a counselor. But none of them did; none of us did," said Lawson. "Then, about a month passed, and I asked a psychiatrist to come to one of our meetings to talk with us as a group. As it turned out, there were a lot of issues that needed to be addressed. Individuals had visual images, disturbing images they could not get out of their minds. Others had feelings of being left out of the loop."

One of the problems was that when the accident occurred, Lawson, not knowing the full extent of the tragedy, telephoned two members of

her staff immediately. One of them picked up another en route to the site. Hence, there were four members of the Office of University Relations involved from the beginning. The rest of the staff arrived at the office at 8 a.m., as usual, to find that things were already in progress without them. "Some of them had difficulty finding tasks that were useful or helpful," said Lawson. "They felt left out. Somehow, getting lunch for everyone or doing what they called 'menial tasks' made them feel guilty because they were not pulling their weight."

Although no task is meaningless in a crisis, Lawson said almost 4 weeks passed before these staff members realized their value to the crisis communications. One of the most important functions of a crisis communications plan is often overlooked—that everyone has a valued role in the communications process. Before the crisis, each person on the crisis communications team should know what his or her role will be in the event of a crisis and how important that role is in the management of a crisis.

All of these issues had to be addressed by the psychologist. In addition, Lawson spoke about the sheer exhaustion they experienced: "I cannot begin to describe the pressure 'not to lose it' because you are in a managerial position, because you must appear before the news media, and because you are simply a professional. A time to cry is critical. A time to mourn is mandatory." Lawson recognized her personal breaking point on the Sunday following the Thursday accident. She told the following story:

> I was walking out of church when a young A&M student came up to me. Physically, he looked like a linebacker. He shook my hand and thanked me for representing the university and the students so well. As he said this, his voice trembled. Then, he wrapped me in his arms and sobbed from deep inside his soul. Then, I broke too. I buried my head in his chest and cried. There we were ... two strangers brought together by an unbelievable tragedy, two people who felt the need to be so strong for others at the expense of our own personal needs. We cried together for 15 minutes. He had his release; I had mine. I was okay after that. People need to take time to cry. I feel I should have taken this release earlier, even if privately.

Another problem Lawson related was being in the middle, between grieving parents and the news media. The news media wanted all the information they could get. When you are in the position of providing or not providing information to the news media, providing it is usually the right thing to do. People have a right to know. It is our right under the First Amendment. But, it is not always the thing you want to do. Although most reporters are very responsible and do not speculate or

resort to sensationalism, some others are not. Some documents can easily be taken out of context by irresponsible or unprofessional news personnel. This can cause additional pain to the families of an accident's victims.

One example of misquoting occurred when President Bowen was interviewed by Kelly Brown, a reporter for the *Eagle* in College Station. The reporter asked, "If the Commission's report were to find that the administration was at fault, and if the Board of Regents asked for your resignation, would you resign?" Lawson was present and heard the question and the answer. She said Bowen simply answered, "Yes." It was the only answer to the question. If the Board of Regents asks for a resignation, nearly anyone employed by the university would resign. But some newspapers did not print the first part of the question, "If the Board of Regents asked for your resignation." They ran the headline, "Bowen to Resign." That was not what he said. As Lawson explained:

> Not wanting to bring undue attention to the whole issue, I did not attempt to correct the quote. However, my concern was that in the aftermath of the report, the misquote could create some problems for us. If the report were to cite any administrative oversight, the news media would attempt to pressure Bowen into resigning. They can be relentless about these things. President Bowen has provided exemplary leadership for this institution prior to the bonfire as well as during the crisis. His absence would be a great loss for Texas A&M.

Lawson added that phone calls and e-mail messages primarily supported Bowen.

Another media problem occurred when the *Arizona Republic* published an editorial cartoon that compared the Texas A&M bonfire accident with both the 1993 Branch Davidian inferno and the 1999 brutal murder of a black man in Jasper, labeling all three events "Texas Bonfire Traditions." The university community and Aggies everywhere were incensed. The newspaper pulled the cartoon from its website and apologized for having published it. Then the editorial page editor apologized and sent Bowen a $10,000 peace offering to be placed in two memorial funds. Bowen returned the checks, saying "it would do violence to our ethical standards to accept it from the *Arizona Republic*" (Kirsch, 1999a). It didn't end there. A columnist for the *Arizona Republic*, whose column was published in other newspapers as well, charged that Bowen, "other grown-ups," and the university could have prevented the bonfire tragedy, but "[Bowen] wants people to be upset about an editorial cartoon" (Montini, 1999).

Negative News Stories

As stories negative to the university or to the bonfire tradition emerged (see Figure 8.9), the University Relations Office rarely responded other than simply stating that the university did not want any responses that could potentially influence the commission's report.

On December 3, a headline, primarily in Texas newspapers, was "A&M Student's Use of Crane May Have Violated Bonfire Rule." There was an apparent rule that only professional operators could run the crane. University spokesperson Lane Stephenson, on Lawson's staff, was quoted in the story as saying the student "had 200 hours of experience, sufficient

A&M BONFIRE SAFETY RULES WERE BROKEN

A&M student's operation of a crane may have violated Bonfire rules

2 BONFIRE VICTIMS WERE LEGALLY DRUNK

FACULTY DOUBTED BONFIRE'S STABILITY
A&M engineering faculty doubted bonfire's stability

Photos Show Bonfire Leaning Before Fall

Texas bonfire surpassed 55-foot limit
A&M's tab for Bonfire aftermath: $292,000 and growing

REPORT:
BONFIRE ROPES WERE CUT

Bonfire logs appeared to be leaning, report says

Figure 8.9 Headlines from several negative news stories that Cynthia Lawson and her staff had to contend with during the Texas A&M bonfire crisis.

to satisfy federal requirements for operating the equipment." Because there was no information that the operation of the crane had anything to do with the collapse, Lawson told another reporter, "The commission will delve into each aspect of the incident" (Slover & Lee, 1999).

On December 5, when headlines read, "2 Bonfire Victims Were Legally Drunk," Lawson told reporters, "There's a real danger of getting off point. It isn't that these things aren't important or shouldn't be looked at. But the major issue is, what caused this thing to fall?" (Ball, 1999).

On December 10, news stories, in Texas and nationally, related allegations made by e-mail from members of the engineering faculty at A&M to the president that the bonfire design was unstable. Certain faculty members admitted they kept quiet and ignored colleague T. J. Hirsch, a former member of the faculty, who had been complaining for years that the structure was "fatally flawed." Stephenson did not comment on the e-mail messages and was quoted as saying, "Basically, we're going to let the commission appointed to investigate the accident do its work" (Haurwitz & Copelin, 1999).

When the headline on December 15 was "Photos Show Bonfire Leaning Before Fall," Stephenson was quoted by the Associated Press as saying, "Now that the commission is at work, everything having to do with the bonfire accident will be deferred to the commission" (Associated Press, 1999). After repeatedly referring reporters to the commission, the university noticed that news articles began to include sentences such as the following one: "University officials have referred all questions to the commission, which will not speculate on a potential cause until the investigation is complete" (Brown, 2000).

Lawson took a stand on January 7, 2000, when reports circulated that the investigation of the collapse would cost more than $292,000. She was quoted as saying, "We're committed to do what needs to be done under the circumstances. I haven't heard anyone asking, 'How much will it cost?' or 'How are we going to pay for it?' or 'Who's going to pay?' We're doing it because it's the right thing to do" (Ward, 2000).

Lessons Learned

When asked if she would do anything differently if she had to endure the crisis again, Lawson listed the following:

1. "I would have called all of my staff out immediately."
2. "I would have called in a lot of other PR folks on campus to assist us with answering media calls."
3. "I would have had one or two staff members dedicated to watching the media reports and providing me with any inaccurate information being disseminated."

4. "I would have had one or two staff members developing 'other' stories for the media and lining up prospective interviewees for the immediate aftermath of the crisis. During a crisis, there is such a feeding frenzy of information. When the crisis is over, there is immediate famine. But the media still needs to continue the story. I would prefer to have provided a bunch of stories for them that I wanted to 'get out,' thereby not forcing them to 'go get any story' they could to keep the momentum going."

5. "There will be a crisis communications plan. Once it is written, we will 'exercise' the plan, just like we did at Detroit Edison."

In May 2000, the commission reported that the bonfire collapsed due to a combination of factors: Students cut corners; school officials failed to adequately supervise students; there were organizational failures; and there were structural problems. Student drinking and horseplay were not deemed direct causes. The commission's leader said a safe bonfire would have been possible had school officials taken necessary precautions. The latter pronouncement met with "whoops" from students who filled a basketball arena to hear it.

Lawson said that, now that she had been at the university through this crisis, she understood the "Traditions" (always capitalized in Texas A&M publications) at the core of Texas A&M University. The notion "Tradition" has its roots not only in the longevity of the university itself but also in the fact that many of the opportunities for student involvement are major events or projects that involve a large percentage of the student body. These students thus have many "shared experiences"—Bonfire, Fish Camp, Muster, Elephant Walk—where lifelong bonds are created. Texas A&M probably offers more opportunities for shared experiences than most other higher education institutions. And the students probably do a better job perpetuating those traditions than do their counterpart schools less rich in tradition.

President Bowen announced, in June 2000, that the traditional bonfire would continue, but in 2005 Texas A&M had another president, Robert Gates, who said a decision on whether a campus bonfire would continue would not be made until litigation was settled between the university and the families of students killed or injured in the 1999 collapse.

Parents of students injured and killed in the collapse filed lawsuits against President Bowen, numerous other university officials, and the university. In 2006, 36 of the 64 being sued settled at a total of $4.25 million paid by their individual insurance companies. A U.S. Circuit Court of Appeals dismissed the remaining lawsuits in April, 2007. In October, 2007, the U.S. Supreme Court declined to review the appeals court ruling.

Meanwhile, since 1999 students have built and burned bonfires off campus, bonfires not approved by the university. Sometimes there are

more than one, all on private ground. In 2003, more than 10,000 people turned out to see a "Student Bonfire." In 2004, students raised $60,000 to fund the construction of the 42-foot stack supervised by Houston engineer Will Wilkenson, a former Aggie who worked on Bonfire in the 1990s. He said that all logs touch the ground and thereby eliminate the stress between tiers that contributed to the 1999 collapse. Student Bonfire leader Paul Harding said, "We're serious about this. This isn't some type of rebellion. We just don't want Bonfire to fade away."

In 2005, there were two problems with the off-campus bonfire. A district court judge initially issued an order to stop the lighting. And when the judge finally lifted the injunction, the bonfire was lit but the flames kept dying when heavy rains caused the stack to billow smoke. Eventually the logs were doused with diesel fluid and continued to burn. Some say about 10,000 Aggies watched the bonfire burn, but the number could not be verified.

Cynthia Lawson left A&M and was named Vice President of Communications and Strategy Development at the University of North Carolina.

Environmental Crisis

Case: Häagen-Dazs and Honey Bees

This case study shows the extensive research sometimes necessary before a plan of communications can be developed to emerge from a crisis. It also shows how a company/organization can develop a project of corporate social responsibility (CSR) that demonstrates to its consumers that the company is a good citizen concerned about issues that affect us all and that profit is not everything.

The honey bee is vanishing.

When many people contemplate the disappearance of the honey bee, they think, "We'll be out of honey and honey products." This is a very short-sighted attitude. A beekeeper from Savannah, Georgia, Brother Chuck aka Buzza Shuck, says, "One honey bee only produces half of a teaspoon of honey in its lifetime of six weeks. But that same bee can pollinate up to 3 million blooms."

Many foods rely on the work of bees. Apples, asparagus, avocados, berries, broccoli, celery, cherries, citrus fruit, coffee, cucumbers, kiwi, melons, peaches, peppers, squash, tomatoes, and many nuts are in danger if the honey bee crisis is not solved. Not only flora but also fauna are affected since livestock feed on alfalfa and fruit, which depend on pollination. Kevin Hackett, national program leader (in 2007) for the bee and pollination program of the U.S. Department of Agriculture (USDA), said, "The honey bee is responsible for 80% of that pollination" (see Figure 9.1).

Zac Browning, vice president of the American Beekeeping Federation, said, "Every third bite we consume in our diet is dependent on a honey bee to pollinate that food." Hackett said, "This is the biggest general threat to our food supply."

School children learn early the cycle of life of fruit-bearing plants. A plant grows, bears a flower, then a seed-bearing fruit develops and falls and another plant grows from it. You can't tell the kids the truth.

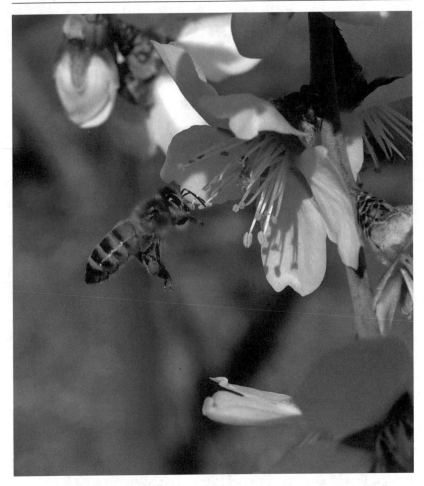

Figure 9.1 The honey bee helps provide one-third of all foods when it pollinates flowers. Beekeepers report a great decline in the numbers of honey bees and hives. Häagen-Dazs, with 40% of its ice cream flavors dependent upon pollination, decided to commit to funding research on the disappearance of the bees as a CSR project.

The pretty flower is not the goal; the purpose of the flower is basically sexual. The flower exists to exchange genetic matter with other like flowers and from that exchange, fruit is produced.

However, just because there is a flower does not mean there will be fruit produced. Pollen (which is male) from a flower must travel to another flower and come in contact with the stigma of the pistil (female) and from there to the ovules and ovary. Then, a seed and later fruit develop.

Help is needed to get the pollen of one plant to the pistil receptor of another. Wind can do it when growing grains. So much pollen flies in

the air that connections are made. Author Rowan Jacobsen, in his book titled *Fruitless Fall*, likens this process to direct mail and Internet spam. "You need to send out a million if you hope to get a single hit."

Insects are what Jacobsen calls "sexual handmaidens." They visit the flower for food and, in the process, the sticky pollen gets attached to them and is passed to the next flower they seek for nectar. "Honey bees," he said, "are the most enthusiastic, best organized migrant worker the planet has ever seen . . . large scale agriculture can no longer exist without them."

Crisis is Widespread

The decline began in the U.S. in 2006 when migratory beekeepers along the Atlantic seaboard states reported declines in their honey bee population. Beekeepers said they opened their bee boxes and found no bees. In 2007, 35 states reported an average decline of 30%. In California, David Bradshaw said it threatens not only his livelihood as a beekeeper but also the California almond.

U.S. honey bees pollinate an estimated $15 million worth of fruit, seed, and fiber crops each year. As the bee population decreases, the beekeeping industry is endangered.

In Canada, 29% of all honey bees were reported lost in 2007 compared to previous years. In the province of Ontario, 35% of the bees were lost. In Alberta, there was a one-quarter reduction in honey production between 2007 and 2008, due partly to losses.

In 2008, more than 7,000 beekeepers in Germany reported losses of nearly 500,000 bees. In November, 2008, the British Beekeepers Association (BBKA) reported that its honey bees could be wiped out in 10 years.

In Uruguay, beekeeper Daniel Rey, with 400 boxes in 2007, lost 50%. He believes the ozone hole directly over his country is responsible. In 2003, all the honey bees in Uruguay died and the country had to be re-stocked with imports from the U.S. and nearby Argentina, but this re-stocking will not be possible if all countries are affected.

In Europe, there was an average of a 40% loss in France, Greece, Italy, Poland, Portugal, Russia, Ukraine, Spain, Sweden, and Switzerland. In Asia, heavy losses were suffered in Thailand, South Korea, and China.

What is the Cause?

The crisis has been termed Colony Collapse Disorder (CCD). The word "collapse" in the term is problematic according to some researchers. The colonies do not actually collapse. The primary symptom is simply no adult honey bees present in the hive—or a low number—but with a live queen and no dead honey bees present. Often, there is still honey in the hives and some immature bees.

There were rumors and talk that cell phones were causing the crisis. While experts do not agree on the cause, they seem to agree that cell phones are not the cause. A German researcher, Stefan Kimmel, did a study of whether a particular base station for cordless phones could affect honey bee homing systems. Kimmel himself announced, "There is no link between our tiny little study and the CCD phenomenon. Anything else said or written is a lie."

The following are the leading suspects:

- Parasite, mites, and disease.
- Emergence of new virulent pathogens.
- Poor nutrition of the bees.
- Contaminated water supply.
- Lack of genetic diversity and lineage of bees.
- Level of stress in adult bees (transportation on truck beds, over-crowding, confinement, other environmental or biological stressors).
- Environmental chemicals such as pesticides to control parasitic moths.
- A combination of factors.

The leading possible combination seems to be a parasite, an unknown virus, a bacteria, and pesticides. One of the four could weaken the bee and the second kill it. Still, where are the dead bees?

The most prevalent bee parasite in North America is the varroa mite, which can infest colonies and suck blood from the bees, causing weight loss, deformities, diseases, and reduced life span. These mites can wipe out an entire colony within a few months.

The Colony Collapse Disorder Working Group

The Colony Collapse Disorder Working Group was formed in January, 2007, and is a collaboration of researchers from the U.S. Dept. of Agriculture, many universities, state departments of agriculture and other related organizations. The team is led by Diana Cox-Foster, a professor of entomology and CCD research at Pennsylvania State University, who has been actively involved in honey bee research for 10 years and was interviewed for the PBS documentary *Silence of the Bees*.

In 2007, the Colony Collapse Disorder Working Group reported a strong correlation between CCD and the presence of a pathogen called Israeli acute paralysis virus (IAPV). When introduced to a colony, the virus resulted in "dramatic bee mortality." However, the team advises that this is not the sole cause of CCD, and that additional causes are needed to trigger CCD, such as pesticides and poor nutrition.

The National Honey Board (NHB), in 2007, approved funding of $100,000 for research on CCD. This was added to $58,000 already awarded to the CCD Working Group. The CCD Working Group's plan includes the following crisis management and crisis communications components. Notice that crisis communications is primarily internal until conclusive data is revealed and at the point that there are steps citizens may take to protect bees, national and international communications can and should be made:

1. Share all communication regarding our investigations into CCD with one another.
2. Establish standardized sampling protocols and collect samples for all CCD working group members whenever feasible.
3. Clearly define areas of responsibility and research effort.
4. Share results of analyses with the entire working group for discussion and integration.
5. Regularly distribute summary reports to the beekeeping community.
6. Work together to secure emergency funding and future sustainable funding to investigate the causes of CCD and treatments to prevent CCD.
7. Deliver by meetings, reports, and publication the findings of the groups to beekeepers and appropriate scientific audiences.
8. Develop an agreement on how involvement in the research will be appropriately acknowledged and cited in any oral or written presentation of the research, in order to circumvent any misunderstandings among the members and maximize the likelihood of finding answers to aid beekeepers and the health of the pollination industry.

U.S. Government Actions

In June, 2007, U.S. Senators Barbara Boxer of California, John Thune of South Dakota, and Bob Casey of Pennsylvania introduced legislation to help research, protect, and maintain America's bee and native pollinator population and ensure the viability of crops that rely on bees.

In July, 2007, U.S. Senators Charles E. Schumer and Hillary Rodham Clinton announced that the full Senate Appropriations Committee approved a bill that would provide $1.5 million for the Pollinator Recovery project, which would address CCD and other threats to the nation's honey bees.

In April, 2008, Senator Max Baucus of Montana, a member of the Senate Agriculture Committee, backed by 35 other U.S. senators, spearheaded a letter to the USDA demanding to know what actions were being taken to investigate what is destroying the bee population.

In May, 2008, Max Baucus and Senator Saxby Chambliss of Georgia introduced to the Senate the Pollinator Habitat Protection Act aimed at improving habitat and food sources for pollinators. The act will reward farmers whose conservation practices are beneficial to pollinators.

In July, 2008, then Agriculture Secretary Ed Schafer announced that more than $4 million would be awarded to the University of Georgia to study the causes of CCD and other diseases affecting bee populations. This is the Protection of Managed Bees Coordinated Agriculture Project (CAP), and the team includes 17 universities and colleges. Professor Keith Delaplane, an entomologist who directs the four-year investigation, said the research will focus on a handful of bee viruses, the varroa mite, and new categories of pesticides such as flea killers for pets. Articles about the grant ran nationally in newspapers and on news websites.

Brother Chuck aka Buzza Shuck, in Savannah, said: "Georgia and Florida are the main states where a very large population of honey bees used for pollination are wintered. Georgia passed what is called the Georgia Bee Laws several years ago. This law protects honey bees and the rearing of honey bees by beekeepers. We [the state's beekeepers] want to institute a protective law so that all bees are protected. There are people out there who will call an exterminator for bees; this law will fine all pest control companies and home owners, anyone who is cruel to honey bees. There should be a national protective law."

Actions in Other Countries

In the United Kingdom, in November, 2008, BBKA beekeepers from all over the country demonstrated outside 10 Downing Street, the prime minister's residence, to get the government to increase funding toward research into the issue of the diminishing bees. They wanted the annual state budget for bee health research to be raised from £200,000 to £1.6 million. More than 83,000 signatures were collected and delivered to the prime minister. The BBKA chapter held education sessions for beekeepers to make sure that the crisis was not compounded by poor care for bees. As of May, 2009, the BBKA felt awareness had been improved, but no increase in government funding had resulted.

Researchers with the Canadian Association of Professional Apiculturists announced it would remain in close contact with U.S. scientists, particularly the CCD Working Group, and that it would continue to monitor the status of bee health across Canada.

Other Actions

Photographer Richard Knox Robinson's short film titled *The Beekeepers* was chosen to be shown at the prestigious Sundance Film Festival in 2009.

The film, according to the filmmaker, "is an artistic, experimental film that blends the history and Zen of beekeeping with the crisis posed by a malady called Colony Collapse Disorder that's decimating hives around the globe." The project was a product of Robinson's thesis in his filmmaking graduate studies program at Virginia Commonwealth University.

Burt's Bees (www.burtsbees.com), manufacturer of earth-friendly personal care products (many dependent upon flowers and bees), announced, in 2007, it was funding research by the Honeybee Health Improvement Project to help find a solution. It also spoke to the U.S. Congress to urge the allocation of additional funding and to heighten awareness of CCD.

The company directed 5% of profits to the North American Pollinator Protection Campaign (NAPPC) and gave away 95,000 packets of wildflower seeds, urging consumers to plant millions of flowers. The giveaway also educated consumers about the plight of the honey bee and the honey bee industry. A Burt's Bees 60-second public service announcement outlining basic steps that concerned citizens can take to protect bees was played in movie theaters as a lead-in to Paramount Pictures' *Bee Movie*.

The NAPPC has, on its website, a page titled "Honey Bee Disappearances and What You Can Do." It urges individuals to learn about creating a pollinator-friendly habitat in one's backyard by accessing instructions from www.pollinator.org.

Häagen-Dazs Enters the Fight

When some ice cream lovers think of the Häagen-Dazs brand, they assume it's a premium brand of ice cream from some Scandinavian country. Mercedes-Benz comes from Germany, Evian water comes from a spring in France and Häagen-Dazs ice cream must come from Oslo or Stockholm, or probably Copenhagen. This is far from true—many miles away.

Häagen-Dazs was started in the Bronx, New York, by a Polish immigrant, Reuben Mattus, who after selling ice cream from his mother's horse-drawn wagon in the 1920s, dreamed of an ice cream business with the finest ingredients from all over the world. He began to live his dream in 1961, when he and his wife, Rose, started Häagen-Dazs ice cream. The name meant nothing at the time; he made it up to capture a feeling of old world traditions, craftsmanship, natural ingredients, and quality production.

His vanilla ice cream, for example, was from hand-picked vanilla beans from Madagascar. The chocolate ice cream included dark chocolate from Belgium. The coffee ice cream used carefully selected beans from South America. Many of today's numerous flavors are based on the

original vanilla, chocolate, and coffee flavors. The end product is rich and dense (very little air is used in the mixing process). No emulsifiers are used, and no stabilizers other than real egg yolks. The words "Häagen-Dazs" are supposed to mean "superstar of ice cream" no matter where people think the ice cream originates.

The business was sold first to Pillsbury (in 1983) and is currently owned by General Mills, Inc. In the U.S. the trademark is licensed to Nestlé and sublicensed to Dreyer's. The devotion to quality has remained.

Public Relations

Diane McIntyre is Senior Public Relations Manager for Dreyer's in Oakland, California. She represents not only the Häagen-Dazs brand with its own PR program but also separate programs for The Skinny Cow, Dibs, Fruit Bars, and Frosty Paws. She has an in-house assistant and they work with a team from Ketchum Public Relations on the Häagen-Dazs account and another team on Skinny Cow. Another manager and her assistant handle Dreyer's/Edy's, Drumstick, and Eskimo Pie. They report to Dora Sera Bailey, the Director of Consumer Communication, who oversees the company's public relations, interactive, consumer relations, and community relations functions. She reports to the Executive VP of Marketing who, in turn, reports to the CEO. Dreyer's employs 7,000 employees nationwide, 350 of which are in the Oakland corporate office.

Häagen-Dazs has only occasionally had to use its crisis management plan, developed generally for all types of crises. "We developed crisis management messaging for our internal team, consumers, and the news media regarding the 2009 pistachio recall because we use pistachios in two flavors—one for Dreyer's and one for Häagen-Dazs," said McIntyre. "However, while none of our products used any of the recalled pistachios, we offered to replace consumers' ice cream if they preferred to exchange it for a non-pistachio flavor. The peanut butter recall also required media messaging although none of our products were affected."

The honey bee crisis had not yet affected Häagen-Dazs ice cream either. The company *chose* to join the fight to help restore the honey bee colonies. In the fall of 2007, staff members from the brand's advertising agency noticed an increasing number of blogs on Colony Collapse Disorder. "This is a real risk to U.S. agriculture and specifically to Häagen-Dazs," said McIntyre. "Ingredients in more than 40% of our all-natural flavors require honey bee pollination. Without bees, many of the fruits and nuts we use in our ice cream would no longer be available. No more Häagen-Dazs Strawberry or Vanilla Swiss Almond ice cream."

The company's research shows that the Häagen-Dazs ice cream consumer is more discerning of what they eat and where it originates. The Häagen-Dazs brand saw an opportunity to use the power and

popularity of its ice cream brand to educate consumers on the vital importance of honey bees, and, in doing so, underscore its commitment to using only 100% of all natural ingredients in its ice cream, frozen yogurt, sorbet, and snack products.

Campaign: Objectives

On February 19, 2008, the Häagen-Dazs Loves Honey Bees (HD Loves HB) campaign was launched. There were three sets of goals: business, awareness/comprehension, and behavior.

The business goals were to drive sales and to increase 2008 revenue growth by more than 1% over 2007.

The awareness/comprehension goals were the following: (1) to increase awareness of the honey bee issue and the HD Loves HB campaign; (2) to increase consumer media impressions on the brand by 25% over 2007 levels with a total media goal of 125 million impressions in the first year of the campaign.

The behavior goals were the following: (1) to convince consumers to plant bee-friendly habitats with a first-year goal of planting 1 million bee-friendly flowers; (2) to drive unique visitors to the website helpthe honeybees.com, aiming for an average of five page views per visit; (3) to increase consumer recommendations of the Häagen-Dazs brand.

Campaign: Research

Primary research included focus groups, which were conducted to determine consumer awareness, engagement, and attitude toward the honey bee issue, and the brand's possible role in the cause. Focus group findings were the following:

1. When consumers see Häagen-Dazs supporting the cause and educating people about the issue, they feel positive about the brand and its involvement.
2. Creating awareness about the issue makes consumers feel that the brand truly cares and is not just interested in sales.
3. The cause helps consumers feel more connected to the brand; there is a sense of "we're in it together."

Secondary research showed that while honey bees are essential to the U.S. food supply, no major food brands had adopted the issue. The findings guided the communication strategy. To be authentic and create a reason for consumers to connect to the brand and advocate for it, the campaign needed to help raise awareness, educate consumers about the issues, and engage consumer and community groups. To be successful,

the Häagen-Dazs brand needed to take advantage of its first-mover status and be the first national consumer brand to "own" the bee cause.

The target public was adults ranging from 35 to 54 in age. Most of them had children. Most were highly educated, had active lives, and lived in affluence.

Audience analysis showed that Häagen-Dazs ice cream consumers care about what they eat, and where their food comes from. They pay attention to what they put in their mouths and the quality of food their families eat. They are happy and eager to do their part to contribute to a sustainable society—particularly if they can make an impact through small, enjoyable, hassle-free actions. They're also willing to support causes that are genuine and relevant, and are eager to find ways to teach their children about responsible sustainable living.

Campaign: Planning

The team knew a cause-marketing campaign could help create an emotional connection between consumers and the brand and help make the brand more approachable, but the program needed to be more than just another ribbon on a carton. The cause had to be engaging while still directly relating back to the Häagen-Dazs brand's essence. The plight of the honey bees seemed obscure at first, but after learning that bees play a pivotal role in pollinating ingredients in more than 50 of Häagen-Dazs' ice cream flavors and, moreover, that one-third of all foods are pollinated by honey bees, the team knew the cause was right.

Using the insights from research as a guide, the team set out the following strategies:

1. Give consumers a compelling way to engage more genuinely and frequently with the brand by educating them about the honey bee plight. Show the Häagen-Dazs brand's concern and the brand's authentic reliance on honey bees.
2. Leverage first-mover advantage and become the first national consumer brand to support the issue and put the cause on consumers' radar in a major way, strategically use the brand name to raise awareness and underscore the brand's "all-natural" brand essence by inextricably linking honey bees with Häagen-Dazs.

Campaign: Execution (Tactics)

Donation Towards Research

After a deep-dive assessment of leading universities and organizations working to raise awareness and solve CCD, the brand decided to donate

$250,000 to Pennsylvania State University (PSU) and the University of California, Davis (UCD) for sustainable pollination and CCD research, and an additional $10,000 donation to The Pollinator Partnership, an organization dedicated to preserving honey bee health. Part of the UCD gift was used to hire a postdoctoral research fellow to conduct problem-solving research in honey bee biology and health pollination.

Bee Board

The brand created an advisory board comprised of PSU and UCD scientists to guide the brand and ensure that communication is authentic and factual, and two beekeepers—one East Coast-based and one West Coast-based—to provide insight into the struggles beekeepers face. All Bee Board members serve as media spokespeople to deliver campaign messages related to their specific area of expertise.

The Bee Board includes the following:

- Diana Cox-Foster, head of the CCD Working Group.
- Dennis vanEngelsdorp, bee specialist at PSU, who has worked for the Canadian government as a consultant to the Antigua Beekeepers Cooperative and helped Cornell University develop its master beekeeping program.
- Robert Berghage, a professor of horticulture and bee garden expert at PSU, who is the director of the Center for Green Roof Research and teaches plant propagation.
- Sue Cobey, a bee breeder, geneticist, and leader of the bee breeding program at UCD, who has taught researchers and beekeepers all over the world for 25 years.
- Eric Mussen, apiculturist at UCD, who was named 2006's "Beekeeper of the Year" by the California State Beekeeper's Association.
- Michael Parrella, professor of entomology and UCD dean, who has authored more than 350 publications on entomology.
- Randy Oliver, who has an MS degree in biological sciences, and has been a beekeeper for more than 40 years, running about 500 colonies and researching beekeeping practices.
- David Hackenberg, beekeeping expert and apiary owner, who started with one colony of bees as a high school student and had 150 colonies in 2009.

Flavor Launch

The Häagen-Dazs brand launched a new bee-dependent flavor, Vanilla Honey Bee (see Figure 9.2). It was described as "a rich vanilla ice cream blended with a touch of golden sweet honey. It is a creamy classic with

Figure 9.2 Häagen-Dazs created a new flavor—Vanilla Honey Bee—to commemorate the campaign to create awareness of the plight of the honey bee.

a mouthwatering twist only the honey bee offers." The company pledged to donate a percentage of overall sales of this flavor and all other bee-dependent flavors to go toward CCD research. The brand also created a special logo that was featured on all bee-dependent flavors and printed CCD information under the lid of every bee-dependent carton.

Industry Outreach

Prior to the official launch in early February, the brand announced the campaign to the beekeeping and scientific community at a key industry conference. As a result, experts were ecstatic about the Häagen-Dazs brand's involvement, and served as credible brand ambassadors who later spread the word about the program within the industry and to other influencers.

Media Outreach

A comprehensive media strategy was created to ensure no media stone was left unturned; to expedite mass awareness, the team's strategy hinged on launching the story with a "media multiplier." The team allowed CNNMoney.com to break the launch date embargo, because the outlet directly feeds hundreds of others on the web and drives broadcast and print coverage in local markets throughout the United States.

The Häagen-Dazs brand also understood the importance of education and expanded its media targets beyond the usual food and lifestyle outlets to include scientific, agricultural, environmental, gardening, and beekeeping trade outlets. The team conducted national and regional print, broadcast, radio, and online outreach; it also developed B-roll featuring Häagen-Dazs plant footage, comments from Bee Board members, and bees pollinating crops and flowers, which was distributed to regional and national broadcast networks; and it engaged Bee Board members as spokespeople for magazine, television, and radio media tours.

Million Seeds Challenge

The team outreached to bee supporters online using Craigslist and MeetUp.com and challenged them to help Häagen-Dazs plant one million seeds to create bee-friendly habitats. Enthusiasts received "HD loves HB" seed packets for planting in backyards and gardens.

Ice Cream Social on Capitol Hill

During national Pollinator Week, the brand and The Pollinator Partnership hosted a briefing on Capitol Hill about the plight of honey bees and a Häagen-Dazs brand-hosted ice cream social. Katty Pien, Häagen-Dazs Brand Director, testified before the Subcommittee on Horticulture and Organic Agriculture on behalf of CCD to keep honey bees and beekeepers top-of-mind for legislators and decision makers. Additional media coverage ensued, resulting in two more nationally-syndicated wire stories and a front page *San Francisco Chronicle* feature in the company's own Bay Area backyard.

Campaign: Evaluation and Success

Response to the campaign exceeded all expectations for a first-year cause marketing initiative and goal to change brand perception; "HD Loves HB" (see Figure 9.3) revived consumer interest in Häagen-Dazs ice cream and spiked sales. The following evaluations are measurements of the goals on page 169.

Business Goals

- There was a 5.2% April sales increase—the largest single sales spike in a year—and 4% growth sustained from April to July 2008.

Awareness/Comprehensive Goals

- There were more than 277 million media impressions, worth nearly $1.5 million in advertising equivalencies. The HD loves HB story was featured or included in more than 1,097 unique news placements, including Cable News Network (CNN), Associated Press (AP), National Public Radio (NPR), *Wall Street Journal*, NBC's *The Today Show*, *The New York Times*, *Everyday with Rachael Ray* (the Häagen-Dazs brand was mentioned in the headline or the lead).
- In a media audit and ROI analysis, 93% of all media coverage was overwhelmingly positive toward the brand; virtually 100% carried brand name/product mentions and key PR messages proving Häagen-Dazs dominated the cause.
- A strong 12-point increase in the level of PR and "buzz" was achieved over previous quarters.
- An omnibus survey conducted at the end of year one showed a large increase in honey bee awareness, knowledge and brand recall, an eight-point increase in awareness of the honey bee issue, and a six-point increase in accurate identification of the issue. Häagen-Dazs had the highest unaided brand recall among consumers identifying companies/organizations working to help the honey bees.

Häagen-Dazs loves Honey Bees

Figure 9.3 This logo was designed to name the public relations campaign handled by Häagen-Dazs and Ketchum Public Relations. "HD Loves HB" (Häagen-Dazs Loves Honey Bees) won numerous awards.

Behavior Goals

- The team surpassed its goal for 1 million seeds to be distributed. More than 1,200,000 bee-friendly flower seeds were distributed to community groups and individuals, including local businesses, garden clubs, and teachers.
- 469,798 unique visitors swarmed helpthehoneybees.com, and engagement was high—visitors viewed 8 pages per visit (82% above industry average) and the number of new visits averaged 76% above industry standards.
- More than 950 consumers and organizations contacted the Häagen-Dazs brand with suggestions, offers to collaborate, requests for more information, and compliments on the program.
- Häagen-Dazs experienced a 13% increase in its brand advocacy rating (between Q1 and Q2) to 69%, the highest in the category (exceeding Ben and Jerry's).

Awards Won

The campaign won the 2009 gold Clio Award in the Public Relations Consumer Category, a gold Cannes Lion for Corporate Responsibility and Environmental Issues, a Silver Anvil for Reputation Brand Management, and a 2009 Silver SABRE (Superior Achievement in Broadcast and Reputation) Award in the Food and Beverage Category.

It also won the 2009 *PR Week* award for Cause-Related Campaign of the Year and an honorable mention for Campaign of the Year.

The research continues. No conclusive data has emerged to show absolutely what is responsible for the disappearance of bees. Scientists believe a combination of events and situations are the cause, but they have not yet determined with certainty what those events and situations are.

Natural Disasters

In a study of crisis communications, natural disasters are a key component because even though organizations cannot be blamed for starting them, organizations are blamed if a state of normalcy is not achieved swiftly.

No matter where people live on planet earth, no matter how ideal the setting, how depressed the surroundings, natural disasters may strike. In the United States, the southeastern states, the Gulf Coast, and the East Coast are subject to hurricanes. The West Coast (as well as numerous other places) is earthquake-prone. Tornadoes, floods, and severe snowstorms do their damage on most of the rest of the country.

When lives, homes, and means of livelihood are lost, good Samaritans are often generous in making donations and offering other assistance. However, this creates additional crises. When donor dollars go to victims of natural disasters, other nonprofit charitable organizations suffer. Many donors have X amount of funds for giving and they have to choose which causes are more worthy. Some organizations with very crucial services have difficulty staying afloat. Nonprofits are easily ignored when disasters—natural or man-made—strike.

After the 2005 Asian tsunami, Hurricane Katrina, and Haitian earthquake of 2010, arts organizations scrambled to find ways of raising funds. In one city, the symphony orchestra allied with a retail store planning a grand opening event. The symphony provided the store with its patron list for invitations to the opening, and the store promised the symphony 10% of sales for the weekend event. The partnership was explained in the invitation in hopes that it would encourage symphony patrons to make purchases at the store's opening. It was the kind of creative plan that nonprofits that do not save lives directly must seek in order to survive in difficult times.

Case: Hurricane Katrina and New Orleans

After hitting Florida first, Hurricane Katrina made landfall on August 29 and caused death and destruction in Alabama, Mississippi, Louisiana,

and Florida. The stories are tragic in all the states, but in a study of crisis communications and crisis management, New Orleans stands out. The crisis touched everyone in the state in some way but specifically every person and every business and organization in New Orleans.

There was death and suffering in Florida, Mississippi, and Alabama, but death and suffering were more visible in New Orleans because of the news media coverage. There were bodies floating in the flooded streets, people screaming to be rescued from their rooftops, and thousands of people trapped in unlivable shelters—and it was hot, sizzling hot—exciting news, especially for television and newspaper photography. In addition to the excitement, there was miscommunication and controversy, elements that were not so apparent in the other cities and states where nature did its damage and exited.

There were evacuation plans, but the plans obviously did not consider certain segments of the New Orleans public: (a) people who were too ill to evacuate, even with help from neighbors (some were mute or blind); (b) people with pets who could not bear to leave them (some would volunteer to die rather than leave their pets—pets were not admitted to the primary shelters); (c) people who did not have cars or money for gas to evacuate, or places to go if they had gas (U.S. Census statistics reveal that 112,000 residents did not own cars); and (d) a great number of people who decided to sit out the storm because they had heard warnings to evacuate so many times before and each time before it had been unnecessary. The plans did not include what would be done with these publics, probably because the actual crisis was worse than the worst case scenario imagined by the person or persons who devised the plan.

We know from Chapter 1 that the first stage of a crisis is the prodromal stage, a point before a crisis when warning signs are analyzed and heeded. Crisis management and crisis communications plans are developed based on these warnings and an effort is made to avoid the worst case scenario. That does not mean we ever ignore the worst case scenario. The worst case scenario is the absolute worst tragedy that *can* occur. We make crisis communications and crisis management plans based on likelihood and degree of devastation but we should always consider what will be done if the worst happens.

Let's begin with this narrative:

> It was a broiling August afternoon in New Orleans, Louisiana, the Big Easy, the City That Care Forgot. Those who ventured outside moved as if they were swimming in tupelo honey. Those inside paid silent homage to the man who invented air-conditioning as they watched TV "storm teams" warn of a hurricane in the Gulf of Mexico. Nothing surprising there . . .

But the next day, the storm gathered steam and drew a bead on the city. As the whirling maelstrom approached the coast, more than a million people evacuated to higher ground. Some 200,000 remained, however—the car-less, the homeless, the aged and infirm, and those die-hard New Orleanians who look for any excuse to throw a party.

The storm hit Breton Sound with the fury of a nuclear warhead. Pushing a deadly storm surge into Lake Pontchartrain, the water crept to the top of the massive berm that holds back the lake and then spilled over.

Nearly 80% of New Orleans lies below sea level . . . so the water poured in. Thousands drowned in the murky brew that was soon contaminated with sewage and industrial waste. Thousands more who survived the flood later perished from dehydration and disease as they waited to be rescued. It took two months to pump the city dry, and by then the Big Easy was buried under a blanket of putrid sediment, a million people were homeless, and 50,000 were dead. It was the worst natural disaster in the history of the United States.

(Bourne, 2004)

The narrative continues with "When did this calamity happen? It hasn't—yet." This piece was written by Joel K. Bourne, Jr. and published by *National Geographic Magazine* in October 2004, nearly a year before most of his predictions actually happened. Bourne, not a psychic or a seer, merely predicted the mass destruction.

This mass destruction had been predicted by geologists for years. The state has lost more than a million acres of coastal wetlands in the past 70 years or so. The soil has destabilized for various reasons, including industrial plants, offshore gas and oil particularly (which actually makes the disaster at least partly man-made and not a natural disaster at all). With the eroding ecosystem, the Gulf of Mexico gets closer to New Orleans all the time. In the Gulf, hurricanes are nursed until they make landfall. They grow stronger over water and weaker once they hit land, so the land closer to the coastline stands to suffer stronger hits.

In addition, many experts say global warming had helped the likelihood of a devastating hurricane in New Orleans. Some disbelieve global warming is of any great significance, but those who do say the deep extensive pool of warmer water in the Gulf charged the hurricane.

Levees and floodwalls were built to protect the city from floodwaters from the Mississippi. The levees would work against 95% of all hurricanes. The levees would withstand up to, perhaps, a Category 3 hurricane. If that rare 5% of storms—Category 4 or 5 hurricanes—were to hit New Orleans, engineers warned, the strong storm surge would either pour over the levees or destroy them.

Protecting the city from those strong hurricanes would cost hundreds of millions of dollars. The state could not afford it, and apparently it was not a priority for the federal government.

So the crisis planning went awry in the first stage. Planners just assumed —hoped—that what had never happened would not happen. This is not an unusual occurrence in developing plans. People on the San Andreas Fault in California are not prepared for the earthquake called The Big One. There were no detection or warning devices in the Asian countries hit by the tsunami, even though it was always possible. People build homes and communities under Mt. Rainier, a sleeping volcano in Washington state that could erupt anytime.

However, organizations and individuals should learn a lesson from Katrina and make plans. One should plan for the worst catastrophe—it is easier to adjust down if a lesser one occurs than to adjust up.

This case study deals primarily with the first week of the expectation of Hurricane Katrina and its aftermath. It is concerned primarily with the people of New Orleans and secondarily with observers of the unfolding crisis. We might call it the prodromal and containment stages, but this is a difficult label because the crisis and the crises it spawned will perhaps last for years. When the Asian tsunami hit on December 26, 2004, and when terrorists attacked on September 11, 2001, the attacks were swift, and immediately afterward there was the containment stage. This was also true in the other states struck by Katrina. However, in New Orleans, the discovery of the extent of the tragedy seemed endless.

The Governor Contacts President Bush

Governor Kathleen Blanco, on August 27 before Katrina made landfall, wrote a letter to President George W. Bush. The letter was sent through the Federal Emergency Management Agency (FEMA). The opening, in part, read:

> I request that you declare an emergency for the State of Louisiana due to Hurricane Katrina for the time period beginning August 26, 2005, and continuing. The affected areas are all the southeastern parishes including the New Orleans Metropolitan area and the midstate Interstate I-49 corridor and northern parishes along the I-20 corridor that are accepting the thousands of citizens evacuating areas expecting to be flooded as a result of Hurricane Katrina.
>
> ("Blanco's State of Emergency Letter," 2005)

A section read, "I have determined that this incident is of such severity and magnitude that effective response is beyond the capabilities of the state and affected local governments, and that supplementary assistance is necessary to save lives" ("Blanco's State of Emergency Letter," 2005).

NEW ORLEANS KATRINA: TIMELINE

Friday, August 26:
- Gov. Kathleen Blanco declares a state of emergency in Louisiana.

Saturday, August 27:
- In a letter, Gov. Blanco asks President Bush to declare a federal state of emergency.
- The White House announces a federal emergency is declared and DHS and FEMA are given authority to respond.

Sunday, August 28:
- Mayor Ray Nagin orders mandatory evacuation.
- The *St. Petersburg Times* says Bush, Brown, and Chertoff were warned of levee failure by the National Hurricane Center.
- The *Times-Picayune* reports that water has toppled over a levee.
- The *Times-Picayune* says about 30,000 are in the Superdome with 36 hours worth of food.
- The *Boston Globe* reports that the Louisiana National Guard has requested 700 buses for evacuations.

Monday, August 29:
- Katrina makes landfall as a Category 4 hurricane.
- On NBC's *Today* Mayor Nagin announces that water is flowing over the levee and that a pumping station is not operating in the lower Ninth Ward.
- FEMA Director Michael Brown requests that DHS dispatch 1,000 employees to Katrina-torn areas. AP says the request lacked urgent language, the employees had 2 days to arrive.
- The *Times-Picayune* reports a Bucktown levee is breached.
- Gov. Blanco again requests assistance from President Bush. *Newsweek* reports she said "We need everything you've got."
- 5,700 National Guard members are called up.

Tuesday, August 30:
- Water continues to rise; eventually 80% of New Orleans is underwater.
- TV's *Meet The Press* later interviewed Michael Chertoff who said this was the day he became aware that the levee had failed.
- WWL-TV reports that the Pentagon claimed there were enough National Guard in the region to handle hurricane needs.
- The Associated Press says President Bush was playing guitar with country singer Mark Willis.

Figure 10.1 This is a timeline of major events and actions during the first 2 weeks of the Hurricane Katrina Disaster.

Wednesday, August 31:
- The *Boston Globe* reports that National Guard troops had arrived. WWL-TV showed a local emergency director advising that the food and water supply was nearly gone.
- Reuters reports that former mayor Sidney Barthelmy estimated that 80,000 people were trapped in the flooded city.
- The *Times-Picayune* reports that 3,000 are stranded at the Convention Center without food or water.
- On CNN, FEMA Director Michael Brown says, "I must say this storm is much bigger than anyone expected," and "You can tell them, you've talked with the FEMA director and it's going to happen."

Thursday, September 1:
- The *Washington Post* quotes President Bush as saying, "I don't think anybody anticipated the breach of the levees."
- Mayor Nagin blasts Bush and Blanco saying, "Get off your asses. . ."

Friday, September 2:
- *Newsweek* reveals that President Bush's staff made up a DVD so Bush could see "horrific reports coming out of New Orleans as he flew down to the Gulf Coast the next morning on Air Force One."
- Bush praises Brown with "Brownie, you're doing a heck of a job."
- National Guard arrives in force and brings food and water.
- Commercial airplanes begin flying evacuees to sites all over the United States. Some had no idea where they were going until they were enroute.

Saturday, September 3:
- President Bush blames state and local officials for the New Orleans slow response.
- The *Wall Street Journal* says FEMA finalizes a request for 1,335 buses.

Sunday, September 4:
- The Superdome is completely evacuated.

Monday, September 5:
- A breach is closed and water begins to be pumped out of the city.

Tuesday, September 6:
- Mayor Nagin orders forced evacuation because the city is not safe.

Friday, September 9:
- FEMA director Brown is removed from the Katrina relief efforts.

Monday, September 12:
- Brown resigns as Director of FEMA.

Figure 10.1 continued

The letter went on to cover various specifics and estimates and what the state could and would do. (See Figure 10.1 for the Katrina timeline and other actions of the governor.)

The Mayor's Communication Problems

Also on Saturday, August 27, Mayor Ray Nagin and his team set up a command center in the Hyatt Hotel because it was only a block from City Hall and it had a backup generator for power and food. Much of his staff had been evacuated safely out of town. Only a skeletal team remained in New Orleans.

On that team was Sally Forman, the mayor's Director of Communications. Forman said there was a crisis communications/management plan. However, she said:

> We had never considered there would not be a way to communicate. All of our resources were wiped out. We could occasionally call out on a land line in the power company's command center. I got a few SOS messages to someone on my staff and those messages were released to the news media.
>
> Another call was to a local AM radio station. I was only able to form a Joint Information Bureau (JIB) once the military arrived and provided support. [The military apparently had the only satellite phone in the city.]

On that same day, Nagin, in a joint news conference with Governor Blanco, told those of his constituents who hadn't left town already to evacuate, saying, "This is not a test. This is the real deal. Things could change, but as of right now, New Orleans is definitely the target for this hurricane."

As winds began to grow in strength, he said, "We want you to take this a little more seriously and start moving—right now as a matter of fact." He told them the Superdome would be a shelter of last resort for evacuees with special needs and advised people seeking refuge there to bring their own food and drinks for 3 to 4 days and comforts such as folding chairs, as if going camping.

He said "Looters will be dealt with severely and harshly and prosecuted to the full extent of the law." This was necessary to ease the minds of evacuees that their homes would be safe if they left.

On Sunday, August 28, according to a New Orleanian who evacuated and later wrote a blog, "It was 8 o'clock in the morning and Mayor Nagin's concerned face looked directly into the television camera as he pleaded with the citizens to please leave as soon as they could." That

blogger did as the mayor asked, but many felt as some of her family members: "They were certain that this was another Ivan" (a previous hurricane that bypassed the city). A writer for the *Times-Picayune* said: "I don't always defend the mayor, but considering the number of hurricane threats we've had, he might have had to put people on buses 3 times each year. How can a city do that? How many times will people cooperate after so many false alarms? Also, how many times can you ask people on high ground to keep 10 extra people in their houses? The concern on the mayor's face was real because maybe this storm was the big one, but maybe it was not. People are using hindsight when they say what he should have done."

Also on that Sunday, Nagin ordered a 6 p.m. curfew and said that emergency services would be provided until winds exceeded 45 mph. He dispatched firefighters and police to use sirens and bullhorns to urge people to leave.

Meanwhile, both landline telephones and cell phone towers were out and there was no way the mayor's team could communicate to the outside world. Mayor Nagin said: "All communications broke down. I got cell phones as high up as the White House that did not work. My Blackberry pin-to-pin was the only thing that worked. I saw the military struggle with this, too. No one had communications worth a damn."

Greg Meffert, the mayor's right-hand man and chief technology officer, said the emergency communications plan basically depended on phone service—at least cell phone service—being functional. The mayor and his staff were able to learn what was going on from police radios. Looters were raiding the hotel while they occupied it.

On Monday, August 29, Katrina made landfall. Winds had already taken away one side of the hotel. Both the Superdome and the Ernest N. Morial Convention Center were filled beyond capacity with those who couldn't or didn't evacuate. Thousands of others were still in their homes. After the hurricane passed, they thought everything would return to normal and power would be restored. That was not to be the case.

On Tuesday, August 30, the levees broke and water began to flood the city, even around the Hyatt.

On August 31, the mayor's team was finally able to make a call outside from an Internet phone account set up recently by technology team member Scott Domke and linked to his laptop. They used an Internet connection at the Hyatt and eventually linked eight lines through a single Vonage Internet phone account. Meffert, realizing he needed more lines and more phones, went out with others to a nearby Office Depot where, with the aid of Chief of Police Eddie Compass, they "officially looted" the store for the supplies.

President Bush had flown over the New Orleans scene and seen some of the disaster. The president telephoned that night and Nagin said he

told him that "flying over New Orleans in Air Force One did not do the crisis justice."

In an interview with radio station WWL on September 1, the mayor lost his patience and said of President Bush and Governor Blanco, "Don't tell me 40,000 people are coming here. They're not here. It's too doggone late. Now get off your asses and do something, and let's fix the biggest goddam crisis in the history of our country." Forman said CNN picked up the local piece and broadcast it all over the world.

Also on September 1, the team moved to a higher floor to evade some 200 gang members they heard were en route. They took with them some cordless phones that had a range of only 300 feet—sometimes they had to lean over a balcony toward the inside of the building to use the phones. Meffert said, "It felt like the Alamo—we were surrounded and had only short bursts of communication."

Meffert told the *Wall Street Journal* that the city was unable to spend more on emergency communications because of its budget crisis and also because of cuts in federal assistance. Still, improvements had been made since Nagin had taken office 2 years before. Crime, though still high, was down. The city's website reportedly ranked first out of 70 major cities. The site stayed up throughout the hurricane and its aftermath because Domke shifted it to a Dallas server.

Forman said if she could do it over, she would have had bullhorns and satellite phones. Forman said she is developing a new plan. She says the office should have its own generator to power up a copy machine and should explore some type of alert system during evacuations.

"Cities are not prepared for great disaster," she said. "If you are hit in more than one place, you are up a creek. Plans must include alternate locations outside of the city that may be in crisis. A lot of people compared our situation with Mayor (Rudy) Giuliani in New York. This is an unfair comparison; as tragic as the September 11 attack was, Mayor Giuliani could go to his office and work."

Warnings by the News Media

The *Times-Picayune* is the metropolitan newspaper in the Big Easy. People who actually read the newspaper in the days leading up to the hurricane were aware of just how big the threat was. Those who merely glanced at the newspaper may not have been persuaded because the headlines and front-page stories were not alarming. It must be emphasized that even though it was possible that the destruction would be as bad as it was, it was by no means certain that the levees would be breached and the city would flood. It was also not known, at first, how many people had remained in their homes. It is possible, even likely, that persons who chose not to evacuate had not read the newspaper.

On Saturday, August 27, Katrina had hit Florida and was headed toward Louisiana and, if it continued in the same direction, the eye of the storm would hit New Orleans. The headline on page A1, occupying two-thirds of the page above the fold, read:

KATRINA PUTS END TO LULL

STORM'S WESTERN PATH PUTS N.O. ON EDGE

Hurricane lashes south Florida, leaves six people dead

There was a map showing the storm's path but nothing alarming on page A1. However, in the jump story on page A10, there was a map showing evacuation routes to Interstate 10 to Baton Rouge, and halfway through the story that occupied nearly half of the 6-column page lengthwise, there was a paragraph that said that "if" the storm hit the city, it would be a Category 4 with a storm surge of 18 to 22 feet, several feet more of waves, and winds greater than 131 mph.

In the story, Mayor Nagin was paraphrased as saying he was alarmed about the potential path and the lack of time to prepare fully. "This storm really scares me," he said. The story added that city officials would make a decision about mandatory evacuations later that day. Because the city had escaped hurricanes earlier in the season and some people had evacuated without cause, Nagin wanted to be sure that it was necessary.

The newspaper that day had a story about the five people killed by Katrina in South Florida. There was a story saying Governor Blanco, expected to be named chair of the Southern Governors Association in Atlanta, might not be able to make the trip for the swearing-in ceremony because of the coming storm. Interestingly, the front page of the local section had a story about Mayor Nagin, indicating he would not seek a race for a possible open seat in Congress despite the suggestion by political handicappers that he would be a contender due to his "pro-business stance."

The newspaper also printed its Sunday, August 28 edition. The banner headline (in 1½-inch bold letters) and subheads on page A1 were the following:

KATRINA TAKES AIM

AN EXTREME STORM
Monday landfall likely to be as strong Category 4

GET ON THE ROAD
Officials strongly urging residents to leave area

WALL OF WATER
Levees could be topped in the entire metro area

These were the three foremost warnings: (a) the storm is huge; (b) evacuate; (c) there may be great flooding. The lead indicated the storm would make landfall on Monday. The hurricane was, at the time, a Category 4 that "could build to a top of the chart Category 5 with winds of 155 mph or higher." Below the fold was a second story with the headline:

Katrina bulks up
to become
a perfect storm

The lead indicated the storm surge could "flood much of eastern N.O." The National Hurricane Center Director said, "I don't remember seeing conditions as favorable as this for a strengthening hurricane for a long time." A color photo occupying much of the front page showed cars evacuating to the west in the normally eastbound lanes of I-10, a contraflow. Page A15 had a full-page ad from Entergy, the power company, urging residents to be prepared for long power outages and advising them of how to be safe when lines and poles are down.

The jump stories from page A1 had a banner headline 1½-inch bold letters reading:

PREPARING FOR THE WORST

It included the mayor's warning, "This is the real deal," made the evening before. The coming hurricane was called "a threat of first magnitude." The mayor's spokeswoman Tami Frazier was quoted as saying that people should not plan to retreat to the Superdome, but should evacuate the city. The Superdome was to be "a special-needs shelter of last resort," for persons who absolutely could not evacuate the city. Ten buses with lifts for disabled people in wheelchairs were sent to take prequalified people to the Dome. The regular city bus system would pick up people at 12 locations and take them to the Dome. Another story on the same page revealed that oil rigs in the Gulf would be closed because the storm is "coming right on top of us."

A half-page color map on page A21 showed a projected aerial view of what might happen if the wall of water surged against the levees and the city flooded. On page A23, next to the final page of the section, there was a warning from hurricane researcher Ivor van Heerden: "The bottom line is this is a worst-case scenario and everybody needs to recognize it. You can always rebuild your house, but you can never regain your life" ("Katrina Takes Aim," p. A23).

In the sports section, the headline story was that the New Orleans Saints would evacuate that day and head to Oakland, California, where they

had a game the following weekend. Tulane University's football team was to evacuate to Jackson, Mississippi.

The Sunday paper also urged readers to e-mail their hurricane experiences to the newspaper at talkback@timespicayune.com. Many people, when safely evacuated, did that, and NOLA.com, the online paper, carried their poignant blogs later. On Monday, August 29, the day Katrina made landfall, the newspaper was out. The large banner headline, in 2-inch bold uppercase letters read:

GROUND ZERO
SUPERDOME BECOMES LAST RESORT
FOR THOUSANDS UNABLE TO LEAVE
NEW ORLEANS BRACES FOR NIGHTMARE
OF THE BIG ONE

A large photo taken the day before showed lines of New Orleanians filing into the Superdome—people carrying plastic bags, cases of bottled water, and hand luggage. The estimate then was 10,000 people; eventually 25,000 people took refuge there. A smaller photo showed an empty highway after evacuees had left. The city was awaiting the storm. Most people expected to be in the Dome a few hours, not days. Even on that first day, some complained to reporters that no food or water was being provided. One person brought food only because she expected the lines to the concession stands would be long; but warnings from the mayor by television and newspaper urged people to bring food, water, and clothing—that none would be provided.

Page A3's major headline spanned four-fifths of the page and dominated the middle of the page under a photo of a mother and baby who had found safety in a Red Cross shelter:

Surge likely to top
N.O. levee system

The story, a jump from page A1, made it clear that the worst case scenario that was about to occur was no surprise. A story occupying the entire left column indicated that the utilities already knew there would be no electricity or landline phone service "for weeks, or even months" if flooding and damage hampered repair crews. The Convention Center, where thousands more were gathered, was not mentioned as a shelter, but the mayor had said that additional buildings and boats would be commandeered for shelter.

The other stories on pages A4 and A5 were about the success of the contraflow of traffic out of the city, the downtown hotels housing only

stranded tourists, and a Carnival Cruise ship that had been diverted to Galveston.

The flooding began that day, and the newspaper's circulation was immediately and perhaps permanently changed. The staff were forced out of the newspaper's building because it was taking on water. There could be no home delivery, no hawking at newsstands. Instead, the newspaper communicated in a way it could not have if the disaster had occurred just a few years earlier. It also set a precedent for other cities that may suffer similar tragedies. The newspaper already had an online version, NOLA.com. After Katrina, it had only the online paper until Thursday, September 1. The web-published paper provided regular updates of news events, much more regularly than a printed newspaper could do. Fortunately, NOLA.com's headquarters are in New Jersey so it was not affected by the flooding when other websites were down; it had more bandwidth.

In addition, not only did the regular readers who had evacuated have access to information but also the hundreds of thousands of people all over the world who wanted to know what was going on in New Orleans from New Orleanians.

In addition to news, NOLA.com had photographs, details of housing available, and forums on topics such as tracing missing persons—this forum was titled, "Tell Them You're OK."

Frances Spencer was an external web producer for NOLA.com during the disaster. She and others were taking urgent phone calls from people saying things such as "Help my grandmother in the Ninth Ward," or "An insulin-dependent man is still in his house." Spencer said, "We would get word through to emergency response teams to find these people."

Then, she saw an e-mail from a woman in Illinois whose 6-year-old daughter had just died after a trauma-filled life. She had been shaken by her father as a 9-week-old infant and was thereafter blind, brain-damaged, and bed-ridden. The father had been given a 25-year prison sentence. Just a few days before Katrina hit, the child had died—according to the mother, due to an injury caused by a careless health-care worker. The mother had sent the child's body to a New Orleans' funeral home/cemetery for burial in a family crypt. The family was to gather for a funeral and burial in a few days. When Katrina and the flooding occurred, the mother could not reach the funeral home. She did not know if it was underwater and whether her child's coffin might be floating in the New Orleans muck.

Spencer wanted to put the message on the NOLA.com blog page, but a temporary editor thought the story was so outrageous it had to be an urban legend. So Spencer researched the incidents of the child's life and found news stories in Illinois and Missouri from when the child was injured 6 years earlier, then found stories about the child's death a few days earlier, and the missing coffin more recently.

Armed with these stories, she brought them to the attention of NOLA.com editor John Donley who permitted the blog to run the piece. Bloggers began to respond and offer assistance. Soon, the funeral home responded to the mother, saying the coffin had been sent to Lutcher, Louisiana before the hurricane and that it was intact.

Ashton Phelps, Jr., publisher of the *Times-Picayune*, said some of the journalists on the staff had lost their homes and had only the clothes on their backs. They were determined to continue to work, to deliver information to the public. They evacuated the building, and some set up shop at the *Houma Courier*'s offices while others worked from Baton Rouge on the campus of Louisiana State University.

From their temporary digs, the staff members wrote a newspaper circulated in areas where persons gradually returned home after the flood water was pumped out. The paper also was distributed to displaced New Orleanians in Baton Rouge.

The September 2 edition declared, in red letters over the name of the newspaper, "Katrina: The Storm We've Always Feared." This tribute of sorts ran for weeks, at least, because the city would not soon recover from the crisis, if ever. The headline taking up nearly a third of page A1, quoted a desperate woman pictured, in another third of the page, on her knees at the Convention Center, praying:

'HELP US, PLEASE'

The emphasis of articles was the need for assistance with the efforts to rescue people from the Superdome, the Convention Center, and homes all over the city. Buses and planes had begun to transport people to Houston and other cities, but the move was slow. National Guard troops were needed to assist Louisiana Guardsmen and local police to combat looting and violence. Prominent in the paper were full-page ads from insurance companies promising to be there to help.

On September 3, the newspaper concentrated on President Bush finally recognizing the conditions and promising support and relief. Photos of troops were seen arriving. Numerous ads ran from companies seeking employees and offering assistance.

The September 4 and 5 newspapers centered on more evacuations and the uncertainty of recovery. There was no healthy running water, no power; the streets were still flooded with a gumbo of sewage, vermin, dead bodies, gasoline, and oil. The mayor was calling for total evacuation, which was not to be, as some people began to return to their homes even when there was nothing for them to retrieve.

The disaster was not a surprise to the staff of the *Times-Picayune*. It had run a story warning city, state, and federal government of the

likelihood of the tragedy 3 years before in an award-winning series of articles. The articles read, "Eventually a major hurricane will hit New Orleans head on . . . It's a matter of when, not if."

The *Times-Picayune*, in a crippled advertising economy with a diminished subscriber base, as of early 2006, kept most of its staff members on salary, and continued to put out the newspaper, an online edition, and a blog page.

TV News Warnings

Dave Walker, a TV columnist for the *Times-Picayune*, on the evening of Friday, August 26, was attending a taping of the syndicated game show *Wheel of Fortune* in the Ernest N. Morial Convention Center. When he arrived home, he learned Katrina was headed toward New Orleans.

He would evacuate later, but his immediate action was to monitor TV news broadcasts of three local stations—WWL Channel 4 (CBS), WDSU Channel 6 (NBC), and WGNO Channel 26 (ABC). Walker has high praise for the newscasters, who, despite having to cope with the disaster as it impacted their own families, struggled to serve their viewers. WVUE was off the air for about 2 weeks, but its meteorologist, Bob Breck, broadcast from Dallas. Throughout the critical period of the crisis, the other stations were able to broadcast by moving their operations to other sites.

On the Saturday morning, Margaret Orr, from WDSU, told viewers, "Dallas is looking good at this time"; Walter Maestri, a local disaster specialist, talking about the hurricane, said, "This is a bad lady"; WWL anchor Eric Paulsen interrupted meteorologist John Gumm and said to the viewers, "Would you go ahead and leave now?"

Later that day, Breck at WVUE suggested the viewers take their kids' cell phones to free up airspace for crucial calls. By Saturday evening, Walker said, "CNN was airing a prepared piece spelling out the well-known worst case scenario for poor New Orleans and its even poorer below-sea-level citizens." At the end of the piece, the CNN anchor said, "That'll make you sit up and take notice, won't it?" Walker replied, "If you're in charge of FEMA, evidently not."

As the cable networks arrived to cover the crisis, Walker's family evacuated. He stayed as long as he could to monitor coverage.

On Sunday morning, WDSU's Ed Reams warned, "What you love about New Orleans may not exist 24 hours from now." Reams then covered the Superdome where Walker said everything was already "coming apart at the seams." By late Sunday, Walker evacuated himself to Baton Rouge. He said his notes changed from "New Orleans pounded" to "New Orleans dodges bullet" to "New Orleans swamped."

He saw the first of many boat rescues that day on WWL. WBRZ's helicopter toured the flooded city at dusk. Meteorologist Bruce Katz,

narrating the live tour of the city, realized on air that his own home was flooded. Katz also narrated the sight of early looting and expressed outrage.

Walker found the debate over the word *refugee* trivial in describing people like himself. He said he was "more concerned with words like 'dewatering' meaning removing the water from my street and 'civil unrest' meaning civilians pillaging a defenseless city."

Walker's house had some flooding, and he and his family lived on the second floor of the house for months while the ground floor was being restored. He said, "It's the worst thing that's ever happened to us, but we're the luckiest people we know."

Wheel of Fortune cast and crew Pat Sajak and Vanna White, along with the big wheel and letter board, escaped the Convention Center just in time. The show had planned to do a series of 10 episodes but cut it short and made 9. About 100 staff stayed over Saturday night, and their Sunday flights were cancelled, so they were bused to Texas, then flown back to Los Angeles. The week of shows aired in November showing New Orleans landmarks before flood damage.

Radio station WWL managed to stay on the air throughout the crucial periods of the disaster. Many New Orleanians had battery-powered radios, and those who did not evacuate found this their only source of news. This was also true of people in nearby cities and towns, such as Baton Rouge, which also lost power. The wind caused some damage there, but many people talk of visiting neighbors with generators to watch newscasts.

The New Orleans Culture

The culture of the residents of New Orleans is not that of the French Quarter. New Orleanians like jazz and Creole music but rarely do they go to the Quarter unless they are entertainers. They like their "second-line dancing," but they only do it in the Quarter if they are entertaining for events such as Mardi Gras. They do not eat at Emeril's. This is partly because many cannot afford French Quarter prices, but they also like to prepare their own gumbo and shrimp creole and pralines. They have their own recipes, their own combination of ingredients and spices, and when they do venture out to eat, it would be to neighborhood spots such as Barrow's Catfish Restaurant, a New Orleans eatery for generations.

The French Quarter is for tourists who come in and out of New Orleans and never see where the people in the city live; the only New Orleanians they see are maids in the hotels, employees in the restaurants, taxi drivers, and musicians in the clubs and on the streets. Many people who visited New Orleans never heard of the Lower Ninth Ward, the poorest neighborhood, until it was flooded and its people were homeless or dead.

Louisiana has the largest percentage of native-born residents of any state in the union. Many family lines, black and white, date back to French settlers who founded the city in 1718. New Orleans was 67% African American when Katrina hit, and their culture is different from African American culture in other U.S. states. They not only have roots in West Africa but also in France, Spain, and Italy. They have names such as Thibodeaux, Rousseau, and Etienne. For many years, they clung to their European heritage. They were mulatto (half-black), quadroons (a quarter black), octaroons (an eighth black) and the children and grandchildren of mulattoes, quadroons, and octaroons. They understood and cherished this heritage and would explain their ancestry to anyone who would listen. Then they developed more black American pride during the Black Power Movement of the 1960s and 1970s. According to Lolis Elie, a columnist for the *Times-Picayune* and a lifelong New Orleanian, there has been a resurgence in creole culture to embrace both the European and African heritages. This cultural difference separates black New Orleanians from white residents, though the two groups share some love for music and cuisine.

The Lower Ninth Ward was once swampland, and houses were built usually with stilt-like foundations and high porches in case of moderate flooding. According to Elie, 30 years ago the working poor—longshoremen, teachers, factory workers—were able to purchase homes in the ward. This is how 45% of the homes in the ward were owned. In the poorest neighborhoods of most U.S. cities, nearly all of the residents are renters. However, the children and grandchildren of N.O. homeowners have not had the skills or employment to keep up the houses. They also have not had the financial ability to purchase hurricane insurance, not to mention flood insurance. Property taxes are nonexistent or very low. New Orleans has one of the highest unemployment rates in the United States. When unemployment is high, crime rates are usually high.

All these statistics and facts explain why a number of residents did not want to leave their precious homes, the homes they or their families have owned for years. They wanted to protect them from looters; looters were thought to be more likely to take over a house than a flood. There were problems with getting police protection, even in the best of times. The New Orleans Police Department had been suspected of corruption for years and that suspicion continued through the Katrina aftermath when police officers did not show up for work to protect and serve the people.

Also, New Orleanians were evacuation-weary. They had been warned numerous times to evacuate and each time, the storm had blown in another direction. Some recalled Hurricane Betsy in 1965, which had caused some flooding, and said, "I lived through Betsy so I'm not leaving" (see Figure 10.2).

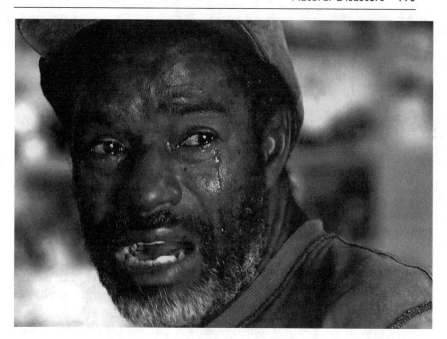

Figure 10.2 George Stewart, 57, is a former Marine who served in Vietnam and an alumnus of Southern University in Baton Rouge, Louisiana. When his wife and sister evacuated their home in New Orleans, Stewart elected to ride out the storm. He had done that during previous storms, but, he said, "You couldn't ride this boy out. My instinct kicked in from military experience. It told me when you're in enemy territory, you keep moving until you feel safe." So Stewart put a change of clothing, three bottles of orange juice, and $15 in a backpack and walked 85 miles to Baton Rouge where he knew someone at Southern University would help him. The trip, in smothering heat, took 2 days (he got rides for about 20 of the miles). He said he put his left foot in front of his right and prayed 12 times a day until he made it. One of his professors from years ago did help find him shelter. Excerpt from an article by Brandi Worley in *The Southern Digest*, September 9, 2005. Photo by Douglas Toussaint, *The Southern Digest*, Southern University, Baton Rouge, LA. Reprinted by permission.

Stranded New Orleanians Communicate

Approximately 50,000 New Orleanians who, for various reasons, stayed in their homes rather than evacuate, realized the flood waters were not going away soon and later wanted to be rescued. Many had battery-powered radios, a staple in a city prone to storms and power outages, and were told the water level would not soon subside and would probably increase. Some called 911 as the water seeped or poured into their homes and were told it was too dangerous for emergency workers to attempt

the rescue. One blogger wrote "The 911 operator told me, 'You should have listened when you were told to evacuate.'"

The 911 operators working downtown had a dilemma they will never forget. Realizing it was impossible to rescue people as the hurricane-force winds roared and the water rose, they took calls from frantic, desperate, doomed people. They tried to calmly give good advice such as, "Go to your attic," and the caller would say, "I'm already on the roof and the water is rising." One caller said she had a handicapped girl and a baby on a pump machine and said, "We're on the bed and the water is coming up." They promised to help as soon as possible, knowing there was no one to send. The 120 operators said they could only handle calls for 15 minutes at a time, then they had to take a break to recover composure. Eventually, they had to evacuate as their center flooded and as they left, the phones were still ringing.

As flood levels grew, it was not possible to use most landline phones, but a few continued to work, especially those that did not require electricity. In some areas, pay phones worked longer than home phones. Cell phones worked for a while, but cell towers were soon down and cell phones went dead. In other areas, especially the Lower Ninth Ward, the houses were nearly submerged except for roofs. Sadly, more than 1,000 people died. Some swam to safety on a highway overpass or at the Convention Center or the Superdome.

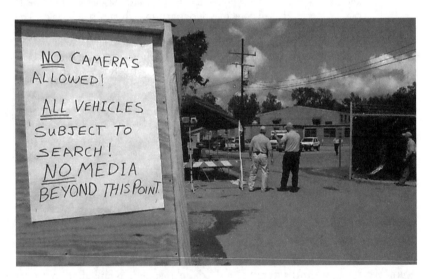

Figure 10.3 After the flooding devastated the city of New Orleans, a sign warns the news media at the entrance of the morgue installed in St. Gabriel, Louisiana. The death toll was over 1,000 but, fortunately, far fewer than the predicted 10,000. Photo by Omar Torres/Special Collection/Getty Images. Reproduced by permission of Getty Images.

Survivors retreated to their attics and, in many cases, broke through to their roofs. News helicopters captured shots of stranded people with signs large enough to be seen by pilots. Many later said they wondered why the news helicopters did not attempt to save them, but these choppers are not equipped for rescues. Many news cameramen in the helicopters did say they told rescue people where to find people. It is interesting that people would have had supplies for signs in their homes, even more surprising in their attics. These were people who did not expect a great flood, so it seems they would not have anticipated rescue by helicopter. After the flooding that was swift, there was no time to search for paintbrushes, posterboard or cardboard, and paint, so these supplies had to be readily available. Some people painted signs directly on their roofs.

Communicating with Persons in New Orleans

People who had fled from New Orleans knew from the news media that the city was flooding. But they were as frantic about finding news of relatives and friends as they had been to find safe shelter and food. Many wondered if they would have been less stressed out if they had stayed home and weathered the storm with loved ones who couldn't or didn't evacuate.

At the same time, families and friends who lived in other parts of the United States and the world were stressed because of the lack of communications. For a while they managed to get through on cell phones, but service was intermittent. They might connect, but the connection would die before a conversation could be made or completed.

Ham radio operators revealed that people dialed random numbers on their cell phones hoping to reach anyone who could send word to help trapped people. A man in Oklahoma got word by cell phone that his New Orleans relatives were trapped on the second floor of their home and their cell phone had died. The man called the Red Cross, which was instrumental in contacting an organization of ham operators who specialize in emergencies. The organization was unable to reach ham operators in New Orleans. However, one of them was able to connect with another operator in Utah who was able to reach operators in Louisiana. Subsequently, emergency personnel rescued the Oklahoma man's aunt and about a dozen others.

Mobile phone providers urged consumers to use text messages instead of voice calls because they are sent in packets of data that use less bandwidth to get through overloaded lines. However, text messaging is so impersonal when lives are being lost. It was necessary to actually hear a person's voice, to not only know the words that were being said but to ascertain frame of mind, mood, and fear from voice tone.

One man in Washington, DC, said he was comforted when he finally heard the voice of his stubborn aunt who had refused to leave her apartment until the levees broke. His calls had not been getting through; he had tried postings on the Internet, which did work for some people, but no one had responded to him.

Many people outside the hurricane-stricken area were irritated with the news media for its concentration on looting and the blame game when there were still people camping out on highway overpasses and on their roofs, not to mention the thousands of people in the nightmare that was the Superdome and the Convention Center.

Lack of Communications in the Superdome and the Convention Center

The Superdome and the Convention Center are the two places in New Orleans that will hold the most people. Many locals who could not afford to evacuate went there before the storm. Others retreated there after the floods began to overtake the city. Estimates are that 25,000 were in the Superdome and the Convention Center.

Even though Mayor Nagin asked people to bring food, water, and comforts for 3 to 4 days, many people felt that they would be there for a few hours; the storm would pass and they would return home. So there was no food, no water. There was great shock when they found out that most of the city was underwater. Apparently there was no official announcement of what would happen to them. No one was in charge.

With no air conditioning, the heat was unbearable. There were no bathing facilities. The toilets, which often backed up during sports events, were useless. Sickly people died and were just covered in sheets and blankets, but their deteriorating bodies remained among the living. There was crime—stealing for sure, and some reported murders and rapes.

There were no television monitors giving people information. A few—too few—members of the Louisiana National Guard, patrolling the buildings, told the persons they encountered that buses would "soon" come and take them away. They didn't know when "soon" would be.

Evacuees housed in the Dome and Convention Center were eventually taken to Baton Rouge and Houston by buses. Many were taken by plane and bus to cities all over the United States where many still reside. Courtney Scott, a mass communications student at Louisiana's Southern University who had family members housed in the Convention Center, said some buses left passengers standing on I-10 to wait for other buses to rescue them, buses that never came.

Scott also said, "National Guardsmen 'protected' the evacuees from harm but some also took bribes to provide food and other amenities and to load certain passengers on buses first."

Cell phones were out. Pay phones did not work. The primary source of communications was rumor. People did not know they would be rescued until they actually were. It would seem that there should have been someone in authority who could have utilized low-technology tools, such as a bullhorn, to inform the people.

One rumor was greatly exaggerated, and this was the number of deaths in the Superdome and the Convention Center. Many people who took shelter in these places spoke about seeing murder and rape, and one estimate was that there were as many as 200 bodies either from natural causes or murder or suicide.

When the buildings were emptied, the Louisiana National Guard brought in a refrigerated 18-wheel truck to transport the bodies. They reported finding only 10 at the Dome, and 4 of those were found in the street near the Dome. Four persons died of natural causes, one overdosed, and there was one suicide. The number of atrocities reported by the news media and some evacuees turned out to be false. An officer who played a key role in the security at the Dome said that "99% of the people were very well-behaved."

At the Convention Center, four bodies were discovered, and one was apparently slain, according to law, military, and health officials. The crime rate in New Orleans was high before the disaster; in 2003, the murder rate was eight times the national average and 52 more per 100,000 citizens than in New York. There were 5,000 murders in 2003 and all this happened in a city plagued by charges of police corruption. So, in a pressure-cooker situation such as that in the Dome and the Convention Center, some crime would be expected.

World News Coverage

While the people of New Orleans were suffering in a kind of fishbowl, the whole world was watching round the clock, helplessly. All the world's viewers knew more about the disaster than the people trapped in New Orleans. Viewership was up 371% on CNN, 165% on Fox News, and 191% on MSNBC. The networks broadcast news bulletins often and had preempted regular programming with special news broadcasts in the evening.

At first, the TV news reporters and anchors seemed to blame the people for not evacuating; then, apparently, they learned that some actually were incapable of evacuating. Reporters on the scene waded through the gumbo of flooded streets, taking some risks themselves to tell the stories. Word was that there were rats and snakes swimming through the toxic muck along with bodies and sewage. One report said a shark was sighted. The stories were very poignant until it became apparent that the federal government had not taken steps to rescue the people in the Superdome

or the Convention Center. Then the coverage turned to the blame game, and it was the main storyline until the people were transported to Houston and other cities and even afterward.

Looting and crime were reported widely, and as mentioned in the previous section, much of the reporting of crime was overblown. There were reports of shooting and speculation was that this might have been why President Bush did not fly to the site immediately, but flew over. There were shots of looters taking items such as television sets, and reporters wondered aloud what they could do with them in a city with no power, no people, and few homes.

Information also came from blogs and websites in New Orleans and later sprang up from all over. Again, this information was accessible to the world but not to the people struggling to fulfill their basic needs.

Crises of Words

Mini-crises within the crisis erupted over comments made and words used by both news reporters and newsmakers.

Bloggers on various sites, including Yahoo.com (August 31), Boing boing.net (August 30), and salon.com, complained that the news media, particularly the print media, were racist in photo captions. A black man hauling food through the flood waters was called a "looter." However, a white man and woman who were doing the exact same thing were "finding" food. There were no stores visible in the photos, and all were carrying food products. The photo of the black man was an Associated Press photo and the other was shot by APF/Getty Images.

Rapper Kanye West was one of several celebrities who appeared on an NBC special fundraiser for Katrina victims on September 2. West was supposed to read a script prepared by the show's producers; the script was about the impact of Katrina on the Gulf states. Instead, he complained about black families being called "looters" by the news media. He did urge viewers to make donations. But then he said, "George Bush doesn't care about black people." This also was not in the script, and, at this point, the director cut him off and went to another celebrity. The show was live, so it was seen by East Coast viewers with a disclaimer from the network saying, "Kanye West departed from the scripted comments that were prepared for him, and his opinions in no way represent the views of the network." The rapper's comments were cut entirely from the West Coast broadcast. This made news nationwide. Some columnists and editorials, especially in African American newspapers, praised him, whereas others criticized him.

What some critics of the news media did not understand is that journalists are not one body working together to label people. If one

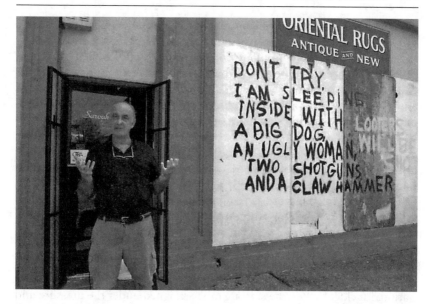

Figure 10.4 Knowing looters and robbers were having their way while the city was crippled, New Orleans rug store owner Bob Rue, like numerous other business-owners, put a warning sign on his boarded store windows. Photo by Nicholas Kamm courtesy of Getty Images. Reprinted by permission.

reporter or one newspaper were to categorize blacks taking food as "looters" and whites as "surviving," it would indeed be cause for concern and claims of racism would be understandable. However, if the two photos and captions on the sites are the only photos in question and they originated from different sources, the racist claim is unfounded.

Considering the situation in New Orleans with no stores being open, it is likely that all the people pictured did not purchase the food, so they are all technically looters. Eventually news media and TV viewers came to comprehend the dire circumstances and realized that stealing food was necessary for survival. So we have "understandable looters."

Other comments were termed insensitive. President George W. Bush was caught by a television crew engaged in small talk. He mentioned that Senator Trent Lott had lost "one of his homes" but that it would be replaced with a "fantastic house—and I'm looking forward to sitting on the porch." This made the President seem oblivious to the thousands of people who would never recover from the tragedy as easily as Lott.

The President's mother, according to John Kass of the *Chicago Tribune*, put her "silver foot" in her mouth, too. Barbara Bush, after touring the Houston Astrodome where thousands of evacuees had to live, said to a TV news reporter, "And so many in the arena here, you know, were underprivileged anyway, so this is working well for them."

Probably the most interesting faux pas in the spoken/written language of Hurricane Katrina was the word *refugee* used to describe the displaced persons. The *Random House Dictionary of the English Language* defines refugee as "a person who flees for shelter or protection from danger or trouble, like a storm." Then it adds "especially to a foreign country."

Critics argued that the word *refugee* was condescending and negative, and that its connotation signals second-class citizens, not Americans who had lived in the United States all their lives and paid taxes. Most news organizations stopped using *refugee* and started using *evacuee* because arguing over the use of a word would be counterproductive to their purpose as news disseminators. It just was not worth it.

The furor over the word is reminiscent of the incident in 1999 when a staff member of Mayor Anthony Williams of Washington, DC, used the word *niggardly* in a meeting with other staff members. The word means "miserly," and the staff member used it correctly, but the others were not familiar with it and felt it was a racial slur. It became a concern of which the news media became aware, and it turned into an international incident when the staff member resigned under the pressure and the mayor accepted his resignation. People were furious that the man would be losing his job when he had used the word correctly. So the mayor urged him to return and he did. Nevertheless, many who argued on behalf of the staff member agreed that *niggardly* is a word one can easily omit from conversation if there is a chance that it will be misunderstood.

Images and Sound Bites

The images of the disaster, seen over and over on television and the print media, were of rescues by helicopter and boat, people on their rooftops waving to news helicopters not knowing they could not make rescues, President Bush hugging two young black sisters, President Bush looking at the flooded city from a window on Air Force One, dead bodies floating in the toxic flooded water, a parking lot full of school buses that ostensibly could have been used to evacuate people, helicopters dropping MREs (meals ready to eat) and water and victims scrambling to catch them, a woman sitting on the ground next to the body of her husband wrapped in a sheet, a dead person in a wheelchair.

A memorable sound bite was President Bush congratulating FEMA head, Michael Brown, saying, "You're doing a great job, Brownie," when the, whole world knew Brownie was not doing such a good job. He would later be demoted, and he then resigned from FEMA altogether.

News anchor Ted Koppel on *Nightline* said to Brown, who didn't know about the thousands of people seeking shelter at the Convention Center, "Don't you guys watch television?" (see Figure 10.5).

NEWS AROUND THE WORLD

Israel's news program Channel 2 News: Footage of the destruction and uncovered corpses were shown with commentary saying no one was tending to the dead. The newscaster's narration suggested that the Bush Administration placed a higher priority on ensuring a steady flow of gasoline than on saving lives.

Michael Streck in Germany's *Die Welt*: Hurricane Katrina will bury itself into the American consciousness in the same way 9/11 or the fall of Saigon did. The storm did not just destroy America's image of itself, but also has the power to ring an end to the Republican era sooner than expected. America is ashamed.

Jean-Pierre Aussant in France's *Figaro*: This tragic incident reminds us that the United States has refused to ratify the Kyoto accords. Let's hope the US can from now on stop ignoring the rest of the world. If you want to run things, you must first lead by example. Arrogance is never a good adviser!

Robi Ronza in Italy's *Il Giornale*: Everything can be used in Europe to bad-mouth Bush, so it may be worth clarifying a few key points: New Orleans was below sea level even before drilling for oil began. Second, there is no certain proof that the increase in mean global temperature is a consequence of the emission of so-called greenhouse gasses. Finally, the federal government has no specific responsibility for the post-hurricane chaos.

Yildirim Turker in Turkey's *Radikal*: The biggest power of the world is rising over poor black corpses. We are witnessing the collapse of the American myth. In term of the USA's relationship with itself and the world, Hurricane Katrina seems to leave its mark on our century as an extraordinary turning point.

Editorial in Iran's *Siyasat-e Ruz*: Hurricane Katrina has proved that America cannot solve its internal problems and is incapable effacing these kinds of natural disasters, so it cannot bring peace and democracy to other parts of the world. Americans now understand that their rulers are only seeking to fulfill their own hegemonic goals.

Shen Dingli in China's *Dongfang Zaobao*: Katrina is testing the US. Katrina is also creating an opportunity for world unity. Cuba and North Korea's offer of sympathy and aid to the US could also result in some profound thinking in the US, and the author hopes that I will not miss this opportunity.

Figure 10.5 These are comments of the Katrina aftermath from editorials and columnists in various foreign newspapers and a television news program. The undated excerpts were taken from Sullivan (2005).

Editorial in Malaysia's *Berita Harian*: What's more saddening is that there have been riots and looting in New Orleans. It turns out that in a developed country with the most powerful economy in the world, some of its citizens are not much different from the poor in the third world countries.

Editorial in *Media Indonesia*: The superpower United States has finally succumbed to natured wrath. The US must eventually admit that it is unable to deal with the victims itself. Something has changed: Hurricane Katrina has destroyed some of the US's arrogance.

Venezuelan President Hugo Chavez, quoted in *E Nacional*: The rich were able to leave, the poor stayed there, and it is now that they are evacuating them, four, five days later. That is the model they want to sell to us. Racial segregation—the mayor of New Orleans said it—is a question of social classes; the rich were able to leave, the poor were left, enduring the hurricane. It is capitalism, in its extreme individualist phase.

Editorial in Pakistan's *The Nation*: The U.S. government for three days sat smugly apathetic to the people's plight.

Editorial in London's *The Guardian*, Sept. 3: Such is the scale of this disaster that Mr. Bush would probably have been criticized however he had responded... Still, there is a widespread perception that the sheer scale of the problems reflects a shuffling of resources—to pay for tax cuts and the Iraq adventure—that has left the US far too vulnerable.

Melbourne's *The Age*, Sept. 3: How could it happen? Six days after hurricane Katrina swept in from the Gulf of Mexico, America is waking up to a reality as frightening in its force as the storm and flooding themselves. It is that America has been humiliated by its inability to prevent, or then deal effectively with, a natural disaster in its own back yard; and, worse and more important in the long term, that the world's richest nation has been exposed, in a most brutal way, as a society still divided by race and possessing an underclass.

Toronto's *Toronto Star*, Sept. 3: "A just anger is rising across America at the official incompetence that Katrina has exposed. A vacationing Bush made a tardy post-disaster appearance. The Federal Emergency Management Agency failed to speedily organize an effective command and control system. And the National Guard was deployed after Katrina hit, far too late. By then 100,000 people had flouted the evacuation orders and were in peril. Even then, troops, helicopters, buses and trucks were slow arriving. And the Army Corps of Engineers had no effective contingency plan to repair broken levees. Katrina is proving as much a man-made disaster, as a natural one."

Figure 10.5 continued

Mayor Nagin peppered some of his emotional comments with expletives such as, "I don't want to see anybody do any goddam press conferences. No press conferences until we get some supplies down here." He later said, "The president told me he appreciated my frankness and bluntness and I told him I was sorry if anything I said had been disrespectful."

Locating People

As people were evacuated from the Superdome by bus, desperate parents passed their children overhead to assure them places in the bus and did not make the buses themselves. In other cases, helicopters and boats rescued children first from rooftops and homes and promised to come back for parents. But they did not. Some people did not know to what cities they were being transported until they were en route. So in these cases, children sometimes ended up in different places, even different cities than their parents. The same was true for various other family members.

Mayor Nagin said, "I saw stuff that I never thought I would see in my lifetime. People wanting to die. People trying to give me their babies … It was a helpless, helpless feeling. There was a lady waiting in line for a bus who had a miscarriage. She was cleaning herself off so she wouldn't lose her place in line. There were old people saying, 'Just let me lie down and die.' It's unbelievable that this would happen in America."

The American Red Cross, the Salvation Army, and organizations such as Craig's List, the National Next of Kin Registry, the National Center for Missing and Exploited Children, as well as TV cable stations and networks helped connect families. All had websites, but some actually talked face to face with missing family members and used photos to help find loved ones. Many complained that the news media spent too much time with the blame game and looting rather than being instrumental in locating people.

A website, tattoo.about.com, catered to the tattoo community. One blog was about a man with a crown tattoo who had apparently had a stroke and could not communicate. The site sought the artist who created the tattoo in hopes that he might know him and might be able to notify his family where he was. Other messages offered jobs to displaced tattoo artists.

A site, www.katrina.com, was the business site for a web designer named Katrina who lent it to the cause because she was getting hits anyway. She provided links to various help organizations and agencies and a message board.

When evacuees settled in Houston, the newspapers there ran stories about what was going on in New Orleans. They helped locate people but they also told stories of rebuilding and recovery, stories that helped displaced persons know whether to return or not, whom to contact about jobs, insurance, housing, and so on.

FEMA E-mails

After much national and international criticism of the federal government's handling of the crisis in New Orleans, FEMA head Michael Brown was removed from the leadership position of the Katrina relief on September 9. Then on September 12, he resigned from his position as Director of FEMA.

In October, the Senate Homeland Security and Governmental Affairs Committee made public 19 pages of e-mail communications between a FEMA official on duty in New Orleans and Brown and his staff. Marty Bahamonde, a public affairs officer from Boston, was the first FEMA official to survey the crisis developing in New Orleans. He sent the first message on August 28, the day before the hurricane hit. The messages support critics of the government and its failure to be concerned about the plight of the victims.

On August 28, Bahamonde wrote on his Blackberry, "Everyone is soaked. This is going to get ugly fast." On August 31, in a message directly to Brown, he wrote, "Sir, I know that you know the situation is past critical. Here are some things you might not know. Hotels are kicking people out, thousands gathering the streets with no food or water, hundreds still being rescued from homes . . . Estimates are many will die within hours."

Brown's press secretary, on the same day, wrote to Bahamonde, "it is very important that time is allowed for Mr. Brown to eat dinner . . . He needs much more than 20–30 minutes." She went on to talk about the woes of dining in a busy restaurant. Indignant, Bahamonde's response to other FEMA staff was the following: "I just ate an MRE (military type meals-ready-to-eat) and crapped in the hallway of the Superdome along with 30,000 other close friends so I understand his concern about busy restaurants." Later news vindicated Brown to an extent showing he sought aid earlier.

Companies and Organizations in Crises

It would be hard to even imagine a company, business, or organization in New Orleans that was not affected by the hurricane or its aftermath.

The following are some of these businesses and organizations, and what they did to communicate.

Charity Hospital

Charity Hospital was a Level I trauma center that treated people despite their inability to pay. After the hurricane blew through the city, the hospital was without electricity to operate monitors and ventilators and air conditioning. The temperature was 100 degrees. There were no working toilets, no elevators.

After the water began to rise, the medical personnel carried 50 patients up a flight of stairs. They tried to call FEMA and the Louisiana National Guard to no avail. One doctor said they were promised FEMA would rescue them but 2 days later, he said, "We've been forgotten . . . we've disappeared from the radar screen for five days. It's unbelievable."

They put a sign hanging outside a high window reading, "God of Abraham, Help Us O God." In desperation, they went to the news media and the news media got help to get the medical personnel and patients evacuated.

AARP

The American Association of Retired Persons (AARP) was planning a convention in New Orleans beginning September 29. Actually it was more like a party for 20,000 people of retirement age. Most people had already paid for the 3-day bash, had airline tickets, and were beginning to pack their bags when Katrina changed their plans.

AARP staff members stopped the news releases promoting the event and its highlights: a concert, a lecture by Maya Angelou, a swamp tour, great meals in French Quarter restaurants, pigging out on beignets at Cafe du Monde. An announcement was posted on the AARP website telling members they could get refunds. The organization threw away some pamphlets and other promotional items that were relevant only to 2005 and New Orleans and saved other materials that could be adapted to future conventions. Trinkets being trucked to Louisiana were halted. New Orleans tee shirts, beads, and hurricane glasses (a Louisiana souvenir for many years) had been loaded into souvenir packages. The shirts were retrieved and were sent to clothing drives in Louisiana. The enameled logo pins were sent to registrants with a letter of explanation.

On a positive note, hundreds of registrants sent e-mails refusing the refund and asking AARP to forward their fees to relief efforts instead.

Other Organizations that Helped Alleviate the Crisis

Numerous employers engaged in employee relations and/or community relations programs.

Wal-Mart, often under fire itself for employee problems, was the first major company to step forward and offer jobs to its displaced employees wherever they might be. Also, Wal-Mart employees whose stores were closed due to the storm received their salaries for 3 days whether they were scheduled to work or not. After 3 days, they were offered temporary work at other Wal-Mart or Sam's Club stores. Financial assistance was offered for lodging and food; $250 cash was available from store managers for food and clothing.

Harrah's Entertainment, which operated casinos in New Orleans, Biloxi, and Gulfport (which were all closed after the hurricane), offered employees emergency supplies and money. Employees were paid for up to 90 days.

Prior to the hurricane, museums in New Orleans sent e-mail messages to institutions further inland requesting space to store valuable art objects. The pieces were transported to these places safely so that most museums could return to normalcy sooner than many city attractions could.

Mortgager Freddie Mac and Fannie Mae urged lenders to excuse late payments. The Internal Revenue Service (IRS) offered extensions to taxpayers who requested more time to file returns or pay taxes. BellSouth set up mobile units in Louisiana and Mississippi so that affected employees could rest and do laundry, and their families could eat three meals a day.

In Houston, before evacuees arrived there in great numbers, an organization called NOAH (New Orleans And Houston) was formed to secure gigs for transplanted musicians. The organization's founder developed a website (www.noahleans.com) with a database linking New Orleans musicians to professional Houston players. He also urged music store owners to offer free rentals of musical instruments because most musicians lost their instruments in the flood. The founder said, "Just think of the music of New Orleans on the streets of Houston."

Habitat for Humanity deployed teams to check and repair homes the organization had built. Many were lost, and the organization hopes to build more.

When evacuees settled in Houston, the newspapers, particularly the *Houston Chronicle* and the *Houston Defender*, ran stories of what was going on in New Orleans. They helped locate people but they also told stories of rebuilding and recovery, stories that helped displaced persons know whether to return, or not, whom to contact about jobs, insurance, housing, and so on.

Fundraising Scams

The list of organizations raising funds for Katrina victims ranged from single individuals to the American Red Cross, the agency that led the relief effort and raised nearly $2 billion.

Most of the fund collections were run by concerned, honest citizens, but the news media urged people to donate to the American Red Cross or the Salvation Army because there were numerous scams. The Federal Bureau of Investigation (FBI) said 60% of the 2,000 sites it reviewed were registered to persons outside the United States and were expected to be fraudulent.

Scam artists were primarily persons or organizations purporting to be raising funds for Katrina victims; they reached people in person, by mail,

and online. However, *PC World* also warned against the sale of flood-damaged cars from Louisiana being sold as if they were in pristine condition.

There were many websites with Katrina names, such as katrinahelp.com, katrinadonations.com, and katrinarelief.com, and many were scams.

Florida's attorney general took action to shut down the sites and filed a civil action against the webmaster. There was a phishing scam in which donors divulged their credit card numbers or PayPal accounts, not knowing the donation was being made directly into the webmaster's private PayPal account.

Also, some sites were set up to look like news reports, but if one clicked on "read more," one was then linked to sites that secretly installed Trojan horse software that give hackers control over computers. There was another scam, promoted through faxes and e-mail, urging investing in post-Katrina stocks. The fax stated, "Any company that gets a tiny slice—even 1%—of this business could add a minimum of $260 million to its bottom line."

Crisis Begets Crises

At the end of 2005, the disaster that is New Orleans was still at crisis point and had spawned other numerous crises with no end in sight. There was uncertainty that all bodies had been recovered from once-flooded homes. There was great uncertainty over the reconstruction of the levees. Some members of the U.S. Congress felt rebuilding the city would be useless if the levees were not rebuilt to withstand Category 5 hurricanes ... and there seemed not to be funds for such a restructuring.

The people of New Orleans were displaced and living, permanently or temporarily, in all 50 states. Some had not located their families and loved ones at the end of the year. Out of 200,000 homes, 120,000 were damaged by flood waters. Approximately 80,000 homes had no insurance at all. Most with hurricane insurance were told by insurance companies they were not covered by floods.

FEMA's assistance to displaced New Orleanians was sporadic and slow. The people were encouraged to find work and housing. Some did; some did not for various reasons. President Bush's approval rating dipped considerably because of his and the government's failure to respond adequately and swiftly, and partly because of the public attitude toward the war in Iraq.

In December 2005, the president of the American Red Cross (ARC), Martha Evans, resigned after the organization drew criticism for its internal conflict, for moving too slowly in response to the crisis, for having poorly trained volunteers, and for seeming to be disorganized. The ARC took in $1.8 billion in donations after Katrina. Four presidents have

ONE KATRINA VICTIM'S STORY

Gloria Juluke Scott was one of the New Orleans residents who did not evacuate. "I'm 60-years old. I've never evacuated and I've never had an inch of water in my house," she said, "but this time it was different."

In her two-story house in the Lake Bullard sub-division of New Orleans East, she had enough food for a week and all the hurricane preparation equipment. "I checked the attic and made sure I had the hatchet, the hammer, the crowbar, the white flag, all the stuff we've always been told to keep."

Two days after the hurricane hit, she needed the white flag. Water in her backyard pool had spilled over and was taking over the first floor of the house. Soon, she and her 80-year-old mother and two teenaged nieces made a pact that they would not be separated and were rescued by boat and taken to a dry highway where a bus was supposed to pick them up and take them to a shelter. They had only the clothes they were wearing and no food.

The bus never came so, with 200 other people, all African-Americans, left on the highway, they broke into a nearby church where they stayed a day and a half. "This was the nicest shelter we had. The people were very supportive of each other. There was no crime. I even slept," she said. "Some young men went to a Winn-Dixie and got us some food." New Orleans police later made them move because more flooding was expected. Before leaving, all the people put the church furniture back in place and swept the floors.

After another wait at another location, a Ryder truck took them to the Convention Center which, as most reports say, was fearful. "There was all kinds of disorder, fights, stealing, all in darkness and heat. I didn't sleep. I was afraid to blink. If they had told us there would be buses in 10 hours, it would have been OK, but we knew nothing."

She and her family went to Harrah's Casino nearby where someone told her there were tourists nearby and he was certain the buses would transport them first. So, she and her family joined the tourists and sure enough, boarded one of the early buses.

Eventually, she was on a plane heading somewhere. "We had no idea where we were going. They didn't tell us anything. No one in any of the lines at the Dome or the convention center knew anything either. When you've lost your whole world and then no one will respect you enough to tell you where you're going, it's inhumane."

Fortunately, she was flown to San Antonio where she called family member in Dallas and settled there. Her house in New Orleans, valued at $210,000 was partly insured; as of January, 2006, she was not sure what she would do. However, she said, "I love Mayor Nagin. I love Gov. Blanco. I even love Pres. Bush. I count my blessings! I'm here; I survived!"

Figure 10.6 Every New Orleanian had several stories to tell. This is merely one of them.

HURRICANE KATRINA'S
13 CRISIS COMMUNICATIONS LESSONS

1. Heed prodromes.

2. Anticipate and plan for the worst case scenario. You can always adjust down to a lesser crisis but not to a greater crisis.

3. Always have alternatives. If plan A cannot work, there must be plan B and C.

4. Align the crisis communications with crisis management. What you say should be what you do and vice versa.

5. Have several places pre-selected for a crisis center or work site. All sites should not be in the same neighborhood or even the same city.

6. Have an e-mail address, phone number or voice-mail number (perhaps out of town), where employees may report their whereabouts.

7. If possible, monitor television, radio, and Internet, and print news. The news media may know something you don't know.

8. Always, the most crucial action is protecting lives in jeopardy.

9. If the story is negative, it is best that the organizational spokesperson reveal it. Tell your own bad news.

10. Plan on not having electricity and other necessities like landline telephones and cell phones. Be prepared to utilize low technology — bullhorns, walkie-talkies, manual typewriters, etc. But have effective hi-tech equipment available. Have power packs.

11. Do not guess statistics. In a great tragedy, the news media will want to know how many people lost their lives. Any guess made is bad. A large estimate gets headlines, but you look uninformed when it's over. A low estimate also insults your knowledge of the situation.

12. If you will depend upon the resources of others (governmental and non-governmental agencies and organizations), know what you can expect from each and how to seek those resources.

13. Just because a crisis has never occurred does not mean it never will.

Figure 10.7 Communications professionals should learn these lessons from the mis-communications of the Hurricane Katrina aftermath in New Orleans.

resigned since 1991, citing conflicts with the perhaps overly large, 50-member board.

In conclusion, 25 to 30 square miles of Louisiana land is swallowed each year by the Gulf of Mexico; this makes New Orleans closer to being a beach-front city, and therefore more and more susceptible to hurricanes. The hurricane season runs from summer through fall every year.

Hurricane Katrina: What's Going Well 5 Years Later?

In late 2009 the French Quarter and the Garden District, the primary tourist sections of New Orleans, for the most part look and seem to operate as if the disaster never happened.

Some residents of the Lower Ninth Ward, the hardest and poorest neighborhood hit by Katrina flooding, have rebuilt their homes. Some had insurance; others were aided by families and friends, charities, churches, and some good Samaritans. The rebuilt homes are scattered over a huge expanse of land, larger than it seemed when it was densely populated. New Orleanians estimate that by 2015, it will look like a neighborhood again.

Actor Brad Pitt and his Make It Right Foundation are building 150 homes for the Lower Ninth Ward (see Figure 10.8). Pitt and producer Steve Big donated $5 million each, "Idol Gives Back" on TV's *American Idol* donated $10 million; more than $10 million more has been pledged by companies, organizations, and individuals. The homes are equipped with solar panels so residents can produce most electricity needed. Some are up and occupied. On narrow lots, they are long and narrow and stand eight feet from the ground with rooftop escape hatches just in case there are future floods. Many in the ward died because they could not get to their roofs in the 2005 flooding. Pitt's project calls for houses to cost no more than $150,000, and he hopes buyers will be able to put up 85% from insurance and government assistance. The Pitt houses, if placed in one corner of the vast wasteland left by the flood would be the size of a postage stamp on a large envelope (www.makeitrightnola.com).

The New Orleans Public Library system lost all books in certain areas of the city, and every building was either damaged or destroyed. Soon after the hurricane, an e-mail from a public relations professional working in the library went out to her contacts seeking books of all kinds, and those she e-mailed forwarded the message to their contacts and those to even more. By July, 2007, more than three million primarily second-hand books were received, 2.2 million more than the pre-Katrina libraries held. As the books continued to arrive, in 2008 the libraries had to discourage donations of used books and encourage new volumes and donations for other resources and equipment lost. In late 2009, the library system announced in a letter to donors that six new libraries had been built and

Figure 10.8 One of the houses built by actor Brad Pitt's foundation in the Lower Ninth Ward of New Orleans. Notice the house is built high off the ground to offer protection against minimal flooding. Many residents have rebuilt but have been concerned about the height. Photos by Gerald Brown. Permission granted.

that a new public media campaign was under way titled "Imagine That," which will engage community members.

Reconcile New Orleans, an organization of concerned citizens in and near the Central City section, had already spent several years helping at-risk youth learn life skills when it opened Café Reconcile in 2000. The meals are prepared by youth trained for entry into the hospitality and restaurant business that makes New Orleans famous. Though it existed before Katrina, it grew appreciably afterwards, partly because the city needed trained employees to keep the restaurants and the tourist trade; partly because the youth needed jobs. The eatery is a non-profit restaurant serving delicious and inexpensive midday meals including fried catfish, gumbo, bread pudding, peach cobbler, and other New Orleans cuisine. The youth, referred by school counselors and word of mouth, take turns serving as chefs, sous-chefs, waiters, cashiers, dishwashers, and greeters. Some of the trainees plan to go to college and major in culinary arts; others want to get local jobs right away. They are required to take lessons in life skills for three weeks—being on time, appearances, and social graces. Then they do four weeks in the café and two weeks of internships.

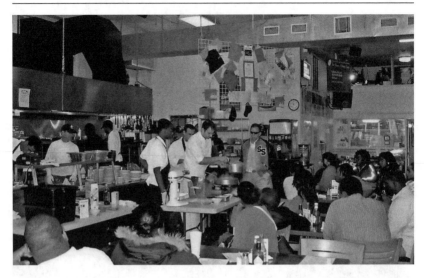

Figure 10.9 At Café Reconcile in New Orleans, youth learn the restaurant business and many are able to get positions in local restaurants after the training. This helps the youth and the city's premier attraction, food. Some of the students go on to college and major in culinary arts. In this photo, a leading chef in a local restaurant teaches the students dishes popular in New Orleans cuisine. Photo by Gerald Brown. Permission granted.

Figure 10.10 Many houses in the Lower Ninth Ward sit just as they did after Katrina's waters damaged them. Local residents say some of the families never returned to see what happened to their houses . . . and, of course, some died in the flooding. Photo by Gerald Brown. Permission granted.

Figure 10.11 Numerous residents who did return had their damaged homes razed, and all that is left is the slab foundation (painted pink by surveyors) and shade trees. Often, the lawns are carefully manicured and cared for by the residents who post signs reading, "This property belongs to _____." Photo by Gerald Brown. Permission granted.

On graduation day, tips earned during the four weeks are divided among the trainees. Supervised closely at every step by Sister Mary Lou Specha, executive director Reconcile New Orleans and her staff, many students have graduated from the program and transitioned into employment in the local restaurant industry.

What Is Not Going Well?

Thousands of displaced New Orleanians were scattered all over the United States in desperation after the floods. Some have made new lives elsewhere and are content; many want to return to the city if they can resume their lives and get their homes back. Some returned to take a chance and found the government housing projects in which they lived torn down. Arguments abounded that the housing projects were not beyond repair and the city did not want them to return, preferring to eliminate a chunk of the city's poor population. For a while, people camped out under a freeway overpass near the downtown area.

Not all of the displaced people were from the projects. Many were homeowners from the Lower Ninth Ward, which was one of the first neighborhoods where African Americans could buy property in the

1920s. In some cases, homes had been passed down for generations, sometimes without documentation. Since there was no property tax on homes with low valuation, there were no records. These people had and some still have great difficulty proving ownership. An officer in the Lower Ninth Ward Homeowners Association said they have received little or no assistance from federal, state, or local government. Part of the reasons for slow growth is that politicians and urban policy experts fear future storms.

The children who lived in FEMA trailers for years following Katrina were described in *Newsweek* ("Katrina kids sickest ever," 2008) as suffering from illnesses caused by living in the trailers. Irwin Redliner, president of the Children's Health Fund and a professor at Columbia University's Mailman School of Public Health, examined 261 displaced children and found that 41% were anemic, half had mental health problems, and 42% had respiratory infections and disorders linked to formaldehyde from the trailers. Government trailers were supposed to be closed down in May, 2008, but some remained in use because people said they had nowhere to go. Redliner said, "As awful as the initial response was, it's been dwarfed by the ineptitude and disorganization of the recovery."

Meanwhile, a series of articles in the *Times-Picayune* in December, 2008, warned that Louisiana is the fastest sinking land in North America and that the Gulf of Mexico, to the south, is rising. And that does not take into account hurricanes.

Chapter Eleven

Transportation Crises

This chapter involves crises and near-crises relating to transportation. They show that crisis communicators must cope with near-crises and preventing crises, and that job is nearly as demanding as actual tragedies. The case study, "Metro Transit: Driver Shot, Bus Flies Off a Bridge," on page 275, could also have been in this category.

Case: Holland America Line and Cruise Crises

This crisis features the multitude of crises one corporation can face. It advises and warns all organizations to be aware and prepared for all possibilities.

When cruise lines do crisis communications and crisis management plans, the worst case scenario is the sinking of a ship and lives lost. The last luxury liner to sink was the *Andrea Doria* in 1956. It collided with another ship (the *Stockholm*) en route from Italy to New York. Unlike the Titanic, there were enough lifeboats for all passengers—the 46 fatalities (out of 1,706 persons aboard) resulted from the collision.

Like the Titanic, the *Andrea Doria* was considered "unsinkable." Because of these two sea tragedies, cruise lines don't use the word "unsinkable" in their marketing. Advances in shipbuilding and strict safety precautions have made the loss of lives due to sinking very unlikely.

However, cruise lines (as well as many other companies and organizations) must expect the possibility of numerous crises, and publics expect a response from their crisis communicators. Crises or negative news stories about any one cruise line can affect future bookings. Any crisis at sea deters potential passengers from taking cruises on any cruise line. Unlike flying, cruising is an elective form of travel; no one has to cruise. Therefore, cruise lines such as Holland America Line must do their best to persuade past, current, and future customers that cruising is safe, luxurious, relaxing, exciting, enjoyable—all the positive adjectives that add up to making cruising popular.

Some call cruise ships floating hotels, but others go so far as to describe them as contained floating cities. As a form of transportation, almost anything can happen. Storms, hurricanes, collisions, hijackings, drunkenness, missing persons, person overboard, fire onboard, sickness of many kinds, food poisoning, natural deaths, spousal abuse, airport shutdowns, power outages, oil spills, kidnapping, theft, and violence are some of them.

Holland America Line is owned by Carnival Cruise Lines and is registered in the Netherlands. In 2010 there were 15 ships offering nearly 500 cruises to 320 ports in more than 100 countries in all seven continents. Passengers come from all over the world. The ships must follow law in the Netherlands and typically the United States as well as in the countries of port cities.

Under the leadership of Sally Andrews (see Figure 11.1), Holland America Line manages its crises and issues through the Public Relations Department. Sally and director Erik Elvejord (see Figure 11.2) act as its primary crisis communicators and spokespeople. The department includes the following areas: Media Relations, Social Media, Crisis Communications, Internal Communications, Corporate Giving, Event Planning, Inaugural Events, and Writing.

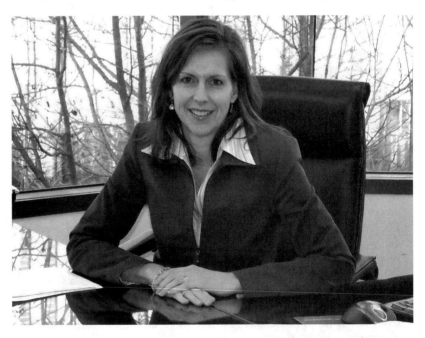

Figure 11.1 Sally Andrews heads Holland America Line's Public Relations Department as Vice President. She usually learns about crises first and passes the information to the rest of the staff. Photo courtesy of Holland America Line.

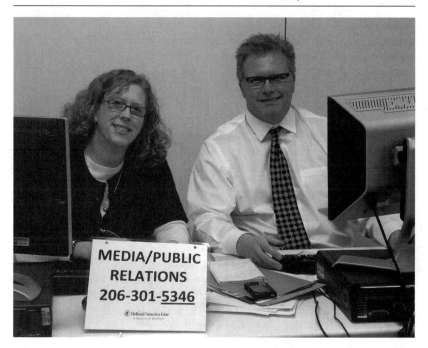

Figure 11.2 Erik Elvejord is Director, Public Relations, Holland America Line, and Mary Schimmelman is Manager. They are seated at the media relations station of the company's incident command center. Photo courtesy of Holland America Line.

Each area serves the company proactively in building good relationships with publics—customers, travel agents, port officials and employees, news media, and others. Each area also serves to prevent crises. If all the areas run smoothly, crises are less likely to occur. However, when a crisis does occur, the PR team is usually front and center as the primary spokespersons and communicators.

The Public Relations Department reports to the Executive Vice President, Marketing, Sales and Guest Programs, and to the CEO of Holland America Line who reports to the CEO of Carnival.

Case 1: Passengers as Non-Expert Experts

The *Titanic*'s officers had to use Morse code to notify other ships that it was in trouble, and the world did not know the full story until the surviving passengers reached New York, days after the ship sank. Just a few years ago, the company and the Public Relations Department would be notified by ship personnel when a crisis occurred. Today, with cell phones and computers, news media and people worldwide often know

of an incident at sea before the cruise line company does. This compounds the crisis, because people frequently do not get the facts correct, and undoing false information is extremely difficult. Non-expert experts are people who speak as if they are knowledgeable and have authority when actually their appeal is based on emotions and excitement (see page 229). These passenger non-expert experts are the spokespersons who often use exaggeration when describing situations to the news media.

Also, the news media, especially television news reporters, seek stories from "real people" because they are perceived to be more interesting than a boring spokesperson with facts.

Onboard illnesses such as the Norwalk-like Virus (NLV) are probably the most expected crisis when hundreds of people are gathered in one place for a long period of time. The ships take precautions by washing down the ship after each cruise; they even wash the poker chips in the casino and throw away the playing cards (see Figure 11.3). Viruses are spread when individuals, even though they are warned, do not take precautions to avoid communicable diseases. So the diseases spread despite the fact that the cruise ship staff do all they can to prevent them.

Elvejord was in San Diego in spring, 2009, to meet the news media at the port where a Holland America Line ship had Norwalk virus victims.

Figure 11.3 After a ship returns from a cruise and passengers disembark, the crew washes all the poker chips and throws away all the playing cards in the casino so that new passengers are not exposed to germs left by previous guests. That's a small part of the stern-to-bow cleanup process.

A passenger had sent e-mails to the news media that two people had died, 200 were sick, and the ship was in quarantine. The "facts" were erroneous. No one had died, there were 106 who were affected during the entire length of the cruise. The ship was not quarantined. The passenger spokesperson also falsely claimed to be sick and quarantined. When Elvejord arrived, he found reporters who wanted to believe the passenger—the non-expert expert—and not the cruise line as it was a much more interesting news story, so he had to battle cameras and a barrage of questions.

Elvejord checked the websites of three of the news organizations and found the incorrect facts and also a quote attributed to him that he knew nothing about. He was quoted as saying, "They were puking, having diarrhea and in quarantine." Holland America Line received many calls from other news organizations and individuals who had seen this misinformation.

Knowing that the reporting was misinformation, he contacted the news organizations and corrected the information. He said that after that incident, he always checked the websites first and made sure the online information was correct sooner.

Case 2: The Bungee Jumper

A 36-year-old would-be stuntman/daredevil sought to get attention to his bravery and skills by jumping from the middle span of the Lions Gate Bridge in Vancouver, British Columbia, Canada, to Holland America Line's ms *Veendam* as it passed under the bridge.

There was a stuntmen's convention nearby, and the man, Dean Sullivan, thought if he succeeded at the stunt, he would get the attention of people at the convention.

Sullivan said, "This was no way some whimsical thing." He said he had planned it for more than two years. He checked traffic flow charts figuring out how to get to the bridge on time, reviewed tide times and boat layouts including the location of boat mainstays. He said, "The planning also included security protocols for the port of Vancouver and research on where people stood on cruise ships leaving the port of Vancouver." He found out that people gather at the bow or the stern, so he prepared to reach the ship in a less populated spot so no one would get hurt. He said, "I would rather hurt myself than someone else." He studied weather and itineraries for the ship, had custom anchors for the bridge built, two-way radios secured, and he said he practiced.

On the chosen day, the weather was overcast, which was perfect for Sullivan because few people would be on the deck. He had a driver get him to the bridge on time, secured himself to the span with 227 feet of rope in a custom-made bag. He knew the *Veendam* would pass under

the bridge 270 feet above the water. He had a knife attached to himself so he could cut the rope once onboard. So he jumped.

The bag holding the rope did not deploy on time, putting the jump off by mere seconds. By the time he jumped, the ship had traveled about 12 knots. He said, "Holy s***! I was flying towards the deck of the ship at an incredible speed." He bounced off the netting covering the ship's tennis court, struck his head on a railing, and the ship sailed off leaving him dangling in mid-air. He was not seriously injured; a witness said he saw him light a cigarette after being picked up by a water taxi. He said his face was "cut pretty good." He was arrested and charged with criminal mischief. Evaluating his feat, he said he was on the ship's netting for about two seconds, so technically he made it. If he had not lost those few seconds and landed successfully, he had planned to stay onboard until he was forced to leave.

Passengers on the back deck of the ship saw the incident and told the crew. The Coast Guard, advised by passers-by, told the captain. It could have been so much more unfortunate. A man hitting the side of a cruise ship is similar to a mosquito hitting the windshield of a moving car. Sullivan was very lucky. This could have been a tragic story with the Holland America Line name in it, something the cruise line would never welcome though it was totally innocent.

Elvejord was contacted by a Vancouver television station. He answered questions about the ship's route, what was happening onboard, that no one on the ship was injured, etc. He told the news media that the ship followed standard procedure, that the incident slowed the ship down— inconveniencing passengers—because the Coast Guard asked the ship to dock.

Case 3: Immigrant Rescue

Holland America Line experienced a crisis of sorts after a ship's crew members thought they spied a man overboard and soon found themselves involved in rescuing refugees immigrating to seek a better life.

The ms *Noordam* was approaching Kusadasi, Turkey, in the Aegean Sea early one morning when crew members cleaning the deck heard a shout in the distance and saw a person in the water. Notifications were made and personnel began its man overboard (MOB) procedure returning to the site of the sighting. The captain sent a fast rescue boat to search for the person in the water. Then, suddenly, they saw three persons wearing life jackets yelling for help on the port side of the ship, then there were more on the starboard side and others in front of the ship.

One officer said he thought they were survivors of a sunken pleasure boat. The rescue boat holds only six passengers and there were many more people needing to be rescued. The ms *Noordam* sent a Mayday

signal asking for assistance, but no other vessels would stop. The ship's hotel manager explained, "The other vessels are so used to people in the water that if they have brown skin, they just call the Coast Guard." So the ms *Noordam* sent out additional rescue boats and plucked 22 persons out of the sea. One infant had drowned.

The survivors were taken to non-public areas of the ship, fed, clothed, and seen by a medical team. They were from Somalia, Iran, Iraq, and Palestine and had been in a refugee house in Turkey. They wanted to go to a Greek island where they hoped to get jobs and live under human rights laws, but the motorboat they hired had capsized in rough seas.

Over the last decade, thousands of people have died attempting to get to better lands of opportunity in unseaworthy boats. The ship morally was obligated to save the refugees from what would have been certain death, but it was obligated by international law to disembark rescued persons at the next port of call, which was in Turkey, from where the people had fled.

Holland America Line held the ship in Kusadasi an extra day while diplomats from the Netherlands, the United States, and Great Britain took up the issue of repatriating the refugees with the Turkish government. This delayed the ship's schedule and meant that the cruise would have to skip one of its ports of call, angering passengers who were looking forward to going to Malta. Some of them may have considered Malta to be the highlight of the trip, and now they would not get there. It also meant that Holland America Line would lose revenue on shore excursions and vendors in Malta would suffer economically.

Andrews said, "Holland America Line has a very deep sense of its humanitarian role as well as a commitment to service and our guests. As this situation played out, we kept our guests informed so they understood the situation. Even though we missed a port, they did understand the reasons behind it and nearly everyone supported this."

The ship's hotel manager said they sent out to guests several statements from the captain, both written and verbal, to apologize and give partial refunds. At the end of the cruise, the ship's officers and staff made a presentation to the passengers relating details of the incident, and they received a standing ovation.

The Public Relations Department issued a news release to travel media and those who were following the story.

Nature's Crisis

Cruises are often affected by severe storms and hurricanes. Executive management and crisis teams make decisions about alternate routes and changes of itineraries to ensure the safety of passengers while providing them with a pleasurable experience. Crisis communicators regularly disseminate messages to several stakeholders.

Key among them are: persons aboard ships directly affected by an impending storm; employees who live in the path of a storm; families of employees who live in the path of a storm; travel agents with clients currently aboard affected ships; travel agents whose clients' future travel plans may be affected; and the travel industry news media.

Elvejord and Andrews say they use virtually all news media, travel desks, and news desks: "We use PR Newswire and post on our website if the event is large enough, then we keep a log of those working the story to always send updates. We now use social media—Twitter and Facebook—though we did not at that time. Other publics we have to reach are port officials, airlines, travel agents, vendors, visitors, and shore excursion operators."

Case 4: Hurricane Changes Ship's Itinerary

September 2

When Hurricane Frances threatened the coast of Florida in September, 2004, the staff on the ms *Zuiderdam* delivered a letter to passengers on September 2, reading that the Coast Guard had closed Port Everglades (at Fort Lauderdale) to incoming vessels. The ship would be unable to dock there as the scheduled point of disembarkation two days later.

The letter indicated Holland America Line would re-book passengers on later airlines if flights were missed. Also, Holland America Line would provide motor coaches to other airports when it could dock in Fort Lauderdale. Further, it gave passengers a website and a toll-free phone number they could pass on to family and friends to keep them updated on the changing situation.

On the same day, letters were sent to travel agents with clients booked on the September 4 sailing, informing them that the cruise would be shortened from 7 to 6 days and there would be one less port stop. It gave each passenger a choice of a total refund or a discount and onboard credit for a future cruise. Whenever passengers are inconvenienced, benefits are offered.

A news release to consumers, the travel trade, local reporters, and the website was sent announcing the itinerary change due to the hurricane and why. It stressed that safety was paramount and that the passengers were enjoying an extra day of cruising in calm seas away from the storm.

September 3

By the next day, Hurricane Francis had weakened, and the plan was that the ship would dock in Fort Lauderdale on the morning of September 5

—a Sunday—a day later than scheduled. The letter that day also offered passengers an opportunity to stay onboard for the next sailing at a reduced rate. Several took advantage of the opportunity.

A letter went to travel agents with clients aboard the then current cruise advising them of the situation and the air travel issue. A letter went to Holland America Line employees and their families living in the path of the hurricane; the letter informed them that if they were thinking of evacuation, they might think of evacuating to the safety of the *Zuiderdam* at a greatly reduced rate ($149 per person for a one-week cruise) since several passengers would likely cancel. Employees enjoy those special benefits regularly.

September 4

An early letter on September 4 indicated the plan was still to dock in Fort Lauderdale the following morning, and that, until then, the ship would be navigated far from the storm and would cruise the beautiful calm seas and sunny skies of the Gulf of Mexico until it could safely approach Fort Lauderdale. However, it was later announced that nature had made its own plans and that the ship could not dock until Monday, September 6 and that the scheduled Saturday departure would depart on September 6, two days later than scheduled and with a change of ports of call.

Again, passengers were offered an opportunity to stay onboard for the next cruise if staterooms were available, anticipating that some of the booked passengers would cancel because they were unable or unwilling to take the delayed shortened cruise and/or unable to get to Fort Lauderdale.

Another announcement news release went out explaining the extended delay and the change of ports.

September 5

The *Zuiderdam* actually reached port on Sunday September 5, a day earlier than predicted, and delivered letters to thank guests for their patience and give them instructions to make disembarkation and re-booking of flights easier.

Some stayed onboard for the Monday embarkation and a five-day cruise. Some Holland American employees made quick decisions to take a few days off and join the cruise at a discounted rate (a perk of the job). The company communicated with cruise customers through sales representatives so that they received the communications in their own languages.

Crisis Management Also Includes Communications

Holland America Line's 13,500 seagoing employees on all 15 ships must participate in fire and "abandon ship" drills monthly. Upon boarding a vessel, crew members receive crisis management and human behavior training in accordance with the Standards of Training, Certification and Watchkeeping (STCW) convention mandated by the International Maritime Organization (IMO). Key issues taught are for crew members to be firm in their actions and self assured.

An example of problems faced in the training is that 60% of guests in an emergency situation do nothing at first. They find the situation unbelievable and continue to gamble, drink, sleep, eat, do whatever they were doing or maybe just stare into space. So the crew must be able to persuade them to take action swiftly.

For those employees that are shore-based, Michiel Versteeg, Director, Compliance Programs, manages the Incident Command Center and organizes periodic drills and exercises so that, in the unlikely event of a shipboard emergency, adequate assistance can be provided.

There are various contingency plans for different types of crises. There may be incidents on board ships or ashore, or there may be natural disasters such as earthquakes, tsunamis, and mudslides that affect company employees. International maritime law requires a ship to render assistance whenever another ship is in distress. Rescue Coordination Centers all over the world have the authority to do so. In particular, cruise ships with large numbers of supplies, medical assistance, and other facilities onboard are likely to be assigned to take charge of on-scene rescue until the Coast Guard arrives. As an example, one of Holland America Line's cruise ships was called to the site of a cargo ship taking on water off the coast of Cuba. The crew members rendered assistance by providing dewatering equipment, which kept the cargo ship afloat.

Rescuing persons at sea is an expected but not common event, but it is a part of maritime law. Elvejord said, "You help your brothers, like using your cell phone when you see an accident on the freeway."

So assimilated drills and exercises are critical for emergency preparedness and Holland America Line's business operation. Some are as long as 2 days; others take 2–3 hours. Participants in shore-based exercises not only include land-based employees but may also include external partners such as the U.S. Coast Guard, U.S. Customs, FBI, FEMA, state (Department of Public Health, state troopers, Department of Environmental Conservation), and local agencies (firefighters, police, etc.).

To facilitate any interaction with these agencies, the cruise line adopted the Incident Command System in accordance with the National Incident Management System. This provides a systematic, proactive approach to guide departments and agencies of all levels of government, non-governmental organizations and the private sector to work seamlessly to

prevent, protect against, respond to, recover from, and mitigate the effects of incidents regardless of cause, location, or complexity in order to reduce the loss of life and property and harm to the environment.

In August, 2009, a simulated exercise was held in Juneau, Alaska, aboard Holland America Line's *Veendam*, together with the local authorities. The created scenario was that there was a fire aboard the cruise ship, and the local fire department as well as the Coast Guard participated. For 3½ hours, the participants tested communications, equipment, and response skills and simulated getting passengers away from the fire and the ship, and safely evacuating them to a nearby school.

A larger multi-agency 2-day exercise was conducted in April, 2009, and organized by the U.S. Coast Guard, Holland America Line, U.S. Customs and Border Patrol, and local authorities in Ketchikan. The exercise consisted of a tabletop exercise and an actual simulated exercise involving about 100 volunteers that acted as guests and responded to a simulated incident with a large passenger vessel.

Each organization in the drill has its own set of objectives in the drill plus objectives shared by all participants. The shared objectives include but are not limited to the following:

- Coordinate rescue and assistance action plans for the evacuation and transportation of evacuees from the incident site to designated landing/recovery sites.
- Account for passengers and crew with 100% accuracy by the end of the exercise.
- Implement a shore-side support plan for evacuees that includes triage and medical services, local transportation, sheltering, and personal care.
- Establish and operate a joint "media plan" for response to an elevated public affairs demand to the given scenario.
- Establish timely communications and information exchange between the ship, industry Emergency Operations Center, response agencies, and impacted port community.
- Establish an Emergency Call Center and an industry website to serve as a point of information for family and friends and crew members sheltered at the location.

Holland America Line's objectives include the following:

- Improve overall Incident Command Center readiness and effectiveness.
- Activate an Emergency Call Center and a Holland America Line website to serve as a point of information for family and friends of guest and crew members.

- Coordinate a public affairs plan for the planning and execution phases of the event.
- Establish video conferencing with the Coast Guard command. Exercise and evaluate the system if the technology is available.
- Provide all Holland America Line Crisis Action and Emergency Response Team members with incident response training.

Incident Command Center

The company also maintains a fully equipped, ready to use Incident Command Center in case of major news-making crises or disasters. The center has established stations for various department representatives (media relations, guest programs, risk management, etc.) who will need to be present during a crisis. The stations have computers and telephones; supplies; LCD television screens that can be tuned to different networks and cable stations; video conferencing equipment; surround systems; organizational charts; clocks set for various time zones including the site of the crisis; everything needed. Employees from Public Relations such as Andrews and Elvejord need only come into the office and they can immediately begin the media relations aspect of the crisis communications. Every four weeks, the equipment is tested for readiness.

The center is located in Holland America Line's headquarters in Seattle; Versteeg said the company is looking towards establishing a similar setup off site in case of the unlikely event that the headquarters office is not usable. This is an advisable preparation—as businesses in New York's World Trade Center realized after the 9/11 tragedy. When there is no office, no command center, no phones or computers, what happens? Management needs to communicate not only with the news media but also with employees and perhaps their families as well as other publics.

Holland America Line has consistently been rated among the top cruise lines by Condé Nast Traveller Readers' Choice Awards and *Travel & Leisure* World's Best Awards. It earned the High Deluxe Five-Star Rating by the World Ocean & Cruise Liner Society, and for 17 consecutive years it was the Best Overall Cruise Value by the World Ocean & Cruise Liner Society and *Ocean & Cruise News*.

Case: US Airways and the Emergency Landing in the Hudson

James Olson joined US Airways as Vice President, Corporate Communications, in April, 2008, from Waggener Edstrom Worldwide, a technology-focused PR agency based in Seattle. One of his first tasks was to consider the company's crisis communications plan. The plan had been developed years before and basically suffered from additions deemed

important by later teams. It was 125 pages and Olson said, "Every name was out of date."

So, in October, 2008, he and his department organized to make the plan more user-friendly. It was cut to fewer than 15 pages and included only elements needed if there was a crisis "now."

In mid-December, 2008, the company had a "tabletop drill." The drill was a simulated catastrophic accident. The corporate communications team also had a half-day summit that involved first-responder teams from other areas of the company, including marketing, emergency planning, information technology, and the external crisis response agency, Weber Shandwick.

The drill was just in time. Each executive and each member of the communications team recalls where they were and what they were doing on January 15 when they learned that US Airways Flight 1549 leaving New York's LaGuardia Airport for Charlotte, North Carolina, was down.

Elise Eberwein (Executive Vice President, People and Communications) was on a flight from Phoenix to Charlotte heading for a vacation. As soon as she landed, she abandoned thoughts of vacation and took the next flight to LaGuardia.

Michelle Mohr (Senior Manager, Corporate Communications) was in her office at the Charlotte hub. The troubled plane was heading to Charlotte so Mohr began to prepare for the local news media that would descend on the airport.

Morgan Durrant (Senior Manager, Corporate Communications) was based in Philadelphia and was in his office. On hearing the first report, he caught the next flight to LaGuardia to provide on-site support.

CEO Doug Parker was in the Tempe, Arizona, headquarters company boardroom meeting with bankers. Senior Vice President of Public Affairs C. A. Howlett entered the room and told Parker there was a report that a plane was down. Parker dashed back to his office and saw the Airbus 320 floating in the Hudson River on television. He told the bankers the problem and dismissed them immediately; the boardroom was the designated corporate command center.

Olson was meeting in his Phoenix office with the Director of Information Technology to discuss the technology and phone demands and needs of the war room should there be a crisis. The IT director had just said that it would take about three months to install the needed equipment.

Suddenly, a colleague burst into the office and said, "Jim . . . sorry to interrupt but I think you'll want to take this call. It's Reuters (Wire Service) wanting a comment about one of our planes floating down the Hudson River." Olson turned on the television, which is generally always on CNN. Without a word, the team went about setting up the crisis war room. The phones were installed within minutes (rather than months).

Participants in the December drill were warned that despite the company's sophisticated notification system, if there were an actual crisis, they would probably be notified by the news media. Reuters called and they tuned in to CNN and received confirmation when they saw the plane afloat.

Olson and the communications team activated the emergency response plan immediately. He said his Blackberry was "burning in my hand with people seeking information."

He rushed back to the office where the rest of the Phoenix-based Corporate Communications staff of six were already writing the first news release. Olson said, "It is our goal that the initial news release should go out within 15 minutes of a crisis. There are templates for press releases that were available, but this was a 'moving accident site.' All the templates did not fit the situation."

The site and the information were changing rapidly. So updates were made as information was confirmed. Information had to be substantiated by the airline before it could be distributed. News media often go with one source in the interest of immediacy and beating the competition, but the Corporate Communications team at US Airways was determined to be more accurate than fast.

Even though numerous media outlets were reporting that all passengers were safe within 90 minutes of the emergency landing, US Airways could not make that announcement on its website or on social media networks until it had confirmed personally with each passenger or a family member. This could not be done immediately because the ferries that rescued passengers took them to various places. As the ferries took them to both sides of the Hudson River, the passengers dispersed to hotels or the homes of friends and family, and some even headed back to the airport to catch the next flight to Charlotte.

The news media, especially television and online media, often get facts wrong in their quest to be first rather than factual. An organization in crisis cannot afford to take this chance. It serves its customers and employees first or it will lose customers and the respect of employees—reactions organizations cannot or should not risk. It cannot guess or estimate when lives are in question.

When News is Wrong, When Experts are Not Experts

An illustration of this dilemma took place on November 5, 2009, when 12 people were killed and 31 wounded at Fort Hood, the military base in Killeen, Texas. CNN—on the air with continuous coverage—and networks reported that Major Hassan, the gunman, was himself killed by civilian police.

For more than four hours, this "fact" was reported over and over. Also, the anchors advised viewers repeatedly that there would be a news conference "at any minute." At about 9:15 p.m. EST, Fort Hood finally held the news conference, led by spokesperson Lt. General Robert Cone. Cone and the Public Affairs staff had without doubt monitored television news, saw the errors, and felt the pressure to make announcements. Nevertheless, they did not come forward until they had facts. The first fact was a correction of the error made all evening. Hassan was not killed, but injured and in custody. Cone said, "I would say his death is not imminent."

A few minutes later, *The Larry King Show* was broadcast, and King mentioned again that the gunman was not deceased and said something about how it is expected that errors will be made in breaking news. That seems to be the nature of today's news media, in the post-Cronkite era.

King's show that night had as guests Dr. Phil McGraw, former POW Shoshana Johnson, and Tom Kenniff of the U.S. Army. The conversation was why Hassan had shot so many people, or shot anybody. Certainly none of them knew why, but it was exciting conversation about a timely issue. Kenniff said Hassan was an Islamic committing a terrorist act. The others were incensed at Kenniff and said Hassan had a mental health problem. None of them actually knew. All of them were *non-expert experts* in this arena.

The non-expert expert, seen on television and online frequently, appeals to viewers on emotion not fact, a threat to any organization or individual in crisis. The term "non-expert expert" was coined for the first three editions of this textbook in a case titled "Cellular Phones and the Cancer Scare." Ken Woo, then a media relations manager for Cellular One, used the term to describe David Reynard, a recent widower and a father whose wife had died of brain cancer. On *The Larry King Show*, he blamed the cancer on her usage of a cellular phone, which, he said, she held near the tumor. Also on the show was a scientist who had studied cellular technology for years and said the power output from cellular phones was too low to damage human tissue. However, viewers chose not to believe any of her scientific data because, after all, Reynard's wife had died. He was sad. He had a motherless child. The show even showed video of the wife before she died saying she used the phone "a lot." As the phone calls poured in, the cellular phone crisis was born for cellular carriers. They all developed crisis communications campaigns, but basically the crisis ended because people did not really want to give up the convenience of cell phones.

Getting It Right Takes Time

So US Airways wanted to get the facts right. An emergency response "bridge line" was established, through which key company personnel—

Operations, Customer Relations, Corporate Communications, Legal and Regulatory teams—were either participants in the phone calls between key first responders who were communicating with the crew and the Federal Aviation Administration (FAA) or listening to the conversations.

It was during this call that Olson learned that all 150 passengers and the five members of the crew had been safely evacuated. Olson said, "One of our guys at the OCC (Operations Control Center) came on the line and said, 'This is preliminary, but I just spoke to the captain [Sullenberger]

US AIRWAYS PRESS RELEASE

US Airways Flight 1549 Initial Report

Tempe, Ariz.—(Business Wire)—Jan. 15, 2009—US Airways (NYSE: LCC) flight 1549, an Airbus A320 en route to Charlotte from LaGuardia, has been involved in an accident in New York approximately 3:03 p.m. Eastern Time.

Airline officials are in direct contact with local, state and national authorities and are cooperating fully with emergency response efforts. US Airways' primary concern at this time is for those on board the airplane and their families.

US Airways is confirming passenger and crew on board the aircraft and will issue additional information as soon as possible. At this point, no additional details can be confirmed.

Individuals who believe they may have family members on board flight 1549 may call US Airways at 1-800-679-8215 within the United States. This number can be reached toll-free from international locations though AT&T's USADirect(r). Then contact an AT&T operator—please visit www.usa.com/traveler for USADirect(r) access codes.

US Airways will provide additional information as it becomes available. Please monitor usairways.com for the latest information. (LCCG).

—LCC—

CONTACT:

US Airways

Media Relations

Source: US Airways

Figure 11.4 This news release was the first one that US Airways disseminated after Flight 1549 made an emergency landing in the Hudson River. Courtesy of US Airways.

and he tells me he walked up and down the aisle and he thinks everyone is off the plane safely.'" People watching television news and computer reports also heard about Captain "Sully" Sullenberger going back through the plane to make sure all were off. Fear at US Airways turned to relief shared by people everywhere as they watched the passengers standing along the slightly submerged wings seemingly standing on water.

Corporate Communications put up its customer and media website dedicated to Flight 1549 within 30 minutes of notification of the accident. This was the initial primary source for customers and the news media. The first news release was issued in 45 minutes (see Figure 11.4). The CEO conducted a press briefing covered by nearly every network and news outlet within about 90 minutes. As more information was learned, additional news releases and internal messages followed in the hours and days that followed (see Figure 11.5).

Olson recalled, "The Corporate Communications team also worked with our marketing team to leverage search engines like Yahoo and Google by purchasing key word terms related to the Flight 1549 emergency landing and directing them to the dedicated Flight 1549 micro site."

Several crisis management/communications actions emanating from the company took place immediately. The Care Team of employees trained from various work groups was dispatched to New York, where they provided cell phones and clothing for passengers, and to Charlotte, to provide on-site support to family members. The Family Support Hotline

CONTINUING PRESS RELEASES

Our goal is to issue the first press release (which acknowledges the accident and provides initial details) within 15 minutes of notification.

Press Release #1: Initial report. Flight number, aircraft type, O&D, location of accident, time, time zone

Press Release #2: Includes initial report information, adds number of passengers and crew

Press Release #3: Follow up release containing remarks from initial press conference

Press Release #4: Information on aircraft (age, hours, last checks)

Press Release #5: Details on crew

Figure 11.5 As new information was available, that information was added to subsequent news releases.

was a special toll-free phone number set up for family members to call to get information on the status of their loved ones. The Passenger and Crew Manifest Reconciliation is a crucial process of confirming the whereabouts and safety of all passengers and crew. The confirmation from Captain Sullenberger was assumed to be correct, but each and every person had to be accounted for and confirmed to have survived. Someone had to determine where they all were and make contact with them. Olson said this process took 24 hours.

Later, in an article in *Business Week*, writer Dean Foust praised the airline's care of passengers, calling the process "a model of crisis management" (Foust, 2009). In the article, James J. Hanks, Jr., a Baltimore attorney, was quoted as praising not only the pilot and crew but also the US Airways Care Team for providing free hotel rooms, warm meals, and dry clothing.

FLIGHT 1549 LESSONS LEARNED

Be Prepared.
- Have an integrated plan.
- Test it!
- Use It!

Be Fast.
- First press release issued 40 minutes after accident.
- First CEO press briefing within first two hours of accident.

Be Accessible.
- 100+ calls an hour.
- Established media war room within ten minutes of accident.
- Established PR presence at origin, destination and crash site (in part through PR agency support and local team members).

Be Engaged.
- Share information with employees early and often.
- Partner with NTSB, FAA and manufacturer PR teams.

Be Compassionate.
- Balance facts with emotion.

Figure 11.6 James Olson, US Airways Vice President, Corporate Communications, developed this list of lessons learned based on challenges he faced in handling crisis communications after the emergency landing. Courtesy of James Olson.

The Go-Team consisting of CEO Parker, a managing director of the Finance team, members of the Care Team—about 50 employees altogether—carried special emergency credit cards and cash to first responders to be used to book hotel rooms and to buy clothing and other essentials for passengers whose personal belongings, including wallets, were left on the plane. Passengers were ordered to leave everything not attached to them on the plane.

Before the day of the emergency landing was over, New York Mayor Bloomberg informed officials that there would be a news conference the following morning, and he wanted CEO Parker to be present to honor the crew as well as the first responders.

The January 26 news conference was announced in a news release along with the CEO's remarks applauding the crew, police, ferry boat operators, water taxis, EMTs (emergency medical technicians), the Office of Emergency Management, the American Red Cross, the Salvation Army, and others.

On January 17, a letter from the CEO was sent to Flight 1549's passengers informing them how they might get their personal belongings from the plane and what the process would entail. A check for $5,000 was enclosed to cover immediate expenses and a separate check to reimburse the costs of the original airfare. The services of the airline's Family Support Center were offered.

On January 21, another letter went to passengers again offering the services of the Customer Care Team and promising to make efforts to recover personal items from the submerged plane. All passengers were informed that they would be extended Chairman's Preferred status, the most prestigious flier level, through March, 2010.

There was some success recovering passengers' belongings (see Figure 11.7). YouTube showed a dramatic video of the plane being raised.

The Corporate Communications team's work was not done even after passengers and crew were safely at home. The entire Flight 1549 crew appeared on CBS's *60 Minutes*, about a month after the incident. They were interviewed by Katie Couric in one of the airline's maintenance hangars in Charlotte. In the 12 months after the emergency water landing, the crew conducted dozens of interviews and were reunited in New York City with many of the passengers and first responders on the 1-year anniversary. Captain Sully again made news when he returned to the cockpit on October 1, 2009 (see Figure 11.8). The 1-year anniversary activities included a trip back out on the Hudson River at the precise time of day and the precise location where the plane landed a year earlier.

The incident soon became known as "The Miracle on the Hudson," a term that Parker does not like. "I believe that 'Pride' is a better

FLIGHT 1549

Returning (to Charlotte) from the New York-based investment company that she is president of, (Maryann) Bruce had schlepped through LaGuardia Airport with a . . . laptop, briefcase, purse, a mink coat and a carry-on suitcase.

The diamond ring she . . . received on her 25th wedding anniversary " . . . must've smashed my finger," says Bruce. "By the time I got to the plane my finger was black and blue."

So she stashed the ring in a jewelry pouch in her carry-on in the overhead compartment. When the plane landed and the flight attendant ordered everyone off, "I knew I had to get off the plane even though the ring was up there."

After being rescued, I thought I might get my suitcase back," she says "but I thought someone might steal the jewelry . . ."

. . . US Airways' (Deborah) Thompson flew to Charlotte to personally deliver Bruce's . . . ring . . . and (it) looked like new. "Oh my God, I got it back," Bruce says she thought.

. . . Another item that came back, a little worse for wear but still legible: Bruce's boarding pass for seat 5D, Flight 1549.

"I plan on framing that," she says.

Excerpt from "Belongings Once Lost Are Found Again" by Marilyn Adams, *USA Today*, Wednesday, May 20, 2009

Figure 11.7 This excerpted story in *USA Today* tells a positive story of the efforts US Airways made to satisfy customers on flight 1549 (Adams, 2009).

characterization," he said. There was nothing miraculous about the flawless efforts of the crew. He preferred to think that all US Airways pilots and crews would perform in the same excellent manner. As Capt. Sullenberger said, "I know I can speak for the entire crew when I tell you we were simply doing the jobs we were trained to do."

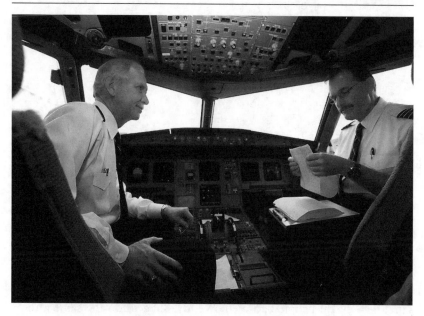

Figure 11.8 Captain Chesley "Sully" Sullenberger (left) became a celebrity after safely landing the US Airways jet in the Hudson. He made numerous public appearances and his return to work on October 1, 2009 made news again. Here, he and co-pilot Jeffery Skiles prepare for the October 1 flight. Reproduced by permission of Getty Images.

The company hosted an employee ceremony praising the many employees who were directly involved in the response. A special video of the event and media coverage was distributed on DVD to all 33,000 employees. It was also available on the company intranet.

Product Failure and Product Tampering

The cases in this chapter center on problems and perceived problems of products and what was done in the areas of crisis management and crisis communications in order to convince consumers that the problem had been eliminated. Yuhan-Kimberly in Korea had a crisis when consumers believed its wet wipes were not safe for infants. Maple Leaf Foods, Inc. in Canada had to make changes to convince consumers its products were safe after several people had died. Wendy's had to do the same after a customer tampered with its chili.

Case: Yuhan-Kimberly and Baby Wet Wipes

Yuhan-Kimberly is a leading health and hygiene company that manufactures and sells diapers, tissues, sanitary napkins, and wet wipes. The company was established in Seoul, Korea in 1970 as a joint venture of Kimberly-Clark and Korea's Yuhan Corporation. Its major products make up more than 50% of the market share in Korea.

SeungWoo Son is public relations manager for Yuhan-Kimberly and EunWook Lee is vice-president (see Figure 12.1).

The 2005 crisis centered on the Yuhan-Kimberly product, Huggies baby wet wipes. Wet wipes were originally classified as a cosmetic product in the United States, Europe, and several Asian countries. Because Yuhan-Kimberly also sells diapers, the wet wipes were marketed in Korea for baby care.

The crisis began March, 2005, when a consumer activist organization discovered through its research that there was formaldehyde in Yuhan-Kimberly wet wipes. It announced its findings through the mass media —newspapers, TV cable channels, and radio—all over Korea.

Son said there was a standard of formaldehyde used in cosmetics, but there were no regulations in place for wet wipes for babies. Yuhan-Kimberly took the position that the wet wipes had only one-tenth of the formaldehyde permitted in cosmetics, therefore there was no danger.

Figure 12.1 Crisis communicators at Yuhan-Kimberly in Seoul, Korea handled the wet wipes crisis. EunWook Lee (in front) is vice president of the company. SeungWoo Son (rear) is public relations manager. Photo printed with permission. Courtesy of Yuhan-Kimberly.

Cultural Concern

In order to comprehend Yuhan-Kimberly's position, Son said one must first understand aspects of the Korean culture. The Ministry for Health, Welfare and Family Affairs reveals that the Korean people consider the ideal birth rate to be 2.54 children per family. However, the actual birth rate is lower than what people consider ideal; it is 1.19 children per family. The reasons, according to Son, are financial burdens, including the value and importance of private education and insufficient infra-structure for child care. In addition, public opinion can quickly spread through Internet networks due to Korea's 80% use rate and top class IT infrastructure.

Consequently, Son said, parents are extremely sensitive about the safety of babies and want to take all precautions and no risks to protect babies from illnesses and infections.

This does not suggest that parents in other countries do not care as much for their children, but the formaldehyde scare did not arise in other countries where wet wipes were sold, probably because they were marketed as a cosmetic product.

The level of formaldehyde in Yuhan-Kimberly's wet wipes did not please parents even though it was one-tenth of the permitted level. Nearly 50,000 consumers filed complaints via telephone, e-mail, and a website bulletin board. In addition, comments were posted on portals and community sites; an anti-website was launched. This put Yuhan-Kimberly in a challenging situation. Not only was there concern for the sales of wet wipes but also fear that sales of other products would drop. Yuhan-Kimberly is also the leading diaper manufacturer. In fact, it began manufacturing wet wipes for hygiene purposes as an extension of its Huggies diaper business, which accounted for 60% of the market share of all diapers sold in Korea. As consumers complained about the wet wipes, there was concern that the diaper business would begin to fail because they were connected. The market share of the wet wipes went from 50% to 26% and 21% in April and May, respectively. The possibility of widespread criticism of the company was a dire situation.

Son said, "Yuhan-Kimberly is one of the most respected companies in Korea and has earned high consumer confidence as a company that is strongly dedicated to fulfilling its corporate social responsibility." Corporate social responsibility (CSR) is very important to Koreans, who have high expectations of ethical behavior in large companies. CSR asks for a high standard of social contribution in addition to fulfilling ethical and environmental requirements. Just before the crisis in 2005, the company ranked sixth on the list of "Most Respected Companies in Korea" by the Korea Management Association. "We did not want to lose this position in the eyes of consumers," said Son.

Customers had begun asking for refunds on wet wipes and then also began asking for refunds on diapers. There were signs that consumers were planning to launch a boycott campaign of all products. "Whereas companies with a good image can achieve high marks from consumers, when consumers are disappointed, the effect can be much more negative in relative terms," said Son.

Crisis Management and Communications Plan

Yuhan-Kimberly had a crisis management policy that included crisis communications. It included crisis prevention and crisis response if a crisis developed.

When the formaldehyde issue became problematic, the company set out to follow its plan:

Step 1 The company created the crisis management team, which included the CEO, a spokesperson, and the business leader.

Step 2 The spokesperson (EunWook Lee) was responsible for communication with all publics, external and internal, to be certain to have what Yuhan-Kimberly calls "one voice, one channel."

Step 3 The crisis management team oversaw the monitoring of all reports in newspapers, television, radio and Internet sources, particularly websites. Persons directly monitoring media made reports back to the crisis management team.

Internal publics were informed of outlooks and outcomes. A product safety survey was conducted by authorized research facilities.

Step 4 A standby statement was carefully written as swiftly as was possible (see Figure 12.2). A Q&A was prepared for each stakeholder: employees, news media, customers, vendors, government, and consumer protection organizations.

There was great concern to protect Yuhan-Kimberly's reputation and the confidence publics have in the company. There was determination to avoid any public misunderstanding and thereby minimize the impact of the crisis.

Step 5 In an effort to convince the publics that the product was safe, data was collected to prove the points and avoid further widening of the crisis. This data was written in a news release to the media. Questions were expected and interviews with staff members, shareholders, and partner companies were conducted to add to the persuasion. One interview with experts was posted on the website for consumers who sought details online.

In addition to the standby statement, medical and chemical professionals gave objective evidence of product safety on a video interview. They had studied safety regulations of Korean and international agencies.

Step 6 The company refrained from making individual responses to prevent friction and the dissemination of ungrounded data. The team did, however, make efforts to control information on anti-websites by politely providing the site webmaster with the company's position and objective data to resolve misunderstanding.

In response to the third party complaints on the web, the team used the standby statement as well as convincing information from the medical professionals.

Step 7 If consumers made requests for exchanges or refunds after learning of the explanations, the company complied with their requests to prevent the spread of complaints.

The company handled its own exchange and refund process rather than turning it over to external agencies so that the crisis would be contained and the "one-voice" could be maintained. Also, the company delivered its statement and Q&A to wholesalers and direct accounts including discount stores, and asked for their cooperation in dealing swiftly with exchanges without inconveniencing consumers.

유한킴벌리 물티슈는 안전합니다.

물티슈 제품은 미국, EU 등 선진국에서는 화장품류로 분류되어 일반공산품보다 더욱 엄격한 품질과 안전성 관리를 받고 있습니다. 이때 허용되는 포름알데히드의 기준은 2000ppm입니다.

국내 화장품의 허용 기준 역시 미국, EU, 캐나다, 호주 등과 같이 2,000ppm이며, 유한킴벌리의 아기용 엠보싱 물티슈는 이러한 기준보다 훨씬 강화된 품질관리와 안전성관리를 통해 생산되어 지난 5년 이상 최고의 소비자 만족도를 지켜왔습니다.

한편, 소비자시민모임의 최근 조사결과에 따르면 유한킴벌리의 엠보싱 물티슈에서 210ppm 정도의 포름알데히드가 검출되었다고 합니다. 이는 앞서 언급한 주요 선진국 및 우리나라의 화장품류 허용 기준 2,000ppm의 약 10분의 1 수준으로, 안전성을 재 확인 받았습니다. 다만, 소비자시민모임에서 물티슈의 자율적 검사제도인 항균(S)마크를 위해 정한 가이드라인 30ppm을 국내 제품에서 맞추기를 바라는 요구가 제기 된 바 있습니다.

이에, 유한킴벌리는 주요 선진국 물티슈 및 국내 화장품 허용기준에 따라 생산 판매된 회사의 엠보싱 물티슈 제품의 안전성을 거듭 확신하고 있지만, 국내 항균(S)마크의 자율적 사용을 위한 가이드라인을 존중하는 입장에서 원하는 거래선과 고객들께 반품, 교환을 해 드리기로 결정하였습니다. 고객들께서는 사용하시던 제품은 그대로 사용해도 무방하며, 원하실 경우 교환해 드릴 것입니다.

별도로, 주요 선진국의 공통적인 허용기준이자 국내 화장품의 허용 기준인 2000ppm과 상기 국내 자율 안전마크 사용을 위한 30ppm의 가이드라인 간에 있는 현격한 차이에 대해서는 향후 관련 기관 및 단체와 긴밀히 협의해 나갈 것입니다.

Figure 12.2 This is the message, in Korean, used on the news release to explain the wet wipes situation. There was never a danger, but consumers did not understand this. Courtesy of Yuhan-Kimberly.

YUHAN-KIMBERLY WET WIPES ARE SAFE!

In the developed countries such as United States, EU, and etc, wet wipes is classified as cosmetics and its quality and safety are rigorously controlled by administration than any other industrial products. Here, the maximum permissible level of formaldehyde in cosmetics is 2,000 ppm.

Use of formaldehyde in the local cosmetics is also allowed by 2,000 ppm just like United States, EU, Canada and Australia. With much reinforced quality and safety control than regulation, Yuhan-Kimberly's baby wet wipes has become the most loved one over the past 5 years.

According to the recent examination of one consumer organization, 210 ppm of formaldehyde as detected in the Yuhan-Kimberly's baby wet wipes. As noted before, this amount is only 1/10 of both local and other developed countries' regulation, and it had been reconfirmed as being safe. However, the consumer organization asked the local companies to adjust the amount not exceeding 30 ppm once in the past, which falls into the guideline for the 'voluntary safety mark' of the wet wipes.

Though Yuhan-Kimberly is convinced of the safety of baby wet wipes, we decided to accept return or exchange products, with respecting the 'voluntary safety mark' guideline. The consumer who is currently using the product can either keep it or replace.

Separately, we will closely work with the related organizations to close the gap between 2000ppm, which is the common regulation in both of the developed countries' and the local cosmetics, and 30ppm, which is the 'voluntary safety mark' guideline.

Figure 12.3 This is the news release in Figure 12.2 translated into English by the Yuhan-Kimberly executives. Courtesy of Yuhan-Kimberly.

Step 8 The business leader prepared his department for development of wet wipes without formaldehyde even though legal regulations did not make this requirement.

Step 9 A rebuilding program was executed to recover corporate and brand reputation. There were five steps, all designed for a return to normalcy.

1. Maintain consistency in communications until the close of the crisis.

2. Develop and launch a new product that not only meets legal standards but also consumers' expectations.

3. Re-examine social commitments such as ethical management, environmental management, and corporate social responsibility.

4. Expand social contributions activities and reinforce public relations activities. Reinforce corporate public campaign "Keep Korea Green," which existed before the crisis onset.

5. Make an announcement on the increased investment and enhance reporting on the company and products.

Observations

1. The crisis was kept at a minimum by speedy communications and effective crisis management. The market share recovered in a short period of time. The wet wipes market share recorded 50% in February, 2005, and dropped to 21% two months later; however, it recovered after that and recorded 30% in June and 40% in October. The 2008 market annual share recorded was greater than 46%. The general evaluation is that the company's communications program received high trust due to the company's reputation of being concerned with the consumer.

2. Although the reputation of the company was partly damaged, consumer confidence was recovered in a short period of time thanks to prompt and consistent response, a reputation rebuilding program, and the longstanding high reputation of the company.

3. In the list of Korea Management Association's Most Respected Companies in Korea, Yuhan-Kimberly slipped from #4 in 2004 to #6 in 2005. It recovered the #4 position in 2006 and advanced to #3 in 2008 and 2009.

4. Research in 2009 conducted by crisis management experts headed by Professor Hyun Ou Lee of Hanyang University revealed that Yuhan-Kimberly's long-standing good corporate image had helped it withstand the crisis with less damage to its corporate reputation than a company with a not so stellar image.

Conclusions

Yuhan-Kimberly's reputation based on social contributions and responsibilities is the best asset and value in the face of a crisis.

Approach with a human face is the basic part of crisis communications.

Setting crisis management techniques and appointing a spokesperson swiftly minimizes confusion. Even prior to the crisis in 2005, Yuhan-Kimberly had a well-managed crisis management system including a crisis management team. However, the company took the opportunity to be stronger when facing a crisis. The company reinforced crisis prevention activities and an early warning system with issue monitoring and tracking.

Prompt responses minimize negative opinion.

Yuhan-Kimberly's crisis management was successful in that it minimized negative public opinion and sentiment efficiently with clear and honest communication, and it also prevented problems, all according to its prepared crisis manual.

Case: Maple Leaf Foods and the Battle Against Listeria

Maple Leaf Foods, Inc., headquartered in Toronto, Ontario, Canada, packages food products for distribution in Canada, United States, United Kingdom, Asia and Mexico. It is Canada's largest food processor and its origins date back more than 170 years to a company called Grantham Mills in St. Catharines, Ontario. After several mergers, Maple Leaf Foods was founded in 1961. It is publicly traded under the company symbol MFI on the Toronto Stock Exchange (TSX).

The food products distributed from Maple Leaf are organized in three major groups: meat, bakery, and agribusiness. The meat group includes fresh meats, chilled and ready to cook products, and packaged meats. The bakery group includes various kinds of breads, pastas, and sauces. The agribusiness group includes rendering, biodiesel and hog production operations.

The crisis centered on sliced meats that bore the establishment number of the Toronto facility, 97B, on the packaging. These recalled meats were produced under three dozen brands and were sold at retailers, mass merchandise outlets, institutions and food service outlets including McDonald's, Boston Pizza, Pizza Nova, Shopsy's, and Tim Hortons.

Listeriosis is very rare, affecting 1 to 5 out of 1 million people per year and can result in death. Listeriosis usually occurs in people with weakened immune systems such as AIDS patients, the elderly, and pregnant women. In pregnant women, it can spread to the fetus and cause premature

delivery or it can infect the newborn. The infection can begin with fever and gastrointestinal symptoms, and can spread to the circulatory system and/or the nervous system. Headaches, neck stiffness, and nausea occur from 30 to 70 days after consuming contaminated foods.

A crisis fell on Maple Leaf in August, 2008, when a number of deaths and illnesses were linked to products produced at one of its plants. Dennis Schroh's 82-year-old mother had Listeriosis and was one of the first cases to be reported after the link was confirmed on August 24. She died after being fed the contaminated Leaf cold cuts while she was in a hospital.

Listeriosis is a serious infection caused by eating food containing the strain of bacteria called Listeria monocytogenes, which is one of six strains of the Listeria bacteria and the only one that causes human illness. Listeria can be found in processed foods such as deli meats, hot dogs, cheese, and ice cream as well as in some raw vegetables and some unprocessed foods such as raw dairy, meat, poultry, and fish.

Maple Leaf released a fact sheet informing the public of its safety procedures. It was important to inform the public that safety measures were in place even if a glitch had occurred. Federal Health Minister Tony Clement announced that several cases of Listeriosis had been reported and that the number of cases was expected to rise. Maple Leaf voluntarily chose to close the Bartor Road plant as a precautionary measure.

With the plant closed on August 20, 2008, Maple Leaf cooperated with investigators from the Canadian Food Inspection Agency (CFIA) to determine the origin of the bacteria. All 220 packaged meat products produced at the plant dating back to January 2008 were originally recalled from retail stores, warehouses, distributors, and 9,000 food service establishments and institutions. (Actually, the number of products recalled turned out to be 191 rather than 220 because some products were duplicates.) The recall cost an estimated $20 million, not to mention loss of sales and costs of advertising to recover from reputation loss. A "deep sanitization" was done of the plant and equipment; in fact, six sanitization cycles were completed. All 84 slicing machines, the most likely problem area in the Maple Leaf network, were comprehensively inspected. All were completely disassembled, deep sanitized and swab tested. Then the company made deep sanitization part of its regular cleaning protocols.

The company went public with its crisis communications. It responded to approximately 50,000 calls in August alone. All the information mentioned here about inspection and sanitizing was posted in greater detail on the website in a media backgrounder as were photos of the sanitizing process. CEO Michael McCain (see Figure 12.4) held several news conferences. Spokespersons did interviews and responses to numerous print,

Figure 12.4 Maple Leaf President and Chief Executive Officer Michael McCain was the primary communicator on the website and at news conferences after the Listeria crisis. He came forward with several explanations and apologies as the crisis unfolded. Reproduced by permission of Bloomberg/Getty Images.

broadcast, and online media requests. Regular news releases that repeated key phrases were distributed:

- August 20: "We believe it is important to take these broader preventative actions to respond to this situation promptly, comprehensively, and in the best interests of our consumers."
- August 23: "We know this has shaken consumer confidence in us. Our actions will continue to be guided by putting their interest first."
- August 24: "Our actions are guided by putting public health issues first."
- August 25: "We remain steadfast in our belief that our actions must continue to be guided by what is in the best interests of public health."

- On the website, MapleLeaf.com: "Our management of the Listeria outbreak will be motivated by one thing only—the best public health interests of Canadians and specifically, our customers."

With the food products already distributed and the victims already sickened, 22 people died. This was a tragic blow to the company and its 23,000 employees, not to mention all the families and friends of the victims. Maple Leaf CEO Michael McCain made three statements. They were placed on YouTube, released to the broadcast media on video news releases, and posted on the Maple Leaf website. The first aired on August 23, the second on September 18, and the third on December 12, all in 2008. The second statement follows:

> I'm Michael McCain.
>
> For the past three weeks, we've worked with authorities to determine exactly how Listeria appeared in our sliced meat products at one of our plants. You deserve to know what happened.
>
> Listeria is everywhere in the environment, which makes it challenging. Our investigation found spots deep inside the slicing equipment where the Listeria could have avoided our rigorous cleaning procedures.
>
> We fixed that by something called a deep sanitization and then we tested it thoroughly. We've also done this at each of our other plants and made this special procedure standard.
>
> Our actions will not stop there. The recall product is off the shelf. We believe we know what caused the problem and we believe we have corrected it. Now, I know these efforts can never make up for what has happened and I deeply regret this. We will always be guided by putting your interests first and doing everything we can to build your confidence in us once again.

The Bartor Road plant began phasing in production in mid-September within a highly controlled and monitored environment with daily on-site inspection by federal inspectors to ensure the effectiveness of its food safety protocols. A news advisory went out on September 17, announcing that McCain would talk to the news media, and a news release was distributed announcing the resumption of production (see Figures 12.5 and 12.6).

In October, 2008, Maple Leaf issued another backgrounder explaining the progress of the investigation. Environmental and product samples were being tested. Most samples were negative, and those few products that did test positive were not released for distribution in accordance with

Maple Leaf MapleLeaf.com

NEWS ROOM

Urgent News Advisory—Maple Leaf President and CEO to Address Media

Toronto, September 12, 2008—Maple Leaf Foods (TSX/MFI) will hold a media briefing in conjunction with Bartor Road reopening.

- Who: Michael H. McCain, President & Chief Executive Officer
- When: September 17, 2008 at 4 p.m. Eastern – TODAY
- Where: 16th Floor, 30 St. Clair West, Toronto ON
- How: In person, or to participate via conference call, please call 416-███████ / 866-███████
- For those unable to participate, playback will be made available an hour after the event at 416-███████ / 800-███████ (Passcode 3270923 followed by the pound sign.)

Registration required:

Please contact Caroline Spivak at 416-███████ to register.

Maple Leaf Foods Inc. is a leading food processing company, headquartered in Toronto, Canada. The company employs approximately 23,000 people at its operations across Canada and in the United States, the United Kingdom, and Asia. The company had sales of $5.2 billion in 2007.

Source: Maple Leaf Foods Inc.

Media Inquiries contact: Caroline Spivak 416███████

Figure 12.5 A news advisory informing reporters of a briefing by the Maple Leaf CEO announcing that the plant closed after the Listeria crisis would reopen.

the company's new food safety protocols. The incidence of Listeria in food products ranges from 1% to 10%, according to Health Canada, or, put another way, one in every 200 products will test positive for Listeria. Also, Maple Leaf cited reliable sources that indicated that 5% of humans carry Listeria in their intestine without ill effects.

Maple Leaf MapleLeaf.com

NEWS ROOM

Maple Leaf Bartor Road Plant Resumes Production

Toronto, Sep. 17, 2008—

Maple Leaf Foods (MFI: TSX) today announced that it is resuming production at its Bartor Road facility in Toronto, following the completion of a comprehensive pre-operation inspection conducted by the Canadian Food Inspection Agency ("CFIA"). Maple Leaf voluntarily closed the plant after products were found to contain listeria.

"This plant has undergone intensive investigation, deep sanitations and testing to ensure that the listeria contamination linked to the recent outbreak has been eradicated" said Michael McCain, President and CEO. "While we have always practiced the highest level of vigilance, we are implementing even more rigorous food safety standards going forward, which are the best practice in Canada and the industry."

- The Bartor Facility has undergone six intensive sanitations, well beyond normal cleaning practices, under the supervision of microbiologists and sanitation experts.
- Slicing equipment has been completely disassembled and deep cleaned and tested multiple times. Slicing equipment across the Company is subject to daily disassembly prior to daily cleaning and regularly scheduled intensive disassembly to verify elimination of potential harborage points, well beyond industry standards.
- The effectiveness of the sanitization effort has been verified through recent extensive testing, including more than 1,200 swab tests for listeria from various points on all production lines and throughout the plant.
- We have enhanced our regular environment Listeria monitoring program, more than doubling the sampling sites and frequency of testing.
- The plant will resume production over a phased-in-period. No products will be released until the CFIA and Maple Leaf are fully satisfied that food safety protocols in place at the Bartor Road plant are effective. Test runs of products will also be completed before any new product is distributed from the plant.

"Throughout this incident we have steadfastly placed consumers' interests first," concluded Mr. McCain. "Now we must completely restore their confidence in the quality and integrity of our products."

Maple Leaf Foods is a leading food processing company, headquartered in Toronto, Canada. The company employs approximately 23,000 people at its operations across Canada and the United States, the United Kingdom, and Asia. The company had sales of $5.2 billion in 2007.

Source: Maple Leaf Foods Inc.

For further information:

Investor Inquiries Contact: Lynda Kuhn (416) ███████

Media Inquiries Contact: Linda Smith (905) ███████

Figure 12.6 The news release disseminated with information about the plant opening. It was posted on the company's website. Reprinted with the permission of Maple Leaf Foods.

CEO McCain made the following statement when the company and the CFIA announced they would not distribute any products from the Bartor Road facility until findings and remediation through sanitization had been validated: "We are being ultra cautious in this facility, more cautious than any other plant in North America."

The news media and consumers were carefully educated using Listeria experts. It was explained that the new safety management program's environmental testing would encourage finding Listeria, that this was "a normal and routine finding," also that "if you test for it, you will find it."

Three months after the crisis onset (in November), the message from the CEO was that the recall was over. The changes at the plant were termed "far reaching"—and not only at the Bartor Road plant. The changes also included a company-wide environmental program to serve as an early warning system, with daily senior executive oversight. A new Chief Food Safety Officer would be hired to ensure constant improvement in food safety procedures.

In December, 2008, Maple Leaf reached a settlement agreement of up to $27 million, subject to court approval, with the principal counsel groups that had launched class action lawsuits following the Listeria outbreak. It agreed to pay $750 to individuals who were sickened by the Listeria and $120,000 to the estates of persons who died. The spouses of the deceased would receive $35,000 and a child $30,000.

Dennis Schroh, the first to file an affidavit that his mother died from eating the sliced meats, said "I'm pleased that it's coming to a closure. That's basically what we want, that it comes to an end and everybody can get on with their lives."

Colin Stevenson, a lawyer who represented several plaintiffs, said the settlement would end all litigation against Maple Leaf resulting from the outbreak. "This is a mutually agreeable settlement everybody is happy with." He said that McCain and Maple Leaf had "done the right thing." Stevenson continued, "The fact that it settled so early shows that he clearly wanted to do that." Companies that bought the products that were later recalled also received a settlement.

Dr. Randall Huffman was named and announced as Chief Food Safety Officer effective January 5, 2009, reporting to McCain. This was said to be the first such position in Canada. In addition to numerous food safety responsibilities, including the recently established Maple Leaf Food Safety Advisory Council, Huffman also contributes posts and responds to comments and questions about the company's food safety practices or decisions on the Maple Leaf blog.

After new food safety protocols were set up, the company produced a video, *Our Journey to Safety Leadership*, which was posted on YouTube in July, 2009.

Figure 12.7 Cleaning a slicer machine. The effectiveness of all stages of sanitation was verified through intensified tear-downs and swabbing, involving over 1,000 tests for Listeria from various points on all production lines, and throughout the plant. Courtesy of Maple Leaf Foods.

In its continuing effort to concentrate on safety and to let consumers know how they are directing this effort, in January, 2010, Maple Leaf named Peter Slade as Senior Director, Food Safety Technical Affairs. A microbiologist, Slade came to Maple Leaf with an extensive background in food safety. The announcement posted on the blog page said he would specifically be "responsible for working closely with each Maple Leaf business unit to identify opportunities to further mitigate potential food safety risks."

Blogs

DaveFleet.com has a blog "exploring the intersection of communications, marketing, and social media." Most of the bloggers about Maple Leaf were positive about the company and its response to the crisis. Fleet himself cited seven lessons learned from the crisis:

1. The CEO told his own story.
2. The CEO personally apologized in a video played on mainstream TV and YouTube.
3. The company recalled all of the tainted packaged meats (in question).
4. The company worked to improve inspection standards.
5. The CEO had well-thought out messages.
6. The communication was consistent.
7. The CEO was open.

Study of Consumers' Attitudes

Professor Terence Flynn of the DeGroote School of Business, McMaster University, headed the research team and wrote a study of the perceptions of more than 4,500 Canadians and how they felt about Maple Leaf Foods based on reputational opinions, loyalty, trust, and desire to do business with the company (Flynn, 2008).

Fieldwork was done following each of CEO McCain's thee major video announcements.

- August 27–September 5, 2008.
- September 26–29, 2008.
- January 8–12, 2008.

All persons participating were 18 or over and were stratified according to ages, gender, and the province in which they reside. The same questions were asked of each group. The study was dated January 29, 2009 (Flynn, 2009). Flynn's results are excerpted below.

Results showed that those participants who saw the video news release had significantly higher good opinion ratings of the company than did those who did not see the video (74% vs. 63%).

Of those who had previously purchased Maple Leaf Foods products 83% scored the company higher on credibility, food safety, and doing what they said they would do than those who had not purchased Maple Leaf products.

The study determined that companies should consider the following points in coping with crises:

- The impact of a credible spokesperson.
- The value of being crisis prepared.
- The effect of immediate communications.
- The desire and intention of doing the right thing and being transparent and in light of not only listening to the accountants and lawyers.
- The power of ongoing consumer/customer relationships and the value of a healthy and strong reputation.
- The connection between public relations/communications management and customer loyalty.

Case: Wendy's and the Finger-in-the-Chili Hoax

Denny Lynch, as Senior Vice-President of Communications for Wendy's International, faced a crisis that innocent food-based companies fear—a consumer commits a vicious act that causes other patrons to turn away from the restaurant or product.

In March 2005, Anna Ayala, then 39, a Las Vegas resident visiting San Jose, California, went to a Wendy's with relatives. She ordered a bowl of beef chili. She said she bit into a spoon of chili and "suddenly I chew something that's kind of hard, crunchy. I spit it out." She said that's when she realized the crunchy item was a 1½ inch human finger with a well-manicured nail. She hired a lawyer and sued.

Lynch received a phone call that night from Bob Bertini, Wendy's director of communications, explaining what happened. Lynch said he had no time to make a plan of action; he had to act immediately—the news media were calling. For the next 60 days, Lynch and Bertini spent many hours talking to the news media. Lynch said, "The pace was nonstop. Even when Pope John Paul II died, the incident still got coverage."

At first, sympathy was with Ms. Ayala. The Santa Clara County Health Department said she was ill and distraught. The spokesperson said, "She was so emotionally upset once she found out what it was. She was

vomiting." It also hurt Wendy's efforts when the health department immediately released photos of the finger to the news media. This made the picture people imagined very real, and national news coverage intensified. The health department did announce that there was no public health risk, but that was never the issue anyway.

Lynch was not new to crisis communications. In his 25 years at Wendy's, he was on the job when five workers were shot and killed in a Wendy's in Queens, New York.

So a Wendy's regional management team set up a makeshift control room in a franchise office in San Jose. The local police were involved, as was the coroner. Wendy's cooperated fully with the police and health officials, and did everything possible to assist them with their investigation from the earliest stages of the crisis.

As the news spread, patrons fled. A human finger found in food was not life-threatening—as in the Tylenol case when capsules had been laced with poison (see Chapter 7)—nor was it as frightening as a fear of AIDS—as in the Snapps case (see Chapter 6) when restaurant patrons heard a rumor that a manager with AIDS had bled into a hamburger. However, it was still a picture that people could not get past. "It was the gross-out factor," Lynch said. People could not eat chili without imagining there was a finger in it. Even people who knew it was extremely likely that it was a scam were still affected by the gross-out factor.

Wendy's is based in Dublin, Ohio, with 6,600 locations in North America. All its restaurants were affected but particularly those in the San Francisco Bay area. The company lost 20% to 50% of its business in the Bay area in the first month after the incident.

The *New York Times* called the crisis campaign "CSI: Wendy's." Wendy's checked its own employees and the employees of all its suppliers and quickly determined that no one in Wendy's supply plants or the restaurants had a missing finger. Lynch announced to the press, "All of our employees have ten digits." In addition there had been no reports made to the Occupational Safety and Health Administration of injuries at any supplier of the ingredients of Wendy's chili. (Wendy's chili is made from scratch in each restaurant.) The employee who prepared the chili had been with the same restaurant for 10 years and was respected for his dutiful work.

Wendy's crisis management strategy centered on four areas:

1. Conducting due diligence to establish the brand was not at fault.
2. Ensuring that Wendy's key company values drove all decisions and activities.
3. Briefing and mobilizing team members for quick action and response as events unfolded.
4. Building a post-incident campaign that enhanced Wendy's brand.

"Our position was that based on all the information we had, we strongly believed Wendy's was not responsible," Bertini said. "We cautioned the news media not to jump to conclusions, while deliberately avoiding fraud accusations against Ms. Ayala. We did not want to do anything that could jeopardize the police investigation."

So, feeling confident about Wendy's position, it became necessary to find out to whom the finger had belonged and vindicate the company publicly. In the spirit of a true TV mystery, talk went to "Where is the rest of the body?" Wendy's offered $50,000 and later a $100,000 reward for information leading to positive identification of the finger and announced that to the news media. Wendy's also contracted with an outside source to man a "tip line" operating 10 hours each day for reports.

Copycat cases sprang up with people claiming to have found other items in food at Wendy's—bones and fingernails were mentioned. The finger was fuel for jokes on late-night TV talk shows and conversation for daytime call-in radio shows. Jay Leno, on NBC's *The Tonight Show with Jay Leno*, said "I didn't know Wendy's sold finger food."

Immediately following the alleged incident, Ms. Ayala scheduled an appearance on ABC's *Good Morning America* to tell her story. This was the only such national program to have booked an interview with her. Wendy's tried to dissuade ABC from airing the interview because the story, at that point, would make Ayala look credible and would give her a national forum. However, the show refused to curtail its plans, and Wendy's representatives opted not to appear on camera with Ayala.

Nothing good could come from a conversation about the incident, especially as the police investigation was ongoing and the origin of the finger was still a mystery. Nevertheless, Lynch spent 3 hours on Easter Sunday night preparing a written statement that was read in its entirety on the show. The company's basic position was that the finger did not enter the food chain in its ingredients.

The employees at the San Jose restaurant had all their fingers, and no suppliers of Wendy's ingredients had any hand or finger injuries. If a Wendy's spokesperson had appeared, it could have left the viewing public with the attitude "Big company attacks poor innocent woman and won't admit it is wrong." Still, Ms. Ayala and her lawyer appeared, and anyone who had never heard the story before now heard it, and she was still considered the victim in the case.

People began to claim the finger and the reward. In one of the many bizarre twists in the case, a woman claimed she lost a finger in a leopard attack at an animal compound near Las Vegas. The woman said she last saw her middle finger when it was packed with ice in a plastic bag in hopes of reattaching it. When doctors told her it could not be reattached, she said she had "no idea what happened to the finger." The hospital

confirmed that she was there for a leopard attack and that it could not account for where the finger was. Her lawyer came forward saying, "She wants to participate in DNA testing and any final resolution of that matter." He stressed that his client had no connection with Ayala. This was investigated, but the woman's finger was longer than the one supposedly found in the chili, and the fingerprints did not match.

Then the story began to turn. The police continued to investigate, and the coroner began an investigation. In considering the preparation of the chili, first, the raw meat is turned into ground beef at the meatpacking plant. Nothing as long as one inch survives the process. The ground beef used in the chili is chopped into small chunks with a spatula, not even a sharp knife. The beans, from cans, are added along with seasonings and tomatoes. Then, the chili is made in a 22-quart pot and cooked for 4 to 6 hours; it is stirred every 15 minutes. The coroner said (and the health department concurred) that the finger "was not consistent with an object that had been cooked in chili at 170 degrees for hours."

The police discovered that Ms. Ayala was experienced at filing lawsuits against companies. She had been involved in at least six such cases, some in the San Francisco Bay area. One involved a sexual harassment suit against an auto dealership. That case ended when she had a dispute with her lawyer.

In another suit, she won a settlement against an El Pollo Loco restaurant in Las Vegas. She charged that her daughter became ill after eating in the restaurant, and she was paid for medical expenses. Police investigators said they found 13 civil actions involving Ayala and her children. She was involved in a criminal complaint charging that she sold a trailer she did not own to a woman in San Jose.

In early April, police went to Ayala's home to question her and, according to Ayala, she asserted that they were out to get her and were unnecessarily rough as they executed a search warrant at her home. The Associated Press reported that she said, "Lies, lies, lies—that's all I am hearing. They should look at Wendy's. What are they hiding? Why are we being victimized again?" A few days later, her lawyer said she had decided not to sue.

In mid-April, there was a press conference with Wendy's officials and the police. The police told the news media that they considered the claim a hoax. Ayala was arrested and held without bail at Clark County jail in Las Vegas. She was charged with attempted grand theft stemming from the fact that Wendy's had lost millions of dollars in sales because of a hoax devised by her.

Police said they found in their investigations that two people who knew Ayala said she described putting the finger in the chili. The descriptions were similar and the two people did not know each other. Also, Ayala's

family members who were with her at Wendy's said they did not see the finger in her mouth and noticed it only after she pointed to it in the cup. Two family members said they saw her spit it out and she vomited, but there was no evidence of that at the scene.

In May 2005, Wendy's was fully vindicated when police discovered the owner of the finger. A phone call to the hotline tipped police to speak to a male friend and coworker of Ayala's husband, Jaime Plascencia. The friend—Brian Rossiter—had lost a finger in an industrial accident the previous December. The finger was positively identified as belonging to Brian Rossiter, who had sold it to Plascencia for $100. Rossiter cooperated with police and told them the couple had offered him $250,000 to keep silent. The husband was arrested on identity theft charges unrelated to the Wendy's case, but was later also charged with conspiracy to file a false insurance claim and attempted grand theft with damages exceeding $2.5 million.

San Jose Police Chief Rob Davis declared, "The jig is up! The puzzle pieces are beginning to fall into place, and the truth is being exposed."

Soon afterwards Wendy's made a customer relations move, reaching out to customers in 50 Bay Area restaurants and offering each one a free Frosty and coupons. The approach was later expanded nationally with Wendy's giving away more than $15 to 18 million during a weekend to thank customers for their loyalty (see Figure 12.8). A column by Wendy's Chairman Jack Schuessler appeared that same week in the *Wall Street Journal* explaining how Wendy's defended its brand, at great cost, and would emerge stronger and better.

Both Ayala and Plascencia entered guilty pleas in September. At their sentencing hearing in January 2006, the Wendy's cashier, Jose Pacheco, said Ayala had asked whom he killed to get the finger and made him bear the brunt of her complaints. Hector Pineda, who made the chili, said "I felt so bad for the fear of what people would think of me. We are the ones who suffered."

Ayala was sentenced to 9 years in prison while her husband received a 12-year sentence. They also must pay $170,000 in restitution for the San Jose Wendy's workers' lost wages and $21.8 million to Wendy's International and JEM Management, which owns the restaurant. Both corporations agreed not to collect from the couple if they never benefit from the scam, including books and movies.

Lynch asked the judge to send a message that "consumer fraud is a serious crime that demands a severe penalty."

Looking back at the crisis, Lynch says that Wendy's "moved from a place where many people thought we were guilty to a point where they realized our employees and our brand had been victimized. Because of our actions, we hope people also now see us as a company that stood

Figure 12.8 The Dublin, Ohio-based fast-food chain gave away as many as 18 million frozen desserts on the weekend after the sentencing. "The turnout for the promotion exceeded our expectations," said spokesman Bob Bertini. "Throughout the weekend, there were long lines in our restaurants across the country." The company gave the desserts away to thank customers for their loyalty. Courtesy of Wendy's.

Figure 12.9 The celebration at the Wendy's restaurant following the hoax proved to be fun and uplifting for employees as well as customers. After struggling through the crisis, employees enjoyed hearing all of the positive reaction from the customers. Courtesy of Wendy's.

by its principles and endeavored to do the right thing when faced with enormous challenges."

In talking to *USA Today* about the crisis, Schuessler said, "We believe our reputation is the most important thing we have." He also said that during a crisis situation, companies have to have a set of core values because "there's no playbook that's been written."

Mini-Case: Domino's Pizza

Wendy's gross-out crisis was trumped in 2009 by a Domino's Pizza chain crisis that played out and was appropriately battled on social media networks.

Two Domino's employees (a man and a woman) in a Conover, North Carolina, restaurant filmed a tasteless extremely graphic prank and posted the video on YouTube. As the man defiled the delivery foods, the woman provided voiceover while operating the camera saying, "In about five minutes, it'll be sent out on delivery where somebody will be eating these, yes, eating them, and little will they know that the cheese was in his nose and that there was some lethal gas that ended up on their salami. Now, that's how we roll at Domino's."

The video soon became the hit of YouTube and was seen by millions of viewers and, no doubt, described to numerous others. Though disgusted, people would still look and still talk, even though reviled. At the time, a search of Google for "Domino" turned up stories of the incident on five of the 12 results on page one. On Twitter, there were many discussions about it.

A blogger alerted Domino's, and the two employees were immediately fired and arrested on felony charges. The woman issued an apology, which, naturally, was not accepted by Domino's or its consumers. The two said the tainted food products had not been delivered. Yet that disclaimer was not enough to prevent serious damage to Domino's reputation or its financial stability.

Domino's spokesperson Tim McIntyre said, "We got blind-sided by two idiots with a video camera and an awful idea. Even people who've been with us as loyal customers for 10, 15, 20 years are second guessing their relationship with Domino's, and that's not fair."

At first, Domino's chose to lay low and let the controversy die, but that didn't work even though YouTube removed the video. "What we missed was the perceptual mushroom effect of viral sensations," said McIntyre.

Scott Hoffman, chief marketing officer, Lotame, a social media marketing firm, said, "In social media, if you think it's not going to spread, that's when it gets bigger." In that respect, social media can be a modern form of spreading rumor (see Chapter 6).

Questions on Twitter were basically, "What did Domino's do about it?" So Domino's created a Twitter account to address comments. It also posted its own YouTube response featuring President Patrick Doyle who said:

> We thank members of the online community who quickly alerted us so we could take immediate action. The independent owner of that store is reeling from the damage that this has caused and it's not a surprise that this has caused a lot of damage to our brand. It sickens me that the actions of two individuals could impact our great system where 125,000 men and woman work for local business owners around the U.S. and more than 60 countries around the world.
>
> The store has been sanitized from top to bottom. Nothing is more sacred and important than our customers' trust, and we're examining our hiring practices to make sure that people like this don't make it into our stores. We have auditors in our store every day of the week making sure our stores are as clean as they can possibly be and that we're delivering high quality food to our customers, day in and day out.

Death and Injury

The following cases were prominently played in the news media because of the old saying in journalism circles, "If it bleeds, it leads." This means that news in which persons are killed is usually first on television news and headlines in newspapers. Such stories require careful communications.

Public relations professionals are expected to handle crises of violence, death, and injury with sensitivity that must be learned; it does not come naturally. Public relations organizations such as the Public Relations Society of America (PRSA) as well as large companies should offer employees simulated training in handling such crises . . . just in case it is necessary. Most professionals who have had these experiences speak of sleepless nights, nightmares, nervousness, and other symptoms of trauma.

Communications professionals must also realize that when their crises involve violence, death, and injury, reporters, though they may appear to just want the facts and to be indifferent to the incident, are often as emotional as the people about whom they write.

The case "Maple Leaf Foods and the Battle Against Listeria" on page 243 could also be in this category.

Case: Columbine High School and the Shooting Tragedy

To Rick J. Kaufman, APR, Executive Director of Jefferson County Public Schools in Colorado, April 20, 1999, began like many other work days. On this day there was a special community event. He and most of the district's administrative team attended a county-wide celebration of individuals and community groups for their outstanding contributions to Jefferson County.

When he returned to the office around 11 a.m., there was a call from a radio station. The station had heard on a police scanner that there had been a shooting at a school in the south part of the school district. Media calls of this nature were not an everyday occurrence, but it was not overly alarming either. Kids do have guns occasionally.

He and Barb Monseu, an assistant superintendent who oversaw the region of the county that included Columbine High School, immediately left for the school. Kaufman, who had been in his current position only 7 months, was not yet familiar with all 145 schools in the district. He only knew that Columbine was one of the high schools in the south area of the county and recalls, "We believed that a student had fired off a gun in the parking lot, or that there had been some sort of altercation. This was a school that, up to that time, we just did not believe something as tragic as the shooting would happen."

Columbine High School is one of the sprawling school district's top-performing schools, and has been rated among the top high schools in both academics and athletics in the state of Colorado. Its students come from upper middle-class families and it had a reputation as a "community-centered school" with a lot of parent involvement. It didn't fit the perception of an inner city or rural school where violence could occur.

"Columbine High School is a 30-minute drive from the district's educational services center (central office). We made it to the school in 15 to 20 minutes," said Kaufman. "We topped speeds of 100 miles per hour en route. All the way, we were trying to establish contact with the principal or someone at the school to determine what was taking place."

They had no idea why they couldn't reach anyone. They soon learned why. Columbine High School sits on a portion of Clement Park, a large community park and open space bordered by a residential area to the south, Pierce Street to the east, and Bowles Avenue, a six-lane highway, to the north. There were so many emergency responders—fire, police, paramedics, emergency helicopters to transport victims, and police helicopters trying to find the location of the shooters—that Kaufman and Monseu couldn't get close enough to the school. So they parked on Bowles Avenue and ran toward the school. "We heard what sounded like gun shots and explosions as we neared the building, though we didn't know if that was coming from police or someone from within the school," said Kaufman. "It was a very unsettling, and yet surreal experience."

Parents, who by now had heard media reports of shots fired at Columbine High School, were racing to the school as well, leaving parked vehicles on the two highways bordering the school and park. Students and school employees were fleeing out of the school in every direction throughout the park, having either witnessed or heard shooting. At this point, police did not have a perimeter secured around the school as they were trying to locate where the shooter or shooters were and tending to wounded students who had escaped the building. So Kaufman, a former emergency medical technician who had trained to be a paramedic,

went to the aid of a student who had been shot multiple times, and remembers:

> I checked his vitals, and when we couldn't get a pulse or response from this young man, with the help of two other first responders we basically dragged him and put him in a rescue vehicle. The rescue guys asked me if I wanted to ride along to the hospital, but there was nothing more I could do, so I said, "No." I did check his wallet for a student ID so I could write his name and address down, in case we would need to contact his parents. I truly thought he had perished but as it turns out, thankfully, he did survive after being shot seven times, including a shotgun blast to the face.

Eventually, responding law enforcement personnel from multiple agencies established a safe perimeter around the building to keep parents, bystanders, and media out of harm's way. Students and school staff continued to escape on their own, or were aided by police who had entered the building. Columbine High School principal Frank DeAngelis was able to escape, but not before encountering one of the shooters and then helping a number of students escape. Kaufman states:

> With Mr. DeAngelis' help, we were working with law enforcement drawing up a schematic layout of the school to be relayed to police who were inside of the building looking for the shooters and freeing students and staff who were trapped. We also started identifying potential students who might be responsible for the shooting, based on eyewitness accounts from those who had safely fled.

Kaufman also communicated information back to his office where a crisis command center had been established by the district's communications team and superintendent. In the immediate hours after the shooting began, Kaufman served as the liaison between school personnel and law enforcement at the crisis site and the district's command center.

Asked if he had a crisis communications plan or a crisis management plan, Kaufman replied, "The district certainly had a crisis plan in place and I had written a number of crisis plans for other school districts, but as the events unfolded, we didn't take the opportunity to pull out the plan and follow it to the letter." Kaufman did call on lessons learned from a mock crisis drill he had developed while working for a school district in Wisconsin prior to moving to Colorado in 1998:

> I had developed the first mock crisis drill of an attack on a school with the help of a local technical college and representatives from law enforcement, fire and hospital. We created a full-scale mock shooting

on a school to determine the effectiveness of our newly written crisis plan. We wanted to make sure the plan was sound. I learned a tremendous amount from that drill, and I called on what I had learned throughout our work and response to the Columbine tragedy.

What was most problematic at the time was that I was not in the district long enough to have conversations with law enforcement and public information officers to determine, in advance, what would be done when multiple agencies needed to respond to a crisis or emergency at one of our schools. We did not have the opportunity to determine, who does what, where, and when before the shooting.

Kaufman said that as the afternoon wore on, attempts to communicate with the district's command center or other responders via cell phone were nearly futile because of the sheer volume of cell phone traffic in the area:

Whenever we were able to establish a connection, there were times when we would be cut off in midsentence. Often, it took repeated calls to give or receive information from the command center, or request assistance. That was one of the most frustrating aspects of our work that day—the lack of the ability to communicate information as well as access to things we needed.

Kaufman said he knew early on that the news media's focus would be on events as they unfolded and that the criminal aspect would require law enforcement personnel to respond initially. The news media, after such a violent incident, were interested in what was happening, who was killed, who was injured, and who was responsible. From the school district's perspective, media needed only the basics, such as the size and layout of the school, the number of students attending, the staff who worked in the building, and names of students who might have been injured or killed.

Said Kaufman, "I knew early on that we would not be media's primary focus. It was really the police, the public information officers who would take the lead in disseminating the initial information because this was a major crime scene."

Kaufman, and later Marilyn Saltzman, a staff member of the district's communications department, were the initial district spokespersons. Saltzman, manager of communications, worked with the news media that had sent teams of reporters and photographers to the site, while Kaufman continued to assist law enforcement at the school: "We established a location near the school, but outside the police perimeter, for media to gather and receive updates from both law enforcement and district personnel" (see Figure 13.1).

Figure 13.1 Rick Kaufman answers questions from the national media gathered at a news conference about the shooting at Columbine High School. Years later, Kaufman and his staff still get questions from publications and other school districts about the incident. Courtesy of Jefferson County Public School.

At the district's Educational Services Center, communications department staffers, with help from school public relations professionals from Denver metro-area school districts, established a volunteer phone bank to handle the hundreds of calls that were coming into the district asking for information and offering help.

Superintendent of Schools Jane Hammond had also pulled together an emergency response team of school board members, principals, and central office administrators who worked to calm the fears of other school personnel and parents throughout the district. Early on, a rumor had circulated that the Columbine shooting was a coordinated attack and that others might have planned similar attacks at multiple school sites throughout the district.

"Remember, this was before the 9/11 attacks so there were certainly no thoughts that this was a terrorist attack. But rumors were quick to be formed and shared because of the awful news coming out of what was happening at Columbine High School. Those rumors had to be refuted at the other schools as well as to the mass public," said Kaufman.

The attack on Columbine High School garnered national and international media attention, as well as round-the-clock coverage in Colorado. Kaufman said, "It was one of those seminal events that dominated media attention 24/7. It was crucial to dispel any erroneous information before

it got out. We weren't necessarily successful, but we worked very hard to ensure that whatever information the school district shared publicly was corroborated and not based on hearsay."

Parent relocation sites were set up at a nearby elementary school and a public library. Students who were able to flee the school were reconnected with their parents at these two sites. At the same time, Kaufman and others were attempting to account for all students and staff. "It wasn't until early evening, 5 or 6 p.m. [Mountain Standard Time], that we received word there were multiple fatalities. It wasn't until much later in the evening that we were able to account for those who had made it out safely." However, school district leaders still did not know the condition of those hospitalized, or even how many had been transported to medical facilities. So the information was still incomplete.

It was also that night that the district learned the names of the alleged shooters. There was still concern, however, that there might be others involved, and that information was not easy to reveal. Kaufman said:

> We had pretty good knowledge based on law enforcement sources that [Dylan] Klebold and [Eric] Harris [both seniors attending Columbine High School] were the alleged shooters because they had committed suicide in the library. Law enforcement didn't feel comfortable confirming this information because this was still a very active crime scene and, after all the shooting had stopped, the investigation was just getting underway.

Later that evening, Kaufman returned to the district's command center where he briefed the superintendent and the assembled district emergency response team on the day's events from the school. He also coordinated the development of initial information that would be disseminated to parents, the community, and the news media the next day. The reporters and photographers who responded to the shooting were, for the most part, local media or national news bureaus based in Denver who fed other national affiliates with the stories and pictures. But Kaufman said that on Day 2, the morning after the shootings:

> The nationals were already setting up in the park adjacent to the school when I arrived at 3 a.m. We were getting a lot of requests to do interviews or to arrange to have students and staff go on these national morning news shows. We refrained from doing that because we were still in the mode of collecting information and trying to determine what happened. We didn't have a complete account. We were not going to provide information that could have been perceived as speculative still at that point. It would not have served us well to do that, so we limited our access to interviews, and those we did, were very brief factual statements.

On Day 2, a joint press conference was held with the Jefferson County Sheriff's Office, the lead law enforcement agency; the Jefferson County District Attorney's office; and the school district. Kaufman said:

> It was our first opportunity to express our condolences to the families of those murdered and our concern for those students and staff who were injured, to put a human face to the sadness we were feeling and experiencing. We used the opportunity to share some information about what we knew had happened, but more importantly how we were responding to students and staff needs. We wanted to be up front with as much information as we could as it became available, and when we could corroborate it and substantiate it, and that's what we shared.

On the third day after the shooting, the weather turned to dark skies and heavy snow. "The weather was a reflection of what we were feeling. Our hearts were very heavy for the victims and the community, and we knew we were entering into some very difficult days ahead with the funerals," said Kaufman. It was also at this time that Kaufman realized he didn't have enough staff trained in crisis response to adequately manage the crisis. He turned to his friend and colleague, Rich Bagin, the Executive Director of the National School Public Relations Association based in Rockville, Maryland, to help coordinate school public relations professionals from across the country who would commit their time and expertise to aiding Kaufman's crisis response team.

Superintendent Hammond created two emergency response teams. One, headed up by Kaufman, concentrated on all the media relations and communications and worked directly with schools, parents, community, religious organizations, and others. The second response team, headed up by assistant superintendent Monseu, coordinated the mental health and grief counseling for students and staff, and worked to arrange for Columbine students to return to a neighboring school for the remainder of the school year.

The following is Kaufman's report of the campaign and is reproduced with Rick Kaufman's permission.

The Columbine Tragedy: Managing the Unthinkable— Project Summary

Assessment

The tragic shooting of 12 students and a beloved teacher at Columbine High School on April 20, 1999, created unforgettable experiences for the thousands of students, staff, and community residents of Jefferson

County, Colorado. The tragic events of that day and subsequent weeks thrust the Jefferson County Public Schools' Communications Team into the spotlight as the core communicators for a community and organization in crisis. While managing speculation and rumor perpetuated by more than 750 media outlets from across the world, this team of public relations professionals helped to restore calm and confidence to their organization and healing to the community during what history may label as the defining tragedy of our time.

The Jefferson County Public Schools' Communications Services team developed a crisis communications structure that established key duties and protocols in a crisis. This plan was adapted as a result of the nature and magnitude of the Columbine High School tragedy and continues to be revised to reflect lessons learned from this tragedy and its aftermath.

The Jeffco Public Schools' Communications Team consisted of six professionals and support staff when the tragedy struck, but received volunteer assistance from members of the Colorado and National School Public Relations Associations.

COMMUNICATION OBJECTIVES

The overall public relations objective throughout the crisis was to quickly adjust the school district and community's position from one of response and reaction to one of proactive control, enabling the team to aid in school and community healing. To attain this objective, the Jeffco Public Schools' Communications Team:

- Provided onsite guidance and leadership to students and staff.
- Developed key communication vehicles to reassure parents and the community.
- Strengthened proven strategies to propel those affected beyond the crisis to learn and grow stronger.
- Communicated the school and district's point of view with professional grace and insight.
- Reinforced the healing process, while aiding in return-to-education objectives.
- Cultivated a semblance of triumph in the face of tragedy.

While juggling demands from the news media at an unimaginable rate, the driving force behind every decision and event remained the motivation to help students and staff heal and return to the learning process as quickly as possible.

Another objective was to demonstrate and emphasize the school district's commitment to the emotional and physical needs of affected faculty, staff, students, and the families of the murdered and injured students and teacher.

TIMELINE OF COLUMBINE TRAGEDY AND ITS AFTERMATH

The attack on Columbine High School on April 20, 1999, left 12 students and a teacher dead, and 23 others wounded. Some liken the attack to an "earthquake" because of its devastation on individuals, families, and a community. As the days, weeks, and months following the tragedy came and went, so too did the "aftershocks" that have impeded the students, staff and community's ability to heal and return to normal.

To follow is a timeline of highs and lows in the year after the tragedy.

April 20, 1999
Two students attack Columbine High School killing 12 fellow classmates, a teacher, and wounding 23 others in the worst school shooting in U.S. history.

April 25, 1999
Statewide memorial service pays tribute to the fallen students and teacher with then-Vice President Al Gore and other state and national dignitaries. Over 75,000 people attend the event.

May 2, 1999
Jeffco Public Schools holds special remembrance memorial for the victims of the Columbine tragedy at Red Rocks Amphitheater. Several hundred students, staff, and community members attend the solemn event.

May 3, 1999
Columbine High School students and staff return to classes at sister school Chatfield Senior High.

May 20, 1999
On the 1-month anniversary, President Bill Clinton and First Lady Hillary Clinton visit the Columbine victims' families in a private meeting, then pay tribute to the victims and survivors at a special memorial.

August 17, 1999
Columbine High School students and staff return to "Take Back Our School" for the start of the 1999–2000 school year.

September 24, 1999
CBS News airs portion of cafeteria surveillance videotape it obtained from an Albuquerque, NM television station that captured the chaotic scenes of students fleeing the school. The videotape was being used as part of a law enforcement training exercise.

October 20, 1999
Columbine High School marks the 6-month anniversary with news that a student who was a friend of the killers has been arrested for allegedly making a threat at the school.

Figure 13.2 This was the timeline of the work of Rick Kaufman and his communications staff at the Jefferson County School District in Colorado for the first year after the tragedy that resulted in the deaths of several students and a teacher and the injuries of others. Courtesy of Jefferson County School District.

October 22, 1999
The mother of critically injured student Anne Marie Hochhalter commits suicide at an area store.

December 4, 1999
Columbine High School captures 5A high school football championship, capping season dedicated to Matt Kechter, one of the slain students and a member of the football team.

December 13, 1999
Time Magazine cover story carries excerpts from videotapes made by murderers outlining attack on Columbine High School, including cover photo of perpetrators in the cafeteria. Article surprised community, and students and staff, who were caught off-guard by the release of the information. Neither Jeffco Public Schools nor Columbine High School had been given advance warning of the contents of the article.

December 15, 1999
Student receives Internet threat that claims to "finish the job begun" on April 20, 1999. District cancels classes at Columbine High School for next 2 days, sending students and staff to an earlier than expected holiday break.

February 14, 2000
Two Columbine students found murdered in Subway Sandwich Shop located near the high school. Students informed by teachers of identity of the murdered students during second period class, prompting many students to leave the school or seek counseling. No arrests made to date.

April 20, 2000
Columbine High School and community mark 1-year anniversary with private and public events. Many students choose to stay away from public events because of the intense media coverage.

April 27, 2000
Jefferson County district attorney makes available to public (for $25) a videotape of Littleton Fire Department "training" video that depicts graphic scenes from the library and other parts of the school and video footage from a news helicopter. Columbine High School staff is shown the tape and a warning is issued to parents of the impending public release.

May 4, 2000
Popular student-athlete commits suicide at his home.

May 15, 2000
The Jefferson County Sheriff's Office releases its long-awaited report—by court order—on the tragic events of April 20, 1999. The report is issued on a CD-ROM because of its extensive notes and information, including videotape footage, excerpts from 911 calls, and law enforcement traffic and audio recordings.

Figure 13.2 continued

Planning

- Assisted, prior to the tragedy, in the development of a district crisis management plan, including an emergency response checklist of steps for the first 24- to 48-hour period after a crisis.
- Consulted with school administrative and PR officials from each of the prior school shooting sites, and with the National School Public Relations Association, the National Organization of Victims Assistance, and the Crisis Prevention Institute to identify strategies of crisis response and management.
- Organized briefing with district management team, school board officials, employee association representatives, and community leaders to review responsibilities outlined in the crisis management plan, including the establishment of two command centers—an on-site communications center (near Columbine) and a central operations center.
- Participated in daily briefings with law enforcement, state and federal emergency management agencies, and governmental groups to coordinate the ongoing crisis response and management.
- Created a database of media outlets that contacted the district for information and interviews, and used this list to distribute updates on the district's response to the tragedy and its efforts to help the community heal and return to normal. The media list was used frequently to distribute information on how the school's students and staff, and the community were healing and moving forward.
- Analyzed media coverage daily throughout the crisis to evaluate how Jeffco Public Schools' messages were received and to assess changes in media attitude and public perception.

Target Audiences: Parents, students, faculty and staff, media, state and federal legislators, the Jefferson County community, and the residents of Colorado.

Communication

STRATEGIES

- Implemented a Crisis Communications Command Structure. The structure designated primary functions for managing the crisis, including strategic communication counsel, internal and external communication, media management, research and media monitoring, event management, and coordinating volunteers.
- Created several methods for communicating with parents, students, employees, business and community leaders, political and govern-mental officials, and the public, and continually updated those methods for efficacy.

- Responded promptly and honestly to requests for information and interviews from the media, and anticipated changes in news cycles and demands.
- Apprised daily all staff throughout the 89,000-student district of the status of the investigation and recovery milestones. Spoke with "one clear voice" and "stayed on message" as determined by the district's management team and developed by the district's communications team.

TECHNIQUES/ACTIVITIES

- Responded to more than 1,000 inquiries a day from local, national, and international media outlets for the first 4 weeks after the tragedy, and continued to maintain contacts to update media about recovery efforts. Coordinated the media efforts for the special first day back to school event in August 1999, and planned all events to mark the first through fifth year anniversaries.
- Managed all communications, including twice-daily press conferences and daily fact sheets and news releases, distributed throughout the state and nation. Drafted daily talking points for district spokespersons.
- Established one-on-one opportunities with local reporters to interview key district personnel involved in the recovery efforts, and to strengthen the relationships with local journalists who remained long after national and international media left.
- Created weekly talking points for administrative staff at 143 other district schools to share with staff and parents.
- Met daily with legal and administrative management teams to formulate key messages and address emerging issues.
- Created a community hotline designated to accept offers of monetary contributions, donations of materials, and services from around the world. In the first 3 weeks after the crisis, the crisis command center received over 1,000 phone calls a day.
- Assisted in the development of a Columbine Tribute Web Page, and created a videotape showing the positive images of recovery to replace the negative images that were repeatedly aired on local and national media.
- Coordinated special events, including two large memorial services, separate visits by then President Bill Clinton and Vice President Al Gore, tours of the reconstructed school, and the "Take Back Our School" first day of school assembly.
- Developed a presentation—*The Columbine Crisis: Managing the Unthinkable*—for school district officials, emergency responders, and law enforcement officers.

Evaluation

The school district's communications and management team personnel did their solemn, professional best in a difficult situation and emotional environment. In the ongoing efforts, the team focused on the district's mission to help students, staff, and the community heal and recover, and share the story of our efforts with all key audiences. Further examples of how we achieved our objectives:

- We always kept the feelings of the victims' families in the forefront. Today many of our district leaders have personal relationships with families of the murdered and injured students and teachers based on our work with them.
- Target audiences read or saw Jeffco Public Schools' messages in more than 1,550 print stories (primarily local and large national publications) and 450 broadcast stories. A database of all the media coverage was created and exceeds 700 pages.
- Public perception both locally and nationally was positive and supportive of the district's crisis response based on letters from former President Bill Clinton, private organizations, national media, and community sentiment.
- A strong working relationship was developed with the Jefferson County Sheriff's Office, the Jefferson Center for Mental Health, the Jeffco and Federal Emergency Management agencies, and the FBI.
- Hundreds of requests have been received from organizations for crisis management training. Members of the district's communications and management teams have presented nearly 100 seminars and training sessions since August 1999. Organizations requesting presentations/training include the FBI, Los Angeles County law enforcement agencies and school districts, state emergency and educational associations, and the U.S. Department of Education.
- A special "Welcome Back to School" event and picnic for all staff was developed to celebrate the accomplishments of recovery. Over 2,000 staff attended the event, which included the planting of a tree and placement of a commemorative plaque on a large boulder in memory of Dave Sanders, the only teacher killed in the April 1999 tragedy.

The tragedy was very emotional for everyone connected. No one on Kaufman's staff had family at Columbine, but that didn't eliminate the emotional impact. Kaufman said one of his staff members had to be put on a medical leave of absence for a brief time because of the heart-wrenching concern for others had impacted on him personally. Grief counselors helped employees deal with their emotions throughout the response effort.

Kaufman himself said he ran on adrenaline, like most crisis communicators. He said:

> I didn't sleep for the first 4 days. I mean, I literally did not lay my head down to sleep for 4 days. In hindsight, that was dumb, because when you start coming down off that adrenaline, you're going to crash and make mistakes in your work and decision making. I was responsible for so many people that we started to work in shifts. I forced people, including myself, to start rotating work on and off times. Often we would only get 3–4 hours of sleep, but it was enough to keep us going. We needed to take care of ourselves because it was apparent that this tragedy had legs far beyond anything we had ever experienced.

The media calls continued long after the students returned to school. Marilyn Saltzman had a friendly wager with a friend in the media: The day that the district's communications team did not receive a call or request for information about the Columbine shooting would be the day she and her friend would go to lunch. It was June 2000, a year and 2 months after the incident that the communications team went a whole day without a single inquiry about the tragedy.

Today, the inquiries continue. "I receive, on average, at least one to two Columbine-related calls or e-mails each week," said Kaufman, who continued:

> It might be a parent asking if we can help them because they learned a student in their school had a hit list, or a teacher or emergency responder that wants to know what we did, or what policies we have put in place to prevent another tragedy. I feel a sense of responsibility to never turn away a request for information. We aren't experts at crisis management and communication, but we learned enough about it to help others. If nothing else, callers have told me it is comforting to them to know that we endured and we survived.

And then every year, the news media does their anniversary stories.

Update: Recent Commentary

Dave Cullen, author of *Columbine* and a journalist who covered the massacre, followed his original coverage with 9 years of research including hundreds of interviews, 25,000 pages of police evidence, video and audio tapes, and numerous articles and reports by other journalists.

Cullen praised much of the news coverage; many, he felt, were deserving of the numerous awards won by journalists and photographers.

DANIEL
ROHRBOUGH, 15,
pitched in at his
dad's electronics
shop and the

Kansas. He was
shot after doubl
back to the
cafeteria to h

Figure 13.3 In Littleton, Colorado, a memorial to a student killed in the Columbine High School massacre is adorned with flowers by loved ones. This photo was taken in 2000 on the first anniversary of the incident. Sisse Brimerg. Permission by Getty Images.

However, he writes also of the media errors. He said the most accurate story was the first story in the now-defunct *Rocky Mountain News*. The special edition of the newspaper covered the incident on day one before the bodies had been found.

Often, the first news story after a crisis is full of "holes." Facts have not yet been determined and assumptions, observations, and often opinions of police and other experts are used to put together the most reasonable story possible. The story is chock full of "he said" and "according to" phrases. In the Columbine massacre coverage, Cullen believes the opposite was true. That first story was accurate; then the errors began.

In later news stories, the two shooters were called members of the Trench Coat Mafia (TCM), a band of gay Goths with heavy makeup who were school misfits. This was discovered later to be untrue. There was a TCM presence at the school, and since the shooters wore trench coats, a few students assumed they were part of the group. The news media repeated the claim. Then more students "knew" it was true because the news media said so. The error was repeated so often that most people all over the world still believe the killers were members of the TCM.

There were other media mistakes. The killers did not target jocks, people wearing white hats, or minorities. One emotional survivor had

said that, but what she apparently meant was they were shooting randomly, that among those shot were athletes, hat wearers, and minorities. In this situation, the survivor speaking was a non-expert expert. She was widely believed because people wanted facts and because she had been in the midst of the massacre and survived.

When Columbine High School was scheduled to reopen, the school community planned a ceremony to be titled "Take Back our School" (see the timeline in Figure 13.2). The students felt the school was synonymous to "mass murder" and that they had been termed bullies or pompous rich kids. In the ceremony of "Take Back our School," they had to take back the school from an enemy. The news media was chosen as that adversary. Cullen said, "The news media had made their lives hell." The coverage was never-ending, both local and national. "How do you feel?" was asked over and over. However, when reporters converged this time, a shield of parents and community members blocked reporters from the event.

Kaufman bluntly told reporters that the human chain was there to shield students from the news media. Reporters were, of course, angry. Eventually, a compromise was made and students who wished to were permitted to approach reporters; reporters agreed not to approach students. Cullen and Kaufman said the school felt victorious.

Case: Metro Transit: Driver Shot, Bus Flies Off a Bridge

It was November 26, the day after Thanksgiving, 1998. Dan Williams, media relations specialist for Metro Transit in Seattle (a division of the King County Department of Transportation), was preparing to take his children to an afternoon movie when the phone rang. It was a reporter from the *Seattle Post-Intelligencer* asking if Williams knew anything about an accident involving a bus on the Aurora Bridge (see Figure 13.4).

Williams had been with the county agency for 15 years, 12 as media relations specialist in the office of the director of Metro Transit. He was one of only two media relations specialists who reported to Ron Posthuma, assistant deputy director of Metro Transit, who reported to Director Paul Toliver.

Williams first thought that the call was routine. In a city where buses are so crucial, accidents happen. Metro Transit had 1,600 full-time drivers and 750 part-time drivers. Also, it was after 3 p.m., peak traffic hours. Approximately 1,000 buses are in operation during peak hours, most of them heading into or away from the downtown area. Because of the holiday weekend, traffic was somewhat less congested. Williams told the reporter he hadn't heard anything, but promised to get back to him. It also was not unusual to get calls about accidents from reporters because newsrooms regularly monitor (police) radio scanners.

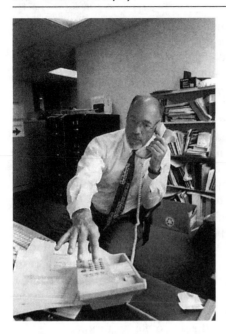

Figure 13.4
Dan Williams, media relations specialist for Metro Transit, served as primary spokesperson during the 1998 bus tragedy, in which a Metro bus driver was shot and the bus plunged off Aurora Bridge in Seattle. Reprinted with permission of Dan Williams.

"I called our control center not really expecting anything out of the ordinary," said Williams. "Our coordinators have a lot of people to notify in case of an accident, and they must also communicate by radio to personnel at the scene of the accident. Calmly, the coordinator told me that the driver of a bus southbound on Aurora Avenue had been shot, the bus veered off the bridge, the driver had been ejected and was receiving medical treatment on the roof of a building where he fell, and there were multiple injuries to passengers."

Aurora Bridge is one of the tallest bridges in Seattle, a city of bridges. It is commonly called Suicide Bridge because it is the bridge of choice for people who want to take their own lives. There were so many suicide jumps from the Aurora that the news media stopped covering them for fear that the victims, through jumping, were seeking a strange kind of publicity or fame. The bridge is also part of Aurora Avenue, a major thoroughfare connecting the northwest section of the city to the downtown area. On both ends, the bridge spans houses and other structures; in the center, it towers 175 feet above Lake Union (see Figures 13.5. and 13.6).

After learning of the accident, Williams said:

> My immediate reaction was to suppress whatever shock I was beginning to feel and do whatever was necessary to get to the scene as soon as possible. I made a quick call to neighbors and dropped

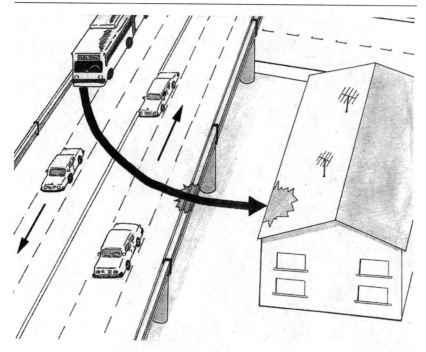

Figure 13.5 Sketch of route of bus headed over the bridge embankment. The 60-foot Metro Transit bus was traveling southbound toward downtown Seattle when a passenger in the front of the bus shot the driver. The bus then swerved into oncoming traffic on Aurora Bridge, crashed through a guardrail, and plunged about 45 feet, striking the roof of an apartment building before coming to rest on the front lawn of that building. The driver, the assailant, and another passenger died of injuries. Drawing by Gina Arnold. Reprinted with permission.

my kids at their house. Television news helicopters were circling the accident scene, just a half mile from my house. I didn't call the reporter right away because I didn't have enough information.

Williams arrived at the scene about 30 minutes after the time of the accident. He described the scene as follows:

The bus was resting upright in the front yard of a house. Emergency medical crews were removing victims from the bus and laying them on blankets and stretchers under the bridge; two or three of the most severely injured had already been taken to hospitals. The rest were being evaluated and treated at the scene. The bus driver was still receiving treatment on the roof of the house [where he had landed]. The Seattle Police Department had taped off the area, keeping media

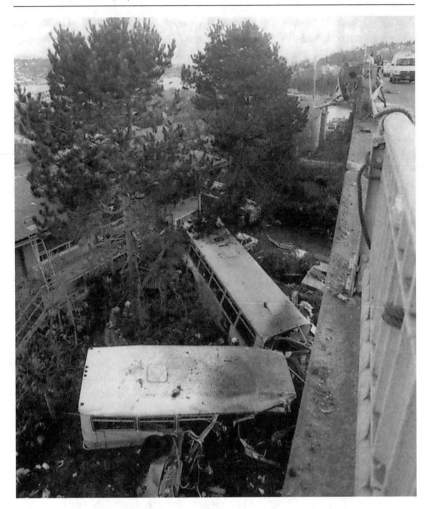

Figure 13.6 The 40,000-pound Metro Transit bus broke into two after it fell from Aurora Bridge in Seattle. Three people died and 29 passengers were injured, some seriously. Fortunately, no one on the ground was injured. Reprinted with permission from the *Seattle Post-Intelligencer*.

and onlookers about a block away. Detectives were beginning their investigation.

Williams learned that an assailant had shot the bus driver, sending the southbound 60-foot-long (so long it bends in the middle), 40,000-pound bus across oncoming northbound traffic, traffic that would have been heavier at that time of the afternoon had it not been for the holiday. The bus crashed through two sections of iron and concrete guardrails and

shot through the air, temporarily landing on top of a two-story apartment building near the bridge, where the driver was ejected. But then the bus bounced off the roof and broke in two: The front part of the bus landed on the steps of the apartment building, and the back part landed upright on a front lawn.

The driver, 44-year-old Mark McLaughlin, died of his injuries. The assailant apparently died of a self-inflicted bullet wound, but his identity was not known until the next day. The 33 passengers had various injuries; one later died of his injuries. Miraculously, no non-passenger was injured.

The Friday following Thanksgiving is normally a "slow news day." Very few events, press conferences, or speeches are scheduled because many people take the day off as part of a 4-day Thanksgiving weekend. Newscasts usually consist of soft news and features; it's a good day for public relations professionals to get their video news releases aired. But this was not a typical holiday weekend. Soft news, features, and video news releases were bumped by this breaking news event. Because the combination of a shooting, an accident, a bus off a bridge, and relatively low loss of life was so unusual, the story was carried by news outlets all over the United States.

The accident occurred at 3:15 p.m., and shortly thereafter local television news operations began covering the accident with live breaking news reports. Some stations preempted regular broadcasting and were on the air continuously through their evening newscasts. After the network news programs (some of which also ran the story), the local stations returned to air more live coverage from the scene.

Precrisis Customer Relations

Before the accident, Metro Transit had established a customer relations program that included three separate phone lines: (a) a 24-hour telephone service providing bus route information and trip planning called "Rider Information"; (b) an automated phone system providing bus schedule information called "Bus Time"; and (c) a Customer Service Office handling customer complaints and commendations.

Customers using the Rider Information service were routed to a recorded menu of options without talking to a real person, although it was also possible to talk to a real person. The system was designed to free operators to respond to more complex questions about the transit system. Customers could listen to the recorded information and then stay on the line to speak with a live operator.

Metro Transit received more than 2 million calls in 1998. Williams believed the system contributed to customer loyalty. He also said the drivers were considered an integral part of the customer relations program: "They are the agency's main connection to customers. They are

the 'face' of Metro to the public. Metro's philosophy in hiring and training is that driving skills can pretty much be taught to anyone, but it is people skills that are of primary importance."

Precrisis Employee Relations

Metro Transit bus drivers are members of the Amalgamated Transit Union Local 587. Metro's contract with the union stipulates processes for grievances, complaints, and so on. In addition, there are committees on which employees can serve to work with management on such issues as security and safety. From each of seven bus operations/maintenance bases, a driver and a maintenance employee of the month are selected. At the end of the year, those employees select the bus driver and maintenance employees of the year from among the monthly winners. The winners' photographs are posted on all the buses, along with a blurb citing their outstanding work.

Precrisis Community Relations

At the time of the accident, Metro Community Relations was in the midst of conducting a hands-on planning process in communities throughout King County. In addition, Metro Community Relations developed and staffed the Public Safety Partnership program, wherein volunteer bus drivers attended community meetings to discuss ways to make buses safer for customers and drivers, what people could do to protect themselves, and how they could help Metro Transit identify and prosecute people who committed crimes on the bus.

Prodromes

Metro's history of assaults and robberies during the 1980s resulted in demands from the drivers for better security. Metro then developed its own security force for its buses, patrol cars, and bus stops. There were seven traffic-related fatalities involving buses in the 1990s, prior to the accident; none involved passengers. There were serious bus accidents causing injuries to passengers. In 1978, five people were hospitalized and 67 were injured in three buses involved in a sequence of rear-end collisions on a freeway. In 1981, a bus with defective brakes crashed into a collapsible barrier, slightly injuring 20 passengers. In 1979, two cars collided with a bus, hospitalizing six people. In 1967, a driver was shot and killed after an assailant had committed a robbery on a bus.

Williams said that Metro took security issues very seriously and was continually improving its programs: "Our system is relatively safe, compared to similar systems in other cities. Assaults are rather infrequent,

considering the amount of service on the streets and the number of passengers carried. We consider crime a community problem, not just a transit problem." Following the 1998 crisis, Metro Transit distributed a chart to the media showing the relative safety records of public bus systems in Seattle and other cities (see Table 13.1).

Media Relations Ideology

Williams had established relationships with news media personnel and believed he and his office were known for their credibility. Many of these relationships developed over years of working for the same agency, whereas others with key news media personnel he purposefully developed. He described his media relations ideology as follows: "Honesty and responsiveness are key to good media relations. If you adhere to those two concepts, you develop trust and credibility with reporters and editors."

Crisis Management Plan

In 1998, Metro Transit did not have a crisis communications plan. However, its emergency procedures included a plan for notifying top management and media relations personnel in the event of a crisis. The media relations personnel were to take appropriate action: notifying the news media, reporting to the scene of the emergency, contacting other staff members, identifying a spokesperson, and so on. The Media

Table 13.1 National Transit Database—1996 Security Statistics

Transit Systems (Comparable Cities/Fleets)	Robbery		Aggravated Assault	
	Drivers	Passengers	Drivers	Passengers
King County Metro (Seattle)	1	0	0	3
Phoenix	7	4	2	0
Oakland	8	11	1	35
Houston	3	2	3	17
Salt Lake City	5	0	0	0
San Diego	18	48	0	8
Boston	63	18	0	10
Minneapolis	45	11	2	26
Pittsburgh	16	3	0	6
Portland	1	7	0	7
Tacoma (Pierce Transit)	1	0	3	3

Note. This chart was effective in getting positive coverage of Metro Transit's security system after the 1998 bus tragedy. Reporters and editors were able to see how the city's bus system compared to other bus systems in cities of comparable size.

Source: Printed with permission of Dan Williams.

Relations Department followed its own guidelines, which stated that its personnel would be available to respond to emergencies 24 hours a day.

Steps after the Tragedy

Williams said that at the accident scene, his first step was to find Metro personnel who could give him details of the accident:

> After about 10 minutes, I learned that the driver was dead. After establishing some very basic facts—bus route number, direction of travel, circumstances of the accident—I went to look for the police department public information officer, Christie Lynn Bonner. Bonner told me that the fire department had established the initial command post, so together we went to look for the fire department public information officer, Sheila Strehle.

Williams, Bonner, and Strehle met briefly to share information about the cause of the accident, the crime involved, the number of injured passengers, and so forth. They knew that each of them would be approached by the media and that it was imperative that they all had the same information. It would have been disastrous if they had told different stories; the reporters would then not trust any one of them.

Together, the three PR people for Metro Transit, the police department, and the fire department faced the media. Each answered questions specific to his or her respective agency. This was an excellent professional move. No one was trying to be the star of the crisis; their shared goal was to get the story told accurately and to help ensure that each agency would be perceived well by the media and the public for effective communications. As Williams explained:

> Our initial news conference was held around 4 p.m., about 45 minutes after the accident. The five local television stations—KING-5 (an NBC affiliate), KOMO-4 (an ABC affiliate), KIRO-7 (a CBS affiliate), KSTW-11, and KCPQ—each had at least two crews at the scene. The local papers—*Seattle Times*, *Seattle Post-Intelligencer*, and *Tacoma News Tribune*—were present, as was the *New York Times*, the Associated Press, the television news magazine *Dateline NBC*, and several radio stations.
>
> After the initial news conference, I spent the rest of the evening gathering information as it became available, communicating with agency personnel at the scene and by cell phone, conferring with the other agency public information officers at the scene, doing interviews with reporters, and making plans for the next day. I communicated with Rochelle Ogershok, public affairs coordinator for [the] King

County Department of Transportation, by phone. She worked with Elaine Kraft, communications director for King County Executive Ron Sims, to issue a statement from Sims expressing sorrow for the victims. Sims and Transit General Manager Rick Walsh visited victims at Harborview Medical Center and spoke to reporters there.

The primary demand for information was in three areas—the homicide, the rescue-medical operation, and transit security. After the initial news conference, Williams said, the three primary spokespeople—fire department, police department, and Metro Transit—responded to media questions about their own areas and issues in separate interviews. He said, "The three of us would get together throughout the evening to compare notes and exchange information. We had an agreement that we would stick to our own areas of expertise and refer reporters to each other rather than answer questions about each other's areas."

Most of the printed material that Williams distributed to the media in the days following the accident included statistics from the transit security database, in response to specific requests from reporters. The statistics covered things such as bus routes with the most security incidents, the frequency of particular kinds of incidents, and the number and categories of incidents that occurred on Route 359 (the route of the bus in the accident). Williams said he turned over the entire security database to the *Seattle Times*.

Some of the written documents included the following: (a) a security program fact sheet, (b) security statistics from the National Transit Database (see Table 13.1), (c) a joint management–union statement on transit security, (d) incident reports by a Metro bus driver who identified the assailant as a person who had pulled a gun in a previous incident, (e) reports from Metro agents detailing follow-up surveillance work after that incident, and (f) an op-ed piece written by Metro Transit Manager Rick Walsh summarizing Metro's security improvements over the past years.

There were also impromptu briefings of the media at the accident site and at Harborview Medical Center, where most of the injured passengers were taken. There was a joint news conference on Saturday, the day after the accident, with Walsh and Barry Samet, president of the Amalgamated Transit Union Local 587. On the following Monday, there was another news conference for the distribution of the joint statement on transit security.

Newspaper Coverage

On Saturday, November 27, the day following the shooting and accident, coverage in the city's two major daily newspapers, the *Seattle Times* and *Seattle Post-Intelligencer* was extensive.

The *Seattle Times'* front page, which was devoted primarily to the incident, featured this banner headline:

Rider Shoots Driver: Two Dead, Dozens Injured
Bus falls from bridge

Two related stories began on the *Times'* front page: One told what happened; the other told what happened from the point of view of the passengers who were on the bus. The front page also included a large 5-column color photo (roughly 10 inches by 6 inches) of police and firefighters rescuing victims from the mangled bus, a 2-column color photo (4 inches by 3½ inches) of the bridge site where the bus went through the guardrail, a half-column headshot of the bus driver, and a series of three drawings showing the route of the bus from the point that it entered the bridge to where it landed after the fall.

At the bottom of the *Times'* front page were two unrelated stories: One was on the President Clinton–Monica Lewinsky situation (with a half-column color headshot), which probably would have been the major story had the accident not occurred, and another about an accountability system set up by the Washington legislature for judging how well the state's six public universities served students. Both of these stories were continued on other pages.

Inside the *Seattle Times*, on pages A19, A20, and A21, following world and national news, was a feature piece entitled "The Aurora Bus Tragedy." On these three pages were: (a) seven black-and-white photos, which dominated the pages; (b) the jump stories continued from page A1; (c) a long story about security on the buses, quoting Barry Samet, president of Local 587, Amalgamated Transit Union (the bus drivers' union); and (d) a list of the passengers on the bus, including their names, ages, conditions, and which of six hospitals treated them. In addition, there was the expected article about the driver and what a wonderful person he was.

Also in the *Seattle Times*, TV critic Kay McFadden's column was on the "human touch" of KOMO-TV's coverage of the tragedy. She noted that KING-5 was first on the air with the news that the bus had plunged off the bridge, but that KOMO-TV was first to break the news that someone had been killed and, later, that the driver had been shot. Various KOMO-TV news personnel were praised by the columnist for their "dogged reporting, superior productions, and rock-of-Gibraltar-like narration by anchor Dan Lewis." One reporter was praised for "button-holing officials as they arrived on the scene" and for seeming like an old friend of the police department spokesperson, Christie-Lynn Bonner. The columnist wrote that all the other stations' reporters seemed to get to

people of interest only after the KOMO-TV reporter had already done so. McFadden praised Lewis and his staff at KOMO-TV for being armed with data, keeping the story going "even when there [was] nothing to report," and for maintaining a "human touch." Lewis apparently signed off the newscast with this comment: "A quick prayer for the people involved would probably not be a bad idea right now" (McFadden, 1998, p. 21).

In the *Seattle Post-Intelligencer*, the front page was similar to the *Times*, with the Clinton–Lewinsky story at the bottom. The banner headline read as follows:

A HORROR SCENE IN FREMONT
Shooting triggers bus plunge off Aurora Bridge: 2 dead, 33 hurt

There were three stories about the accident beginning on page A1. One was about the bus driver and his family; another was on the story from inside the bus. The lead story was the basic five Ws and H (who, what, where, when, why, and how). As in the *Seattle Times*, there was a color drawing showing what had happened to the bus on the bridge, a 3½-column (7 inches by 8½ inches) color photograph showing the damaged bridge and the bus broken into two pieces, and a map of the accident site.

Inside the *Seattle Post-Intelligencer*, following the national and international news, on pages A4 and A5, was a spread entitled "Aurora Bridge Bus Plunge." This 2-page spread included: (a) the jump stories continued from page A1; (b) an entire column listing quotes from witnesses; (c) an article on how disaster drills helped prepare the Harborview Medical Center staff to handle the disaster (a very positive story for Harborview); (d) a story about how residents near where the bus fell described the accident; (e) a history of Metro Transit bus accidents, marking this one as the worst in Metro's 30-year history, but showing a relatively good accident record and few injuries to passengers; (f) a story on how traffic was affected by the accident; and (g) a list of victims' names, ages, and conditions, as well as the hospitals at which they were treated. There were also six black-and-white photographs.

Both newspapers included quotations from Dan Williams; Christie Lynn Bonner; Sheila Strehle, spokesperson for the Seattle Fire Department; Elaine Kraft, spokesperson for King County Executive Ron Sims; Tina Mankowski, spokesperson for Harborview Medical Center; and L. G. Blanchard, spokesperson for the University of Washington Medical Center. Although they all had important jobs to do and they could all be criticized if the communications did not go smoothly, Williams was

more in the hot seat than the others and was quoted most often. After all, it was his agency's bus that crashed and killed people, and it was one of his employees who was killed. In addition, all of the spokespersons scrambled to get representatives of their respective organizations—firefighters, police officers, bus employees and officials, witnesses, victims willing to talk with the media—to make sure the public knew they were all on their toes and doing the best possible job.

Saturday's news coverage also indicated that the bus driver had been shot but that the identity of the assailant was still unknown. On Sunday, November 28, the accident story had become second in importance to a story about the death of the charismatic public school superintendent, John Stanford, who had lost a long and well-publicized battle with leukemia. However, two new developments about the bus accident were reported: the name of the assailant—Silas Cool—and the bad news that another victim had died.

In both Seattle newspapers on Monday, November 29, the accident shared front-page prominence with the death of Stanford. The articles on the bus accident in both newspapers were concerned with painting a picture of Silas Cool: Who was he? What was his problem? Who knew about his problem(s)? A spokesperson for the Union Gospel Mission, Bill Whipple, came forward to provide some of the answers. Although not homeless, the unemployed and troubled Cool had frequented the mission for food. Security on buses was also an important story for several days.

As expected, on the 1-year anniversary of the tragedy, the Seattle newspapers revisited the crisis. The *Seattle Post-Intelligencer*'s front-page story ran the following headline:

BUS CRASH NIGHTMARE WON'T LET ITSELF BE FORGOTTEN

One lengthy article included extensive interviews with survivors—who talked about their inability to sleep, nightmares, and recurring injuries—in its retelling of the story of the accident. Another article was about how the driver's family had worked to adjust to life without him. Both stories were predictable but nonetheless heart-wrenching. Neither article was critical of Metro. There were a few paragraphs that mentioned claims and suits and that noted the county had settled some claims and had "helped some victims financially." The two most critically injured passengers got lump-sum settlements and would receive monthly payments as long as they lived. One had his right arm and leg amputated; the other suffered a very serious brain injury. There were also claims from residents who had some simple complaints such as broken windows (Sunde, 1999, p. A1).

The article about the survivors mentioned that some of the victims argued that the State of Washington, not Metro Transit, was responsible for the bridge, that the guardrails had not been strong enough, and that the northbound and southbound traffic should have been divided by concrete barriers. Some victims filed suits against Cool's estate.

In January 1999, *Seattle Weekly* praised Metro Transit in an article entitled "King County—Too Nice to Sue" (Fefer, 1999).

Communications with Lawyers

Williams said he had no contact with legal counsel until several days after the accident. Metro Transit's legal counsel was provided by the King County prosecuting attorney's office. "At no time did legal staff try to prevent me from media contact," said Williams. "When they did get in touch with me, it was to brief me on the county's plans for providing financial assistance to the victims. Naturally, there was concern over liability issues, and they did suggest ways that the county could express regret and sorrow without admitting liability. But they were sensitive to the media's and public's need to know, and they agreed it was in the county's best interest to be as forthcoming as possible."

Challenges

Williams described his primary challenges as follows:

> Responding in a timely and effective manner to the overwhelming number of requests for information, getting the information quickly from internal sources and passing it along to the media with appropriate explanations and interpretations. I received an estimated 500 media inquiries in the 10 days following the accident.
>
> Television reporters created problems by showing up on buses and at bus bases, wanting to interview employees. They were focused on getting their stories and didn't seem to understand that they might be causing disruptions for employees and customers. It was also difficult to be patient with reporters and editors who keep their ears glued to their police scanners and wanted to pursue every security-related incident on the transit system, no matter how routine or trivial. It was a challenge to make the media understand the routine nature of those incidents without coming across as trying to discount or minimize the importance of security.

Williams also said it was a challenge throughout the crisis to find the time to produce good written material that would shed light on Metro's security program, to convince the media to analyze rather than

sensationalize, and to remain patient and unemotional. Even so, he said he never felt—or allowed himself to feel—traumatized at the scene:

> It was in the week to 10 days following the accident, while media pressure was intense for an extended period of time, that I had periods where I couldn't think clearly enough. I overlooked important details and had trouble controlling my emotions, post traumatic stress. I think I gained some insight, because I was very much in control at the scene of the accident. I have even felt very emotional at times since then while writing or talking or viewing television coverage about the accident.

Evaluation

Customer Service

According to Williams, the Customer Service office's effort to respond to customers' inquiries contributed to customer support after the accident. Tom Randall, chief of customer service, reported that about 80% of the hundreds of callers to the office following the accident expressed sympathy with Metro and/or the driver and his family. About 10% of all callers expressed anxiety about bus security and safety, and another 10% said rude bus drivers were to blame for most altercations. Overall, however, Williams pointed out that "the rapport between drivers and customers contributed to public support for Metro after the accident. Some drivers complained that Metro management failed to protect drivers adequately, and I'm sure that influenced some people, but I think that generally people saw the whole agency as a victim of this crime."

Media Relations

Williams noted that Metro's pre-established relationships with the news media paid off, but he added that quick response to media requests was probably more crucial to the satisfying symbiotic pairing with the media during the crisis:

> Most of the reporters sympathized with what Metro was going through. And I think, in the aftermath, it was important to have credibility with the media as I tried to make the case with reporters and editors for the effectiveness of our security program. For the most part, I believe reporters accepted the information I provided at face value. I can think of only one reporter who was suspicious and antagonistic, and it was a reporter I had never [before] worked with on a regular basis.

Williams feels certain that if the news media had not been able to get the on-site information they needed on that first day, the negativity would have carried over and made it harder for Metro to deal with reporters and editors in the aftermath of the accident:

> Getting the union and management together to face the media early on was good. It minimized finger-pointing. It avoided having reporters running back and forth between the various camps, repeating accusations and denials. I think that, while far from perfect, our general ability to respond to the media went well. There were no stories about Metro's unwillingness or inability to respond. I think that Rick Walsh and Ron Sims both were excellent at being available and willing to talk to reporters. Both came across well and established good rapport and credibility with the media and, through them, [with] the general public as well.

Community Relations

"I think the improvements we were in the process of setting up before the accident added to our already-strong community relations, public outreach program," Williams said.

Government Relations

Williams noted:

> Since we are a government agency, the contact between Metro management and County Executive Ron Sims was [a kind of] government relations as [was] the contact with . . . 13 members of the County Council. The latter communication included members of the County Council's Transportation Committee, primarily to chair Rob McKenna and Greg Nickels, who had been active for years in transit security matters. I worked directly with Sims and his staff and with staff from the prosecuting attorney's office. I also had at least one conversation with an official from the Federal Transit Administration.

Employee Relations

Williams was not involved in activity with employees, but he knows that funds were established for the crash victims and the family of the slain bus driver. "There was quite a bit of communication about that through e-mail and the county's intranet website," recalled Williams. "I also know there were meetings at the seven bus bases with operations managers,

security personnel, and drivers to discuss the incident and Metro's security program. Each base already had a security committee and, within a week after the accident, these committees were assigned tasks to work toward some long-term security improvements."

Williams went on to say that "Amalgamated Transit Union Local 587 was instrumental in establishing a fund for [the bus driver's] family and organizing a memorial service for [him] that took place 10 days after the shooting. The union and management worked together on a plan for continued improvements to the transit security program."

Williams said, "I think that communication and coordination among our department, the prosecuting attorney's office, and the county executive's office went very well. This was critical in dealing with sensitive questions about liability and victims' claims."

"If I Had To Do It Over . . ."

Williams said, "If I had to relive the experience, I would be better prepared and have better knowledge of our security program, with up-to-date handout material readily available and better access to the security database. I would also take the time at the very beginning to assemble a team—probably four or five people at the most—that would devote itself to external and internal communication on the issue for as long as necessary."

The team, he said, would be based on a kind of corporate communications model:

> I would like at least one person for internal communications, probably two or three for external communications (media, public affairs, publications), and one person to develop and maintain a website. There would also be a supervisor or manager to oversee everything, and an . . . administrative assistant. This team would be centralized in the director's office. It seems like a good way for the same messages/information to get out simultaneously to multiple audiences.

Individuals in Crises

Before he was the seventh President of the U.S., Andrew Jackson married a woman named Rachel who was not divorced from a previous husband. Though he was unaware of her marital status, this was scandalous and was a challenge he had to battle in his presidential campaign in the election of 1818. He still emerged victorious.

When Grover Cleveland was running for President in 1884 the public learned that he had had an affair and the woman had given birth to a son. The woman claimed Cleveland was the father and he agreed to pay child support even though he never actually admitted to being the child's father. A chant spread by word of mouth throughout the country: "Ma, Ma, Where's my pa? Gone to the White House, ha, ha, ha!" Cleveland still won the election, possibly because the people felt he took the honorable road under the circumstances.

In the next century, President John Kennedy reportedly had affairs with several Hollywood blonde bombshells, among them Marilyn Monroe and Angie Dickinson. The public did not know of these infidelities until after Kennedy was assassinated despite the fact that many journalists and White House "insiders" were aware. Recent pundits have indicated that the news media protected Kennedy and his reputation. All journalists and all newspapers were not Kennedy fans. What is more likely is that the news media in the Cronkite era rejected such news because it was distasteful. "Taste," "distasteful," "tasteful," and "tacky" are words not in the current lexicon of most news media, who give the public what it wants to know.

During the last decade of the 20th century and the first decade of the 21st, so many politicians, entertainers, and athletes fell from grace due to personal choices that one could wonder why scandals make news at all. Most scandals are and have been sexual misconduct, drug abuse, and making insensitive comments.

President Bill Clinton had what he termed an "improper relationship" with an intern. Senator John Edwards had an extra-marital affair that killed his quest of the U.S. presidency. New York Governor Eliot Spitzer,

in 2008, patronized a prostitution ring called the Emperors Club and was customer #9. The *New York Times* investigation revealed that a "model" named Kristen from the Emperors Club met with customer #9 for three hours, and $4,300 was paid. Kristen subsequently had a few minutes of fame.

In 1993, the *Washington Post* ran an article saying Senator Bob Packwood reportedly made unwanted sexual advances to at least 10 women on his staff. Senator Larry Craig pleaded guilty to disorderly conduct involving a homosexual signal witnessed by a police officer in an airport restroom, then later retracted the plea. Detroit Mayor Kwame Kilpatrick had an affair with a staff member and denied it. The *Detroit Free Press*, obviously on a mission, found and released text messages the mayor exchanged with the staff member. Kilpatrick pleaded guilty to obstruction of justice and was ousted from office in 2009, served time in jail, and was ordered to pay a hefty fine.

After his death in 2003, it was revealed that legendary conservative Senator Strom Thurmond of South Carolina fathered a daughter whose mother was his African American maid. The fully grown woman had DNA proof.

In sports, Alex Rodriguez and more than 100 major league baseball greats were revealed to have tested positive for the use of steroids. Football great Michael Vick went to prison for holding dog fights at his home.

In entertainment, an inebriated rapper, Kanye West, blasted country singer Taylor Swift at the widely televised MTV Video Music Awards in 2009 claiming Beyonce was more deserving. Actor Mel Gibson, while being arrested for suspicion of drunken driving made offensive remarks about Jews, according to the arresting officer. The story was released first by the then-fledgling celebrity news website TMZ.com. Since spicy stories were the website's claim to fame, the owner was extremely proud to have released it. Shock jock Don Imus (see Figure 14.1) made slurs about the Rutgers University women's basketball team. Champion golf pro Tiger Woods was crucified by the news media for being a womanizer.

Actor Isaiah Washington called fellow actor in the series *Grey's Anatomy*, T. R. Knight, a faggot and was dropped from the series after a great uproar from viewers, including gay and lesbian organizations.

Crises of the mouth are not limited to the U.S. Popular German talk show host Eva Herman was fired for praising Hitler. South African soccer player Irvin Khoza, a black man, was sharply criticized for calling a black journalist by a term perhaps more despised in South Africa than the "n" word in the U.S. Martial arts star Jackie Chan was in trouble with Chinese government officials when he told them, "we Chinese need to be controlled."

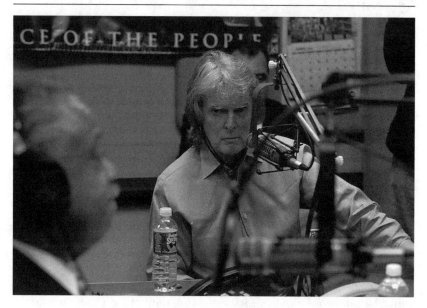

Figure 14.1 Don Imus was one of numerous celebrities who have felt the need to make public apologies. Some exude sincerity and others do not. The news media demand apologies and seek interviews even if the answers are often very personal and humiliating. Photo by Spencer Platt/Getty Images.

The Public Person

Public people—individuals whose positions are determined by judgments of the public—must adhere to the rules and guides of organizations also judged by the public. Their most appropriate behavior is transparency. Their publics should witness their true attitudes. Constituents and fans like to feel that public people are "open books." Actually, such celebrities never are open books but as long as they never disappoint, the public approves.

Often the public person is still in good standing if they are translucent—something of a mystery to publics but not negative in any way. Publics realize they do not fully or actually know the translucent person, but they "feel" that if they did, their opinions would be just as positive.

Opaque public persons are totally hidden, totally a mystery and are hard to judge. They take a risk in being favored or not favored, supported or not supported. Rarely does an opaque public person achieve longtime success. Occasionally, however, an opaque person can be so appreciated for an exceptional talent or skill that the public wants to believe they are perfect in every way. That works well until a crisis brings out human frailties.

Building one's image as a public person takes place when there is no crisis, but when a crisis hits, a person's image can be destroyed or enhanced, just like a company's image. When a public official or celebrity is caught with his/her hand in the proverbial cookie jar, the public makes a judgment. Sometimes the individual's skills, talent, history, and contributions are so great that the individual is easily forgiven, and reputation is diminished only slightly. Often, a public individual can merely wait until the crisis ebbs—when talk subsides—and he or she can rise to the top again in the eyes of their publics. At other times, actions must be taken to correct new found negative images.

Publicist or Lawyer?

Lawyers and public relations professionals often lock horns on methods of addressing crises (see pages 44–47). The public person should, when there is no crisis, make sure he or she has a legal team in place as well as a public relations team.

When the news media are out to get them, often celebrities hire high-powered public relations agencies thinking they can get them out of the news and restore their reputation. Perhaps so. Perhaps not.

When a law has been broken, a charge of crime is imminent, or lawsuits are pending, the best PR guru is one who has connections to a top lawyer who will work in tandem. Legal issues, courts, and prison terms are the job of the lawyer. Reputation is the job of the public relations professional. When a person is undeniably and absolutely guilty, when not only reputation but prison and/or lawsuits are pending, the lawyer is paramount.

When the crisis attacks one's image, when the issue is either ethical or moral, responsible public relations can explain negative actions and lessen the intensity of the bad action making news. However, it cannot change the fact that a deed was committed. Public relations usually disseminates information about good deeds, good performance. However, if a public official is accused of taking city funds, taxpayers don't want to hear about the potholes he filled last year.

Apologies

The principal method of correcting negative image is the apology. Recalling apologia theory (see Chapter 2), apologia is an effort to defend reputation and protect image. Sometimes it is a full, contrite apology. Sometimes it is an effort to explain or deny—to show that one did not intend to perform a misdeed, but that some exterior force swayed them. Or one might have appeared to have committed a faux pas, but actually did not. Most of the public persons described in the opening paragraphs of this chapter delivered some kind of apology (see Figure 14.2).

APOLOGIES AFTER SCANDALS

President Bill Clinton said in a 4-minute speech delivered to Americans: "Indeed, I did have a relationship with Miss Lewinsky that was not appropriate. In fact, it was wrong. It constituted a critical lapse of judgment and a personal failure on my part for which I am solely and completely responsible." Then he went on to explain further, expressed love for his wife and daughter, and a desire to be left alone about the issue. "It's nobody's business but ours."

Major League baseball player Alex Rodriguez came clean and said there was "an enormous amount of pressure" and the times were "loosey-goosey."

After pleading guilty, Idaho **Senator Larry Craig** later retracted the plea and apologized at a news conference (with his wife at his side) saying that he "overreacted and made a poor decision," that it was spurred by stress.

New York Governor Eliot Spitzer (with his wife by his side) said at a news conference, "Over the course of my public life, I have insisted— I believe correctly—that people regardless of their position or power take responsibility for their conduct. I can and will ask no less of myself. For this reason, I am resigning from the office of governor."

Actor Mel Gibson issued a statement through his publicist: "I'm not just asking forgiveness, I would like to take it one step further and meet with leaders of the Jewish community, with whom I can have a one-on-one discussion to discern the appropriate plan for healing . . . There is no excuse, nor should there be any tolerance, for anyone who thinks or expresses any kind of anti-Semitic remark."

After pleading guilty and before being sentenced, **football player Michael Vick** apologized, at a news conference, "for all the things I've done and that I've allowed to happen." He said he was "disappointed in myself" and that "dogfighting is a terrible thing and I . . . reject it." He also included, "Through this situation I've found Jesus" and "I take full responsibility for my actions. Not for one second will I sit right here and point the finger and try to blame anybody else for my actions or what I've done."

Radio talk show host Don Imus made the following apology on-air: "Want to take a moment to apologize for an insensitive and ill-conceived

Figure 14.2 Apologies made by celebrities involved in scandals. Notice the methods and judge the sincerity.

remark we made the other morning regarding Rutgers women's basketball team. It was completely inappropriate, and we can understand why people were offended. Our characterization was thoughtless and stupid, and we are sorry." In a classy response, the Rutgers coach and team publicly accepted the apology.

Rapper Kanye West apologized on his blog with "I feel like Ben Stiller in *Meet The Parents* when he messed up everything and Robert De Niro asked him to leave. That was Taylor's moment and I had no right in anyway to take it from her. I am truly sorry." He made an emotional apology on Jay Leno's show and later personally apologized to Swift by telephone; she accepted.

Actor Isaiah Washington issued an apology through *People*: "I sincerely regret my actions and the unfortunate use of words during the recent incident on-set . . . Both are beneath my own personal standards . . . I have nothing but respect for my coworkers . . . and have apologized personally to everyone involved."

Figure 14.2 continued

Once you're in deep dirt, there is no bath of truth that will clean up one's reputation. People, inquiring minds, will want to know. "I'm sorry" is so easily said in all these cases, but not easily believed.

Whatever is said, not only the words must be carefully crafted but also the body language, humility, honesty, and sincerity. The carefully crafted words must not seem carefully crafted by publicists and lawyers. Inserting an "if" in the apology is a sign of insincerity, for example in phrases such as "If I offended anyone, I am sorry." The apology must be heartfelt. A smile in the wrong place can be perceived as not fully accepting the severity of the bad deed. It could mean, "I was told I have to make this apology but I really don't think this is a big deal." It could mean, "I'm sorry I got caught."

On the other hand, tears can be overly dramatic. It depends upon the misdeed, the occasion, the amount of time that has passed, and what the public's opinion is of the public person. Coming forward early in the crisis is usually advisable because one's emotions are fresh and therefore more believable than days or weeks later when it is obvious the individual has been coached.

Faking sincerity is difficult even for an Academy Award winner. Humility is difficult to show if the person feels he or she is superior to

the common man, those often called "the little people." The little people
are the people who vote for the politicians and buy tickets to the sports
events and films. There is an expression, "Be kind to people you meet
on the way up because you will meet the same people on the way
down."

If the public is very much concerned, it expects something to show
that the misdeed will never occur again. They want to know there is a
plan to assure everyone there will be no repeat offense or the image of
the public person may be damaged. Also, when a public person falls from
grace and makes a confession or apology at a news conference, the
person's spouse will be asked to be present. Lawyers want that if possible
because it says "If the spouse is still supportive, so should you be." The
spouse may be filing divorce papers as soon as the news conference ends,
but often, even usually, they stand stoically, looking to be in silent
support and love. They could actually be supportive; it may depend upon
why they married. If reason #1 or #2 is financial support, then they don't
want that well to run dry. They may want their family to remain intact
and will settle to suffer long. They may have married the spouse because
of the connections he/she can provide for their own careers. Whatever
the reason, the spouse is usually part of the in-person public apology.

Talk or Keep Silent?

Public officials have the obligation to respond to charges. The John Does
who put them in office can take them out again. Only U.S. Supreme Court
justices have positions for life; all others can be terminated. After sex
scandals, sometimes politicians are humiliated to the point of resigning
or they are not reelected. Gov. Spitzer, for example, resigned. Others
manage to stay afloat and even popular. President Clinton, for example,
is still popular with many people after his indiscretion. Many say he could
have been reelected.

It is not so clear with entertainers and sports figures. True, they depend
upon public support, but the public is usually fickle about their enter-
tainers. Hollywood's bad boys and girls—Robert Downey Jr., Lindsay
Lohan, Britney Spears, Charlie Sheen—don't need to do a lot of
apologizing or responding. They have been in trouble so much no one
is paying attention to apologies. Will people tire of them and stop buying
their music or seeing their films? Every time there is a misdeed, some
fans turn away. Can they continue and lose all support? Maybe—but
probably not as long as they are entertaining. Downey is widely praised
as one of the best actors in Hollywood. It's laughable when he gets drunk
and crawls into bed in someone else's house, but then you see him in
another film and you say he deserves to be famous. He's so good he

deserves to be a little crazy. However, once these celebrities make lousy productions, the game is over. But that's true of people with stellar reputations. You're only as good as your last album or movie.

Responding to a Scandal

Tiger Woods was rarely in the non-sports news until late 2009. Except for people in the golf world, few people knew his persona. After Woods' wife beat up his Escalade with a golf club and paramours showed up like bugs in a slum tenement, many crisis communications experts wrote on blogs that he should come forward and be interviewed on some TV talk show. Why? What was he going to say? What could possibly make the picture better? What would the questions be? What was the disagreement with your wife? Was the fight about your affairs? When you married her, was there a pre-nuptial agreement? How many affairs did you have? Why did you marry your wife? Why don't you have some educated girlfriends? Are some of these women lying? Is one more special than the others? Certainly few, if any, questions would be about golf. What service to Woods or the public would answers to these questions serve?

After admitting an affair with missing intern Chandra Levy, Congressman Gary Condit was interviewed by Connie Chung on TV's *Primetime* on August 23, 2001. (Levy's body was discovered much later but Condit was not a suspect.) Every question Chung asked was about the degree of intimacy of his relationship with Levy. "Did you have a romantic relationship with Chandra Levy? Was she in love with you? Did she want to marry you and have your child? Did she want you to leave your wife?" Condit answered the questions with a prepared type of "I refuse to answer" response. These questions were obviously prepared by Chung and others on the ABC show. Condit's sole response was obviously prepared by his legal and PR team. If Condit had answered even one, a more intimate question would have followed. Condit's advisers, no doubt advised him to do the show because in crisis communications, it is understood that you tell your story and tell it as early as possible. But a stronger rule is that you control your message. Controlling a network television program is not easily accomplished. The interview was an embarrassment to Condit, Chung, ABC, and broadcast journalism.

If a celebrity can do an in-depth interview on *Oprah* or *Ellen* or *Larry King Live* and explain their dilemma, that's another story. If having enough time to thoroughly present one's case to the viewing public is the problem, then the public relations team can try to make that happen. Michael Jackson and Princess Diana of Great Britain did long interviews explaining their crises.

Also, if the public person has a personality that lends itself to humor, one might turn the incident (if it's a sex scandal) into a joke. Actor Hugh Grant picked up a lady of the night in Los Angeles; it was considered newsworthy. While it was still being talked about, the actor appeared on *The Tonight Show with Jay Leno* and Leno asked, "What in the world were you thinking?" The studio audience laughed; Grant smiled like a mischievous little boy and said, "I did a bad thing. There you have it." And it was over.

Many public persons, especially entertainers, use various social media. If they have Facebook friends (supporters, constituents, fans), for example, and they keep up a regular communication with them, when a crisis occurs, these "friends" are likely to be more supportive than they would have otherwise been (see Chapter 5, "Social Media and Crisis Communications"). But these "friends" must be in place before a crisis, and they are only there if there has been regular communication, regular news to which they are privy or news they get earlier than regular people who get their information from the news media. When a scandal hits, they will expect a response, and the celebrity has then a tool to explain his or her story. The "friends" will see to it that it is distributed to others.

Some celebrities have their own blog pages. Rapper Kanye West posted his apology to Taylor Swift on his blog. People who follow the page or who followed it because of the scandal had some interest in the situation; they wanted to see how he would respond. But not all of his public—the people who like his music—would search out the blogs, so he also apologized on Jay Leno's primetime show and knew various news media would write about it. Does that mean he is forgiven by all? Not at all. Some people have a negative opinion of him that will never die. Others feel less negative toward him after the numerous attempts at apology. Also, he blamed his behavior on being inebriated. People seem to accept the "I was drunk" excuse amazingly often, perhaps because it's a common human frailty. "He's just one of us."

Some of Tiger Woods' contracts with brands were cancelled, not because he didn't talk about sordid affairs but because he had sordid affairs and did not deny any of them. As a brand representative, he is expected to have an exemplary image. By not saying anything, it made the over-coverage of the news media seem accurate. If the news and talk-TV coverage were exaggerated, a statement could have been carefully written and somehow disseminated so as not to acknowledge any of the women and apologizing to his wife because she is his wife and the most affected by the problem becoming public.

What people did not seem to consider was that just because Woods apparently had many women in his life did not mean he would choose to discuss them. He was not obligated to kiss and tell. Public persons must understand that as individuals, they have the right to be private,

to refuse to reveal details about their personal lives. However, they must also realize that the news media have the right to investigate and reveal. If the person is certain—and certainty is difficult—that information that would be detrimental to his image cannot be discovered, then he may refuse to address it, to reveal it. However, a secret is only secret if only one person knows it. Once two, three, or more are aware, the chances of protecting privacy are lost.

Public persons should know that when they have illicit affairs, their sexual partners are likely to talk to somebody. In fact, sharing that juicy information with their friends is a primary reason for having an affair. They become in demand for conversation. Their stock goes up in the community. Just as TV viewers enjoy watching news about celebrity affairs, they doubly enjoy hearing about their associates and friends who have affairs with famous and/or powerful people.

Last, if the public person can sit it out, the scandal sometimes goes away, especially if the person is careful that a misdeed never recurs.

Chapter Fifteen

The Crisis Communications Plan

Crisis Inventory

Before an organization can develop a crisis management plan or a crisis communications plan, it must determine which crisis or crises the organization is most likely to face. A crisis communications plan's usefulness is directly associated with how specific it is to a particular type of crisis.

The workbook for this text takes the user through a step-by-step process of developing the crisis communications plan. Although there are several items in the plan that are mutual to all types of crises, varying information is needed for each type of crisis for maximum effectiveness. For example, a restaurant chain may decide that food poisoning and fire are its most probable crises. If a food poisoning crisis occurs, the media will want, and the public relations department should have, the following items readily available and in its crisis communications plan: recipes, a list of ingredients stocked, a list of vendors used, kitchen precautions and procedures, names and contact numbers of chefs and all other personnel handling food, and a list of medical experts for consultation and as spokespersons.

If a fire occurs, the public relations department should have, in a specific crisis communications plan, information about its evacuation procedures, its policy on using nonflammable decor items (such as window coverings and tablecloths), the floor plan of the structure, and fire experts for spokespersons.

The following list enumerates common types of crises. There are, of course, numerous others. Companies and organizations are advised to consider the list carefully and add types of crises specific to their operations.

Common Types of Crises

acquisition	bankruptcy
age discrimination	boycott
alcohol abuse	bribery

chemical spill or leak
computer failure
computer hacking
contamination
data loss/theft
drug abuse
drug trafficking
earthquake
embezzlement
explosion
fatality
fire
flood
hacking
hurricane
kickbacks
kidnapping
lawsuits
layoffs
merger

murder
negative legislation
plant closing
product failure
protest demonstrations
racial issues
robbery
sexual discrimination
sexual harassment
strikes
suicide
takeover
tax problems
terrorism
tornado
toxic waste
transportation accident
transportation failure
workplace violence

Some crises will involve more than one of the types listed, such as workplace violence and fatality, or boycott and sexual discrimination.

Perhaps the involvement of the entire company or of representatives from each department can help determine the crises the company is likely to face. Then each unit's selections could be compared and compiled into a company-wide list. When done properly, this can be an effective proactive employee relations program, a way of creating "we-ness," a way of including all of the employees in the company's decision making. Janitors, executive assistants, blue-collar and white-collar workers, midlevel executives, as well as top executives can have a say. After all, each employee stands to suffer if the company should go under after the most serious of crises. Furthermore, employees in each position classification have unique perspectives on things that can go wrong. Janitors are more aware of heating and cooling equipment, possible gas leaks, and so on. Workers on an automobile assembly line know more about the quality of cars than managers in carpeted offices.

However, if a company-wide crisis identification program is not feasible, a meeting of key employees familiar with all facets of the operation can determine the crises the company is likely to face. Such a meeting should certainly include more than public relations staff members. You do not want the company blaming the public relations staff for the failure to recognize a possible crisis.

Frequently, ascertaining probable crises can point out problems that prevent crises from occurring. This is the primary reason for company-wide involvement. The second best reason is being able to manage a crisis once it occurs.

Every company and organization can experience many types of crises. Two questions must be answered: (a) How likely is this crisis? and (b) how devastating can the crisis be? Crisis communications plans should be developed for all crises believed to be both most probable and most devastating. To do this, the public relations department, with its key executives, must take an inventory. Each possible crisis must be ranked as follows:

0—Impossible; that is, the crisis has basically no chance of occurring.
1—Nearly impossible.
2—Remotely possible.
3—Possible.
4—Somewhat probable; has happened to similar companies.
5—Highly probable; may or may not have previously occurred in the company, but warning signs are evident.

Each crisis also should be ranked according to its potential damage to the company. The rankings in this category are as follows:

0—No damage, not a serious consequence.
1—Little damage, can be handled without much difficulty, not serious enough for the media's concern.
2—Some damage, a slight chance that the media will be involved.
3—Considerable damage, but still will not be a major media issue.
4—Considerable damage, would definitely be a major media issue.
5—Devastating, front-page news, could put company out of business.

For added security, when in doubt, rank a crisis in the next highest category. For instance, Company Z determines that there are five crises it could face: workplace violence, fire, protest demonstrations, negative legislation, and tax problems. Each of these crises might be ranked as shown in Figure 15.1.

Keep in mind that a crisis you determine to be unlikely simply because it has never happened before can happen tomorrow. Both human nature and mother nature are very unpredictable, so natural disasters (e.g., earthquakes, floods, and hurricanes) and human failures should be expected to some degree.

After rankings for probability and damage are made, bar graphs should be made to clearly see and consider each crisis and compare it to others. (Bar graphing can be done on various computer programs or by hand.)

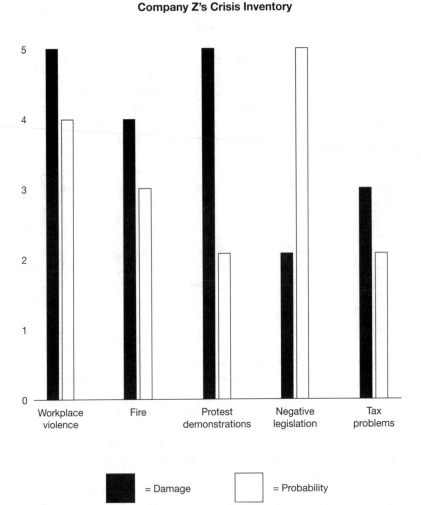

Company Z's Crisis Inventory

Figure 15.1 A sample bar graph showing how an organization might assess the probability of, and degrees of damage resulting from, various types of crises.

At the base of each graph, write the name of each type of crisis. Plot the height of each bar according to numbers attributed to each crisis in the probability and damage rankings. Choose different colors or shadings for probability bars and damage bars.

When Company Z plots its data on a bar graph, it resembles Figure 15.1. Considering Company Z's graph, we see that the probability and

seriousness of a crisis relating to tax problems is not as crucial as in the other crises. This does not mean that a crisis plan is not important for tax problems; it's just not as important as for other issues, and not a priority.

According to the graph, the possibility of Company Z's suffering a crisis resulting from negative legislation is likely, though not particularly critical. On the other hand, protest demonstrations are critical, although not very likely. Workplace violence and fire seem both likely and critical.

Most organizations plan for crises ranked high in both probability and damage. In this case, Company Z would probably develop crisis management and communications plans for workplace violence first, then for the other crises in descending order of importance: fire, protest demonstrations, negative legislation, and tax problems.

Sometimes organizations make crisis plans for the most devastating crises no matter how probable or improbable they may be. In this case, Company Z would develop plans for workplace violence first, followed by protest demonstrations, then fire. Naturally, a version of Murphy's Law can be expected: That crisis for which you have no plan will likely happen. However, you will find that any plan, and the process of developing that plan, will make you more prepared for crises generally.

Some organizations, having several crises classified with similar rankings in all categories, make general crisis communications plans with detailed information for all types of crises, although sometimes the detailed information is omitted.

Many companies, fearing all possibilities of crises equally, merely adopt a policy of "open and honest response" with the media and all publics, and plan to be in a total reactive mode during a crisis.

The importance of the crisis inventory is to force organizations to think about the possibilities. Sometimes the most ridiculous crisis occurs, something no one in the company could predict. Pepsi probably never dreamed that it would have a crisis about hypodermic syringes in its cans. On the other hand, Foodmaker and Jack-in-the-Box could certainly have anticipated children dying from eating hamburgers, and Exxon could have anticipated a devastating oil spill.

The ranking procedure may introduce ideas for prevention programs. You also may realize that your organization is more vulnerable than you anticipated.

Considering that the toll of stress and emotion during a crisis necessarily affects one's thought processes, a carefully developed crisis communications plan is the best substitute for a fully functioning brain. Even if you remain cool and calm under pressure, others in the company may not. The crisis communications plan alleviates this problem, too.

Developing the Crisis Communications Plan

Once likely crises have been identified, the crisis communications plan can be written. A crisis communications plan can be part of a larger crisis management plan (CMP) or it may be a stand-alone document to help public relations practitioners handle crises more effectively.

The CMP includes information such as evacuation procedures, emergency staffing of various departments of a company, and places to purchase or rent emergency equipment, tools, or vehicles—all the things a company may need in a crisis.

Public relations during a crisis focuses on communications with the company's publics during the crisis—for the most part, the same publics to which normal PR activities are directed.

The CMP is sometimes a large volume of instructions, whereas a crisis communications plan should be a more manageable, easier-to-read document. After a crisis has erupted, employees are likely to look at a large volume and say, "We don't have time to read this now," and then proceed to handle the crisis by "winging" it. The crisis communications plan should be organized in such a way that the practitioners can quickly turn to each section. Some professionals use tabs in a notebook; others use a table of contents. Keeping the crisis communications plan on a computer can be dangerous because many crises prevent access to offices (fire, earthquakes, explosives, etc.).

Many companies (such as Johnson & Johnson after the Tylenol crisis) urge employees to keep copies of the plan in various key spots—the office, at home, near the night stand, or in the car. That way, the odds are good that at least one copy will be readily available should a crisis or disaster occur.

If a crisis inventory determines, for example, that there are three likely crises, the organization should draft a crisis communications plan for each type. A plan for an earthquake must be different from a plan for a product failure. The publics may be different; the media may be different; the message must be different.

The crisis communications plan states purposes, policies, and goals, then assigns employees to various duties. It generally makes communication with publics faster and more effective and should help end the crisis more swiftly than without a plan.

When a crisis communications plan is ineffective, it is usually because the type of crisis was not anticipated or because variables arose that were not anticipated. For example, spokespersons or supplies may not be available. The crisis communications plan sometimes fails because it is outdated. Such plans should be updated regularly.

Even if unanticipated variables do arise, the crisis communications plan should be more effective than having no plan at all. Still, it must be

remembered that a crisis communications plan is not a manual guaranteeing success, with everything done "by the book," but rather a guide that must be flexible.

An effective crisis communications plan should have the following components, arranged in an order that best suits the organization and the particular crisis or disaster:

- cover page
- introduction
- acknowledgments
- rehearsal dates
- purpose and objectives
- list of key publics
- notifying publics
- identifying the crisis communications team
- crisis directory
- identifying the media spokesperson
- list of emergency personnel and local officials
- list of key media
- spokespersons for related organizations
- crisis communications control center
- equipment and supplies
- pregathered information
- key messages
- website
- blogs and social media
- trick questions
- list of prodromes
- list of related Internet URLs
- evaluation form.

Cover Page

The cover page of a crisis communications plan is similar to the cover page of a term paper. There are as many ways of doing one as there are ways of doing crisis communications plans. It should include at least the date when the plan was written as well as revision dates.

Introduction

The head of the company or organization usually writes the introduction (or the PR practitioner ghostwrites it for the CEO with his or her approval). The purpose of this component is to persuade employees to take the crisis communications plan seriously. It stresses the necessity and

importance of the plan and it emphasizes the dire results possible when a plan is not followed.

Acknowledgments

This crisis communications plan component takes the form of an affidavit signed by all crisis personnel as well as by key executives, indicating that they have read the plan and are prepared to put it into effect. The signatures assure management that its personnel have read the plan.

Rehearsal Dates

Dates of rehearsals for all crises are recorded here. The most damaging and most likely crises should be practiced at least annually if not every 6 months. Rehearsal for any type of crisis is helpful even if an eventual crisis turns out to be somewhat different.

Purpose and Objectives

The purpose statement details the organization's policies toward its publics. It might say, for example, "In a crisis, an open and honest disclosure with the media shall be stressed." The purpose is an expressed hope for a recovery and return to normalcy, to get out of the media. The objectives are responses to the question, "What do you hope to achieve with this plan?" Objectives should not be overly ambitious in difficulty or number. For example, a company may adopt the following goals:

1. To be seen in the media as a company that cares about its customers and employees.
2. To make certain that all communications are accurate.

List of Key Publics

The key publics list should include all publics, both external and internal, with which the organization must communicate during the crisis. The list varies with organizations, but may include the following as well as others:

- board members
- shareholders
- financial partners
- investors
- community leaders
- customers

- clients
- suppliers
- vendors
- neighbors of physical plant(s)
- competitors
- key management
- employees
- legal representation
- media
- union officials
- retirees
- government officials (city, state, county, federal).

Although all publics need not be notified in every crisis, the list of key publics should be comprehensive. It is easier to eliminate unneeded publics at the time of crisis than it is to think of all the crucial publics during the stress of a crisis.

Publics fall into the following categories:

- Enabling publics—those people with the power and authority to make decisions: the board of directors, shareholders, investors, and key executives. Notifying enabling publics is a priority.
- Functional publics—the people who actually make the organization work: employees, unions, suppliers, vendors, consumers, and volunteers in the case of nonprofit organizations.
- Normative publics—those people who share values with the organization in crises: trade associations, professional organizations, and competitors.
- Diffused publics—those people linked indirectly to the organization in crisis: the media, community groups, and neighbors of the physical plant.

Notifying Publics

To notify publics, a system must be devised for contacting each public, and that system should be described in the crisis communications plan. Social media networks such as Facebook groups can be used if people use computers constantly. For internal publics, many companies use a chain procedure, such as a telephone tree, in which each person is specifically designated to call others. The person who learns about the crisis first notifies the CEO, the head of public relations, and the head of the department that may be involved. The chain should be clear and error-free, even in the event that certain individuals are not reached.

An appropriate means of notification must be decided on for each public. A news release, for example, is appropriate primarily for the news media, not for other publics.

Board members are often reached by telephone or fax. E-mail or other computerized communications are also used. The media can be notified by way of telephone, wire service, fax, press conference, e-mail, or news release. Other methods used for notifying publics include telegrams, personal visits, letters, advertisements, bulletin boards, and meetings (see Figure 15.2).

Identifying the Crisis Communications Team

The crisis communications team members, along with back-ups, should be preselected. The team manager is usually, but not always, the head of public relations. He or she has specific responsibilities: communicating with top management, making decisions, drafting or approving major statements, and notifying the rest of the crisis communications team.

YOUR COMPANY

MESSAGE: There has been an explosion in the plant. There are injured employees. We do not know, at this time, the cause of the explosion or the extent of the injuries of the employees. An investigation is underway.

Methods of Communication

PUBLICS

	TELEPHONE	EMAIL	FAX	LETTER BY MESSENGER	LETTER BY MAIL	NEWSLETTER	BULLETIN BOARD	PERSONAL VISIT	NEWS RELEASE	MEETINGS
EMPLOYEES		* J. Naas				*J. Naas	*J. Naas			
EXECUTIVES	*Nelson J.	*Nelson J.						*Nelson J. M. Yerima		*Nelson J.
CUSTOMERS						*Damien L.				
BOARD OF DIRECTORS	*Nelson J.			*Damien L.					*Gina A.	
ELECTRONIC MEDIA	*K. Stone		*K. Sone						*Gina A.	
DAILY NEWSPAPERS	*Gina A.								*Gina A.	
WEEKLY NEWSPAPERS			*Gina A.		*Damien L.					
SHARE HOLDERS		*Ann C.					*Ann C.			
COMMUNITY LEADERS			*Karen N.				*Karen N.			

*Staff member responsible for communications and followup

Figure 15.2 A sample chart showing how an organization might plan to communicate with key publics during a crisis. It includes key talking points and ways of communicating. The lists of publics and types of communication can be longer, shorter, or otherwise different depending on the organization's needs.

The assistant crisis manager assumes responsibility when the manager is unavailable (a second back-up may be beneficial, if possible). The control room coordinator sets up the room with necessary furniture, equipment, supplies, and tools. An efficient executive assistant can be appointed for this position.

Other PR personnel have the responsibilities of preparing news releases and statements, contacting the media, and reporting all actions to the crisis communications manager. These people may notify employees or volunteers through letters or by writing telegrams to the mayor and governor, by telephoning union officials and others, and so forth.

Crisis Directory

The company should prepare a crisis directory, listing all members of the crisis team, key managers in the company, and key publics or organizations, along with titles, business and home telephone numbers, cellular phone numbers, fax and e-mail addresses, as well as business, home, and vacation addresses. It is also helpful to list the phone numbers of friends, neighbors, and relatives who are frequently in contact with persons crucial to the crisis recovery.

The crisis team should be large enough to get the job done, but no larger. Having too many people involved makes it difficult to get tasks completed and decisions made. There is no time in a crisis for egos; each person must be a team player. It is also preferable that crisis team members be generally healthy and capable of working under stress. They should be reliable professionals, whether gofers, interns, or assistants.

Identifying the Media Spokesperson

The media spokesperson must be selected carefully. To the public, this person is the company or organization.

Actually, sometimes several persons are spokespersons. This is an arguable point in the public relations profession. Some argue for one spokesperson per crisis, usually the CEO. Others argue for several spokespersons, depending on area of expertise. Clearly, the decision is a matter of what suits the company and type of crisis best.

Even if the CEO is an effective spokesperson, he or she may not be particularly knowledgeable about a technical aspect of the crisis. For example, during an oil spill, the company CEO is not the only important spokesperson; also needed is a person qualified to talk about what will be necessary for the clean-up. Frequently, university professors are called on for their specific knowledge about technical aspects of a crisis and for their credibility.

Another school of thought is that CEOs have no credibility because they have too much to lose. However, if lives are lost or in danger—including the lives of animals—most professionals agree that the company head must be the chief spokesperson.

In all cases, at least one, and preferably two or three, back-up spokespersons should be preselected in case the preferred person is unavailable at the time of the crisis. Crises can occur when people are on vacation, on business trips, or sick with the flu. When the 1989 San Francisco earthquake struck, for example, the first two designated spokespersons for the Pacific Gas and Electric Company were at the World Series game at Candlestick Park. The third spokesperson on the list was called and pressed into service.

An effective crisis spokesperson must have some position in the company. It is usually not the PR head, even if the PR person is normally the company's spokesperson. The spokesperson must also be articulate, powerful enough to make decisions, accessible throughout the crisis, able to talk clearly in concise sound bites, and pleasant to the eye of a camera. Moreover, the spokesperson in a crisis must appear rational, concerned, and empathetic. He or she should be pretrained, rehearsed well in advance of the crisis, and briefed prior to the crisis response. The organization's legal adviser should be consulted before statements are made.

If the public relations department is a small or one-person operation, it may be beneficial to have capable, trustworthy volunteers to perform some tasks. Outside public relations firms that specialize in crisis planning and handling might be used. A nonprofit organization can often get PR firms to help pro bono (done or donated without charge). Many nonprofit organizations have PR practitioners on their boards of directors, anticipating the need for their assistance during a crisis.

At times, one person may be required to perform all communications roles. On the other hand, in large companies several people may perform each role.

List of Emergency Personnel and Local Officials

If the crisis is a disaster or emergency, various emergency personnel need to be contacted. A list should be made of contact numbers for police, fire officials, hospitals, the health department, utilities, and paramedics.

If the crisis affects large numbers of people or is a threat to the safety of people, government officials must be contacted. This list should include contact information for the mayor, governor, city council members, county officials, state legislators, and U.S. senators and representatives.

Sometimes union officials must be notified, and they should therefore be listed, as well as key citizens groups and community organizations.

List of Key Media

After key executives are called, the media are the next most important public to notify about the crisis. A list of media contacts—newspapers, television, radio, wire services—should be completed and listed in order of importance. If particular editors or reporters are important to telling the story to the organization's benefit, a list of their home numbers and emergency numbers will be advantageous.

The media list should contain contact information for morning and afternoon metropolitan dailies, certain weeklies, all TV news stations, the Associated Press, United Press International, Reuters, all radio news stations, and trade publications.

Spokespersons for Related Organizations

If an organization suffers a severe crisis, there may be spokespersons outside the organization who may be questioned. It may be effective to make a list of who these people might be and how to contact them at any time of day. It also might be effective to meet with them so that they are familiar with your company, with how you will handle a crisis, if it occurs, and with how to reach you.

Sometimes other spokespersons have information you don't have. This information may help you communicate more effectively. So you need to be able to reach them. Because most people have cell phones, this could be a simple task.

In the Metro Transit case in Chapter 13, involving a bus accident and shooting, the news media interviewed the public information officers for the bus company, the police department, the fire department, the hospitals, and spokespersons for county and city officials. The bus company spokesman learned from the news media that a gun was found on one of the victims, and had to scramble to get to the police to find the information. In this case, the spokespersons got together at the site of the accident and determined that they would refer the media's questions to one particular spokesperson. If, instead, the spokespersons had exchanged cell phone numbers, e-mail addresses, or home phone numbers prior to the crisis, they would have been aware of what procedure to follow regarding the media spokesperson.

Crisis Communications Control Center

The location of the crisis communications control center must be determined in case regular office space is unavailable. After disasters and emergencies, offices are often damaged, without power, or inaccessible.

Several possible sites should be listed in the crisis communications plan, as well as the persons instrumental in gaining access to these locations.

Suppose, for example, a local church has offered its conference room. Who gave permission to use the room? Who can unlock the doors of the church and conference room? Does the permission include use of electrical outlets and furniture? Does the site have adequate space for the media to work?

Equipment and Supplies

Determine and list all of the equipment and supplies needed by the crisis team, media, and visiting publics. The list could include, but is not limited to, the following:

- chairs and desks
- bulletin boards
- flip charts and chalkboards
- computers or typewriters (perhaps manual typewriters in case power is a problem)
- computer printers
- telephones and cellular phones
- battery-powered televisions and radios
- maps of the plant or crisis area
- battery-powered flashlights and lamps
- police radios
- walkie-talkies
- company letterhead, pens, and pencils
- telephone directories
- contact lists and media directories
- press kits
- CMPs and crisis communications plans
- street and highway maps
- food and beverages
- copying machine(s)
- first-aid kits
- cameras and film
- extension cords and generator power packs.

Pregathered Information

Prepare and gather various documents that may possibly be needed during a crisis. Keep identical sets of documents in various locales to ensure availability. The types of documents that can be gathered in advance include safety records and procedures, annual reports, photos, company backgrounders, executive biographies, company maps, branch office locations, quality control procedures, product manufacturing procedures,

and company fact sheets (including such data as numbers of employees, products manufactured, and markets served).

Skeletal news releases can be prepared as long as the PR practitioner anticipates the type of crisis and can make a statement on behalf of the company. As shown in Figure 15.3, a news release can be written in advance with blank spaces left for data to be filled in (such as the magnitude of the crisis and relevant dates and names).

NEWS RELEASE

For Immediate Release

Date _____

Contact: _____

(name/phone number)

_____ (name of celebrity) DIES

(SEATTLE) _____ (full name and title) _____ died

today of _____ (cause of death) at _____ (time

of death) _____ at Swedish Hospital Medical Center in Seattle.

He/She was _____ (age).

Further details will be released by _____ (name of person to

make announcement—family member or professional contact) at a news

conference scheduled for _____ (time of news

conference), at Swedish Hospital, Glaser Auditorium, 747 Summit Ave.

#

Figure 15.3 A sample fill-in-the-blanks news release

Key Messages

Under the stress of a crisis, it is easy to forget, or at least fail to state properly, the main points you want to convey to publics or to a specific public. Even when there is no crisis, experienced spokespersons prepare in advance the primary information they want emphasized in what are called key messages or speaking points.

The act of preparing key messages will help you organize your thoughts and will provide consistent information to publics. Each message must be accurate, brief, easy to use in a quote, and memorable. The spokesperson must be easily able to work the key message into responses to questions. Such messages also help reporters— who are looking for great quotes—to do their jobs.

Effective key messages help avoid misquoting, enable the spokesperson to tell his or her side of the story, and give the spokesperson a way to answer trick questions comfortably. Most of all, they establish credibility for the organization in crisis.

Website

Placing news on the organization's website and pre-appointing webmasters to keep updated information on the site will reduce both the number of phone calls from publics and the amount of time put into crisis recovery. The news put on the site should be brief or detailed depending on the nature of the crisis. In the event of an airplane crash, for example, the airline's website would, at first, merely acknowledge the crash. After families of victims are notified, the names of victims would be listed. Regular notices of progress in the investigation would also be posted.

The concern of the company should be expressed and prominently displayed. A statement from the highest executive in the company is expected by the public. The website is an ideal venue for keeping safety rules, security precautions, and health policies posted. Restaurants might keep information posted on training new employees about cooking burgers at the proper temperature, using gloves when handling food, and policies that discourage employees with colds and other infectious diseases from working with food products.

The website is also a bulletin board for informing publics of the organization's community relations projects and other activities that give back to the public. The website can afford your organization the opportunity to be a Model 4, two-way symmetric company (see Chapter 2). It can encourage feedback, comments, and questions from publics and provide publics with responses and explanations. Finally, the website can reveal how the company is making changes as a result of public comment.

Blogs and Social Media

Monitoring blogs and social media channels is crucial. Sometimes the monitoring can be a prodrome (warning sign) and help prevent a crisis. The crisis communications plan should have a list of all blogs and social media networks relevant to the business and relevant to the types of crises. This can be an excellent way of achieving Model 4, two-way symmetrical communications with publics (see Excellence Theory in Chapter 2, "Crisis Communication Theory," pages 20–24).

It is advisable, if social media are used proactively in marketing and public relations campaigning, that they would also be used in the crisis communications plan. Facebook friends and other contacts with whom the organization has built a relationship will spread the news to a wider group of people. For Twitter, prepare key messages in advance when communicators have time to work with the 140 characters. Make this list of key messages separate from the key messages going to the traditional news media but with the same sentiment.

Do not drop traditional news media in order to spend time with social media unless the crisis relates only to online issues and online publics. Crises originating on social media should indeed be battled on social media and sometimes on traditional media. Similarly, crises not related to social media networks might also be fought through social media as well as traditional media.

For example, in 1993, the Pepsi Cola company experienced a crisis brought on by consumers who placed hypodermic syringes in cans and charged they found them there when they purchased them. The fear supposedly was that the syringes would cause HIV/AIDS, but actually the greedy consumers were hoping to get payoffs from Pepsi. Pepsi ended the crisis when it showed on television newscasts the following: (1) surveillance camera b-roll of a grocery store patron placing a syringe in a can; and (2) the canning process that showed how virtually impossible it would be for the syringes to have been placed in the cans at the plant. Today, in addition to television news, the visual pictures could have been shown via YouTube.

An e-blast might be sent to publics who subscribe to the organization's e-mail list. However, e-blasts are being used less than in previous years as communicators employ other methods.

Trick Questions

When a crisis occurs, what questions can you predict the news media will ask a spokesperson? Check Chapter 4 for types of trick questions. Reporters may not ask certain questions intentionally to trick the spokesperson, but the end result—if a question is not answered carefully—can make the spokesperson and his or her organization look bad.

A spokesperson for a restaurant, for example, might be asked the following trick questions:

1. Off the record, didn't you know this might happen?
2. If the fire happened during the lunch hour, how many people might have been killed?
3. Don't you buy your ground beef from the meatpacker who sold bad meat to the other restaurant?
4. As at most popular restaurants, the work here is very fast-paced and stressful, right?

List of Prodromes

Prodromes are the warning signs that a crisis may occur. List these in the crisis communications plan. If any of the prodromes have actually happened, log into the plan what the company did in response and when. This helps the spokesperson answer the media question, "Did you have any warning that this might happen?"

As an example of a prodrome, consider the normally good employee who is unusually tardy and seems stressed out and irritable. Management notices the problem and gets help for the employee. Or take another example, several near-accidents in the organization's parking lot. Management takes notice, determines that the parking lot has confusing directional signs, and has the signs redone.

Heeding prodromes carefully can often prevent a crisis and help show that the organization is concerned with resolving problems. The prodromes section of the crisis communications plan should be regularly updated.

List of Related Internet URLs

List the URLs of organizations and companies that may have information you need during a crisis. Also include brief descriptions of the data available at the URLs. For example, a restaurant might list the URLs for the National Center for Infectious Diseases, the state department of health, the Food and Drug Administration, and the Center for Disease Control.

Evaluation Form

Evaluation is a crucial step in preparing an effective crisis communications plan. As assessment, it is helpful in determining what did and did not work. It also helps plan for, prevent, and cope with future crises by pointing out what needs to be revised in the crisis communications plan.

An evaluation form should be developed and placed at the end of the crisis communications plan for later distribution to internal publics for input. An environment where suggestions are made freely will add to the effectiveness of the evaluation and the crisis communications plan.

Appendix A

Generic Crisis Communications Plan for a Large Company

Contents

Definitions

Communication Objective

Roles and Responsibilities

Notification of a Crisis

Communications Procedure for Handling a Minor Crisis

Communications Procedure for Handling a Major Crisis

Emergency Operations Center (EOC) Activation

Identification of a Spokesperson

Guidelines for Spokespeople

Format for Briefing Someone Identified as a Spokesperson for Interviews/News Briefings

News Release
— Circumstances That May Require a News Release
— Writing an Initial Statement for Release
— Information Appropriate for Release
— Information That Is Not Appropriate for Release
— Writing a News Release

Messages for the News Media During Environmental Crises

Audiences During a Crisis

How People Receive Information During a Crisis

Tools to Use During a Crisis
— Incident Information Sheet
— Telephone Log Sheet
— Example of Initial Statement for Release
— Checklist for Establishing a News Conference Center
— Crisis Contacts

Definitions

Crisis

A *crisis* is an unplanned event that directly or potentially threatens our company's reputations; the environment; the health, safety, or welfare of employees; and the health, safety, or welfare of citizens in communities surrounding our plants.

Events that fall into this category include: fires, explosions, bomb threats, civil disturbances, equipment malfunctions, environmental impacts, widespread illness, hazardous material spills, and other types of incidents.

Minor Crisis

A *minor crisis* is confined to a limited area of a building; results in minimal, if any, disruption of operations; is quickly brought under control; does not require evacuation other than of a few employees in the immediate vicinity; and causes a minor injury or none at all. Media inquiry is possible with events in this category but apt to be minimal.

Major Crisis

A *major crisis* may involve significant injury or loss of life, prolonged disruption of normal operations, substantial property damage, or a significant environmental impact—or holds potential for any of these. Media inquiry is more likely to occur with events in this category, especially if other municipal emergency response groups have been called in for assistance.

Communication Objectives

In the event of a minor or major incident on any of our sites, every effort will be made to communicate as appropriate to employees, management, surrounding communities, other target publics, and the news media promptly and accurately. The appropriate division of communications staff will be the primary information source available to the news media.

When a crisis occurs, it is necessary for communications personnel to gather facts and data quickly, including the nature of our response to the crisis. The following communication efforts will strive to alleviate employees' concerns, minimize speculation by the media, and ensure that our position is presented.

It should be noted, though, that many incidents occur that are relatively minor in nature and are consequently not covered by the media. Nevertheless, it is essential to gather facts about the incidents and have them available to communicate, if necessary, to appropriate audiences.

The nature of that communication is outlined in the following plan.

Each site's Crisis Committee (at the various sites) is responsible for the following: identifying, confirming, investigating crises; developing strategies for managing crises; and developing strategies for recovering from crisis incidents.

As members of the Crisis Committee, communications personnel will:

- Provide a representative at the Emergency Operations Center (EOC) if activated.
- Control the release of information to employees, surrounding communities, and to the news media.
- Maintain contact with media representatives.
- Establish and maintain a news conference center, if necessary.

Two, and in some cases, three communicators may be required for adequate crisis communications response. Those communicators will function in the following roles: Public Relations (PR) Lead, Incident Command (IC) Interface, and PR Back-up.

The responsibilities for each communication role are outlined as follows:

- PR Lead
 — Received initial notification.
 — Designates staff member as IC Interface.
 — Designates staff member as PR Back-up (if necessary).
 — Receives initial facts and updates from IC Interface.
 — Prepares initial statement for release.
 — Fields media inquiries to office.
 — Briefs executive identified as spokesperson.
 — Joins EOC team, if activated.
 — Provides updates to senior executives.
- IC Interface
 — Joins IC team.
 — Gathers and documents facts as they become known.
 — Shares initial facts and updates with PR lead in main office.
 — Prepares initial statement for release (if necessary).
 — Briefs affected organization management and employees.
 — Fields media inquiries (if necessary).
- PR Back-up
 — Updates corporate personnel as necessary.
 — Fields additional media inquiries to office.
 — Fields employee inquiries to office.
 — Conducts in-field interviews with media (if necessary).
 — Sets up media conference room (if necessary).

Notification of a Crisis

Notification is an extremely important process in managing crises and sending the right messages to all audiences. When notification goes well, it makes the rest of the crisis communications job more streamlined and effective than when it doesn't.

Notification of incidents and crises (both major and minor) have been examined by an Ad Hoc Committee to the Corporate Crisis Committee for the past year. Members of this Ad Hoc Committee included PR/Communications, Fire and Security, Facilities, and Emergency Response Coordinators.

This committee has reviewed the entire notification process from the moment a crisis begins to the point that a crisis warrants informing senior corporate executives, including the chief executive officer. This committee has endeavored to determine the most reliable notification process for each site Crisis Committee to use.

Notification Process in Brief

Notification is initiated from the area where a crisis has occurred or been identified. The person who discovers the crisis or incident calls the site emergency number, which is connected to the site Fire Station Dispatch office. A senior Fire Officer is then dispatched to the incident site, evaluates the magnitude of the crisis, and then contacts the Fire Dispatch to notify additional emergency response organizations. From that point on, notification occurs according to defined call lists and through chain-of-command channels.

Site Communications personnel are now notified directly by the respective site Fire Dispatchers. Once that initial notification occurs, the Communications representative receiving the call should, in turn, notify Corporate PR offices and the company switchboard operators as soon as he/she obtains information about the incident, and then follow the procedure noted.

Communications Procedure for Handling a Minor Crisis

Minor Crisis

1. Division Communications receives notification from the Fire Dispatcher and compiles the basic facts and chronology of the event (possibly using an Incident Information Sheet).
2. Division Communications representative becomes the PR Lead and informs other communications team members.

3. PR Lead determines if more information is necessary and if a communicator should be dispatched to incident site (IC Interface).
4. PR Lead calls Incident Commander (this is usually the senior Fire Officer at the incident site).
5. PR Lead notes more details about the incident (type of incident, when and where the incident occurred, chemical involved and potential chemical reactions, emergency response personnel on site, number of employees evacuated, any injuries, work performed in the building, what is being done to mitigate the incident, and who the appropriate contacts are and how to reach them).
6. On-hours, PR Lead notifies and confers with PR Manager (or back-up). Off-hours or on weekends, PR Lead notifies and confers with PR Manager and PR Duty Officer when practical. If the PR Lead determines that the off-hour incident is likely to generate media inquiries, such notification must be made immediately. The PR Duty Officer should notify the Switchboard Operators (555–1000) and tell them to direct media inquiries to the person serving as PR Lead.
7. PR Lead and PR Manager agree to key messages and response to query statement.
8. PR Lead or PR Manager notifies Corporate PR Manager.
9. PR Lead prepares response to query statement, confers with division management, and obtains approval on statement.
10. PR Lead sends statement via fax to PR Manager and to Corporate PR Manager.
11. PR Lead serves as prime contact for media. PR Manager and Corporate PR Manager serve as back-ups.
12. PR Lead fields media inquiries and makes follow-up calls to media if necessary.

Communications Procedure for Handling a Major Crisis

Major Crisis

1. Division Communications receives notification from the Fire Dispatcher and compiles the basic facts and chronology of the event (possibly using an Incident Information Sheet).
2. Division Communications representative becomes the PR Lead and informs other communications team members.
3. PR Lead determines if more information is necessary and if a communicator (IC Interface) should be dispatched to incident site to obtain firsthand information. PR Lead also designates another person as PR Back-up, if necessary.

4. IC Interface goes to site and obtains details from Incident Commander (type of incident, when and where the incident occurred, chemical involved and potential chemical reactions, emergency response personnel on site, number of employees evacuated, any injuries, work performed in the building, what is being done to mitigate the incident, and who the appropriate contacts are and how to reach them).

5. IC Interface calls PR Lead via cellular phone with details of incident. IC Interface should also continue to provide updates to PR Lead every 15–30 minutes or as circumstances change.

6. On-hours, PR Lead immediately notifies and confers with PR Manager (or back-up). Off-hours or on weekends, PR Lead immediately notifies and confers with PR Manager and also notifies the PR Duty Officer. The PR Duty Officer should notify the Switchboard Operators (555–1000) and tell them to direct media inquiries to the person serving as PR Lead.

7. PR Lead and PR Manager agree to key messages and response to query statement.

8. PR Lead or PR Manager notifies Corporate PR Manager.

9. PR Lead prepares response to query statement, confers with division management, and obtains approval on statement.

10. PR Lead sends statement via fax to PR Manager and to Corporate PR Manager.

11. PR Manager informs PR Operations Manager and PR-VP (or acting PR chief) to review the incident, determine the need for additional on-site support, and decide whether the PR news bureau should be opened if it is after working hours. PR-VP decides at this point if executives need to be notified.

12. PR Lead or PR Manager informs Internal Communications Manager who ensures that appropriate internal communications staff will work closely with division communications personnel in collecting data for a timely report to employees.

13. PR Lead and PR Back-up serve as prime contacts for media. PR Manager and Corporate PR Manager serve as back-ups.

14. PR Lead determines if on-site media center is needed and designates PR Back-up to set one up.

15. PR Lead continues to receive information from IC Interface and updates statements accordingly.

16. PR Lead, in turn, provides updates to PR Manager and PR Corporate Manager.

17. PR Lead, PR Manager, and PR Operations Manager confer on whether a press release is needed. If so, PR Lead writes the release, clears it with division management and PR Manager. PR Manager clears release with PR Operations Manager, PR-VP, and other senior officials as required.

18. If incident in on-hours, PR Lead handles follow-up media and employee inquiries and notes incident in report, as necessary.
19. PR Manager and/or Division PR Lead develop report analyzing communications aspects of the incident and lessons learned. Report is distributed to PR Operations Manager and PR-VP, Division Communications staff, and Corporate PR Manager.

EOC Activation

An Emergency Operations Center (EOC) is a centralized location from which emergency response during a very severe crisis is coordinated and directed. A crisis that would force the site EOC to be engaged would be an earthquake or other incident (an act of terrorism) that causes multiple crises at once. Senior emergency preparedness personnel in the company contend that site EOCs along with the Corporate EOC would not be fully activated for a minimum of 2 to 3 hours after the devastating event (i.e., first tremors during an earthquake).

If the site EOC is engaged, all crisis communications would be directed from that point. For adequate communication response, it is recommended that two communicators should be assigned to the center. One communicator would serve as the Communications Manager, who is responsible for coordinating external and internal communications, which may include the use of a runner system, in the event all electronic means of communications are out. The other communicator would serve as the Information Officer, responsible for documenting the sequence of events in support of communications and then generating any statements for release either internally or externally.

Each site EOC will be equipped with maps, stationery supplies, white boards, flip charts, viewfoil machines, telephones, and numerous other supplies. It is recommended that communicators make sure the following items are either stored in the EOC or are available nearby:

- pads and pencils
- laptop computer
- portable printer or some other printing device
- fax machine
- cellular phone(s)
- radio(s)
- Division Crisis Communications Plan

The procedure for communications response should be consistent with the procedure for handling a major crisis, the only difference being that all communications would be directed from the EOC itself.

Identification of a Spokesperson

After an initial assessment of an emergency, the Division General Manager (or designee such as an outplant general manager) will identify the appropriate spokesperson for the division.

Appropriate spokespeople for most divisions are as follows:

- Division Vice President/General Manager
- Plant General Manager (for other sites under division jurisdiction)
- Division Health Manager
- Division Environmental Manager
- Division Safety Manager
- Director of Facilities
- Division Communications Manager
- Public Relations Manager
- Corporate Public Relations Manager

All releases of information outside the division and company shall be by or through the coordinated efforts of Division Communications, Group, and/or Corporate public relations personnel (as noted in the Communications Procedure for Handling Minor or Major Crises). Whenever possible, encourage the various inquiring publics to consult your organization's website for the most up-to-date and accurate content.

All releases of information within the Division will be coordinated by Division Communications personnel.

Guidelines for Spokespeople

1. *Do not speculate.* Always stick to the facts. A more in-depth investigation is required to determine cause.
2. *Focus on two or three key messages to communicate and repeat them during the interview.* Keep answers short and to the point. TV reporters want "sound bites" of no more than 10 to 15 seconds. Try to bridge to your key messages throughout the interview.
3. *Use a technical expert.* There is no substitute for knowledge. If the questions are outside your area of expertise, find an appropriate technical spokesperson within the company.
4. *Speak in simple, common terms.* Avoid jargon.
5. *Remain calm.* Do not be intimidated into answering questions prematurely. You may tell a reporter that you need to clarify an important matter before you can answer questions.
6. *Do not use negative language.* Do not let reporters put words in your mouth.
7. *Consider human safety first.* When human safety or other serious concerns are involved, deal with those considerations first. You can admit concern without admitting culpability.

8. *Do not answer questions you do not understand.* Ask for clarification. Occasionally, this can be used to buy time to think.

9. *Ignore cameras and microphones.* Face the reporter. Don't look away or up at the sky. During videotaped interviews, it's acceptable to stop your statement and start over.

10. *Make only "on the record" statements.* There are no "off the record" statements.

11. *Avoid saying, "No comment."* If you don't know an answer, say so, then bridge to your messages.

Format for Briefing Someone Identified as a Spokesperson for Interviews/News Briefings

Executives scheduled to talk to the media should be provided a background briefing in advance of the interview. This policy should be followed even if the interview is only to be a brief telephone call.

The briefing should include the following 11 items:

- Date, time, and location of the interview.
- Name of the reporter.
- Name of the publication, wire service, station, and so on.
- Our experience with the reporter or publication—to help the executive understand the degree of caution needed in this interview and to prepare for the specific reporter's approach.
- Subjects/issues/questions to be covered as requested by the reporter.
- Our position or recommended response and the data needed to discuss these subjects.
- Top three to five messages we wish to make in the interview (not necessarily based on the reporter's suggested topics).
- List of other executives to be interviewed during this visit, including key topics and messages you suggest the other executives cover.
- Issues, if any, that the executive(s) should avoid, and recommendations on how to sidestep them.
- Background information/statistics that would be useful in preparing for the interview.
- Proposed length of interview.

If possible, this background material should be conveyed in writing so the executive(s) have a chance to review it carefully. Only under exceptional circumstances should you rely on an oral briefing.

In critical situations, it is also useful to prepare a thorough set of questions and answers to define the organization's positions and to use in rehearsing the executive.

News Release

During an emergency situation, it may be determined that a news release should be distributed to the media. The purpose of the news release is to convey written information on the incident and to avoid misinterpretation.

Circumstances That May Require a News Release

- An accident, fire, or explosion that results in serious injury, death, or considerable property damage.
- A health or environmental incident, or discovery of a health or environmental hazard that may affect employees, the surrounding community, or the environment.
- A serious traffic or air accident involving company vehicles, products, and/or personnel.
- Sabotage, abduction or extortion, bomb threats, or acts of terrorism involving company personnel, products, or property.
- News of an incident that is likely to be known by employees or circulated in the community and create misleading impressions.
- News of an event that is unusual enough to cause concern to employees, nearby residents, or community officials.
- Consistently misleading news reports.

Writing an Initial Statement for Release

Often, reporters will call before all the facts have been gathered. In such an instance, a simple statement acknowledging the situation is useful. The short statement avoids "no comment" and acknowledges that our company recognizes the need to cooperate with the media.

Examples:

> "Our company is responding to the situation (or name the emergency). We have trained and experienced people on-site working on the situation."

> "Our first priority is the safety of our employees and the public. We are gathering information, and as soon as details become available, we will inform the media through regular news conferences and updates to our organization's website."

Information Appropriate for Release

During an emergency situation, there will be information that is appropriate to release to employees and to the media. Communications personnel should do the following:

- Tell what happened: Give a description of the emergency situation.
- Tell who is involved: Report how many employees were evacuated and if any have been taken to the hospital for observation or due to injury. Report when emergency team members and/or the various city or county fire departments and police arrived on the scene (if applicable).
- Indicate where it occurred: Give the street address of the scene of the emergency.
- Identify when it happened: Give the time the incident began.

Information That Is Not Appropriate for Release

Obviously, there will be a lot of information that is not appropriate for release until more is known about the nature of the crisis response and the extent of the impact.

- *Do not speculate on why the emergency occurred or what type of hazardous materials are involved.* Likewise, don't make any statement that blames any individual for the accident. (Although the cause of the incident may appear obvious, it cannot be accurately determined without an extensive investigation, nor can the blame be placed on an individual without a thorough investigation.)
- *Do not include "off the record" information* because there is no such information.
- *Do not overreact to or exaggerate the situation.* For instance, during a hazardous material spill, a reporter may ask for the "worst case scenario" of what could happen with the chemicals involved in the accident. It is impossible to determine this until you have specific data regarding the hazardous chemicals involved. Bridge back to facts and messages.
- *Do not minimize the situation.* Never regard an emergency as a minor incident.
- *Do not release the names of injured individuals,* unless Human Resources have authorized it following confirmation that the victim(s)' family(ies) have been notified.
- *Do not release dollar estimates concerning the extent of property damage.* Normally, there is no way to accurately determine this until extensive studies have been conducted.
- *Avoid the "no comment" response because it often leads the reporter to speculate.* If you don't know the answer to a reporter's question or if you can't discuss something, explain why in simple terms.

Writing a News Release

By following a few basic principles when writing news releases, our company stands a better chance of having reporters use the information with only minor changes. Remember to consult the legal department as needed.

1. *Tell the most important information in your lead paragraph.* Your "story" competes with other news and information, so the most important point should be stated clearly in the first paragraph.
2. *Answer four of the five "Ws"—Who, What, Where, and When.* Explain *what* the emergency is. Identify *who* is involved in the emergency as well as the material and equipment involved. Tell *where* and *when* the emergency occurred. Explain *what* action we are taking to mitigate or respond to the emergency. Do not explain *why* the event occurred unless complete information is available.
3. *Attribute information to a qualified source.* A news release is useful only if it conveys credible information.
4. *Write remaining information in descending order of importance.* If the media cuts off the bottom of your story, they will cut information that is least important to the public.
5. *Explain technical points in simple language.* A direct quote can add the human element to otherwise technical information and help explain a situation or event in layman's terms. Tell the real story. Avoid using language that is overly bureaucratic.
6. *Be concise.* A good news release is judged by the quality of information it communicates, not by its length. Stop writing when you've said all you need to say.

Messages for the News Media During Environmental Crises

Mention of the following points during interviews may help the company communicate its position on environmental issues.

- Our primary concern is for the safety of our employees, the communities in which we operate, and the public.
- We operate a state-of-the-art safety monitoring and control system in our factories and laboratories.
- We are prepared at all times to mitigate a chemical spill or leak.
- We work continuously to reduce our use of toxic chemicals in manufacturing processes and to minimize waste.
- Our standards for "worker hazardous materials safety exposure" meet or exceed standards required by the U.S. Occupational Safety and Health Administration (OSHA).

- Our employees who work directly with hazardous materials receive special training in handling the materials safely. It is a mandatory requirement that employees attend such training.
- The company conducts periodic audits of its hazardous materials and hazardous waste installations, equipment, and operating procedures to ensure they comply with environmental regulations and permits during normal and emergency conditions.
- As in the past, the company will continue to work closely with state and federal agencies to meet or exceed environmental regulations, comply with test procedures, and report results to the Environmental Protection Agency (EPA) and the Department of Ecology (DOE).

Audiences During a Crisis

To effectively communicate your message, it's essential to understand who your audience is and how you want your audience to react.

There are two key types of audiences during an emergency.

1. People directly affected by the emergency.
2. People whose attitudes about the company might be influenced by information about the emergency.

These two types of audiences are broken into seven categories. Public Relations objectives in dealing with each of these audiences are listed below:

- *Employees*—We want employees to know that their safety is the number one priority during an emergency. Employees need information regarding the emergency as soon as possible. This must be accomplished in a manner that assures employees that the company has their best interests at heart and that it can effectively handle emergencies.
- *Community Residents*—We want to quell any unnecessary fears. We want the surrounding community residents to know that we take quick, effective steps to protect the health and welfare of community residents and the environment. This can be best accomplished by responding quickly to community concerns and need for information.
- *Top Management*—This group needs to be kept informed in the event of an emergency as well as to be accessible as a resource if necessary.
- *Government Officials*—Key members of this audience need to be kept apprised of the emergency situation, as determined appropriate by the Government Affairs Department.
- *Customers*—Customers need to know that the company is concerned about crises that impact its operating divisions and that may affect production.

- *News Media*—We want the news media to know that the company is credible, concerned, and effective at dealing with emergencies, and that we understand and meet the unique needs of each type of media.
- *Vendors, Contractors, and Suppliers*—We want these audiences to know that we operate state-of-the-art safety monitoring and control systems in our factories and laboratories and that the company takes quick, effective steps to protect the health and welfare of its employees, vendors, and suppliers.

How People Receive Information During a Crisis

In order to determine the most effective ways of communicating during an emergency, it's important to consider how each key audience potentially can receive information. The following sources of information for each audience must be considered in communications strategy for each emergency:

- Employees
 — direct knowledge of the event
 — other employees
 — intercom and phone systems
 — managers
 — electronic mail
 — news media reports
 — fire department/police/hospital spokesperson
- Community Residents
 — direct knowledge of the event
 — neighbors
 — news media reports
- Top Management
 — Company Security, Communications/PR Manager
 — personal call(s) from concerned employee(s)
 — news media reports
- Government Officials
 — Government Affairs
 — news media reports
 — concerned or scared citizen(s)
- News Media
 — Public Relations representative
 — police and/or fire scanners
 — other news media
 — fire department/police/hospital spokesperson
 — eyewitnesses, including employees

— bystanders with knowledge or hearsay
— firsthand view of the situation
— outside "experts"
• Vendors, Contractors, and Suppliers
— direct knowledge of the event
— employees and/or management
— news media reports

Tools to Use During a Crisis

The following documents are recommended tools that each communications group can use or adapt to specific requirements. Note that a few of the tools will definitely have to be adapted, such as Site Map(s), Building Facts and Figures, and phone lists for key emergency response contacts.

These tools can prove very useful for documenting information related to incidents and for keeping track of media inquiries:

• emergency response contacts
• key division directors/managers
• key communications/PR contacts
• incident information sheet
• telephone log sheet
• initial release
• checklist for establishing a news conference center
• maps of division plants
• building facts and figures

INCIDENT INFORMATION SHEET

Complete using ink pen

Date: _____ Time: _____ Initial Report: _____ Update: _____

Describe the incident (i.e., hazardous material spill, equipment malfunction, serious injury, bomb threat, fire, etc.):

Indicate when the incident occurred and when crisis personnel first responded:

Describe which crisis groups are responding:

Indicate where the incident occurred (building number, column number, east or west side of building, etc.):

Describe the work performed in the building(s) where incident occurred (i.e., machining, office functions, mix of factory and office functions):

Estimate the number of employees evacuated:

Estimate the number of employees injured, nature of their injuries (to clarify misleading reports), and where they are being examined/treated (i.e., on-site medical, local hospital):

Describe what is being done to mitigate the emergency:

TELEPHONE LOG SHEET

Priority: _____ Date: _____ Time: _____

Call Received From:

Name _____

Organization _____

Location _____

Message:

Call back by:

Date: _____ Time: _____

Notes:

Example of Initial Statement for Release

At approximately _____ (time) today _____ (date), a _____ (fire, explosion, etc.) occurred on the _____ site of the _____ Division.

Crisis Response personnel are now responding as well as _____ (other support response groups or local municipalities). Our company's response groups include (list appropriate groups such as fire and security officers, medical doctors and nurses, safety personnel, industrial hygienists, environmental engineers, etc.).

Our major concerns are for the safety of our employees and the public and to minimize environmental impact.

We are now involved in determining what has happened and what is being done to mitigate the situation. As more details become available, we will pass them on to the media.

Checklist for Establishing a News Conference Center

In a major emergency, it may be necessary to establish a news conference center. This will be where the company can conduct briefings or news conferences, grant interviews, and issue official statements.

Because time is of the essence during a crisis, communications teams should designate certain locations as potential news conference centers and be prepared to carry out the checklist before an incident occurs.

Preliminaries

1. Check for the best time with company spokesperson.
2. Notify media of time and location.
3. Compile list of names of reporters and editors who indicate they will attend.
4. Compile background information of interest to reporters.
5. Invite outside officials as appropriate.
6. Assign someone to handle the physical arrangements for the news conference.
 - Video services to record event?
 - Junction box for TV and radio mikes?
 - Chairs, tables, podiums as required?
7. Brief staff on the subject, speaker(s), and schedule of events.
8. Prepare opening statement and review with lead speaker.
9. Review anticipated questions and answers with the speaker.
10. Check all sound equipment and tape recorders prior to the conference.
11. Place log sheet in conference room to obtain names and affiliations of attendees.

12. Place all news information and handout materials in conference room.
 - new releases
 - background information, such as fact sheets, maps, statistics, histories, and biographical information
 - copy of opening statement and other briefing materials
13. Escort the media to the conference room.
14. Use sign-in sheet.
15. Distribute background materials.
16. Have assigned staff member open the conference and establish the ground rules.
17. Monitor questions and answers closely. Make any necessary clarifications before the end of the event.

Afterward/Follow-up

18 Handle requests for follow-up information.
19. Monitor coverage received; contact any news organization that has an error in its report.
20. At an appropriate time, when the crisis atmosphere has cleared, contact reporters who attended and ask them what went well in terms of our handling the event and what could have been improved.

Crisis Contacts

	Office	Pager/Cellular	Fax	Home
Key Division Directors				
Jennifer Jones (South)	555-0001	C: 555-4892	555-8101	555-9801
Kourtney Johnson (North)	555-0121	C: 555-4241	555-8294	555-9123
Rebecca Arnold (East)	555-2127	C: 555-4101	555-8711	555-9777
Jeremy Kahlil (West)	555-3122	C: 555-4801	555-8222	555-9554
Key Division Managers				
Mary Bland (South)	555-0092	C: 555-1121	555-8111	555-9682
John Jackson (South)	555-0013	C: 555-6101	555-8221	555-9319
Sarah Yerima (North)	555-1764	N/A	555-8811	555-9276
Jonathan Kyle (East)	555-2809	N/A	555-8611	555-9211
Allison Millet (East)	555-2684	N/A	555-8314	555-9013
Nicholas Michael (West)	555-3093	N/A	555-8781	555-9901
Telephone Operators				
Mary Jackson (Supervisor)	555-2999	N/A	555-8722	555-3994
Fire Dispatch				
Adam Yerima	555-8894	C: 555-8676	555-9467	555-9276
Duane Troy	555-9075	C: 555-0328	555-5541	555-0101
Safety Manager				
Ron Nelson	555-1112	C: 555-3434	555-6875	555-0841
Julius Jones, Jr.	555-3756	C: 555-4441	555-1954	555-2395
Medical				
Ethan Floyd	555-7864	C: 555-3321	555-7764	555-1346
Allyson Bernardino	555-9090	C: 555-8341	555-5603	555-7651
Demetria Rudy	555-5642	C: 555-2390	555-6678	555-6431
Public Relations				
Nelson Johnson II	555-7490	C: 555-4431	555-5505	555-6490
Jerry Brown	555-7456	C: 555-2210	555-9898	555-7069
Corporate Public Relations				
Gina Arnold	555-8754	C: 555-7890	555-2479	555-0956
South				
Regina Arnold	555-8754	C: 555-7890	555-2479	555-0956
Blair Liggins	555-0293	C: 555-7902	555-2478	555-9154
North				
Kourtney Johnson	555-0121	C: 555-4241	555-8294	555-9123
Myrtle Jenkins	555-2123	C: 555-4545	555-9045	555-8456
East				
Beleria Fulks	555-2345	C: 555-7690	555-3147	555-9067
Amanda Johnson	555-0789	C: 555-4680	555-4896	555-3558
West				
Anne Burford	555-1212	C: 555-0097	555-7847	555-0321
O. M. Thornton	555-9557	C: 555-4502	555-5575	555-3498
Katie Marsh (Back-up)	555-9057	N/A	555-0092	555-2664

Crisis Communications Plan for Seattle's Union Gospel Mission

What is a Crisis?

- A significant event that threatens the Mission's reputation, credibility, financial situation, and that the news media are likely to investigate.

The real issue in a crisis is what you say to show that your organization is responsible. Information is the key to resolving any public relations crisis. Impressions are locked-in an hour after the crisis hits. First impressions are important and it is necessary to immediately demonstrate to the news media and its publics that you care.

Examples:

Felonies/Misdemeanors:

- Sexual assault/molestation by a volunteer, staff, resident.
- Physical abuse allegations.
- Murder.
- Any incidents dealing with a weapon.
- Criminal activity by guest, resident, or staff.
- Criminal activity by someone outside the Mission but affects the Mission.
- Issues surrounding domestic violence.

Disease/Sickness:

- Spread of disease (e.g., SARS, TB, AIDS, Swine Flu).
- Food poisoning/E. coli on a mass scale.
- Infestation of bugs (bed bugs, cockroaches, etc.).

Complaints:

- Lawsuits that go public.
- Inquiries regarding mandatory chapel and Bible studies.

- Denial of services to an individual (who goes to media).
- Child abandonment during field trip.
- Fundraising abuse allegations.

Other:

- Fire/Natural disaster.
- Suicide.
- Disgruntled employees or residents.

Notification Procedure

In the event of an emergency/crisis, the employee in charge *must notify THEIR program director AND Public Relations Manager* immediately with all the details of the situation.

Step 1:

- Notify Program Directors and Public Relations Manager. If the Public Relations Manager isn't available, then contact the Senior Vice President who will act as Public Relations Manager.
- Public Relations Manager gets facts about the incident.

Step 2:

A. Program directors call and instruct their front desk personnel

... on procedures to handle incoming calls about the crisis. All calls will be referred to the Crisis Communications Team.

Front Desks:

- Administration 206.723.0767
- Men's Shelter 206.622.5177
- Woman and Family Shelter 206.628.2008
- Son Shine Inn 206.322.6801
- Riverton Place 206.242.5585

B. Public Relations Manager notifies President and Crisis Communications Team

Responsibilities of Crisis Communications Team:

- Investigate and examine the crisis situation and disseminate information to the PR Manager.
- Answer phone calls from targeted audiences and take messages from reporters who are calling so that the spokesperson can get back to them in a timely manner.
- Work with Public Relations Manager and Director of Marketing on the development of messaging as information is obtained.
- Monitor communication channels about incident. This will make sure messaging is accurate and will help dispel rumors.

Crisis Communications Team:

1. President
 - Spokesperson.
2. PR Manager
 - Notification of crisis to Crisis Communications Team.
 - Investigate, evaluate and disseminate information to target audiences through applicable channels.
 - Develop talking points and deliver to spokesperson.
 - Work with spokesperson, media and organize press conference, if applicable.
3. SVP of Recovery Ministries
 - Provide perspective of recovery ministries in crisis, especially if crisis originates from one of the homeless services and/or recovery programs.
 - Second Spokesperson.
4. VP of Outreach Ministries
 - Provide perspective of outreach ministries in crisis, especially if crisis originates from one of the homeless services and/or recovery programs.
5. VP of Human Resources
 - Provide perspective of human resources in case an employee is affected or involved.
6. VP of Accounting and Finance
 - Provide perspective of accounting and finance in case crisis has to do with donations.
7. VP of Development
 - Assists in message development.
 - Provide perspective of finance issues.

8. Director of Marketing
 - Assists in message development and strategy and online technology.
9. Director of Technology
 - Assists with setting up conference room with telephones and any other technical difficulties.
10. Video Production Specialist
 - Videotape and record public statements for website, YouTube and Facebook.
11. Andy Toles
 - Legal Council.

C. Crisis Procedure

1. If President isn't available, an alternative spokesperson will be designated by president or PR Manager.
2. Crisis Communications Team Members will set up and staff an emergency communications center (available to media, staff, clients, donors, churches and volunteers) at the Administration Building.
 - Accommodations: 4+ phone lines; cell phones; paper; pens; computer, spokesperson's business cards.
 - PR manager and Crisis Communications Team to report developments of crisis situation to all members of Crisis Communications Team and spokesperson.
3. Appropriate Crisis Communications Team member will research and obtain all pertinent information to PR manager, other Crisis Communications Team Members and spokesperson. This information will be disseminated to reporters, Mission website, social media, e-blasts, YouTube and all other communications to target audiences. Purpose is to keep all target audiences updated on current information so that accurate information is in the public and to help dispel rumors.
4. PR manager and Director of Marketing will prepare a statement/news release and get approval for its release. Have general brochures available for media.
5. Video Production Specialist will videotape public statement from spokesperson. This video will be uploaded to Mission website, Facebook and YouTube.
6. Determine accessibility vs. news conference route to inform media. If accessibility is chosen, make sure the media is escorted at all times.
7. Continually update target audiences and media on all new developments.

D. Targeted Audiences

Internal

1. Staff members
2. Board members
3. Volunteers
4. Residents/participants in programs

External

5. Donors
6. Media (including bloggers)
7. Facebook fans
8. General public
9. Vendors

E. Guidelines for Handling Reporters

1. Refer all news inquiries to designated spokesperson(s) (usually President and/or someone on the Crisis Communications Team).
2. Do NOT volunteer an opinion or make a statement to any media inquiries. "Off-the-top-of-my-head," "they told me that," etc. answers are suicide answers. State only factual information.
3. Spokesperson obligations:
 * Respond immediately to media requests (helps rumors from starting).
 * Be factual—only offer factual information you have at that time. If the media asks a question you do not know the answer, tell them you'll get back to them.
 * Offer empathy (if applicable) when speaking to the media, especially when something tragic affects another individual.
 * Take responsibility, if applicable.
 * Do not say "no comment" or "off the record"—say instead that the Mission is looking into that matter and as soon as we can get an answer, we'll get back to you.
 * If you can't answer the questions, explain why.
 * Don't be evasive or misleading—make short factual statements.
 * Never speculate—just state the facts that are known at that moment.
 * Don't make light of incidents or accidents.
 * Don't place blame—just state the facts that are known at that moment.

- Eliminate jargon—use simple words that everyone can understand.
- Don't make promises you can't keep.
- Provide evidence, if applicable.
- Don't give names of dead or injured until the family is notified.

F. Consider:

- Running a full-age ad, with a simple, heartfelt apology from the CEO with his photo and his promise to make things work.
- Having the Mission President contact people affected immediately.
- Putting apology, explanations in receipt stuffers, website, blog, e-mails, editorials.

G. Afterwards:

1. Issue a final statement to the media regarding resolutions to prevent a reoccurrence (if appropriate).
2. Compile a record of crisis and Mission's response (i.e., include newspaper clippings, radio/TV reports).
3. Determine if and how the situation could have been dealt with in a better fashion.
4. Make any personnel changes/actions *immediately*.

(The following names would have home, office, and cell phone numbers listed.)

President Contact Information:

Jeff Lilley

Public Relations Manager Contact Information:

Sharon Thomas-Hearns

Program Directors Contact Information:

Mike Johnson
Stacy Cleveland
Deryl Davis-Bell
Larry Joslin
Bobby Martin

Crisis Communications Team Members:

Gary Fast
Marvin Gray
Julie Hong
John Bang
Craig Carpenter
Bob Hall
Andy Toles/Legal Council & Chairman of the Board of Trustees
Lisa White
Glenn Allyn

Crisis Communications Plan for a Fictitious Small Business

UDUB Burger Drive-In's Crisis Communications Plan for E. coli and Hepatitis A

Crisis Communications Plan Team
Department of Communications
University of Washington
Professor Kathleen Fearn-Banks
Written March 10, 1999

Dana Anderson
Jennifer Boyeson
Sarah Doran
Meg Hemphill
Stacy Jaffe
Melissa Jones
Jaime Kennerud
David Masin
Alexandra Ootkin
Danielle Rosenow
Julie Sanders
Diva Sze

Revised May 25, 1999
Sarah Doran
Meg Hemphill
Melissa Jones
Jaime Kennerud
Danielle Rosenow

Revised February 6, 2006
Joel Bellazza
Tested: _____

Contents

Introduction: UDUB Burger's Crisis Communications Plan
Acknowledgments
Statement from Management to Employees
 Purposes
 Objectives
 Crisis Inventory and Results
Warning Signs of a Possible Crisis
Crisis Communications Checklist* (form in Student Workbook)
 E. coli
 Hepatitis A
Telephone log* (forms in Student Workbook)
 Media Lists*
 Local Television News Personnel
 Local Radio News Personnel
 Local Newspaper Personnel
 Local Newswire Personnel
 Public Relations Contacts
List of Key Publics*
 Internal
 External
Crisis Communications Team Directory*
The Media Spokesperson
 Criteria for Selecting
 Interview Tips
 Trick Questions
List of Emergency Personnel
Key Messages
 E. coli
 Hepatitis A
Evaluation of Plan Effectiveness After a Crisis
Methods of Communication
Pregathered Information
 Generic News Release for E. coli
 History of UDUB Burger Drive-In*
 E. coli Fact Sheet
 Hepatitis A Fact Sheet
 Glossary of Food-Related Illnesses
 Community Relations Programs*
 Employee Relations
 Employee Handbook*
 Cooking Procedures*
 Advertising*

Photographs and Memories*
URLs for Food Poisoning

*Item is not included due to its personal nature.

Introduction: UDUB Burger's Crisis Communications Plan

Why is This Plan Important?

With the plethora of controversy and crisis surrounding the food industry, particularly the fast-food industry, it is always advisable to be prepared for any possible emergency that could damage our establishment. UDUB's hamburger stand has a good reputation among fast-food consumers in Seattle, our target market, and we need to make sure that our reputation is not damaged.

What Could Happen If the Plan Is Not Followed?

If this crisis communications plan is not followed in the event of an emergency, the company's good name and reputation in the community could be damaged, which may result in a loss of business. Because trust and reliability are important to consumers, they must feel that they can trust that a certain problem will not reoccur and that they are safe eating at UDUB Burger Drive-In.

Has a Crisis Happened at UDUB Burger Before?

Fortunately, there have not been any reports of food poisoning from our customers. However, we should always be prepared for this type of crisis because it is a common problem in the fast-food industry.

Has a Crisis Happened to Similar Companies?

Yes. The E. coli outbreak that occurred at a Jack-in-the-Box in 1993 was a warning to all fast-food organizations. That crisis, which had a negative effect on the chain's name and reputation, serves as a good example of what not to do when dealing with the media in the midst of a crisis.

Acknowledgments

By signing this statement, I verify that I have read this crisis communications plan and am prepared to put it into effect.

President and CEO

(Signature and date)

Vice President and CFO

(Signature and date)

Vice President

(Signature and date)

Office Manager

(Signature and date)

Statement from Management to Employees

There are many high-risk factors surrounding the fast-food industry, making it necessary for all food organizations to be ready for a potential public crisis at any time. Our risks are heightened by the nature of our industry: We provide quick and simple food service. Especially with meat, there is a high risk of food poisoning if the meat is not cooked properly. Because of these dangers, it is vital that UDUB Burger's employees are prepared to deal with the media and the public quickly and efficiently in the event of a crisis.

We have worked for many years to build an impeccable reputation with the public for providing clean, quick, and quality service and food to our consumers. Because the most damaging scare in the food industry, particularly with hamburgers, is food poisoning—particularly the E. coli virus and hepatitis A—it is crucial that UDUB Burger be prepared for any possible circumstances involving a patron of our restaurant becoming ill from our food. As mentioned earlier, the E. coli crisis that struck Jack-in-the-Box was a prodrome to all fast-food handlers. In order to prevent similar damage to our company, we must take very seriously what

happened at Jack-in-the-Box and what Foodmaker did wrong in communicating with the media and the public.

If this crisis communications plan is not followed in the event of a crisis, irreparable damage to the reputation of UDUB Burger Drive-In is possible. The loss of trust among our consumers could also lead to a large loss of business. In dealing with this crisis plan, we must keep in mind that trust and reliability are incredibly important to consumers when choosing a place to eat, and UDUB Burger must protect its reputation as being a reliable fast-food source. We trust that all employees will keep up their outstanding work in order to protect our company from such a crisis.

Purposes

In the event of an E. coli or hepatitis A outbreak, we must take immediate action to inform our publics of the situation and the measures they need to take. Our open and honest transfer of information to the media and health care facilities will eliminate confusion among our publics. By being truthful and forthright, the crisis situation can be more smoothly resolved and action can be taken to eliminate any future problems.

Objectives

We will make every effort to:

1. Initiate the crisis communications plan within 2 hours of the crisis outbreak in the event of a suspected E. coli or hepatitis A infection from food eaten at one of our restaurants.
2. Inform all health care organizations that might be involved with the situation.
3. Inform all owners and managers within 3 hours of the outbreak.
4. Inform the media and restaurant patrons within 4 hours of the outbreak.
5. Keep the media and all publics regularly informed of updated information through regular news briefs and updates to the company's website.
6. Maintain honesty with the media about all known information.
7. Find the source of the problem as soon as possible.
8. Distribute our findings to the media and all publics.
9. Develop ways to alleviate future problems.
10. Implement necessary changes as soon as possible and resume business as usual.

Crisis Inventory and Results

The accompanying crisis inventory graph (see Fig. C.1) analyzes five possible crises that could occur at a UDUB Burger Drive-In: E. coli poisoning, hepatitis A poisoning, fire, injury, and violence. By studying the probability of each possible crisis and the amount of possible damage that could result if that crisis occurred, it was determined that UDUB Burger Drive-In is more vulnerable to the crises involving E. coli or hepatitis A outbreaks. This crisis plan was created to suit the needs of UDUB Burger Drive-In in case one of these emergencies should occur.

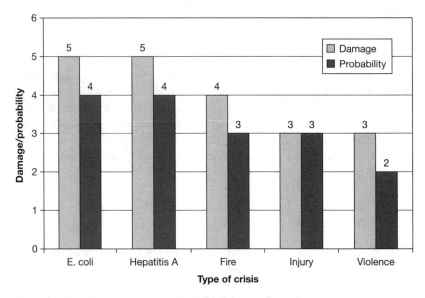

Figure C.1 A crisis inventory graph for UDUB Burger Drive-In.

Warning Signs of a Possible Crisis

E. coli

- The E. coli crisis that occurred at a Jack-in-the-Box cost the company a large number of customers. UDUB Burger can prevent this type of crisis by following proper food-handling instructions and by being aware of the quality of hamburger meat served to customers.
- Employees will be trained in meat-preparation techniques to ensure that the hamburgers reach a temperature high enough to kill E. coli bacteria.

Hepatitis A

- Warning signs of a potential hepatitis A outbreak include employee illness, failure to wash hands, and improper food handling. All employees will be educated in how to prevent the spread of hepatitis A.
- If an employee contracts hepatitis A, the individual will not be allowed to work until he or she is declared "safe" by the Department of Health.

Fire

- The 1968 kettle fire at the UDUB Burger Drive-In in Lake City was a wake-up call to all employees. Five days of business were lost. Employees could have been seriously injured. Instructions for fire prevention can be found in the UDUB Burger Drive-In Employee Handbook.
- Unsafe working conditions or malfunctioning equipment could lead to a potentially dangerous fire. All employees will be trained to recognize possible dangers in the preparation area.

Injury

- Whether involving employees or customers, injury in the workplace can create serious long-term problems, such as loss of business, reduced workforce, negative publicity, and legal repercussions.
- Employees will be trained to take precautions and to notice potentially hazardous areas, such as wet floors, construction areas, and other unsafe areas.

Violence

- Whether involving employees or customers, violence in the workplace is a tragic event with serious consequences.
- Employee training, counseling, and other preventive measures will be taken to curb the possibility of violence occurring at a UDUB Burger Drive-In establishment.

The Media Spokesperson

The media spokesperson represents the company and speaks on behalf of the company. The spokesperson must be selected very carefully. In addition, two or three back-up spokespeople should be selected in advance in case the primary spokesperson is unavailable at the time of a crisis.

Criteria for Selecting

- The spokesperson must have the power to make decisions and be accessible throughout the crisis.
- The spokesperson must be articulate. He or she must be able to talk clearly, concisely, and in a pleasant manner.
- The spokesperson must appear rational, concerned, and empathetic during a crisis.
- Multiple spokespersons, when used, must all be prepared to say the same thing.

Interview Tips

Primary and Backup Spokespersons
Office Phone
Cell Phone
Home Phone
E-Mail

Spokesperson 1: _____

Spokesperson 2: _____

Spokesperson 3: _____

Spokesperson 4: _____

- Prepare for answering who, what, when, where, why, and how questions.
- Focus on two or three key messages to communicate and repeat them during the interview.
- Gather background information that may be useful during the interview.
- Be aware of subjects, issues, and questions that might be brought up.
- Be accessible and pleasant to reporters: Show respect, and remember their names, if possible.
- Avoid saying, "No comment."
- Be honest.
- Remain calm, courteous, truthful, concerned, and, if necessary, apologetic.
- Face the reporter, not the camera or the microphone.
- Avoid jargon: Speak in everyday language.
- Do not speculate. Do not answer questions you don't understand. Ask for clarification.
- Be trained ahead of time, rehearsed well in advance of the crisis, and briefed prior to responding to the media.

Trick Questions

Reporters might bring you into a difficult situation by asking you trick questions. Following are examples of various types of trick questions.

1. Speculative questions that begin with if:
 * "If the hamburgers that were infected were served during the normal lunch hour instead of late at night, how many people would have been infected?"
 * "If the hamburgers had been cooked at a higher temperature, would the E. coli outbreak have happened?"
2. Leading questions:
 * "You do agree that UDUB Burger could have avoided this crisis, right?"
3. Loaded questions:
 * "Isn't it true that you knew there was an E. coli outbreak but couldn't do anything to stop it at once, so it caused so many deaths?"
 * "Isn't it true that you knew of possible E. coli in the undercooked hamburgers?"
 * "Isn't it true that you knew this employee had hepatitis A and that you failed to do anything about it?"
 * "Isn't it true that the shift manager should have been aware of the warning signs of this crisis?"
4. Naïve questions:
 * "What type of food does UDUB Burger Drive-In serve?"
5. False questions (containing inaccurate details that reporters want you to correct):
 * "There were only two employees during the rush hours, right?"
 * "About 90% of your meat comes from the same plant that the contaminated meat from Jack-in-the-Box came from, correct?"
 * "More than seven people have been affected by the virus strain that started here at your restaurant, right?"
6. Know-it-all questions:
 * "We have all the facts. I just need to confirm a few things with you, okay?"
 * "I have all of the details, but could you give me some wrap-up comments about this crisis?"
7. Silence: This tactic aims to get you to "spill your guts."
8. Accusatory questions (designed to make you blame someone else):
 * "Who is actually responsible for this crisis?"
9. Multiple-part questions (designed to be intentionally confusing):
 * "What is the temperature at which you cook your meat, and is that the regulation for Washington? If it is, then how can someone contract this virus if heat is supposed to kill it?"

10. Jargon questions: Make sure to avoid using technical words that can confuse publics.
11. Chummy questions:
 • "Hey Pal, off the record, why do you think this happened?"
12. Labeling questions:
 • "Would you say that the atmosphere here at UDUB Burger is 'stressful'?"
 • "Would you call the fast-paced environment stressful enough for one to lose sight of a specified task?"
13. Good-bye questions (reporters give the impression that the interview is over before asking such questions):
 • "Good-bye. Oh, by the way, how did this crisis actually happen?"

List of Emergency Personnel

Seattle Police Department
610 3rd, Seattle 98104
911
Media Relations: 684-5520
Fax: 684-8197

Virginia Mason
925 Senaca, Seattle 98101
Communications: 583-6082
Fax: 223-6744

Fire Department
301 2nd, Seattle 98104
911
Dept. Info: 386-1400
Fax: 386-1412

UW Medical Center
1959NE Pacific St., Seattle 98105
PR: 543-3620
Fax: 685-3333

Harbor View Medical Center
325 9th Ave. S., Seattle 98104
PR: 731-4199
Fax: 731-8605

Swedish Medical Center
PR: 386-6797

King County Department of Health
206-269-4755

Key Messages

E. coli

In the event of an E. coli outbreak, UDUB Burger employees' first priority is the care of its customers. Warning the public of the symptoms of E. coli is the first order of business. The symptoms can include one or more of the following: abdominal cramps, bloody diarrhea, and nausea. Our primary concern is with those who are infected with E. coli. Without knowing the exact location where the E. coli originated, whether from the meat distributor or inside our store, we promise the public that the

source of the bacteria will be discovered as promptly and effectively as possible.

We will also restate consistently the fact that we are concerned with the E. coli problem and that our primary concern is for those infected. We will restate how careful and cautious UDUB Burger is in preventing diseases such as this one from occurring. We will state that our employees cook meat to the standard temperature set by the FDA and that employees follow proper cleaning procedures outlined by the FDA. We will explain that employees are required to receive a food-handler permit prior to working at UDUB Burger.

The following key messages should be stressed in the order indicated:

1. Our biggest concern is for those affected.
2. We are sorry for what happened and we take full responsibility for what happened.
3. We don't know how it happened, but we are trying to find out and we'll let you know as soon as we know.
4. We maintain a strict and thorough process on avoiding problems such as these from occurring by requiring our employees to receive a food-handler permit.

Hepatitis A

In the event of hepatitis A scare, UDUB Burger employees' first priority is the care of its customers. Warning the public of the symptoms of hepatitis A is the first order of business. The symptoms can include one or more of the following: fatigue, nausea, vomiting, fever/chills, jaundice, pain in the liver area, dark urine, light-colored stools, and/or abdominal pain. Our primary concern is with those who are infected with hepatitis A. Without knowing the exact location where the hepatitis A originated, whether from one of the employees or an external source, we promise the public that the source of the disease will be discovered as promptly and effectively as possible.

We will also restate consistently the fact that we are concerned with the hepatitis A problem and that our primary concern is for those infected. We will restate how careful and cautious UDUB Burger is in preventing diseases such as this one from occurring. We will state that employees are required to receive a food-handler permit prior to working at UDUB Burger and that they must wash their hands before handling food.

The following key messages should be stressed in the order indicated:

1. Our biggest concern is for those affected.
2. We are sorry for what happened and we take full responsibility for what happened.

3. We don't know how it happened, but we are trying to find out and we'll let you know as soon as we know.
4. We maintain a strict and thorough process on avoiding problems such as these from occurring by requiring our employees to receive a food-handler permit.

Evaluation of Plan Effectiveness After a Crisis

After a crisis, the following steps will be followed to ensure that UDUB Burger is better prepared for the future. This evaluation is for looking at what went right and what went wrong during the crisis. It covers all aspects of the crisis, including media relations, community relations, and the crisis management team's performance. It is vital to evaluate the company's CCP while the crisis is still fresh in employees' minds. Thinking about all aspects of the crisis will help determine what we can do better next time.

1. Media relations: Review the media's coverage of the crisis. Were there areas in which we could have received better or more positive coverage of our company? Would the coverage have been better if we had taken more time to build strong media relationships before the crisis?
2. Community relations: Did the community act favorably to how we handled the crisis? If not, what can we do to build better community relations (i.e., public service donations or activities)? If we donate money or services, make sure that the public is aware of it (through media coverage or information at our restaurant locations).
3. Crisis management team: Did all team members perform well under pressure? Were there certain members who should have been put "behind the scenes" or on the "front lines" (speaking to the media, etc.)? Should any members be replaced by others should another crisis occur? Was the crisis control room properly stocked? Was there anything missing that needs to be ordered or created?

Methods of Communication

In the event of a crisis, the following publics should be contacted in the manner indicated in the chart.

Public	Telephone	E-mail	Fax	Letter by Mail	Newsletter	Bulletin Board	Personal Visit	News Release
Meeting								
Owners	•	•						
Executive	•	•						
Employees				•	•	•		•
Electronic media	•						•	
Daily newspapers	•						•	
Weekly newspapers	•						•	
Suppliers	•		•					
Community leaders				•	•			

Pregathered Information

Generic News Release for E. coli

A UDUB Burger Drive-In customer is being treated for symptoms of E. coli at (name of hospital). His/her condition is _____. It is not known at this time if he/she contracted the illness at the UDUB Burger Drive-In location where he/she dined on (date).

"We are very concerned about (victim's name) and we are monitoring his/her condition closely. Whether the illness came from food at UDUB Burger or other causes, we wish for his/her speedy recovery," said _____, UDUB Burger's owner and president.

According to (whom), (victim's name) ate a hamburger at the UDUB Burger Drive-In located at (address or neighborhood). He/she is said to be experiencing (symptoms).

The health department is currently investigating to see if there is a possible link between the burgers served at UDUB Burger and the victim's illness. In the 45-year history of UDUB Burger Drive-In, there have been no other reported cases of this illness.

UDUB Burger Drive-In has a strict sanitary code that requires employees to cook hamburgers to 160 degrees, 10 degrees higher than required by the U.S. Food and Drug Administration. Employees are thoroughly trained in cooking according to safety and health procedures.

E. coli Fact Sheet

Definition of E. coli

E. coli is an emerging cause of food-borne illness. E. coli are germs (bacteria) that normally live in the intestines of people and animals. There is no treatment for E. coli.

What Are the Symptoms?

The most common symptoms are severe stomach cramps and diarrhea. Some people vomit or run a fever, but these are less common. These symptoms usually go away by themselves after 6 to 8 days. In a small number of people, this strain of E. coli can cause a rare but serious problem called hemolytic uremic syndrome (HUS).

What Is HUS?

HUS is a disease that affects the kidneys and blood-clotting system. In severe cases, dialysis is used for a limited time to do the kidneys' work. Some people also develop a bleeding problem or low red blood cell count (anemia).

Where Is E. coli Found?

It lives in the intestines of healthy cattle and gets into the meat when cattle are slaughtered. The germs are killed when the meat is thoroughly cooked. Germs have also been found in raw milk, apple cider, and salami.

How Is E. coli Spread?

E. coli must be swallowed to cause an infection. This can happen if you eat or drink something that contains these germs and is not properly cooked or pasteurized. The germs can be spread from person to person if someone who is infected does not thoroughly wash his or her hands with soap and water before preparing food for others.

How Is E. coli Prevented?

Take the following steps to avoid infection:

- Do not eat nonpasteurized dairy products or undercooked ground beef.
- Do not drink raw milk or apple cider that is made from unwashed apples.

- Always wash your hands with soap and water after going to the bathroom, changing a diaper, or handling raw meat.

Hepatitis A Fact Sheet

What Is Hepatitis A?

It is a highly contagious virus that attacks the liver. It is the seventh most commonly reported infectious disease in the United States (behind gonorrhea, chicken pox, syphilis, AIDS, salmonellosis, and shigellosis). Hepatitis A accounts for as many as 65% of all viral hepatitis cases in the United States each year. It is the most prevalent type of hepatitis.

What Are the Symptoms?

The common symptoms of hepatitis A are fatigue, nausea, vomiting, fever/chills, jaundice, pain in the liver area, dark urine, light-colored stools, and/or abdominal pain.

How Do You Get Hepatitis A?

The hepatitis A virus is transmitted by the fecal–oral route through close person-to-person contact or by ingesting contaminated food or water. Infection has been shown to be spread by:

- Close personal contact with someone infected with hepatitis A.
- Eating foods contaminated by infected food handlers.
- Contact with infected children (who do not usually show symptoms), who can then infect nonimmune children or adults at home or in child-care centers.
- Ingesting raw or undercooked shellfish (e.g., oysters, clams, mussels) from waters contaminated with the virus.
- Ingesting contaminated food or water during travel to under-developed areas.
- Transmission through blood transfusions or sharing needles with infected people using injectable drugs.

What Is the Course of the Disease?

The incubation period for hepatitis A, which varies from 10 to 50 days (mean 30 days), is dependent on the number of infectious particles consumed. Infection with very few particles results in longer incubation periods. The period of communicability extends from early in the incubation period to about a week after the development of jaundice. The greatest danger of spreading the disease to others occurs during the

middle of the incubation period, well before the first presentation of symptoms. Many infections do not result in clinical disease, especially in children. When the disease does occur, it is usually mild and recovery is complete in 1 to 2 weeks. Occasionally, the symptoms are severe and convalescence can take several months. Patients suffer from feeling chronically tired during convalescence and their inability to work can cause financial loss. Less than 0.4% of reported cases in the United States are fatal. These deaths usually occur among the elderly.

What Is the Treatment?

There is currently no treatment for hepatitis A, although rest and proper nutrition can relieve some symptoms. The most important factor affecting the severity of the disease is age.

How Dangerous Is Hepatitis A?

A very small percentage of people infected with hepatitis A are at risk for serious complications. An estimated 100 deaths occur in the United States each year from the virus.

Does It Come From a Specific Food?

The virus has not been isolated from any food associated with an outbreak. Because of the long incubation period, the suspected food is often no longer available for analysis. No satisfactory method is presently available for routine analysis of food. Cold cuts and sandwiches, fruits and fruit juices, milk and milk products, vegetables, salads, shellfish, and iced drinks are commonly implicated in outbreaks. Water, shellfish, and salads are the most frequent sources. Contamination of foods by infected workers in food-processing plants and restaurants is common.

Glossary of Food-Related Illnesses

Botulism—A disease caused by contamination of certain foods by the botulism bacterium commonly found in the soil. The botulism toxin is produced when the bacteria grow in improperly canned foods and occasionally in contaminated seafood. Common symptoms are headaches, nausea, vomiting, constipation, and overall weakness. It progressively attacks the nervous system, causing double vision, muscle paralysis, and difficulty with breathing and speech. Symptoms appear 8 to 12 hours after eating contaminated food. Death may occur within 3 to 7 days without treatment. There is an antitoxin to treat the disease.

Campylocbacteriosis—Bacteria found in the intestinal tracts of healthy animals and untreated water surfaces. Inadequately cooked animal products and nonchlorinated water are the most common reasons for human infection. It can be easily killed by heat above 120 degrees Fahrenheit. Common symptoms are abdominal cramping, diarrhea, fever, headache, muscle pain, and nausea. Symptoms appear 2 to 5 days after eating contaminated food and may last 2 to 7 days.

Clostridium Perfringens—Bacteria found in soil, unprocessed foods, nonpotable water, and the intestinal tract of humans and animals. It is a milder form of botulism. Symptoms include abdominal pain and diarrhea. Symptoms appear 8 to 24 hours after eating contaminated food and may last 1 to 2 days.

E. coli Hemolytic Colitis—Bacteria that come in many forms; most are harmless except the E. coli 0157:H7 strain. Abdominal cramps and bloody diarrhea are the distinctive symptoms of this strain. Other symptoms are fever, nausea, and vomiting. These symptoms appear 3 to 5 days after eating contaminated food. Symptoms may last 10 days.

Hepatitis A Virus—A highly contagious virus that attacks the liver. The virus is transmitted by the fecal-oral route, through close person-to-person contact, or by ingesting contaminated food or water. Common symptoms are fatigue, nausea, vomiting, fever, jaundice, pain in the liver area, dark urine, and abdominal pain. The disease can stay in the body for 10 to 50 days without showing symptoms. Recovery usually takes 1 to 2 weeks.

Listeriosis—Bacteria that live in humans and animals. It is usually associated with cattle and sheep having abortions and encephalitis. The elderly, newborn babies, pregnant women, and people with a weakened immune system are the most vulnerable to this infection. Possible symptoms are fever, headaches, nausea, and vomiting. Symptoms appear 3 days to a few weeks after eating contaminated food and may last several days. Death may occur in rare cases.

Salmonellosis—Bacteria spread through contact with human or animal intestinal contents or excrement, usually found in raw meat, fish, poultry, and eggs. Symptoms, which are headache, vomiting, nausea, chills, fever, diarrhea, and abdominal cramping, appear 12 to 36 hours after eating contaminated food. The symptoms may last 2 to 7 days.

Staphylococcal Intoxication—Bacteria found on the skin and in the nose and throat of most humans. People with sinus infections and colds are high carriers. Infected wounds are rich sources of this bacterium. Sewage, raw milk, and untreated water are carriers. Symptoms are vomiting, nausea, diarrhea, and abdominal cramping. Symptoms appear 1 to 8 hours after eating contaminated food and may last 1 to 2 days.

Employee Relations

- UDUB Burger is an equal opportunity employer.
- UDUB Burger pays at least $7.00 an hour to start. A $1.00 per-hour bonus is paid to employees working between 11 p.m. and 2 a.m., and between 11 a.m. and 2 p.m.
- The opportunity to get raises in pay occurs twice a year at evaluation time.
- Benefits include the following (see the Employee Handbook for more information):
 - Health and dental insurance plan.
 - Employee scholarship plan.
 - Child-care benefit program.
 - Community service plan.
 - 401(k) tax-deferred retirement savings plan.
 - Overtime hours paid at a rate of time and a half (based on the employee's regular hourly wage).
 - Half-price food.
 - Bonus program for new employee referrals.

URLs for Food Poisoning

http://cdc.gov/ncidod.ncid.htm National Center for Infectious Diseases
- Learn about the NCID
- Disease information
- Bacterial information
- Access *Emerging Infectious Diseases* (journal)

www.doh.wa.gov/Topics/ecoli.htm:PublicFactSheetAboutE.coli
- What is it?
- Who gets it?
- How does it spread?
- What are the symptoms?
- How is it diagnosed?

www.doh.wa.gov/Topics/hepafact.html Public Fact Sheet About Hepatitis A
- What is hepatitis A?
- How does it spread?
- How is it contracted?
- Overall history

www.cdc.gov/
- What the Centers for Disease Control (CDC) website does
- Health news
- Hepatitis information
- Ideas for protecting oneself from diseases

www.doh.wa.gov/
- Washington State Department of Health website
- Frequently asked questions about diseases
- Frequently called safety phone numbers in the area
- Current health issues in Washington
- General facts to keep us informed

Sources

Chapter 1: Crisis Communications Today

Barton, L. (1993). *Crisis in organizations*. Cincinnati, OH: South-Western.

Ziakas, T. (1999). Titanic and public relations: A case study. *Journal of Public Relations Research, 11*, 105–124.

Chapter 2: Crisis Communications Theory

Associated Press (2006, September 16) MSNBC.COM. Retrieved December 28, 2009 from www.msnbc.com/.

Barton, L. (1993). *Crisis in organizations*. Cincinnati, OH: South-Western.

Benoit, W. L. (1995). *Accounts, excuses, apologies: A theory of image restoration strategies*. Albany, NY: University of New York Press.

Benoit, W. L. (1997). Image restoration discourse and crisis communication. *Public Relations Review, 23*, 177–186.

Biswas, T. (1997). *Decision-making under uncertainty*. New York: St. Martins.

Castro, H. (2007, October 5). Sheriff apologizes but defends policy. *Seattle Post Intelligencer*, A1.

Fearn-Banks, K. (1996). Crisis communications theory and ten businesses hit by news-making crises. In G. Amin & S. Fullerton (Eds.), *Global business trends: Contemporary readings* (pp. 847–851). Cumberland, MD: Academy of Business Administration.

Grunig, J. E., & Grunig, L. A. (1992). Models of public relations and communications. In J. E. Grunig (Ed.), *Excellence in public relations and communication management* (pp. 85–326). Hillsdale, NJ: Lawrence Erlbaum Associates.

Grunig, J. E., & Hunt, T. (1984). *Managing public relations*. New York: Holt.

Grunig, J. E., & Repper, F. C. (1992). Strategic management, publics, and issues. In J. E. Grunig (Ed.), *Excellence in public relations and communication management* (pp. 117–157). Hillsdale, NJ: Lawrence Erlbaum Associates.

Hearit, K. M. (2001). Corporate apologia: When the organization speaks in defense of itself. In R. L. Heath (Ed.), *Handbook of public relations* (pp. 501–512). Thousand Oaks, CA: Sage.

Marra, F. J. (1992). *Crisis public relations: A theoretical model*. Unpublished doctoral dissertation, University of Maryland, College Park.

Rogers, E. M. (2003). *The diffusion of innovations* (5th ed.). New York: Free Press.

Schick, F. (1997). *Making choices: A recasting of decision theory*. New York: Cambridge University Press.

Ware, B. L., & Linkugel, W. A. (1973). They spoke in defense of themselves: On the generic criticism of apologia. *Quarterly Journal of Speech, 59,* 273–283.

Chapter 3: Communications to Prevent Crises

Bernstein, C. (1994, August 9). Interview. *CBS This Morning*. New York: CBS.

Spector, R., & McCarthy, P. (2000). *The Nordstrom way*. New York: Wiley.

Chapter 4: Communications When the Crisis Strikes

Coombs, W. T. (1999). *Ongoing crisis communication*. Thousand Oaks, CA: Sage.

George, A. (2005, October 20). *Blogs as transformational corporate communication tool: Implications for crisis communication*. Paper presented at the annual meeting of the Association for Business Communication, Irvine, CA.

Internet usage and population in North America (2009, September 30). North America Internet Usage Statistics. Retrieved November 23, 2009 from www.internetworldstats.com.

Media trend track (2009, September 30). TV Basics Television Households. Retrieved November 23, 2009, from www.tvb.org.

Metzler, K. (1994, March). Shooting it out with the media. *Hemispheres Magazine*, pp. 51–53.

Rappoport, P. N., & Alleman, J. (2003). The Internet and the demand for news: Macro-microevidence. In A. M. Nolls (Ed.), *Crisis communications: Lessons for September 11* (pp. 149–166). Lanham, MD: Rowman & Littlefield.

Smudde, P. M. (2005, Fall). Blogging, ethics, and public relations: A proactive and dialogic approach. *Public Relations Quarterly*, pp. 34–38.

Thompson, T., & Hess, J. (1986, November, 15). Delta accused of Jekyll–Hyde behavior in wake of crash. *Atlanta Constitution*, pp. 1–10.

World Internet usage statistics (n.d.). Retrieved May 11, 2010, from www.internetworldstats.com.

Chapter 5: Social Media and Crisis Communications

Avers, C. (2009, March 10). Researchers: Social networking sites critical in disaster situations. *Denver News, Channel 7 News*. Retrieved April 26, 2009, from www.thedenverchannel.com.

Cell phones, blogs enable live reporting of Virginia Tech shooting. TECHWEB. Retrieved March 15, 2009, from www.lexisnexis.com.

Clifford, S. (2009, April 16). Video prank at Domino's taints brand. *The New York Times Online*. Retrieved April 16, 2009, from www.nytimes.com.

Condon, P. (2009, March 27). Wall to wall, Facebook gets word out. *Seattle Times*, A4.

Deutsch, L. (2009, July 3). Judge tosses verdict in cyberbully case. *Seattle Times*, A2.

George, J. (2007, April 18). Facebook makes new connections. *St. Petersburg Times*. Retrieved March 15, 2009, from www.lexisnexis.com.

Griggs, B. (2010, January 14). Twitter hoax spreads rumors of airlines' free flights to Haiti. CNN Tech. Retrieved January 14, 2010, from www.cnn.com.

Higgins, M. (2009, July 5) Twitter comes to the rescue. *The New York Times Online*. Retrieved November 21, 2009, from www.nytimes.com/2009/7/05/travel.

Holland, G. (2009, April 1). College goofs on e-mail to rejected applicants. *Seattle Times*, A5.

Ingram, M. (2008, May 5). Want immediate emergency updates? Go to Facebook. *The Globe and Mail*. Retrieved March 15, 2009, from www.lexisnexis.com.

Luft, A. (2009, November 23). Canada woman to fight insurance co. over Facebook. *Comcast*. Retrieved November 23, 2009, from www.comcast.net.

McAdams, S. (2008, October 29). Twitter proves invaluable in a crisis. *Ragan*. Retrieved March 15, 2009 from www.ragan.com.

Nagesh, G. (2009, February 9). Agencies used social media to manage salmonella outbreak. *NextGov Technology and the Business of Government*. Retrieved March 15, 2009, from www.nextgov.com.

Needleman, S. (2009, August 3). For companies, a Tweet in time can avert a PR mess. *The Wall Street Journal Online*. Retrieved October 23, 2009, from http://online.wsj.com/article.

Pham, M. (2007, April 18). Tragedy unfolds to millions via blogs and websites. *The Irish Times*. Retrieved March 15, 2009, from www.lexisnexis.com.

Ward, M. (2009, March 2). Facebook users suffer viral surge. BBC News. Retrieved March 6, 2009, from http://news.bbc.co.uk/2/hi/technology.

Young, E. (2009, February 11). Crisis puts a new face on social networking. *Sydney Morning Herald*. Retrieved March 15, 2009, from www.lexisnexis.com.

Chapter 6: Rumors and Cybercrises

Battenberg, E. (1999, November). Dealing with cyberspace attacks. *Public Relations Tactics*, 14.

Brown, M. (2005, September 11). I webbed the news today—oh boy! *Seattle Times*, p. D1.

Cancun, A. (2005, November 3). *Blogs as PR tools*. Retrieved April 31, 2006, from www.advertising.about.com/od/publicrelationsresources/a/prbloop.htm.

Cheek, M. (1991, May 25). Student apologizes for AIDS rumor about eatery. *The Stuart News*, p. 1.

Goleman, D. (1991, June 4). Anatomy of a rumor; it flies on fear. *New York Times*, p. C1.

Healy, P. (2009, December 26). Show strives to live down Web-driven rumor mill. Retrieved December 26, 2009, from www.nytimes.com/12/26/theater.

Heires, K. (2005, November 28). Does your company belong in the blogosphere? *Harvard Business School Working Knowledge*. Retrieved August 30, 2006, from http://hbswk.hbs.edu.

Janal, D. S. (1998). *Risky business*. New York: Wiley.

Kimmel, A. J. (2004). *Rumors and rumor control*. Mahwah, NJ: Lawrence Erlbaum Associates.

Knight-Ridder (1991, May 10). Chain denies AIDS rumors. *Denver Post*, p. 18A.

Koenig, F. (1985). *Rumor in the marketplace*. Dover, MA: Auburn House.

Kotcher, R. L. (1999). Surviving a crisis in cyberspace. *The Best of Tactics*, pp. 81–83.

Long, P. (1991a, May 9). Stores business cut 50 percent by AIDS rumor. *The Miami Herald*, pp. 1B–2B.

Long, P. (1991b, May 25). Student apologizes for spreading rumor about restaurant. *The Miami Herald*, p. 1B.

Lucey, R. (1999, July). The truth is out there—On UTMB's web site. *Public Relations Tactics*, 6.

Noack, D. (2000, February 25). Banana rumor called Internet terrorism. Retrieved from www.APBNews.com.

Reeder, J. (1991, May 25). Student apologizes for restaurant rumor. *The Palm Beach Post*, p. 1.

Segal, D., & Mayer, C. (1999, March 28). Sites for sore consumers; complaints about companies multiply on the web. *The Washington Post*, p. A01.

Stiffler, L. (2000, February 4). Fraudulent donation web page is purged. *Seattle Post-Intelligencer*, p. A10.

Wilcox, D. L., Ault, P. H., & Agee, W. K. (1989). Procter & Gamble fights a rumor. In *Public relations strategies and tactics* (p. 620). New York: Harper Collins.

Chapter 7: "Textbook" Crises

Case: Johnson & Johnson and the Tylenol Murders

Goodman, H. (1982, November 12). PR effort launches new Tylenol packages. *Kansas City Times*, p. A3.

Houston, J., & Griffin, L. J. (1982, October 1). 5 deaths tied to pills: Fear killer put cyanide in Tylenol. *Chicago Tribune*, pp. 1–2.

Knight, J. (1982, October 11). Tylenol's maker shows how to respond to a crisis. *The Washington Post*, p. 1.

Shanker, T., & Grady, B. (1982, October 3). Shoplifter is sought in poisoning probe: Reportedly stole Tylenol. *Chicago Tribune*, pp. 1, 4.

Case: Exxon and the Valdez Oil Spill

The big spill. (1990, February 27). Broadcast. Boston: WGBH.

Connelly, J. (1999, May 4). Exxon says it has paid enough for Valdez spill. *Seattle Post-Intelligencer*, p. A1.

Exxon Valdez captain finally will do community service. (1999, February 17). *Seattle Post-Intelligencer*, p. A3.

The Fortune 500. (2009, April 17). *Fortune*, p. F1.

Nalder, E. (1999, March 14) Exxon Valdez captain. Was he the villain or the victim? *Seattle Times*, p. A1.

Richest merger of all time. (1998, December 1). *Seattle Times*, p. A13.

Ruskin, L. (2005, July 13). Protestors: Exxon still owes debt to Alaskans. *Anchorage Daily News*, p. F1.

Sentence upheld over oil spill. (1998, July 5). *Seattle Times*, p. B3.
Serving time. (1999, July 12). *People*, p. 62.
Smith, C. (1992). *Media and apocalypse*. Westport, CT: Greenwood.
Turning Point. (1994, June 15). Transcript of telecast of newsmagazine, p. 1.
Watson, T. (1999, February 11). Wildlife recovering from Exxon spill. *USA Today*, p. 3A.

Chapter 8: Cultures Crises: Foreign and Domestic

Case: Saginaw Valley State University and the Theater Controversy

Martineau, J. (2007, April 14) Angelic alliance. *Saginaw News*, C1.

Case: AIDS in Africa

AIDS Healthcare Foundation/Uganda Care's Stay/Love condoms campaign kicks off in Uganda. (2009, August 6). *Medical News Today*. Retrieved December 8, 2009, from www.medicalnewstoday.com.
African Comprehensive HIV/AIDS Partnerships. (n.d.). Retrieved August 30, 2006, from www.achap.org.
Bell, G. (2005, June 12). Mandela, stars rock out against AIDS. *Seattle Times*, p. A18.
Bobb, S. (2009, December 1). South African President announces expansion of HIV/AIDS testing, treatment. *VOA News.com*. Retrieved December 25, 2009, from www1.voanews.com/English/news/South-African.
Christiansen, J. (2000). Aids in Africa: Dying by the numbers. *CNN In-Depth Specials*. Retrieved August 30, 2006, from www.cnn.com/specials/2000/aids/stones/overview.
Corridors of hope. (2005, April 28). PSI Health Areas. Retrieved August 30, 2006, from www.psi.org/our-programs/coh.html.
Coulson, N. (2004, October 6). Developments in the use of the mass media at the national level for HIV/AIDS prevention in South Africa. *SoulBeat Africa*. Retrieved August 31, 2006, from www.comminit.com.
Cramer, R. (2003, September). Misconceptions, folk beliefs, denial hinder risk perception among young Zambian men. Washington, DC: PSI Research Brief.
Cullen, D. (2009). *Columbine*. New York: Hachette Book Group.
Danielson, C. (2005, October 17). PSI wins Population Institutes Global Media Awards. *PSI Online*. Retrieved August 31, 2006, from www.globalhealth.org/news/article/6747.
DeYoung, K. (2001, August 13). AIDS challenges religious leaders. *Washington Post Online*. Retrieved August 31, 2006, from www.washingtonpost.com/acz/wp-dyn/A6061.
DeYoung, K. (2002, March 15). Mbeki pressured to lead South African fight against AIDS. *Washington Post Online*. Retrieved August 31, 2006, from www.washingtonpost.com/wp-dyn/world/issues/aidsinafrica.
Global Challenges/Report Estimates Significant Impact of Widespread Circumcision Effort in Botswana (2009, May 29). *Henry J. Kaiser Family Foundation*. Retrieved November 11, 2009, from http://kaisernetwork.org.

Kanabus, A., & Noble, R. (2005, August 17). *The ABC of HIV prevention.* Retrieved from www.avert.org/hivprevention.htm.

Goosby, E. (2009, November 27). No hold on PEPFAR funds for Uganda. *Newsweek Online; The Human Condition Blog.* Retrieved December 8, 2009, from http://blog.newsweek.com/thehumancondition/archive/20009/11/27.

HIV and AIDS in South Africa. AVERTing HIV and AIDS. Retrieved May 18, 2010, from www.avert.org/aidssouthafrica.htm.

HIV and AIDS in Swaziland. AVERTing HIV and AIDS. Retrieved December 2, 2009, from www.avert.org/aids-swaziland.htm.

HIV and AIDS in Uganda. AVERTing HIV and AIDS. Retrieved December 7, 2009, from www.avert.org/aids-uganda.htm.

HIV and AIDS in Zambia. AVERTing HIV and AIDS. Retrieved December 2, 2009, from www.avert.org/aids-zambia.htm.

HIV and AIDS in Zimbabwe. AVERTing HIV and AIDS. Retrieved May 18, 2010, from www.avert.org/aids-zimbabwe.htm.

Irin Plus News. (2009, December 8). Uganda: Campaigns tackle "the complexity of sexuality." Retrieved December 8, 2009, from www.plusnews.org/report.aspx?ReportId=84944.

Keller, B. (2005, March 16). AIDS infects education systems in Africa. *Education Week*, pp. 22–23.

Kim, Y., Kols, A., Nyakauru, R., Marangwanda, C., & Chinatamoto, P. (2001, March). Promoting sexual responsibility among young people in Zimbabwe. *International Family Planning Perspectives, 27,* 1.

King abandons campaign for virgin girls to remain abstinent, avoid marriage. (2005, August 23). Retrieved August 30, 2006, from www.kaisernetwork.org.

Koehler, J. (2004, June 9). *Soulbeat Africa.* Retrieved August 31, 2006, from www.comminit.com/Africa/experiences.

Long, J. (2004, September 18). Top players help raise awareness of HIV/AIDS. Retrieved August 31, 2006, from www.icc-cricket.com.

Louw, M. (2005, September). *HIV danger to migrant workers.* Retrieved August 31, 2006, from www.heath24.com.

Machinchick, K. (2003, February 21). Zimbabwean teachers travel to U.S. for HIV/AIDS awareness programs. Retrieved August 31, 2006, from www.usembassy.it.

Mandela's grief. (2005, January 24). *People*, p. 88.

Molomo, B. (2009, May 29). *National Campaign Plan: Multiple Concurrent Partnerships.* Retrieved November 2, 2009, from http://comminit.com/en/node/304747/36.om.

Noble, R. (2005, October 6). HIV and AIDS in Zambia: Prevention and care. Retrieved August 31, 2006, from www.avert.org/aids-zambia.htm.

President's Emergency Plan for AIDS Relief (2009, October 29). *AVERTing HIV and AIDS.* Retrieved November 22, 2009, from www.avert.org/pepfar.htm.

Ramey, C. (2008, July 31). Cell Life Update: Using mobiles to fight HIV/AIDS. *MobileActive.* Retrieved November 2, 2009, from http://mobileactive.org/.

Reducing the HIV stigma by speaking up (2009, August 24). *U.S.A.I.D. for the American People.* Retrieved December 2, 2009, from http://Kenya.usaid.gov/stories/zimbabwe.

Reuters. (2005, August 4). Aids summit opens with accusations. *Washington Post Online*. Retrieved August 31, 2006, from www.washingtonpost.com/wp-dyn/world/issues/aidsinafrica.

Singizi, Tsitsi (2007, November 6). Multiple community programmes simultaneously fight HIV/AIDS in Zimbabwe. *UNICEF Online*. Retrieved December 2, 2009, from www.unicef.org/infobycountry/zimbabwe.

Socio-cultural aspects of HIV/AIDS in South Africa. (2005, April 8). Retrieved August 30, 2006, from www.Health24.com.

Sternberg, S. (2001). Uganda: Deadly traditions persist. *USA Today Online*. Retrieved September 28, 2001, from www.usatoday.com.

Swaziland: Folktales to address modern problems. (2005). Retrieved August 30, 2006, from www.irinnews.org.

Swaziland: New anti-AIDS campaign targets young people. (2005). Retrieved August 30, 2006, from www.irinnews.org.

Swaziland: Tobias undergoes HIV testing. (2005, August 23). Retrieved August 30, 2006, from www.psi.org/news/0805d.html.

Text Messages Are New Tool for AIDS Education in South Africa (2009, March 9). *PBS Online Newshour*. Retrieved November 2, 2009, from www.pbs.org/newshour/updates/health/Jan-June09.

Ugandan condom crisis: Basic facts. (2005, August). Retrieved August 30, 2006, from www.genderhealth.org/uganda.pho.

Ugandan lawmaker to reward virgins with scholarships. (2005, October 16). *Mail & Guardian Online*. Retrieved October 16, 2005, from www.mg.co.za.

UNAIDS: Sub-Saharan Africa. Retrieved May 14, 2010, from www.unaids.org.

UNAIDS (n.d) Zambia. Retrieved from www.unaids.org.

Van Rossem, R. and Meekers, D. (2007, December 18). The reach and impact of social marketing and reproductive health communication campaigns in Zambia. *BMC Public Health*, 7, 352.

Vickers, S. (2009, October 13). Zimbabwe women combat HIV stigma. *BBC Online*. Retrieved December 2, 2009, from http://news.bbc.uk/sport2/hit/football/africa/8304292.

Wax, E. (2005, October 10). Virginity is commodity in AIDS fight. *Concord Monitor Online*. Retrieved August 31, 2006 from www.concordmonitor.com.

York, G. (2009, November 16). South Africa radically shifts thinking in HIV/AIDS. *The Globe and Mail*. Toronto, Ontario, Canada, p. A16.

Youth Love to Scrutinize (2009, July 6). *AllAfrica Global Media*. Retrieved November 2, 2009, from http://allafrica.com.

Zavis, A. (2005, September 29). U.S., South Africa fight AIDS in military. *Los Angeles Sentinel*, p. A-13.

Zimbabwe: Chipawo to present new HIV production (2009, June 15). *AllAfrica Global Media*. Retrieved December 2, 2009, from http://allafrica.com.

Zimbabwe Country Report of the United Nations. (n.d.). Secretary-General's Task Force on Women, Girls, and HIV/AIDS in Southern Africa. Retrieved August 31, 2006, from www.rockofafrica.org/news.htm.

Case: Texas A&M University and the Bonfire Tragedy

Associated Press. (1999, December 15). Photos show bonfire leaning before fall. *Waco Tribune-Herald*, p. 1.

Ball, A. (1999, December 5). 2 bonfire victims were legally drunk. *Austin American-Statesman*, p. 1.

Brown, K. (2000, January 11). Report: Bonfire ropes were cut. *Bryan-College Station Eagle*, p. 1.

Haurwitz, R. K. M., & Copelin, L. (1999, December 10). Faculty doubted bonfires stability. *Austin-American Statesman*, p. 1.

Jones, R. L. (1999, November 19). Collapse kills 11 at Texas A&M. *The Philadelphia Inquirer*, p. 1.

Kirsch, J. (1999a, December 7). A&M refuses money. *Bryan-College Station Eagle*, p. 1.

Kirsch, J. (1999b, November 20). Bush: Bonfire should continue. *Bryan-College Station Eagle*, p. 1.

Montini, E. J. (1999, December 10). A&M can't pass buck in tragedy. *Waco Tribune-Herald*, p. 1.

Nauman, B. (2004, November 23). Bonfire burns despite rain, muck at site. Retrieved August 31, 2006, from www.theeagle.com/bonfire/.

Photos show bonfire leaning before fall. (1999, December 15). Associated Press. *Waco Tribune-Herald*, p. 1.

Slover, P., & Lee, C. (1999, December 3). A&M students use of crane may have violated bonfire rule. *The Dallas Morning News*, p. 1.

Tang, I. A. (2000, March 20). *The Texas Aggie bonfire; tragedy and tradition at Texas A&M*. Austin, TX: Morgan.

Une pyramide meutriere. (1999, November 19). *Le Matin*.

Ward, M. (2000, January 7). A&Ms tab for bonfire aftermath: $292,000 and growing. *Austin-American Statesman*, p. 1.

Chapter 9: Environmental Crisis

Case: Häagen-Dazs and Honey Bees

Borenstein, S. (2007, May 2). Bees, and our diet, on the brink. Associated Press Online. Retrieved December 3, 2008, from www.lexisnexis.com.

Borenstein, S. (2007, May 3). Honeybee die off threatens food supply. Associated Press Online. Retrieved December 3, 2008, from www.lexisnexis.com.

Colony Collapse Disorder Action Plan (2007, June 20). CCD Steering Committee. Retrieved December 2, 2009, from ars.usda.gov/is/br/ccd.

Dart, B. (2008, August 14). Georgia to lead investigation in disappearing honeybees. PalmBeachPost.com. Retrieved February 2, 2009, from http://palm beachpost.printthis.clickability.com.

Garlow, S. (2008, August 29). Honey bee crisis could lead to higher food prices. *USA Today Online*. Retrieved December 2, 2008, from www.usatoday.com.

Kavilanz, P. (2008, February 20). Disappearing bees threaten ice cream sellers. CNN Money.com. Retrieved February 17, 2008, from http://money.cnn.com/2008.

Newstead, S. (2008, November 28). Honeybee crisis could cause chaos for Cumbrian farmers. *News and Star Online*. Retrieved December 2, 2008, from www.newsandstar.com/uknews.

Read, N. (2007, May 19). Honey bee crisis tied to farming, expert says. *Vancouver Sun, Canada.com*. Retrieved December 2, 2008, from www.canada.com.

Chapter 10: Natural Disasters

Case: Hurricane Katrina and New Orleans

Bazar, E. (2005, September 1). Desperate message triggers calls from across USA. *USA Today*, p. 6A.

Blanco's State of Emergency letter to President Bush, August 27, 2005. Archives of the *Times-Picayune*. Retrieved from www.mondotimes.com.

Bourne, J. K., Jr. (2004, October). Gone with the water. National Geographic Magazine [on-line]. Retrieved November 13, 2006, from www3.national geograpic.com/ngm/1410/feature5/.

Connelly, R., Hufner, R., & Spivak, T. (2005, September 8–14). Katrina and the waves. *Houston Press*, pp. 14–17.

Farhi, P., & Wiltz, T. (2005, September 1). Delivering news of the storm that stopped the presses. *Washington Post*, pp. C1, C7.

FEMA E-mails. (2005, October 20). Retrieved October 27, 2005, from www. NYTimes.com.

Frey, J. (2005, September 1). TV networks navigate floodwaters to get on air. *Washington Post*, pp. C1, C7.

Hand, M., & Iacono, E. (2005, September 12). In hurricane's wake, New Orleans-based press relations still chaotic. *PR Week*, 1.

Katrina kids sickest ever (2008, December 1). *Newsweek*, p. 8.

Katrina puts end to lull. (2005, August 27). *Times Picayune*, pp. A1, A10.

Katrina takes aim. (2006, August 28). *Times Picayune*, pp. A21, A23.

Kimzler, S. (2005, September 3). AARP members putting party hats back on shelf. *Washington Post*, p. B1.

Mohammed, A., & Krim, J. (2005, September 1). Communications networks fail disaster area residents. *Washington Post*, pp. D1, D3.

Pierre, R. (2005, September 1). Helpless worry far from New Orleans. *Washington Post*, p. B1.

Rhoads, C. (2005, September 9). At center of crisis, city officials faced struggle to keep in touch, *Wall Street Journal*, p. A1.

Russell, G. (2005, September 11). Nagin: Mistakes were made at all levels. *Times-Picayune*, p. A1.

Scarritt, T. (2005, September 5). Paper sees future of reporting. *Birmingham News*, p. A1.

Sullivan, K. (2005, September 4). How could this be happening in the United States? *Washington Post*, p. A12.

Walker, D. (2005, September 24). The perfect storm coverage. *Times-Picayune*, p. C1.

Chapter 11: Transportation Crises

Case: US Airways and the Emergency Landing in the Hudson

Adams, M. (2009, May 20). Belongings once lost are found again. *USA Today*, IB, 4B.

Foust, D. (2009, February 19). US Airways: After the 'Miracle on the Hudson', *BusinessWeek*. Retrieved June 20, 2009, from www.businessweek.com/magazine/content.

McCartney, S. (2009, February 18). The middle seat terminal, *WSJ Blogs*. Retrieved June 23, 2009, from http://blogs.wsj.com/middlesaet/2009.

Chapter 12: Product Failure and Product Tampering

Case: Maple Leaf Foods and the Battle Against Listeria

Maple Leaf hires food safety officer. (2008, November 5). *Canwest News Service*. Retrieved January 24, 2009, from www.nationalpost.com.

Flynn, T. (2009) *Authentic crisis leadership and reputation management: A study of Canadians' perceptions on Maple Leaf Foods' crisis communications response*. Toronto, Ontario, Canada: Leger Marketing.

Ha, T., Curry, B., and McIlroy, A. (2008, August 27). *The Globe and Mail*. Retrieved January 24, 2009, from www.theglobeandmail.com.

How Maple Leaf Foods is handling the Listeria outbreak. (2008, August 28). *CBC News*. Retrieved January 24, 2009, from www.cbc.ca/money/story.

Meat product recall widens to sandwiches sold at Safeway, Macs. *CBC News*. Retrieved August 25, 2008, from www.cbc.ca/canada/story.

Pitts, G. (2009, April 14). Food safety: stringent testing welcomed. *The Globe and Mail*. Retrieved April 14, 2009, from http://business.theglobeandmail.com.

Walton, T. (2008, December 18). Maple Leaf Listeria suits for $37 million. *The Canadian Press*. Retrieved on January 24, 2009, from www.thespec.com.

Case: Wendy's and the Finger-in-the-Chili Hoax

Clifford, S. (2009, April 16). Video prank at Domino's taints brands, *The New York Times Online*. Retrieved April 16, 2009, from www.nytimes.com/2009/04/16/business/.

Curtis, K. (2006, January 19). California couple get prison for finger-in-the-chili scam. *Seattle Times*, p. A4.

Goldman, A. (2005, April 14). Wendy's Finger finder won't sue. Retrieved from http://signonsandiego.printthis.clickability.com.

LaGanga, M. L., & Simmons, A. M. (2005, April 23). Fast-food, finger-finder arrested; hoax alleged. *Seattle Times*, pp. A1, A12.

O'Hern, M. (2009, April 17). Domino's defends reputation online via Twitter and YouTube response, *Marketing Shift*. Retrieved April 17, 2009, from www.marketingshift.com/2009/4/dominos-defends-reputation-online-via.cfm.

Police call Wendy's chili finger case a hoax. (2005, April 24). Retrieved August 31, 2006, from www.KTVU.com.

Richtel, M., & Barrionuevo, A. (2005, April 22). CSI: Wendy's restaurants. *The New York Times Online*. Retrieved August 31, 2006, from www.nytimes.com.

Ritter, K. (2005, April 9). Woman in Wendy's finger case has litigious past. *Pittsburgh Post Gazette*, p. A8.

Sandoval, G. (2005, May 14). Finger in Wendy's case traced to man's hand. *Seattle Times*, pp. A1, A2.

Search continues for owner of missing digit. (2005, March 24). MSNBC Online. Retrieved from www.MSNBC.com.

Wendy's off hook in finger case. (2005, April 22). *CBS News Online*. Retrieved from www.cbsnews.com.

Chapter 13: Death and Injury

Case: Columbine High School and the Shooting Tragedy

Cullen, D. (2009) *Columbine*. New York: Twelve Hachette Book Group.

Case: Metro Transit: Driver Shot, Bus Flies Off a Bridge

Fefer, M. D. (1999, January 21). King County—Too nice to sue. *Seattle Weekly*, pp. 7, 10.

McFadden, K. (1998, November 28). KOMO-TV led pack with human touches. *Seattle Times*, p. 21.

Sunde, S. (1999, November 26). A year ago today, disturbed rider set off tragic events. *Seattle Post-Intelligencer*, pp. A1, A24.

Chapter 14: Individuals in Crises

Boyle, C. (2009, September 15). Kanye West personally apologizes to Taylor Swift after her appearance on "The View." *NYDailyNews*. Retrieved January 11, 2010, from www.nydailynews.com/gossip/2009/09/15–15_kanye_west/.

Carr, D. (2007, April 7). Networks condemn remarks by Imus. *The New York Times Online*. Retrieved January 10, 2010, from www.nytimes.com/2007/04/07/arts/television.

Exclusive: Isaiah Washington Apologizes (2006, October 25). *People Online*. Retrieved January 11, 2010, from www.people.com/people/article.

Gabriel, T. (1993, August 29). The trials of Bob Packwood. *The New York Times Online*. Retrieved January 29, 2009, from http://query.nytimes.com.

Gibson: I am not an anti-Semite. (2006, Tuesday, August 1) *CNN.com*. Retrieved January 10, 2010, from www.cnn.com/2006/SHOWBIZ/Movies/07/31.

Kocieniewski, D. and Hakim, D. (2008, March 13). Felled by scandal, Spitzer says focus is on his family. *The New York Times Online*. Retrieved January 27, 2009, from www.nytimes.com2008/03/13/nyregion/13/html.

Stadtmiller, M. and Li, D. (2009, September 14). Kanye, Taylor Swift, Beyonce take over the VMAs. *New York Post*. Retrieved October 26, 2009, from www.nypost.com/p/news/local/.

Thornburgh, N. (2008, March 10). The Spitzer scandal: lust plus pride. *Time* in Partnership with CNN. Retrieved October 27, 2009, from www.time.com/time/printout.

Vick pleads guilty, apologizes. (2007, August 27). CNN/com. Retrieved January 10, 2010 from www.cnn.com/2007/US/law/08/27/michael.vick.

Wiener, A. (2006, August 1). Mel Gibson: the speed of scandal. *The New York Times Online*. Retrieved January 29, 2009, from www.nytimes.com/2006/08/01.

Index